WARRIOR CHIEFS

NICK,
BEST OF LUCK
IN YOUR CAREER!

WARRIOR CHIEFS

PERSPECTIVES ON
SENIOR CANADIAN MILITARY LEADERS

Edited by
Lieutenant-Colonel Bernd Horn
and
Stephen Harris

DUNDURN PRESS
TORONTO · OXFORD

Copy-Editor: Andrea Mudry
Proofreader: Julian Walker
Design: Jennifer Scott
Printer: Transcontinental

Published in co-operation with the Department of National Defence

Canadian Cataloguing in Publication Data

Warrior chiefs

Includes bibliographical references and index.
ISBN 1-55002-351-9

1. Canada – Armed Forces – Biography. 2. Canada – History, Military. 3. Generals – Canada – Biography.
I. Horn, Bernd, 1959-   . II. Harris, Stephen John.

U54.C2W37 2000   355.3'31.092271   C00-931875-5

1   2   3   4   5   04   03   02   01   00

THE CANADA COUNCIL | LE CONSEIL DES ARTS
FOR THE ARTS | DU CANADA
SINCE 1957 | DEPUIS 1957

Canadä

ONTARIO ARTS COUNCIL
CONSEIL DES ARTS DE L'ONTARIO

We acknowledge the support of the **Canada Council for the Arts** and the **Ontario Arts Council** for our publishing program. We also acknowledge the financial support of the **Government of Canada** through the **Book Publishing Industry Development Program, The Association for the Export of Canadian Books**, and the **Government of Ontario** through the **Ontario Book Publishers Tax Credit** program.

Care has been taken to trace the ownership of copyright material used in this book. The author and the publisher welcome any information enabling them to rectify any references or credit in subsequent editions.
J. Kirk Howard, President

Printed and bound in Canada.
Printed on recycled paper.

www.dundurn.com

Dundurn Press
8 Market Street
Suite 200
Toronto, Ontario, Canada
M5E 1M6

Dundurn Press
73 Lime Walk
Headington, Oxford,
England
OX3 7AD

Dundurn Press
2250 Military Road
Tonawanda NY
U.S.A. 14150

TABLE OF CONTENTS

Acknowledgements

A NY project of this magnitude owes its existence to a multitude of people. Initially, we wish to thank Lieutenant-General Romeo Dallaire for his support of the idea and its maturation into reality in the form of a two-volume book set. His prescience and zealous efforts at reforming the Canadian Officer Corps will surely be seen in the years to come as a defining moment in Canadian military history.

Next, we would be remiss if we did not thank the wide array of contributors who took the time and effort to share their thoughts, experiences, and ideas. A special thanks must also go to Bernadette Power and Eric Tuttle for their efforts in assisting with the initial formatting of the books as well as helping out with the general administration of the project at large. In addition, we would like to thank Michel Wycynski for his assistance in compiling photographs for the book.

Finally, although too numerous to mention individually, we would also like to thank collectively the staff of the Directorate of History and Heritage, the National Archives, the Royal Military College of Canada, and the Canadian Forces Photographic Unit Central Negative Library for their stellar co-operation and assistance.

FOREWORD

G EORGE Stanley, a leading Canadian military historian, has called Canadians "an unmilitary people." But the truth of the matter is that conflict has shaped Canadians and this nation more than we like to admit. It has been a key influence on our destiny. Although we reject militarism and are not a warlike nation, we certainly are a fighting people.

Over the last century, war and conflict exacted a heavy price in Canadian blood. Of the 620,000 personnel that served in the First World War, 60,000 were killed and another 172,000 were wounded. This represents a casualty rate of approximately 39 percent. During the Second World War, 1.1 million Canadians answered the call to arms. Of this number, 42,042 were killed and 54,414 wounded. The Korean conflict brought the horror of war to 26,791 service personnel, claiming the lives of 516 and wounding another 1,072. Finally, peace support operations since 1950 (not including Korea) cost the lives of an additional 108 Canadian military personnel on 90 different missions.

Clearly, these sacrifices are indicative of the major role Canada's armed forces have played in the international forum. The operations in which the Canadian Forces have participated, whether world wars, lesser conflicts, or peace support operations, have fostered a distinct Canadian identity and pride. Our sailors, soldiers, airmen, and airwomen have always been our most visible ambassadors abroad. They represent Canadian values to the world and contribute significantly to international peace, stability, and human security, whether deterring aggression, assisting in the building of peace, or delivering humanitarian aid.

These accomplishments, however, would not have been possible without strong leadership, particularly that of the generals and admirals who provide the strategic guidance and decisions required for a military force to operate effectively. These leaders are responsible for the stewardship of the Armed Forces. More importantly, they are the ones who must ensure that the Canadian Armed Forces are aligned with the direction and expectations of the Government of Canada and the public it serves.

To lead the nation's sons and daughters to war or on dangerous operations has always been an arduous task. The expectation that this can be done without casualties, collateral damage, or mistakes is unrealistic, but nevertheless makes the challenge all the greater. Thankfully, and as always, there are those who are ready to pick up the gauntlet.

This book examines a number of those leaders who have answered the call to duty and have had the privilege of senior command. It is hoped that their case studies will provide both an historical record and a valuable tool for educating others, including their successors.

Some of the military figures in these pages will be familiar while others will be more obscure. In some cases, the authors have chosen to examine a whole career, in others, they have singled out particular events or periods that best elucidate their subjects' style of leadership. Some readers may object to the numerical imbalance among the Navy, Army, and Air Force officers represented in this book. As it happens, the proportion was not preordained by the editors but was, rather, influenced by a simple fact of our history: being the largest service and having, since the Boer War, been organized in nationally identifiable contingents, the army has had more general officers on active service in command appointments. In other words, there were more cases to examine.

Whether successful leaders are born or can be made is an old question and open to debate. Consequently, the authors were not specifically asked to address this issue. Readers can assess for themselves what shaped the destiny of each of the generals and flag officers studied here. Whether there is a necessary tension between the precepts of the leader and the manager is also an old question. The people examined here, or at least many of them, had to both lead and manage. Finally – and perhaps this is a peculiarly Canadian inclination – there is the question of whether an identifiably Canadian style of leadership and command exists. Again, readers will determine that for themselves. But one thing is clear: all the generals and flag officers studied here understood their responsibilities as *Canadian* leaders.

J.M.G. Baril
General
Chief of the Defence Staff

INTRODUCTION

S ELF-ANALYSIS is always difficult. The military, although not alone, is especially known for its conservatism, insularity, and reluctance at self-scrutiny. In the late 1950s, author and journalist Pierre Berton wrote *The Comfortable Pew*, a critical examination of the Christian Church's complacency and self-satisfaction. In many ways, the Canadian Forces (CF) were in a similar position of self-satisfaction in the late 1980s. To be sure, there was grumbling about defence budgets that were too small, about equipment that was getting old and, in comparison with the "golden" years of the 1950s (when all ranks of regular force strength – Navy, Army, and Air Force – tipped 120,000), about establishments that left something to be desired.

Yet these years were still something of a "comfortable" (or at least a familiar) pew for the Armed Forces. You knew where you stood. Although there were signs of strain in the Warsaw Pact, the Cold War continued, and that gave the Navy, Army, and Air Force their main raisons d'être. The 4th Brigade remained the army's jewel in the crown, and, so long as there were allied politicians like Helmut Schmidt around, the need to maintain Canada's reputation in NATO would eventually result in at least some new equipment. The NATO commitment sustained the Navy too and, combined with NORAD, was the Air Force's main focus as well. Within the cyclical process of capital procurement and defence spending, at some point in every decade one of the elements was the winner – Leopard tanks were followed by CF18 fighter aircraft, and they were followed by patrol frigates. The CF could not claim to be up to date in every respect, but they could still be valued members of the team. And, as members of the team, Canada happily left strategic and operational thought to others with more clout. We really didn't have to think for ourselves.

Peacekeeping was also a routine, especially for the Army. Units rotated in and out of Cyprus and the Middle East, taking their turn on various "green lines" in what were generally predictable deployments. There were surprises from time to time, but nothing earth-shatteringly new, and for the most part the CF took pride (without thinking about it too much) in their reputation as the Armed Forces with the greatest peacekeeping experience and expertise in the world.

Then came the changes and the shocks. The end of the Cold War and the withdrawal of Canadian Forces from Europe demolished old strategic truths: Canada and the Canadian Forces were going to have to think for themselves about their place in the world. Decidedly non-traditional peacekeeping operations in the Balkans, Rwanda, and, worst of all, Somalia produced incidents that equally demolished the old peacekeeping truths and, at the same time, raised questions about moral standards in the Canadian Forces. Further dramatic budget cuts followed, the Department of National Defence (DND) was re-engineered, the regular force grew smaller, and from a public opinion perspective it seemed that Canadians had lost faith in their Armed Forces.

That had never happened before. The country may well have taken the Armed Forces for granted most of the time – and not very seriously, at least in peacetime – but never before had there been any indication of such a loss of faith. Initially, the reaction within the Department of National Defence and the Canadian Forces was to circle the wagons. But some people understood that the status quo had to change, that, like the U.S. Armed Forces after Vietnam, this was a time for professional renewal which went beyond mere organizational change. These individuals saw that there were real lessons to be learned from Somalia, the Balkans, and the Gulf War, and they realized that the way ahead required a fundamental rededication, if not reform, to their profession and to professionalism. They understood that this process required both looking back and looking forward and that, for thoroughgoing change to occur, the general officer corps of the next few years had to be in the forefront of such a transformation – for it was the generals who had the moral authority to translate written and spoken prescriptions (or hopes) into reality.

Warrior Chiefs: Perspectives on Canadian Military Leaders and its companion volume, *Generalship and the Art of the Admiral: Perspectives on Canadian Senior Military Leadership,* together form part of the process of rededication to and reform of the longstanding values of the Canadian military profession. These volumes examine the experience of Canadian admirals and generals in war and in peace – with all their commonalities and differences – to help us understand where we have come from, what the Canadian military profession has been and, by looking at the present and the future, to help us better understand where we may be going and how we might arrive there.

In *Warrior Chiefs*, the idea was to commission articles on leaders from the past to learn the positives and negatives from their experiences, and to see the different styles of leadership that proved successful in given contexts. For example, although Roman Jarymowycz suggests that Guy Simonds was a near-brilliant (yet still tragically flawed) battlefield commander, it is also clear that his style of leadership was not one with which peacetime governments were likely to be comfortable. It was probably for the better that he was not named Chief of the General Staff (CGS) in Canada immediately after the end of the Second World War. Charles Foulkes, on the other hand, has received little praise for his performance commanding 2nd Canadian Infantry Division and I Canadian Corps, but as Sean Maloney argues, he was probably perfectly placed as post-war CGS and, later, Chairman, Chiefs of Staff committee, to lead Canada into the post-war world and thence into the Cold War.

Some of the generals and admirals studied here need little introduction: Sam Hughes, Arthur Currie, Andy McNaughton, Guy Simonds, and Jean Victor Allard have all been the subject of major biographies. Others, like Raymond Brutinel, Leonard Murray, and Charles Foulkes are probably at least recognized by some readers. But some of the commanders included here are likely to be unknown to many Canadians; and, it must be said that some of our authors had difficulty unearthing more than the most meagre biographical details about their subjects. This, in part, is because compared to senior officers in the armed forces of other countries, Canadian generals and admirals have done an execrable job of speaking for themselves in published form – and perhaps even a worse job of leaving behind sets of papers that shed light on what they believed were the touchstones of their professionalism. This may be due to modesty or a host of other factors. Hopefully these volumes will help to rectify this lack and encourage future publications.

BEGINNINGS

CONFEDERATION TO THE END OF WORLD WAR I

Chapter 1

Sir Sam Hughes:
A Canadian General – Why Bother!

Ronald G. Haycock[1]

The Question

THE famous historian Frank Underhill remembered a teacher who lamented that Canadian History is as "dull as ditch water and Canadian politics was full of it."[2] Certainly that description could never be applied to Sam Hughes. He is one of the most colourful – perhaps even bizarre – characters ever to emerge in Canadian politics and the Militia. Though he died in 1921, his name can still conjure up controversy and passion. His long career, in many respects the quintessential story of a poor backwoods Ontario farm boy who made good through his own hard work, continues to exert a fascination which few other Canadian public figures have matched. The purpose of this study is to answer a double-barrelled question: what did this remarkable character contribute to the understanding of Canadian generalship, and was Sam Hughes a "real" general? The answers lie in the history of Canadian generalship and in the life and times of Sam Hughes in particular.

The Setting

Sam Hughes entered Canadian politics during the last years of Sir John A. Macdonald's administration and remained at the centre of the country's politics until his death. He rose through the ranks to become a respected member of his community, and, simultaneously, a Lieutenant-General and Minister of Militia. Then suddenly he was fired unceremoniously from his political post in 1916. Thus, whatever future military input he might have had vanished with his political disgrace. Historians are still unequally divided as to whether or not he was therefore a failure.[3] The events surrounding his demise as minister overshadow both the man and his earlier accomplishments.

One cannot judge Sam Hughes without considering his entire

career in the milieu of both Canadian social and military life. Central to his career and to our understanding of his generalship is an understanding of his fundamental philosophy. It is this: he saw no difference between military and civil functions. Both were simply acts of responsible citizenship and they were symbiotic. For example, the young Sam Hughes joined the Canadian Militia as a boy drummer during the first Fenian threat to Canada in 1866, and he held every rank before his death in 1921. His political career followed the same path to authority. A schoolteacher at the age of 16, he was quickly steeped in the optimism surrounding the creation of Canada, in its historical past, and in Victorian social values. But teaching did not satisfy him, and by the 1880s he was in the newspaper business in Lindsay, Ontario. He was also a Conservative in local politics. As Desmond Morton attests, political activity, social position, and military service were often entwined and mutually interdependent in Hughes' generation of Canadians.[4] Hughes' career followed this pattern.

While Sam Hughes practised teaching and journalism, he served in the Militia. He diligently attended the parades and quickly rose through the ranks to earn a commission. To better himself as a soldier, he took the few military courses available to rural battalions like his 45th in Victoria County, Ontario. These were very lean and difficult years for the forces. The "regular" Army was minuscule; the main line of Canadian defence was held by many like Sam Hughes to be the Non-Permanent Active Militia (NPAM) – part-time citizen soldiers. But the Militia was often ravaged by abject penury and government neglect. So it was the dedicated enthusiasts like Hughes that kept the local battalions together with sheer hard work.[5] It did not take long for Sam Hughes to find that, like the Militia, federal politics was also his passion. He was elected to parliament as a Conservative in 1892. The Prime Minister, Sir John A. Macdonald, died the following year; without the stewardship of the "old man" the federal party fell quickly into disarray, losing to Laurier's Liberals in 1896. In the political wilderness of opposition, Hughes quickly established himself as a talent well above the average Member of Parliament. He continued to blend civil and military functions both in Parliament, where he was the official militia critic by the turn of the century, and in the Non-Permanent Active Militia, where he rose to command the 45th Victoria Rifles as a Lieutenant-Colonel. He was both a good senior parliamentarian and a good commanding officer.[6]

In many ways Hughes was a progressive. For example, he was an enthusiastic promoter of education. As a schoolteacher, he had spent his early years dedicated to the proposition that education was vital for all. Moreover, it made better citizens. He attended courses at the University of Toronto, though he did not graduate. Once in Parliament, he became a vigorous advocate of better schools, especially in technical subjects. He took military development courses where possible and steadily tried to extend their availability to part-time soldiers. Sam sat on the Board of Visitors of the Royal Military College of Canada. He sent his son Garnet there who graduated as the Sword of Honour winner at the turn of the century. Sam Hughes had come from a family which, although poor, valued education and actively sought it as self-improvement. His brother James L. Hughes ultimately became Chief Inspector of Schools. Arguably, he was to Ontario education what Dewey was in the United States. Sam Hughes was completely in favour of an active role for women in certain military efforts before and during the First World War. Prior to 1914, as Minister, he encouraged female participation in the Cadet Instructor Cadre. During mobilization, he ordered that soldiers could not enlist without their spouse's written permission. Although in his declining years he made no comment on the suffrage movement, he did not oppose it either. Certainly, in viewing social issues, he was ahead of his time.

As a progressive, Hughes also comes out favourably in relation to many progressive military and political figures of his day. He was a nationalist, even though he is so closely associated with the jargon of Imperialism. This assertion must be understood. For many Victorian and Edwardian Canadians, Imperialism was a venue for nationalism. It was a forum where the young Dominion could exert a political influence out of proportion with its size. For them, the British Empire was a system in which Canada could influence international affairs. Sam Hughes' knew that Canada alone had no hope of operating in an international setting, nor did it have the machinery to do so. Since this meant staying inside the Imperial alliance, he believed that Canada could revitalize the old Imperium under strong Dominion leadership. Furthermore, Canada could obtain whatever defence she needed by willing, but not blind, co-operation in the defence of the Empire. In fact, Canadians in 1900 viewed the Empire in much the same manner as Canadians now perceive our role in the UN: a venue for statecraft and moral internationalism. Strategically speaking then, Hughes was thinking about Canada's place in the world and ways of improving it. Lamentably, this is a task in which Canadian generals rarely engage.[7]

SOUTH AFRICA

By 1899, it was the mixture of his two roles as parliamentarian and commanding officer that got him his only combat role, which was in South Africa during the Anglo-Boer War. There, as elsewhere, military talent served up with an equal amount of political controversy predictably came out of Hughes' blend of long-held civil and military ideas. Hughes' combat experience simply cemented his ideas in place, especially the one about the efficacy of part-time citizen soldiers. The war also helped his political career, however notorious his reputation was among the regular soldiers both in England and at home.[8]

The Canadian military experience in the South African War, or Boer War, (1899-1902) provides an excellent opportunity to evaluate the development of Canadian generalship for several reasons. First, this war provided the prototype for most Canadian military operations in the next century. Second, it was the proving ground for a great number of Canadians pivotal to the Great War effort. Third, it was an example of the social-political-military triad of Canadian involvement in a limited war, albeit a bloody one. Yet in other ways the Boer War, as with many before and since, taught the wrong lessons on the necessary orders of battle, tactics, and training requirements for an effective force. While not alone in misinterpreting the "lay of the land," Hughes' conclusions were to have a profound impact on the development of Canadian generalship over the next fifty years.

The Boer War would be the only war in which Hughes fought as an active combatant, and he had to struggle politically as well as diligently for the chance to fight. At the war's outbreak Hughes was the Opposition critic in the House of Commons. He was highly critical of Laurier's reluctance to get involved. Hughes was also a Lieutenant-Colonel commanding a local militia battalion. Like some militiamen then and now, he often operated in both spheres at the same time. And like many others, he saw, as a responsible citizen, little contradiction or confusion in mixing the civil and military functions. Such a concoction was not as clear or appreciated by professional soldiers such as W.D. Otter or the imperious British General Officer Commanding (GOC) of the Canadian Militia, the humourless General E.T.H. Hutton. When the war began to affect Canada in the autumn of 1899, there were political and military intrigues at home. A good number of them were of Hughes' own manufacture to get Canada involved officially in the conflict. Consequently influential enemies in both Canadian and

Imperial circles conspired to keep him out of the action. Some did so because they realized that action was what he wanted more than anything, others because they feared he might become unhinged and cost Canadian lives or prestige.[9]

In early 1900, with the sparks from the firing of General Hutton – who had been just as guilty of political machinations as Sam Hughes – still glowing on Parliament Hill, Hughes obtained his first job in South Africa. He got employment for a variety of reasons, some had to do with his military talents, while others did not. Hughes was a good lobbyist. His friend but political opposite, the Minister of Militia, F.W. Borden, privately put a word in for him, and the British were desperate for anyone with a modicum of talent. Moreover, imperial proconsuls, like Alfred Lord Milner in Capetown, noted that Hughes was a supporter of the Imperial ideal. They had yet to feel his nationalism and, when it came, it was always a surprise. In the meantime, as a logistics officer on Lord Roberts' staff, he was responsible for aiding in the supply and communications of Sir Fred's northward "March to Pretoria." Hughes quickly showed a flare for the task, particularly his ability to unravel railway schedules.

Hughes got his second and final operational job because of the competence he demonstrated and the threat of Boer insurrection on Roberts' west flank in northwest Cape Colony. But conveniently for the British – who were suffering badly because of the early incompetence of some of their generals – they made Hughes Chief of Intelligence to General Sir Charles Warren. Warren was by then a bête noire for his earlier mistakes in Sir Revers Bullers' command during the British defeats in Natal known as "the black week." Warren's entire small force was a bizarre mixture of military and political pariahs and others not attached to more formal units in the main theatre for which they were providing flanking support and supply.

Commanding small numbers of mounted troops, Hughes was charged with guarding the supply trains and policing the rear and flank of the main army. This was hardly glorious work in the style of the times, but of vital military necessity. As Hughes well knew, the thinly stretched lines of communication had to be maintained at all costs. A village was likely to revert to rebellion as soon as the last advancing Imperial soldiers disappeared behind the nearest kopje. It was critical to maintain a small but visible British presence in these areas to arrest interloping rebels and to provide warning of any events developing in the British rear. If there were any doubts about Hughes' efficacy or bravery as a field officer, they were quickly silenced over the four months he operated in this role. During these operations, Hughes displayed many aspects of generalship. But whether he balanced these assets with the prudence sometimes required in a general is more debatable.

In all, Sam Hughes proved to be a good soldier in the northwest Cape Colony. His systematic and innovative approach to counter-insurgency proved very effective. It won him the admiration of those who witnessed it. One was Milner back in Cape Town. Another was the young L.S. Amery, a war correspondent for the *Times* of London and later a very famous imperial statesman; and yet another still was Lionel Curtis – later to found the Round Table movement – who considered Hughes to be "one of the ablest persons I have come across out here."[10] At least for a while, Warren himself was quite laudatory of his Canadian lieutenant-colonel. And there is evidence to suggest that Warren had promised to decorate Hughes after some of the serious fights in the northwest Cape. To these people Hughes was innovative, audacious, and – in the case where he captured almost single-handedly an entire Boer commando and tons of their fodder and ammunition – brave nearly to the point of being foolhardy.

There can be little doubt that Hughes had a populist touch which earned him the respect of his troops. In South Africa, a "red-tape be-damned" approach to administration was frequently useful when dealing with the moribund Imperial supply system. Yet this same approach, when applied to the field, proved risky at best and contravened the orders of his superior, General Warren, who in June 1900 suddenly fired the Canadian – ostensibly for an orders infraction. There is ample evidence that the real cause was Hughes' public criticism of Warren's continued incompetence. Again Hughes may have been right in what he wrote, both in official after-action reports and to a host of others. And one must admire him for his solid tactical assessments and his conviction to get the truth out. But in the heady world of Victorian military politics, it was hard for career longevity. Nevertheless, one could argue that his blunt criticism was the healthy sign of a citizen-soldier trying to cure a real problem of professional leadership. However, the immediate effect, especially after Hughes sent the critical letters to the *Cape Times,* was that no one less than Lord Roberts ordered Hughes out of South Africa on the first boat available.[11]

Thus on two fronts Hughes seems to have been defeated in South Africa. Through reckless daring he undermined his superiors' confidence in his judgement and, through his correspondence with the press on some quite correct conclusions about the problems of the British war effort, he made many enemies who sought and achieved his removal.

The South African War provides proof of many positive and negative attributes of Hughes' personality. While undoubtedly brave and loyal to the cause, he was prone to reckless action. That war requires dash and risk is true; it is equally true that a commander must balance that risk against potential consequences. This is the true art. Hughes could not see the need to separate his political and military activities. His experience in the war should have proved the opposite: politician soldiers must restrain their parliamentary tendencies while on active duty. Moreover, the watchword for any general must be "balance."

The war also strengthened Hughes' notions about how wars should be fought and who were the best soldiers to fight them. For him, a guerrilla war required dash, innovation, and field and small arms skills. During his time there, the Imperial effort in South Africa had proven to be amateurish in all meanings of the word, and it provided many superficial examples of generalship at its worst.[12] Thus, to Sam Hughes, a resourceful amateur could do well. But would a gifted novice be able to sift through the lessons and apply them to a far more rigid conflict? The Great War would test this hypothesis fourteen years later.

Back in Canada in September 1900, Hughes was re-elected. His reputation as a loyal and hard-working MP rose steadily as he delivered his riding to the Conservatives election after election. Soon he was seen as a veteran member vital to the fortunes of the federal Tory party. When the Conservatives were elected as the new government in 1911, Robert Borden made Colonel Sam Hughes his Militia Minister. Once in a position where it was possible to operate with real political power, Sam Hughes promoted his inseparable blend of civilian and military ideas with tremendous gusto and enthusiasm, all in the name of responsible citizenship. He set out to build a militia structure that both promoted social values and provided for the defence of Canada. The vehicle was to be a strong Non-Permanent Active Militia. As it turned out this threatened the small Permanent Force and slowed its progress toward professionalism. This was the military picture as Canada entered the cauldron of the Great War in 1914. Few had any idea of what was to happen in the next four years.

MINISTER OF MILITIA

On 28 July 1914, the British flashed a message to the Empire to adopt the precautionary stage of planning war which had been agreed upon two years previously by the Committee for Imperial Defence. Hughes – as Militia Minister – rushed to Ottawa to meet with his staff, absolutely certain that war would mean British involvement and a fighting task for Canada. Mobilization was underway. But how would mobilization be conducted? A few years before the conflict, the British Imperial Inspectors General, first Sir John French in 1910, then Sir Ian Hamilton in 1913, had gone to great pains to warn Canada against the dislocation any impromptu methods would cause. Indeed, in 1911, under General Mackenzie's orders, Colonel W.G. Gwatkin, then mobilization officer, began confidential plans for raising a small force for service outside Canada. This scheme was secret and separate from the already evolving domestic mobilization project. The proposed force would include a division of infantry and a mounted brigade totalling 24,000. The force would either concentrate at Petawawa or go directly to the point of embarkation depending on the season. The scheme was decentralized and dependent on local commanders for most things, including recruiting, remounts, and equipment. Yet by 1914, though the plan was in the hands of some local commanders, it was only half-complete. Thus Hughes had to make a choice: go with the incomplete Gwatkin plan or make his own. This is a choice most military commanders would wish to avoid but, given the incredible constraints, Hughes decided to create his own plan.

Indeed, there is much weight to the argument that Hughes was entirely correct in scrapping Gwatkin's plan, as there were some serious shortcomings which, if time had permitted analysis, might have come to the public's attention. In 1914, unfortunately, there was no time. The plan as it stood meant that the divisional staff for the overseas unit was the same one that governed the domestic forces.[13] To send it out of the country would be to remove the ability of the home forces to mobilize quickly and coherently. In fact, Sir Ian Hamilton had commented on this flaw in 1913; Loring Christie, the Prime Minister's personal advisor on legal affairs, gave similar advice. Several years later, in looking back on those hurried events, Christie also reminded his chief that the legal implications of sending a force to fight outside Canada might jeopardize any mobilization serious doubt, sufficiently so that the Governor-General had to raise the question with the Colonial Secretary on 2 August 1914. In the special war session of Parliament called on 18

August, Hughes told members that there was no authority to send the Militia outside Canada. Consequentially, only volunteers (as distinct from Dominion forces) were acceptable.[14]

These were just two of the major pitfalls of the Gwatkin plan. As Hughes explained in 1916, the plan was simply too slow for the first contingent, but since there was no hurry with the subsequent divisions, normal channels were adequate. By that time as well, the Government had learned from problems encountered during the dispatch of the first contingent. In addition, it is also possible that Hughes the populist had accurately gauged the exuberant, patriotic mood of the Canadian public. He claimed so himself, going so far as to call mobilization a crusade: "really a call to arms, like the fiery cross passing through the highlands of Scotland, or in the mountains of Ireland in former days."[15]

That the practical mobilization questions weighed heavier than Hughes' personal or political ones seems improbable; however, they did exist. In some ways Hughes resembled his British counterpart, Lord Kitchener, who at the same time was also ignoring his professional soldiers and an existing mobilization plan.[16] Yet the best explanation for his action remains the fact that Sam Hughes was an egotistical and grand improviser, led on by an archaic war concept and encouraged by a particular view of a citizen's martial responsibilities, by existing military moods, and by his own experience. Perhaps those very attributes were what the situation required in 1914. To paraphrase Winston Churchill, sometimes a nation needs stinkers and imperfect motives. Without Hughes' drive, energy, and infectious enthusiasm, his single greatest contribution to the Canadian war effort would not have come to pass: the "miracle of Valcartier."[17]

Hughes' greatest achievement in the mobilization process was the establishment of Valcartier Camp. Since 1912, the Militia Department had planned to build a training camp for the Quebec militia and had selected the wide valley where the Jacques Cartier River meets the St. Lawrence above Quebec City. But, as of the summer of 1914, nothing had been done in the area. When mobilization was announced, Hughes decided that, with the British constantly pressing the button to get Canadian troops overseas as quickly as possible, the contingent would be best situated close to an embarkation point. But the Gwatkin plan had the contingent assemble at Ontario's Camp Petawawa. This would have only delayed and complicated things further in Hughes' mind. On 7 August, the Militia Minister ordered a Tory friend from Quebec to begin construction at Valcartier and to have the camp finished by the time the entire force assembled there. It was a tall order, but the newly minted Lieutenant-Colonel Price tackled the project head-on. Hughes offered further help by ordering the contractors, then completing Ottawa's Connaught Rifle Ranges, to move to Valcartier. Over four hundred workmen built the camp in thirty days, including sewers, water mains, rail links to Quebec City, and the longest rifle range in the British Empire. Even some of Hughes' bitterest political enemies grudgingly admitted that it "was a splendid performance all around."[18]

Characteristics of leadership are manifested many ways. Good generals know this. Hughes built Valcartier and this camp gave Canada one of the first symbols that the nation was determined and acting together. At this early stage, the symbolism of the war effort, the nation, and the camp were one. Clearly, Valcartier would decline as that symbol with the onset of the winter of 1914-1915; then it would simply be subsumed by the bloody battles around Ypres in the spring. Yet in those super-charged days of August through October 1914, Valcartier and the departure of the Canadian Expeditionary Force proof of the country's determination.

Never one to leave political hay unstacked, Hughes played his Valcartier triumph card to the limit. His activities were at times a frenetic mixture of civil and military functions. He enjoyed being in the eye of the public hustle and bustle at Valcartier with a long entourage of aids, guests, journalists, sycophants, and Tory businessmen in tow. He meddled in the details of camp life; he did not seem ready to delegate but acted like a commanding officer. Conditions of the stables, a recruit's bayonet fighting style, or a squad's marksmanship, all were personally attended to by the Minister who left confusion and trodden feet in his wake. In short, Hughes, by temperament and training, was incapable of making the jump from tactical to strategic leadership. He was trying to run a national army, the Department of Militia, and be commanding officer to every battalion; he was harming the effort as often as he was helping. Indeed, by mid-September, the Governor-General, the Duke of Connaught, thought Hughes was "mentally off his base."[19] Yet, it was also here that he set the country on the path toward a monumental and lucrative war industry by creating the Canadian Shell Committee that first September. To many applauding Canadians, he was the epitome of the war effort. There was even talk of raising him to the peerage as Lord Valcartier. The real problem was in judging Hughes in any dispassionate way. With him it was hard to tell because there was so little balance in his actions, and most of these seemed so politically partisan.[20]

Amateurism in Action: The Ross Rifle

As the war continued it became increasingly apparent that Hughes' amateur approach would not work. His decisions and actions were sometimes lop-sided and often quite inconsistent on critical issues. One of the clearest examples of this was his handling of the Ross Rifle issue, both in peacetime and in war. This essentially sound idea of having self-sufficiency in rifle production, while originally a Liberal government creation in 1902, was highly charged politically even before the war started. When Hughes became Minister, he only added to that partisanship so that there were very few temperate opinions concerning the rifle at the onset of the hostilities. Early use of the Ross showed that there were easily rectifiable technical problems with it.[21] However, instead of explaining publicly in a calm way what they were and what was to be done about them, Hughes continued to stridently declare that the rifle was the best in the world. He even hinted that there was a conspiracy by the British against good Canadian equipment. To the ill-informed but expectant Canadian public this was not good enough, especially when the rumours after the bloody battles of the Second Ypres had produced so many casualties.[22] But the Minister still gave no reasonable explanation, just more of the same excited rhetoric. There was no balance to his statements. The net result was that both the military and the public did not believe him, even though the solution to the technical flaws for the Ross had been found. By then it did not matter. Confidence was all gone. Both the Minister and the ill-fated rifle were "withdrawn" from active service at about the same time. The perception of scandal was a major reason why Hughes was fired, and the reputation of the rifle and the Canadian company that produced it were ruined forever. We never made another rifle in Canada until the next war and never again one of our own design.

The rifle case only goes to show how Hughes' lack of proportion had such a devastating effect. It aggravated civil-military relations to an almost unprecedented degree, and it caused confusion and embarrassment that impeded departmental administration and military development. Moreover, between 1914 and 1916 he had progressively lost sight of the fundamental principle of collective cabinet responsibility; in short, his actions threatened the continuance of the Borden Government. It was one more reason why the Prime Minister had to fire Hughes from his ministerial job, which he did in late 1916.

Besides lacking proportion, another of Hughes' failures, if that is what it can be called, was to be a humanist in the finest Victorian tradition. He was not alone in this. By 1916, both the war and the people who led all parties to the conflict had changed markedly. Sir Sam did guide Canada through the first difficult phase of the most horrendous war in which we have ever participated, and he did so in an unmatchable manner. The very magnitude of the war changed it into a mechanistic struggle of statistics: the professionalization of violence. Is it any wonder he was eventually outpaced by events? What does it say of generalship in Canada that such a man became one of the nation's senior wartime leaders in an apocalyptic struggle the likes of which the world had not known until then?

SOME "GENERAL" CONCEPTS

In order to set Sam Hughes in context, one has to say a few words about generalship and the specific character of Canadian generalship.

The concept of generalship is vague enough to leave much room for debate. Indeed, both generalship and its relation, the operational art, have been subjects of enormous argument since the Great War. The essence of the purist conceptual form of generalship is about how a general directs his formation, whatever size it may be. In this context the criteria are reduced to answering the question, "Did he win?" But this basic concept is perhaps a faulty one. To assume one individual can make the great difference in a contest of nations is debatable. In fact "success" depends upon the perspective from which the individual or event is viewed. If a general wins, then we must ask what did he win, and for what purpose? In the Canadian tradition, Pyrrhic victories with high casualties are wisely treated with a jaundiced eye.[23]

And yet this crucible test of victory fails to touch on other vital aspects of generalship which are of primary importance to Canadians. War, it must be remembered, is not the normal condition under which a general exercises his craft. How the general relates to his profession along the entire spectrum from peace to war is of primary concern. How does the general balance the often conflicting requirements of managing supply, supporting, and leading his subordinates, accommodating the tempo of battle into his operational plans, incorporating and applying technology in the most effective manner, and dealing with his superiors? Indeed, how does the *Canadian* general do all this and remain true to two chains of command: the alliance and the national government? In addition there is the larger question, recently asked in 1997 by the Minister of National Defence, the Honourable Doug Young, of how to select, train, and prepare the individuals who assume these burdens? In reporting his shocking findings on the failures in education of the officers of the Canadian Forces in his report to the Prime Minister, Young based his information on three reports by Professors Granatstein, Bercuson, and Morton. All of them noted the low level of education in the officer corps as compared to that of other armies.[24]

The art of generalship lies in the path the general follows as he navigates his way through these seemingly impossible challenges. For a great number of Canadian generals in the twentieth century, these challenges have been insurmountable. Sam Hughes is almost alone in successfully orchestrating the transformation of the nation from peace to war.

Twenty-three hundred years ago, Socrates described the ideal general thus: the general must know how to get his men their rations and every other kind of store needed for war. He must have imagination to originate plans, and the practical sense and energy to carry them through. He must be observant, untiring, shrewd; kindly and cruel; simple and crafty; a watchman and a robber; lavish and miserly; generous and stingy; rash and conservative. All these and many other qualities, natural and acquired, he must have. He should also, as a matter of course, know his tactics; for a disorderly mob is no more an army than a heap of building materials is a house.[25]

In discussing generalship as a concept, the first thing that stands out is its holistic nature. As Socrates states, generals must be many things to many people. Indeed, to the list of attributes above can be added public relations expert, politician, humanitarian, and negotiator. Hughes possessed many of these qualities in abundance. In 1914 and 1915, he was hailed as the most important expediter of the war effort. His ability to raise and dispatch troops seemed boundless. By the time of his removal from cabinet two years later, hundreds of thousands had volunteered and the establishment of the Canadian Expeditionary Force (CEF) had confidently been set at half a million men.[26]

While Sam Hughes would not have articulated it in any theoretical way, at the heart of the generalship is command. As British general and theorist J.F.C. Fuller emphasizes, command is the fulcrum where control of people and the control of technology meet.[27] This fulcrum does not cease to exist simply because we are in the midst of a revolution in military affairs (though the evidence for such a phenomena is dubious to say the least).[28] Nor did it cease during the revolution in warfare surrounding the guns of August. Indeed, this convergence of the human and the technological is a constant in military operations. Fuller wrote:

> Though most of the theory I have quoted is drawn from that epoch of war [before] the industrialization of military power, it is no way incompatible with the needs of the modern age. The theory that the three pillars of Generalship are courage, creative intelligence, and physical fitness, is absolutely sound whether shock or missile weapons predominate, or whether missile weapons are of short or long range.[29]

Without a doubt Sam Hughes had these three pillars. But it remains to see whether they make him a first-rate general.

CANADIAN GENERALSHIP

One of the most persistent themes of the Canadian military experience continues to be our reliance on alliance structures in the pursuit of foreign policy objectives. Since the earliest period of *Nouvelle France*, the importance of alliances in the national experience is clear.[30] The post-conquest period re-enforced this phenomenon to the point that if it was not automatic policy, it certainly was a constant. As a small, poor colony, there would have been no way for British North America to withstand the 1812 onslaught from the United States without remaining intimately associated with both Great Britain and various aboriginal coalitions, the Iroquois Confederacy being the most obvious. Indeed, fifty years later, Confederation itself was the creation of an alliance of the various British North America (BNA) colonies to help protect them against the very real threat of the United States.[31]

In the twentieth century, the ideas of alliances have been refined, but the basic concept remains. Canada went to war in South Africa because such action was in the interest of maintaining our defence alliance with the British Empire. As one of the chief architects of the Canadian involvement in Natal, Sam Hughes was simply giving expression to that fact. He saw alliance relations not only as a necessity but as Canada's duty. Overseas involvement was also a chance to learn, if not lead, in the Empire. Without a doubt, there were many that disagreed, especially in the method and amount of the participation. But then alliance participation has many forms and effects, be they Sam Hughes' fighting roles in 1899 and 1914 or Lloyd Axworthy's "soft power" in the year 2000. Whatever the case, alliances are the main stuff of our participation in two world wars, Korea, and the Cold War. Indeed, Canada has never fought independent of a coalition. There is little doubt that this fact has tempered the way our soldiers and their generals see the way ahead. As William McAndrew has noted, "the closest anyone has come to independent [Canadian] command of a [land] campaign was Major-General Sir Fred Middleton in the Canadian Northwest [in 1885], if he can be appropriated as a temporary Canadian."[32]

Alliance dependence has some interesting side effects. Compared to the senior partners in the group, Canada is usually a very junior ally because of limited resources and interests. For Canadian soldiers this has meant that they have been historically valued because of their technical and tactical talents rather than because of their strategic leadership abilities. Interestingly, Canada, unlike more junior members of the Commonwealth, such as South Africa, Australia, and New Zealand, has never produced a Field Marshal. When Canada went to war in 1899, 1914, and 1939, it was her soldiers' common sense and practical skill that was valued over competence in the command dimensions of warfare. This was a competence Hughes understood implicitly and was most comfortable with, even over the need to develop and nurture professionalism in the officer corps. Besides, in 1914, as the spokesman of the major partner, Lord Kitchener asked only for organized troops – suitable for tactical application to be provided quickly as the British Army retreated from Mons. Initially, and for some time after, Kitchener wanted Canadians as "bayonets" and not much else. Other allies have made similar requests both before and after 1914.[33]

What Hughes did know is that within these limitations of decisions and determinants, as Joel Sokolsky and Dan Middlemiss wrote years later,[34] there were some choices. Hughes made them in terms of keeping the Canadian forces together, in making sure that we had access to information and representation, and that the industrial welfare of the nation was promoted. Through Lord Beaverbrook and others, Hughes was a tireless national publicist of Canada's war effort.

Having established the fact that alliances are intrinsic to Canadian concepts of defence in general and the Canadian way of war in particular, the obvious question is what effect has this had on the development of generalship in Canada? That Canada's relations with her allies have had an effect on the development of Canadian generalship is undoubted. Having never been forced to operate alone or think about unilateral defence, our military has become quite adept at manoeuvring within alliance systems.[35] Combined operations have traditionally held little fear for the Canadian general, but have had a detrimental effect on his understanding of other areas of generalship. The role of corps or division commander within a coalition army has required a technical specialist. But the question remains: do technical specialists have the *Weltanschauung* necessary to become army and national commanders? Many have argued that Sam Hughes had no business being Minister of Militia because he lacked the vision for the task. A study of his political thought might very well affirm that he was a tactician: at his best on the riding stump, or commanding a battalion. His abilities beyond this level were limited. but in this "failing" he was certainly not alone. Much of what he believed and saw while on the verge of leaping into an unknown war in 1914 was normal – just as it is portrayed in C.S. Forester's *The General.*[36]

Professor Douglas Bland has noted that three inhibiting characteristics have defined defence planning and, by extension, generalship in Canada: "Canada's defence policy and the main tasks of the armed forces were set by allied strategic appreciation to which Canadian planners contributed very little. In Ottawa most everyone agreed that a national strategy distinct from allied strategy was not only unthinkable, it was unreasonable and, in a sense, disloyal." Further, "Canadian officers, 'gifted subordinates,' were content to follow foreign military leaders." Finally, "Canada's political and foreign policy establishments [have been] inspired by notions of co-operative internationalism."[37]

As mentioned earlier, the Canadian general has had to master many skills above and beyond basic military competency. Indeed, skill as a bureaucrat, as a politician, and as a heroic figure have weighed far more heavily in the selection of Canadian generals than battlefield skill. This is perhaps true of most armies, but in the Canadian context, it is more obvious in that there have always been so few generals – allegations from the press notwithstanding – and so few wars to participate in. The Canadian general must often ply his craft in the absence of war: that politically indefensible position of commanding soldiers when there is no obvious reason to do so.

Conclusion: Sam Hughes – a General?

Finally we are left with the central question: where does Sam Hughes fit into the image of the Canadian general? Was he a "real" general? Hughes' blind faith in the citizen-soldier was dangerous for the country's regular soldiers. Before the war, he had let the Permanent Force dwindle to 3,000 while he had raised the NPAM to nearly 70,064 in the last summer of peace. It is doubtful that he could have ever destroyed the Permanent Force. Countervailing military trends were too strong for that. But he did impede the growth and efficiency of the regular army. In this process, he had strong supporters as well as critics. Yet few of his contemporaries were able to grasp a complete view of the basic contradiction of his military policy. Perhaps this was so because only retrospective insight through four years of bloody war could clarify that the erosion of the professional force would rob Hughes' militia dream of its life-giving fibre and substance. Whatever the case, with his ministerial discrimination, lack of balance, and his confusion of professionalism with red tape, the regulars steadily lost ground as teachers and leaders. This process would continue until the next German War.[38]

As mentioned earlier, Hughes' conception of the citizen-soldier is central to understanding his leadership – indeed his perception of generalship. However, in combining in politics the responsible citizen role with that of the soldier, Hughes joined two ideas which, although superficially attractive, are antithetical in a democracy. The former emphasizes individual responsibility, freedom of action and speech; the latter demand discipline, routine, and subordination to a clearly structured system of authority. Still, at the micro level embodied by Hughes himself, the dichotomy worked very well. On one hand it allowed him to operate as a democratic citizen and to take independent action; on the other, it let him be a militia officer and function authoritatively as a soldier with the full weight of the military structure behind him. Once he gained a cabinet post, this symbiotic combination gained a greater potency. The outbreak of war in 1914 unleashed an even greater multiplication of the dichotomy.

Hughes' drive and energy, his political success, his constant defence of education as a form of social improvement, and his faith in the country were among his many merits. He always had an instinct for what Canada could do industrially, and, as we know, he did something about it when others were hesitant. So too he had some solid military reform notions, however extreme in their implementation. In the last two decades of the nineteenth century, he was a constant fighter for the improvement of the force. In the Boer War, he spotted – and fatefully criticized – archaic British practices so that his voice contributed to the growing crescendo demanding change; once in office he made his policy clear and then carried it out. During the Great War, still profoundly influenced by his earlier South African experiences, he was in the vanguard of the criticism of British practices and the struggle for national recognition. Indeed, in both conflicts, what had appeared to be typical "Hughesian" generalizations proved true. Ultimately his growing disaffection became a succinct statement of Canada's view of things. Even the frustrated and harried Prime Minister admitted in 1916 that Hughes was often fighting for the right principles with the many nationalist rockets he fired at the British.[39] But these talents, whether expressed in military or political ways, were special and limited. He was tough and could inspire, but could never raise himself above the tactical, personal level of a battalion commander on independent service. To some degree, it was much the same in politics. In the end, Sam Hughes was not a good general. Save in name, he was not a "real" general at all, although he did share some of their qualities. In the brief glimpse that we have of his operational experience, he was a competent senior officer.

This assessment, however, does raise the other aspect of the double-barreled question posed at the beginning of this essay: is he worth studying as a general. The answer is yes. Like it or not Hughes held that rank, so some attention has to be given him. Just before the war he had worked on changing the rules that had prevented Canadians, himself included, from holding substantive general ranks. While he did open the ranks, he did not get himself promoted then because of the Chief of Staff's opposition. However, soon after the war started, he did get a hesitant prime minister to agree to the idea. Borden did so because he felt that Hughes deserved it after the miracle of Valcartier. Hughes likely wanted it because it did not seem fitting that as the "war minister" he should be only a colonel. As a general, he could meet the British on par. They thought that it would make him less prickly in London where he was insisting on all aspects of a Canadian identity – however strained. Canadian Chief of the General Staff Gwatkin was promoted at the same time as his minister was to Major-General. And so Hughes became first a Major-General, then a Lieutenant-General. In short, the rise to his highest rank had distinct personal and political causes rather than being based on professional development or other military merits. Without a doubt, to him the assumption of a general's rank bore a relationship to his position as the Minister, and when he was also knighted by George V in 1915 for his accomplishments in rallying the nation, the synthesis of the citizen and the soldier was then complete.[40]

Even in light of these facts, professional soldiers should never be so arrogant to dismiss him as just a militia soldier and only a political hack. Few societies actually have what might be called "pure" generals – that is, generals who are only practicing their craft in war and without other considerations. Furthermore, Canadians do not fight wars frequently. Most of our generals are of the peacetime variety. As Marti Hooker has noted, given this environment, they therefore serve two masters: the socio-political imperatives and the military ones.[41] Most often these are at odds or at least separate and competitive. Frequently, in trying to serve the military imperative, our generals adopt the processes and characteristics of the socio-political form. There are examples, and perhaps General A.G.L. McNaughton is one of them. In the atrophying atmosphere of the twenties and thirties, he moved into the socio-political mold to protect his beleaguered military force. There are many that believe the experience seriously eroded his ability to be an operational general in the Second World War. Sometimes he too, like Hughes, had no hesitation in stepping across the civil-military boundary: to wit, sending the First Canadian Division to France in 1940 without his government's prior knowledge.[42]

Hughes, of course, shared similar experiences a generation before. Whereas McNaughton was a soldier-politician, Hughes was a politician-soldier, a militiaman whose view of the talented amateur, the part time citizen-soldier, dominated his thinking nearly to the point of burying his appreciation of the professional. In mixing the civil with the military in such a lop-sided way, Sir Sam's ideas of citizen responsibility automatically meant having a similar military capacity resident in the same individual. Thus, according to Hughes' logic, the higher one's civil position the higher should be one's military rank. It was simple then: being the Minister of Militia meant being a Lieutenant-General. As the nation found out by the fall of 1916, Hughes' assumption was not true. Moreover, it was not tolerable. Hughes had to go. It is doubtful if he ever realized that truth. He simply did not have that other quality necessary for successful generalship: a sense of balance.

Indeed by 1916, the nature of the Great War was changing so rapidly that even Hughes the politician was having trouble in keeping up with the new socio-political imperatives, let alone the military ones.

While displaying some of the attributes that under other circumstances could have fulfilled the characteristics of a general, such as in South Africa or as a dynamic early war leader, Sam Hughes was never tested in the rank. Save for the clear field competence he displayed in the Boer War in such tactical and technical areas as intelligence, counter-commando operations, and railway and supply functions, Sam Hughes was a general in name only.

In Lieutenant-General Sir Sam Hughes' career, it is how he mixed and balanced the socio-political and military imperatives that make him not a great general – but, rather, worthy of being studied as one.

ENDNOTES
CHAPTER 1

1. The author would like to thank Lieutenant (Navy) Hugh A. Culliton for his contribution to the preparation of this chapter. As one of Lieutenant-General Romeo Dallaire's former aides at NDHQ for eighteen months, he has, like his General, a passion for the theme examined in this book.

2. Frank Underhill, "Some Reflections on the Liberal Tradition in Canada," The Presidential Address in the *Report of the Annual Meeting of the Canadian Historical Association* (Toronto: University of Toronto Press, 1946), 8.

3. For some early examples, see Sir Andrew MacPhail, *The Official History of the Canadian Forces in the Great War: The Medical Services* (Ottawa: King's Printer, 1925); Ralph Allen, *Ordeal by Fire* (Toronto: Doubleday, 1961), 111; and Roger Graham, *Arthur Meighen*, Volume 1 (Toronto: Clark Irwin, 1960), 106. The debate is lop-sided and most are highly critical of Hughes. The most recent representation was aired on the History Channel in February 2000 when Jack Granatstein, Desmond Morton, and Ron Haycock presented the entire spectrum of historical opinion. See CRB Foundation, *The Canadians: Biographies of a Nation.* http://www.heritageproject.ca/learning/lessons/cdns-tv/default.html.

4. Desmond Morton, *Ministers and Generals, Politics and the Canadian Militia, 1868-1904* (Toronto: University of Toronto Press, 1970), 146.

5. Stephen Harris, *Canadian Brass: The Making of a Professional Army, 1860-1939* (Toronto: University of Toronto Press, 1988), introduction and chapter 1.

6. Militia Orders, *1897* (July) GO65; National Archives of Canada, hereafter NAC, RG 9, II B 1, 250, 65436 DA:AG (HQ) to DOC 3 June 1897; Ibid. Cotton to DA: AG(HQ), 7 June 1897, and Public Archives of Nova Scotia, F. W. Borden Papers, Volume 140, f4, 2020, AG, 3 June 1897. Also see Militia Orders, *1897,* GOs 83, 8788 and 106, and NAC, RG 9, II - B 1, Volumes 250 and 256 which contain the

documentation between the Minister, the GOC, and other authorities that saw Hughes promoted to command the 45th Battalion.

7. Carl Berger's *The Sense of Power: Studies in Ideas of Canadian Imperialism, 1867-1914* (Toronto: University of Toronto Press, 1968) is the best book yet on this subject.

8. After the war the various letters were collected for Parliament. In due course, they were used by Sam's friends and foes alike to prove a variety of things. See the NAC pamphlet 2565, *Correspondence Touching on the Conduct of Lieutenant-Colonel Hughes, M.P. in Connection with his Volunteering for Service in South Africa.* Also see L. Drummond to Minto, 12 January 1900 in the files of Dr. C. Miller. This letter is typical of the reaction of some of the English soldiers who did not like the pushy Canadian Lieutenant-Colonel in South Africa.

9. See Haycock, Chapter 5: "The Proving Ground: South Africa 1900" for an analysis of Hughes' ideas and his role while in South Africa.

10. Lionel Curtis, *With Milner in South Africa* (Oxford: Blackwells, 1951), 27, is one example.

11. Great Britain, National Army Museum (NAM), Lord Roberts, papers, 1101-23-111-3, No. 67, Roberts to Warren, 20 June 1900; Ibid., No. 759, Cowan to Warren, 25 June 1900; Ibid., No. 780, A/Mil-Sec Pretoria to Chowder, 27 June 1900, and the *Cape Times*, 13 June 1900, 5.

12. The best assessment of "bad British generalship" is Thomas Pakenham's *The Boer War* (New York: Random House, 1975).

13. See Hamilton's *Report*, and NAC, Loring Christie Papers, Vol. 2, f3, 4039, Memorandum on Mobilisation, nd. and Ibid., 1260–8, Memorandum on Sending Canadian Forces Outside of Canada, 6 June 1917.

14. *Hansard*, 1916, 287.

15. Ibid.; and Haycock, *Sam Hughes*, 181.

16. Philip Magnuss, *Kitchener: Portrait of an Imperialist* (London: Penguin, 1968), 374-5.

17. Domino, *Masques of Ottawa* (Toronto: Macmillan, 1921), 141–152: *CAR*, 1914, 200-202; Ibid.; 1915, 186–187.

18. See NAC, RG 24, Vol. 413, 54-21-1-29, "Report on the Construction of Valcartier Camp": Nicholson, *CEF*, 20, Hansard, 1915, 522-26; NAC, Sir George Foster, diaries, MG 27, 11, D7, September 19, 1914; also *CAR*, 1914, 200–1; and NAC Borden, private diaries, 6 September 1914.

19. Great Britain, Oxford University, Bodleian Library, Viscount Harcourt *papers*, 476, No. 29, Connaught to Harcourt, private and confidential, 5 October 1914, 175-179. Also NAC, Borden, private diaries, 16 and 17, September 1914.

20. Domino, *Masques*, 141-152; and *CAR*, 1914, 200-201. For Hughes' creation of the munitions industry see David Carnegie, *The History of Munitions Supply in Canada, 1914-1918* (London: Macmillan, 1925).

21. R.G. Haycock, "Early Weapons Acquisition: "That Damned Ross Rifle," *Canadian Defence Quarterly*, Vol. 14, No. 3, Winter, 1984/85. For a detailed examination of Hughes' involvement in the Ross Rifle controversy, the reader should see Haycock's *Sam Hughes*.

22. Colonel A.F. Duguid, (Clive M. Law ed.) *A Question of Confidence: The Ross Rifle in the Trenches* (Ottawa: Service Publications, 1999), iv.

23. One does not have to look too much further than the 1920s and 1930s to see the political aversion to any military involvement that might repeat the Great War's traumatic experience. For a recent look at the Great War's effect on the national memory of the generation who fought it, see Jonathan Vance's excellent *A Death so Noble: Memory, Meaning and the First World War* (Vancouver: UBC Press, 1997). Perhaps the fear of casualties has never left the national psyche. Some say that the hesitation of the Mulroney Government to commit Canadian forces to a greater combat role during the Gulf war had the same basis.

24. Report to the Prime Minister on the Leadership and Management of the Canadian Forces, The Honourable M. Douglas Young, PC MP Minister of National Defence, (Canada: DND, 25 March 1997). See appendices by Professors Bercuson, Granatstein, and Morton relating to professional development and education of the officer corps.

25. Socrates as quoted in Sir Archibald Wavell *Generals and Generalship* (Toronto: Macmillan, 1941).

26. NAC, RG 9, III CEF box 203320 HS-20-H-3, and J. Castell Hopkins *The Canadian Annual Review of Public Affairs, 1914* (Toronto: CAR Publishing, 1914), 214; and the entries for the Canadian publics' favourable to Hughes' efforts (Ibid., 200-202). Also see Domino, *Masques of Ottawa* (Toronto: Macmillan, 1921), 141-152.

27. J.F.C. Fuller, *Generalship: Its Diseases and their Cure* (London: Faber and Faber, 1933).

28. For a critical examination of the concept of a revolution in military affairs, see *Army Lessons Learned Bulletin*, Fall 1998. Also see Scott

Robertson and Sean Maloney, "The Revolution in Military Affairs" in *International Journal,* Summer 1999, 443-462.

29. Fuller, 33.

30. Desmond Morton, *Canada and War* (Toronto: Butterworth & Co. Canada Ltd., 1981), 2-8; also see his "Reflections on the History of Canada," in *Canadian Speeches,* Vol. 8, No. 9, 15-20.

31. R.A. Preston, *Canada and Imperial Defence: A Study in the Origins of the British Commonwealth Defence Organization, 1867-1919* (Durham: Duke, 1967), chapters 1 and 2.

32. William McAndrew, *Operational Art and the Canadian Army's Way of War,* in B.J.C. McKercher and M.A. Hennessy (eds.) *The Operational Art: Developments in the Theories of War* (Westport, CT: Praeger Press, 1996).

33. A.F. Duguid, *The Official History of the Canadian Forces in the Great War: 1914-1919* (Ottawa: King's Printer, 1938), Volume 1, appendices, # 64, CO to GG, 14 August 1914; Ibid. No. 65 and Ibid. No. 98, CO to GG, 1 September 1914.

34. D.W. Middlemiss and J.J. Sokolsky, *Canadian Defence:Decisions and Determinants* (Toronto: Harcourt Brace, Janovich, 1989).

35. Harris, 168.

36. C.S. Forester, *The General* (London: Penguin, 1956). While in 1914 both men faced the unknown, confident that their past would be the future, in many other ways Hughes was completely different than Forester's character, General Sir Herbert Curzon. To greatly understate it, Hughes was unconventional and Curzon the epitome of convention. Hughes was a militiaman – Curzon a regular. Neither was stupid. But what they shared was the expectation of coming out of the Boer War. And they shared moral values: in Forester's words about Curzon, "he would give his life for the ideals he stood for.... His patriotism was a real and living force ... his courage was unflinching. The necessity of assuming responsibility troubled him no more than the necessity of breathing." Ibid., 24-25. Indeed, one would have to look hard to find a Canadian anywhere in history who exhibited such prescient qualities. Perhaps only General Guy Simmonds came close. But then again, such political understanding is equally rare at the political level as well. See J.L. Granatstein, *The Generals: The Canadian Army's Senior Generals in the Second World War* (Toronto: Stoddart, 1993), 64-68, and Farley Mowat, *The Regiment* (Toronto: McClelland and Stewart, 1989 paper edition), chapter 3.

37. Douglas L. Bland, *Chiefs of Defence: Government and the Unified Command of the Canadian Armed Forces* (Toronto: Brown Book Company, 1995).

38. Sessional Papers, 1915, No.35, "Report of the Militia Council for the Financial Year Ending 31 March 1915," 24-26.

39. NAC, Borden papers, DC 318, Hughes to Atken, 30 Nov 1915; and NAC, Sir George Perley, papers, Vol. 4, Borden to Hughes, 30 November 1915; Ibid. Borden to Perley, 2 December 1915.

40. NAC, Borden, private diaries, 11 August, 12 September, and 22 September 1914 and 12 October 1914. Militia List, July 1917, 57 and 107; and Haycock, *Sam Hughes*, 156-60.

41. Marti Hooker, "Serving Two Masters: Ian MacKenzie and Civil-Military Relations in Canada, 1935-1939," *Journal of Canadian Studies*, Vol. 21, No. 2, 38-56.

42. Granatstein, *The Generals*, 64-68; and Mowat, *The Regiment*, chapter 3.

CHAPTER 2

THE MILITARY LEADERSHIP OF
SIR ARTHUR CURRIE

A.M.J. Hyatt

S ENIOR Allied officers of the First World War generally have poor public reputations. A prominent critic once wrote that the ordinary soldier did not even see the generals, that "now and again he heard of them far away ... sitting in the chateaux and in the offices."[1] A more recent commentator claims that generals of the First World War had authoritarian personalities, and thus were "dogmatic, inflexible, callous, ethnocentric, conformist, obsessive. The authoritarian soldier yearns for professional success and yet, ironically, is prevented from achieving it because of his personality."[2] The British Commander-in-Chief, Sir Douglas Haig, has been characterized as "a stubborn, fame-hungry, cold-blooded, deceiving oaf, and his [Passchendaele] campaign as a military abortion unparalleled in the history of the western world."[3]

Yet there is a different case to be made – at least for the Canadian generals. For the record, during the First World War there were 126 Canadian generals of whom 69 served in France. If you follow them carefully, 42 percent of these 69 generals were wounded, killed, or taken prisoner.[4] Among the 698,636 Canadians who served in the war the casualty rate was 37.5 percent (232,494).[5] One should be cautious about such comparisons, but these figures are an interesting starting point from which to consider the generalship of the highest ranking officer in the Canadian Forces in the First World War.[6] With 42 percent of participating combat generals becoming casualties, Canadian generals were obviously not "sitting in the chateaux and the offices." Their leader, Sir Arthur Currie, however, has always had a mixed reception among Canadians.

While those who study him carefully find much to admire, his reputation during the war and later in the popular press was subject to controversy. Historian Arthur Lower, himself a participant in the war, spoke for many when he observed that Canadians "became intensely proud of their fighting men, though characteristically took little interest in their generals."[7] Although Currie commanded what was unarguably the most successful large military organization to that point in Canadian history, although he was praised by the British and

Canadian prime ministers and by admiring biographers, he has always had severe critics – particularly journalists and media commentators. Historians, of course, have added to the controversy about both Currie in particular and military leadership in general. But the saving grace of most historical scholarship is that its judgements on leadership, most of the time, seem to be based on the actual record of events and personal performance. This is not always the case with social scientists who colour their judgements with such determinants as genetic factors or psychological theories. And the media's "thirty-second clip" rarely matches the historical reality.[8] The argument in this essay is that any reasonable judgement of military leadership, particularly Currie's leadership, requires a consideration of historical record and context.

Currie was the first, indeed the only, Canadian officer to command the Canadian Corps during the First World War. The achievements of his command were largely responsible for creating the atmosphere which allowed a huge step towards independent nationhood and which fostered a sense of Canadian identity. The Canadian Corps, in short, was a special and important formation even if its size and status within the British Army did not place Currie among the top group of British generals. His command, for example, was sufficiently small enough that he was never required to make strategic decisions. His diary and letters contain many sensible strategic comments, but these were never made with the knowledge that he would have to implement them. He was simply not that highly placed in the British military pyramid, even if he was at the peak of the Canadian pyramid.

In the British Army Currie had many disadvantages. For example, he became Corps Commander with remarkably little experience as a full-time soldier. Long a member of the Canadian Militia – he had joined it in 1897 as a private and in 1914 had reached the rank of Lieutenant-Colonel – he had had no full-time army service before the war, and he resigned from the army within a year of the armistice.[9] His total full-time career service, in other words, was less than five years. Although Lloyd George, the British Prime Minister, would later argue that Currie's success was in large measure the result of being an amateur soldier,[10] the evidence for this is slight. In fact, Currie's amateur status and his lack of experience were substantial disadvantages for him in the British Army.

Currie had other problems. Not the least of these was his appearance; he was a soldier at a time when appearance counted for a good deal more than it does today. Currie was a big man – over six feet tall and well over two hundred pounds. However, because of his shape he seemed conspicuous and awkward rather than dignified and impressive. He had a pear-shaped figure topped with a narrow head, which was emphasized by his long jowls. Currie's uniform always looked uncomfortable; his tunic habitually bunched over the top of his Sam Browne belt, which appeared to encircle his chest rather than his waist because of his large bottom half. According to a young soldier serving in the ranks, "Currie always looked too heavy for his horse."[11] I mention Currie's physical appearance because it too was a substantial handicap and an impediment in his relations with senior commanders in the British Army and his own soldiers. In soldierly bearing Currie was at the other extreme from Sir Douglas Haig, the British Commander-in-Chief. Whatever else may be said of Haig, he looked an impeccable military portrait. Furthermore, he liked his officers to have a soldierly deportment. Currie did not qualify.

Few commanders, indeed few people, are able to conduct their affairs – business, professional, or personal – in isolation from private problems. Throughout the war Currie had a worrisome problem that created difficulty for him. In 1914, when he left for overseas, he had taken more than $10,000 from militia regimental funds to pay personal debts.[12] This was a very large sum in 1914, and the money belonged to his regiment. His action could as easily be called theft or embezzlement as it could be called a debt. At the very least it was illegal expropriation, though he preferred to think of it as a personal loan.[13] Currie made no attempt to repay this money, in spite of substantial salary increases, until 1917. It seems clear that he was motivated then by fear of public exposure. Unknown to Currie, the matter was revealed to the Prime Minister, Sir Robert Borden, and to the Minister of Overseas Military Forces of Canada, Sir George Perley. Both men were appalled by the discovery. Indeed, Perley volunteered to pay off half the debt if Sir Edward Kemp, the Minister of Militia, would discharge the other half. Before any official action could be taken, Currie himself borrowed from two wealthy subordinates and repaid what he had taken. Currie seems never to have learned that Borden and Perley had known of his guilty secret. Indeed the whole matter was simply dropped. It was never mentioned by his first biographer, though he obviously knew about it. Nor is there any mention of the affair in any of the several accounts of the Canadian Corps and its operations. However, the possibility of exposure constantly worried him, and, at the very least, did not make the task of commanding the Canadian Corps any easier. Writing of the debt in a private communication in June 1917, Currie claimed that "for nearly three years the last thing I thought of at night and the first thing in the morning was this."[14] However much this secret bothered him, it seems likely that it had less impact on the way the Corps Commander appeared to his soldiers than did his inability to be charismatic in front of them.

John Keegan argues that a commander "must speak directly to his men, raising their spirits in time of trouble, inspiring them at moments of crisis and thanking them for victory."[15] Currie tried. He was frequently at the front. He carried out thousands of inspections of all kinds of formations. He addressed the troops, encouraged the troops, exhorted the troops, and thanked the troops. But he could never inspire the troops, except on those occasions when he provoked them to anger. This could happen whenever he addressed large numbers of soldiers either in person or in a formal written proclamation. The worst of such occasions was probably his special order of 27 March 1918.

This order, written at the height of German success in the spring offensive of 1918, was intended to raise morale and stiffen resistance. At least one observer insisted that "it evoked a jeer from every trench and dugout."[16] Among other things, the message was too long and the prose was too purple. It was read to soldiers as well as published in all unit orders. It contained segments of Edwardian sentiment, which seem very foreign today, and passages which seem ludicrous even for 1918. A brief sample will suffice as illustration: "Under the orders of your devoted officers in the coming battle you will advance or fall when you stand facing the enemy." This sentence alone would leave the listener with questions, but the speech got worse: "To those who will fall I say: You will not die, but step into immortality. Your mothers will not lament your fate, but will be proud to have borne such sons." On another occasion he told survivors of an infantry battalion returning from the front line, "that is the way I like to see you, mud and blood."[17] By 1918 many soldiers simply could not swallow such prose, and it did not do much for mothers either. The great French general, Marshal Lyautey, believed that first among the imperatives of command was "speaking with all the arts of the actor and orator to the soldiers."[18] Currie was devoid of such arts. As a listener from the ranks put it: "General Currie did not seem to have the gift for stroking fur the right way."[19]

This was not, by any means, the end of Currie's problems. On occasion he was suspicious and jealous of colleagues and barely civil to his political superiors. His difficulties included a longstanding, turbulent relationship with Sir Sam Hughes, a strong prejudice about politics and politicians, and a substantial distrust of the press. Even without going into these problems in detail, the puzzle is how someone with these inadequacies could be successful as a military commander. Although some British officers thought him to be inexperienced, although he was an imposing rather than an impressive figure, although he lacked the flair of a charismatic leader, although he may well have been preoccupied with personal problems which made his job more difficult, nonetheless his formations kept winning. Judged by the records of the formations he commanded, his success was quite remarkable.

Two caveats should be added. First, the records of the formationsthat Currie commanded – the 2nd Canadian Infantry Brigade for twelve months, the 1st Canadian Division for twenty-one months, and the Canadian Corps for seventeen months during the war and nine months after the war – were extremely good, though not the unbroken string of successes some have suggested. Second, the success of any large modern formation or, for that matter, its failure can rarely be attributed solely to its commander. In modern war sheer size of formations and sophistication of weaponry rule out such simplistic attribution. Nonetheless, the records of Currie's commands reflect very well on their commander, and, interestingly, the operations which left Currie most dissatisfied are sometimes those which showed him at his best.

A perfect example of this is the attack made by the 1st Canadian Division on Regina Trench during the Battle of the Somme in September and October of 1916.[20] For twenty-five days the German strong point opposite the Canadians eluded capture. Each attack followed essentially the same pattern: intense artillery bombardment followed by infantry attacking in waves. Each time the barrage ended, the enemy emerged from its dugouts and harvested another crop of Canadians. It was Currie's first severe test as a division commander, and he had been given little freedom in planning his attacks. He was very dissatisfied with the result. He conducted his own post-action investigation and undertook a detailed analysis of a particularly unsuccessful attack on 8 October. Before putting pencil to paper, Currie interviewed all available unwounded officers who had participated in this attack. In addition he talked to at least three men in each participating company. His analysis of the attack spared neither himself nor his subordinates, but he found no scapegoats. There were many deficiencies, which he took up one by one. But, in the end, he concluded, none of these deficiencies, singularly or together, really explained the failure.

In spite of everything left undone, in spite of wire obstacles that were intact, and enemy fire of "hurricane"[21] force, Canadian soldiers did reach the enemy's lines and "did not give up as long as bombs were available."

Yet the attack on 8 October had failed. Here, according to Currie, was the real rub. It was possible, even under the adverse conditions of the Somme, to get into enemy trenches. Once there, the attackers could not hope to hold out unless reinforced and well supplied with bombs and ammunition. In the existing circumstances this had been impossible. Given the fire-power of the enemy, reinforcements could be sent forward only if they could move safely through communication trenches, and communication trenches could be dug only at night. British attacks invariably started at dawn. In future, Currie believed, assaults should be timed so that night would cover reinforcement and supply activities. This suggestion was only one of many sensible observations, and this episode is only one of many such reports written by Currie or carried out on his orders. Collectively Currie's reports and analyses suggest that he was a natural tactician, above all, one who continually sought victory at the lowest possible cost in lives.

Whether or not such activity is great leadership, it goes far in explaining the success of the Canadian Corps, particularly when linked to two other things. First, Currie insisted on training people for the job they were required to do. After 1916, he was insistent that whenever the Corps was out of the front line, they would be resting or training. Indeed, a series of permanent training schools was established by the Canadian Corps in France to compensate for the lack of realistic training in Canada and England. Training, it seems, is a much more useful explanation of military success and successful military leadership than most of the social science paradigms for success. Currie was a fanatic about training.[22] Second, he was equally insistent about communicating clearly down to the lowest level. In his 1916 report, he argued that "to tell a Machine Gunner to take up his position at M14 b2.6. Or a Bomber to establish a block at M8 d3.0. is an absurd order unless some other means of fixing this point has been explained." Currie worried a great deal about the process of getting orders quickly and simply from the top to the bottom of the military chain of command in the Canadian Corps.

The Second World War British general, Howard Essame, described the communication problem facing a junior officer in the First World War. Before every battle, he claimed, "there descended on us an immense spate of paper, operation orders, appendices and sketches, to be followed by amendments and, later, amendments to amendments. By the time we moved back to the line, the file was nearly a foot thick and quite unintelligible."[23] Earlier in the war this procedure had been common in the Canadian Corps. But by August 1918, at Currie's insistence, the process of issuing orders and having them expand as they passed down the line had been virtually reversed. Currie's headquarters would issue a comprehensive battle order to all infantry divisions and supporting arms and services. Each sub-commander would then extract from this general order the purpose of the whole operation and the instructions relevant to his own formation. The latter would be automatically elaborated in sub-formation orders and quickly forwarded to the next lower formation. In approximately three to eight hours the corps commander's orders would reach the lowest private soldier and would do so in an intelligible manner. The infantry private would know the general objective of his own battalion and the specific task of his platoon and company; he knew who was working to his right and left and what support was available to him; he was given special instructions for specific obstacles that lay in his path; he knew when and where he would receive his next rations, the location of the field dressing station, and when he could expect to be relieved. This entire process took place smoothly as the general order issued by Currie's headquarters was expanded and contracted automatically at every level. All of this occurred because Currie, an extraordinarily poor communicator in some instances, insisted on an excellent method of communication in military operations.

Currie was also well known for insisting that sending under-strength units into battle resulted in more casualties, proportionately, than would be the case if units fought the same action at full strength. The accuracy of this proposition, of course, could never be tested, but Currie believed the principle needed no proof. Indeed, he believed this so passionately that he rejected the reorganization of the Canadian Corps proposed in January 1918 by British authorities which would have resulted in the formation of a Canadian army and a promotion for him to the rank of full general and the position of army commander.[24]

The reorganization was the British answer to the increasing severity of the problem of reinforcements. Britain had introduced conscription long before the spring of 1917 when Sir Robert Borden announced that Canada would solve the Canadian reinforcement problem by introducing conscription. This action by the Prime Minister began one of the greatest political crises in Canadian history. For Currie, as for most soldiers in France in the spring of 1917, conscription seemed essential to keep the Corps supplied with reinforcements. When he became Corps Commander in June 1917, he had complied without cavil to Borden's request for a statement that made "clear the need for reinforcements to maintain [the] Canadian Corps as full strength."[25] Thus in mid-June Currie maintained that conscription was essential, and he seemed prepared to do whatever possible to have compulsory military service adopted as quickly as possible. Over the summer, as the debate in Canada grew in intensity, the solution to the problem of reinforcements seemed to him less and less likely to be conscription. While the debate raged in Canada, the Canadian Corps suffered a total of 15,654 casualties.[26] By late Autumn Currie was certain that conscription could not provide reinforcements by the spring of 1918, and he felt that he had been used by politicians. When the British plan for reorganization came along in January, Currie used the British initiative to argue for his own solution to the problem of reinforcements.

He believed that reducing each infantry brigade by one battalion, which in essence was the British plan, would merely result in sending under-strength brigades into battle and thus higher casualties. Moreover, to form a second Canadian Corps and a Canadian army headquarters would increase the Canadian administrative overhead out of all proportion to Canadian fighting strength. He argued that the Canadian Corps should not follow the British reorganization, but should maintain its present organization and use as reinforcements the men of the 5th Canadian Division, which had been confined to service in Britain. This division was at full strength while the four divisions of the Canadian Corps in France were desperately under strength. Currie's idea worked brilliantly. The Canadian Corps was at full strength before the first Canadian conscripts arrived in France, in time to face the crisis caused by the German attacks in the spring of 1918.

There was something else about Currie which is very important in explaining his success as Corps Commander. Currie had the capacity to put together a team of outstanding talent. He was not afraid to appoint subordinates who knew more than he did, and he did not lean over their shoulders while they did their jobs. As a consequence, in small groups he gave a very different impression than he did on formal occasions. General Andy McNaughton has testified to Currie's ability to induce extraordinary loyalty from those he worked with closely.[27] Among friends or in small groups, Currie seemed to lose his stiffness. With his defences down, he could laugh at himself, cuss with salty fluency and be very human. In the words of his post-war secretary who noticed the same transformation, when he was face to face with someone, "all pretentiousness seemed to melt away."[28] He could then demonstrate precisely the characteristics which the troops might have admired but which were so conspicuously absent when he was with them on formal occasions. Currie, according to historian Stephen Harris, "created an atmosphere which allowed for, in fact positively demanded, the movement of ideas from below."[29] Currie's senior subordinates were intensely loyal to him and flocked to his support at the 1928 libel trial.[30] "Tiny" Ironside, later to become Chief of the Imperial General Staff, was attached to the Canadian Corps for more than two years. He claimed that Currie "trusted his staff in an ideal way and yet never ceased to command. Nobody ran Currie." Speaking of the atmosphere among officers at corps headquarters, he said that there "friction could not exist. There we were like a band of brothers."[31] And this band, which included the senior officers in divisions and brigades, was tenaciously loyal to its chief.

Currie's tactical comprehension, his penetrating post-action analyses, his capacity for organization and fanaticism about training and communication, his ability to put together a skilled team of staff officers and divisional and brigade commanders were all important elements in his success as Corps Commander. Even those who were infuriated by his speeches could recognize his leadership capacity. Wilfrid B. Kerr, one of Currie's most intelligent and severe critics wrote that "at no time, even among the men who could not mention his name without some coarse allusion to his personal appearance, [was there] any question of his military skill."[32] Lloyd George, the British Prime Minister, argued in his memoirs that Currie and the brilliant Sir John Monash of the Australian army should have gone to the very top of the military hierarchy. But that did not happen. Currie was a Corps Commander, and a very good one.

From his career I think some generalization is possible. He was clearly not a heroic leader, but he was not one of the "chateaux generals." He was frequently at the front. He knew exactly what was happening there, and he never stopped trying to reduce casualties. Currie's leadership and the success of the Canadian Corps suggest that generalship cannot be measured by a neat and tidy formula. Formulas are too simple for the description of senior leadership in modern warfare. Currie's career speaks more of organizational ability than heroic action, more of endurance than impulsiveness, more of intelligence than instinct, more of careful study and planning than of intuition and sudden action. Currie never had the benefit of a university education, but he never stopped learning. Perhaps he is proof of the proposition that the most important thing a professional soldier can have is an open mind.

Unfortunately Currie's career has not always been studied with an open mind. In general those who are interested in him have found him either totally admirable, to the point where his obvious shortcomings are not merely overlooked but covered up, or, have found him guilty of the most egregious behaviour and have accepted slander as evidence against Currie.

The slander that hurt him most in his own lifetime was the accusation that he caused needless casualties among Canadians during the last hundred days of the war, and particularly that he was responsible for the unnecessary death of many Canadian soldiers during the recapture of Mons on 11 November 1918. This charge was first uttered by an ill and unbalanced Sir Sam Hughes in Parliament in 1918. Hughes repeated his accusation on several occasions in the House of Commons where he was protected from retaliation by parliamentary privilege. His remarks were the foundation for allegations, which were printed in the *Port Hope Guide* in 1927.

Currie sued for libel and won, but the cost was substantial. Colonel Urquhart, the biographer who knew him best, argued that his health at the close of the trial "was already on the verge of a breakdown."[33] Shortly afterward he became seriously ill and remained frail until his death in 1933. Although he was spared repetition of the false charges during his lifetime, they did not go away. A CBC television program, produced some seventy years later and called "The Killing Ground," repeated much of the old slander. A review of the program claimed that on 10 November 1918 Currie "decided that a last-minute assault of the Belgium city of Mons would be a glorious way to close out the war.... His men ... were horrified when the order was given.... When the battle was over 26 Canadian soldiers ... were buried in the fields of Europe.... The circumstances of their tragedy have been distorted and mythologized for 70 years. We may never get the full story, but 'The Killing Ground' is the closest we have ever come."[34]

In fact we had already come much closer. The full story emerges only from the context of Currie's experience. This context first became apparent during the Currie trial when a massive examination of casualties demonstrated that on the 11th of November one man was killed and fifteen were wounded. The trial also proved that the attack was not something that Currie initiated. This was confirmed when the official history was published in 1962 and has subsequently been re-examined and accepted by biographers and other historians. All of this occurred before the production of "The Killing Ground." Context, apparently, is something easily dismissed by the modern media.

During the war Currie was a new general with many problems and difficulties. He overcame many obstacles during his career and, by any standard, showed himself to be a brilliant tactician and a sound military leader. Whatever his deficiencies, he accepted the most difficult responsibility of any military commander – the certain knowledge that in war casualties can never be avoided, only minimized. His slogan became "pay the price of victory in shells not lives." Currie believed that constant planning and preparation were the best way to reduce the imponderables that plague every commander. Good luck was also important. Clearly Currie had more of this during the war in the conduct of operations than he had with his post-war detractors.

ENDNOTES

CHAPTER 2

1. J.F.C. Fuller, *Generalship: Its Diseases and Their Cure* (London: Faber and Faber, 1950), 15.
2. Ronald Lewin, "On the Psychology of Military Incompetence by Norman F. Dixon," *London Times,* 17 June, 1976.
3. Leon Wolff, *In Flanders Field: The 1917 Campaign* (New York, 1958), 241.
4. A.M.J. Hyatt, "Canadian Generals of the First World War and the Popular View of Military Leadership," *Histoire Sociale – Social History,* Vol. XII, November 1979, 425.
5. G.W.L. Nicholson, *Canadian Expeditionary Force 1914-1919: Official History of the Canadian Army in the First World War* (Ottawa: Queen's Printer, 1962*),* 546 and 548. The figure on casualties used here is the sum of the total deaths from all causes and the total non-fatal casualties expressed as a percentage of total mobilization. C.E.W. Bean, the Australian official historian argues that a more accurate percentage of Canadian casualties is 49.74. In either case 42% of casualties among generals who served in France is impressive when compared to the overall casualty rate. See, Hyatt, "Canadian Generals," 425, No.15.
6. It should be noted that lieutenant-general rank was also held by Sir Richard Turner.
7. Arthur M. Lower, *Colony to Nation: A History of Canada* (Toronto, 1957), 456.
8. The basis for this comment is "The Kid Who Couldn't Miss," the controversial National Film Board biography of Billy Bishop, the CBC program called "The Killing Ground," which dealt with Arthur Currie, and finally the McKenna brothers CBC production "The Valour and the Horror."
9. Unless otherwise indicated all biographical details are from: A.M.J. Hyatt, *General Sir Arthur Currie: A Military Biography* (Toronto: University of Toronto Press, 1987).
10. David Lloyd George, *War Memoirs of David Lloyd George,*

(London: I. Nicholson & Watson, 1936), vi, 3423-3, 3524, 3382.

11. General W.H.S. Macklin to author, 10 June 1962.

12. The best account of Currie's debts is in R. Craig Brown and Desmond Morton, "The Embarrassing Apotheosis of a 'Great Canadian': Sir Arthur Currie's Personal Crisis in 1917," *Canadian Historical Review*, Vol. LX, March 1979, 41-63.

13. One of his biographers, Daniel G. Dancocks, called the episode a "minor indiscretion on Currie's part concerning regimental funds" Dancocks, *Sir Arthur Currie: A Biography* (Toronto: Methuen 1985), 202. It was anything but minor.

14. National Archives of Canada, hereinafter NAC, Currie Papers, Currie to Forsythe, 25 June 1917.

15. John Keegan, *The Mask of Command* (New York: Pimlico, 1987), 318.

16. William Benton Kerr, *Arms and the Maple Leaf: Memoiries of Canada's Corps 1918* (Seaforth, Ontario The Huron expositor press, 1943), 28.

17. Hugh M. Urquhart, *Arthur Currie: A Biography of a Great Canadian* (Toronto: J.M. Dent and Sons Ltd., 1950), 223.

18. Keegan, 321.

19. Kerr, 28.

20. See Nicholson, 182-88; and Hyatt, *General Sir Arthur Currie*, 59-61.

21. All quotations are from Currie's report: NAC, Currie Papers, Currie to Canadian Corps, 16 October l916.

22. The best account of technology and training in the Canadian Corps is found in Bill Rawling, *Surviving Trench Warfare: Technology and the Canadian Corps 1914-1918* (Toronto: University of Toronto Press, 1992).

23. Major-General H. Essame, "Second Lieutenants Unless Otherwise Stated," *Military Review*, Vol. XLIV, May 1964, 92.

24. A.M.J. Hyatt, "Sir Arthur Currie and Conscription: A Soldier's View," *Canadian Historical Review*, Vol. L, September 1969, 295-6.

25. NAC, Perley Papers, vol. 9, Borden to Perley, 18 June 1917.

26. Nicholson, 237.

27. Interview with General A.G.L. McNaughton.

28. Dorothy McMurray, "Only Grandfather's Wore Beards" (n.p., Canadian War Museum Library), 7.

29. Stephen J. Harris, *Canadian Brass: The Making of a Professional Army, 1860-1939* (Toronto: University of Toronto Press, 1988), 124.

30. The best account of the Currie trial is by Robert J. Sharpe, *The Last Day the Last Hour: the Currie Libel Trial* (Toronto: The Osgoode

Society, 1988). See also, John Swettenham, *To Seize the Victory: The Canadian Corps in World War I* (Toronto: Ryerson Press, 1965).

31. Cited in Urquhart, 269-70.
32. Kerr, 45.
33. Urquhart, 321.
34. *Calgary Herald,* 7 November 1988.

CHAPTER 3

BRUTINEL:
A UNIQUE KIND OF LEADERSHIP[1]

Yves Tremblay

NORTH America has often been contrasted with "Old" Europe as the young continent on which talent and opportunity – rather than social status and standing – reign. Canada, at the turn of the twentieth century, offered real opportunities of this kind to anyone with talent and the skills to promote it.

Brigadier-General Raymond Brutinel, CB, CMG, DSO (1882–1964), was precisely one of those enterprising individuals who felt constrained in his own nation and would find his true destiny in voluntary exile abroad. Born in the foothills of the Pyrenees, Raymond Brutinel was the child of small landowners of little distinction. His ancestors had been shepherds in Scotland; most of them later became farmers, although some were also sailors, soldiers, merchants, and even missionaries. More recently, various Brutinels had spent less than exciting careers in the Gendarmes (a branch of the French Army) with all that offered in the way of security – a programmed career with a civil service pension following an equally well programmed retirement.

Brutinel's physique was not typically military. He was a stout 5 feet 7 inches tall and weighed more than 180 pounds in 1919. Furthermore, his vision was poor: he wore glasses his entire adult life and would end up almost blind. And, while the future general had benefited from good secondary studies at the Collège des jésuites de Carcassonne (Jesuits' College of Carcassonne), his formal education had stopped there. His only real distinction, then, was his adventuresome spirit. At the age of 16, he left the Jesuits and became a sailor on a three-master plying between the West Indies and South America.

Upon his return to France in 1901, he was called upon to complete his military service, like all young Frenchman of the time. He would make the most of the situation. A mere enlisted man in the 53rd Régiment d'infanterie de Tarbes, he became a drill-sergeant, then fencing master and was finally called out of the ranks and into the platoon of officer-cadets. He then quit the army and emigrated to Canada. In the meantime, Brutinel made what would prove a very promising marriage, although he could not know it at the time. In 1903, he wed Marie Calamun, daughter of a man of high standing from the Hautes-Pyrénées and niece of Colonel Ferdinand Foch, a native of Tarbes.[2] Foch, former head of studies at the École de guerre, stood in disgrace with the Republican lay government of the day because of his devout Catholicism. The French government made him commander of the 35th Régiment d'artillerie in Vannes; thus, they could send him far from Paris. Foch was yet to publish his masterworks, *Des principes de la guerre* and *De la conduite de la guerre* in 1903 and 1904 respectively.[3]

So, why did Brutinel suddenly abandon his military career at that time? In a 1964 letter, addressed to Larry Worthington, General F.F. Worthington's wife, he explained that numerous soldiers of Catholic belief, fed up with the various plots that were being hatched against them, had decided to emigrate en masse to Alberta's Trochu Valley.[4] It would appear that the anti-Catholic policies of the French ministry, which had momentarily slowed the career of Foch, had also compelled the young Brutinel to embark upon a new adventure – emigration. Brutinel left the army and was transferred to the reserves with the rank of lieutenant.

With a young wife and their first child, Brutinel established his family in the Edmonton area in the fall of 1905. But he was not interested in farming and would live by his wits for some time. He worked briefly as a fencing master, which provided initial contact with members of the Canadian Militia interested in his courses. He then became a journalist on a French-language weekly where he met three powerful federal politicians of Liberal allegiance. They were Philippe Roy, Frank Oliver and, most importantly, Clifford Sifton. He next turned general contractor but won no contracts and, finally, became both a representative of the E.B. Greenshields brokerage and a speculator in mining securities. It was through the latter activities that he ultimately achieved financial security in about 1910. Three years later, he moved to the country's financial capital, Montreal, where he built an opulent residence. Then came the summer of 1914.

Still a French citizen and a member of the reserves, he was at least theoretically obliged to report to the 53rd French Régiment d'infanterie on the opening of hostilities.[5] But the prospect of being just one of a vast number of army underlings offered little promise. For a man who professed to be a millionaire, there was nothing very enticing in this situation. His travels within political circles helped sort things out and gave him the opportunity of a lifetime. With the help of the very powerful Sifton, he managed to obtain a special dispensation from the French president by invoking his participation in the war as an officer of the Canadian Army. Once again, through Sifton, he was able to convince the truculent Minister of the Militia, Sam Hughes, to accept his services as the commander of an armoured vehicle force, the first formation of its kind in the British Empire. At the same time, he would provide the Canadian contingent with his technical expertise on machine guns.

The history of the Canadian Motor Machine Gun Brigade and the Canadian Machine Gun Corps have been told many times.[6] Brutinel himself condensed his memories in 1962 and 1963 for a CBC radio show.[7] While taking into account the exaggeration to which Brutinel was particularly prone when in notable company, his contributions to the war effort are worthy of mention. First, he was a technical and organizational innovator and an unrivalled experimentalist. Second, he was without doubt a remarkable instructor who played a key role in the training of machine gunners for the first two Canadian infantry divisions from late 1914 through early 1917 when he became increasingly involved in operational routines. And finally, a corollary of his role of instructor was his ability to communicate equally well with subordinates and superiors.

It is worth noting on this point that Brutinel knew how to solicit the affection of his men. After the war, and despite the distance, he remained in touch with many of them until his death. He also maintained good relations with General Currie and corresponded with him until 1930.[8] In their correspondence, both generals were concerned with the difficulties of reintegrating veterans into civilian life and providing for their most basic needs. Both Currie and Brutinel often opened their wallets to help veterans at a time when the federal government had little concern for this problem. Some of their letters are quite moving.

On the other hand, among his peers, with officers of similar rank, his relationships were often tense and sometimes even insufferable. Accordingly, McNaughton and Brutinel carried on a feud over the effectiveness of machine gun barrage fire until 1963.[9] Both liked to recall how Currie had consulted them. Both were in a sort of competition for the attention of the Commander of the Canadian Corps,[10] as well as for the promotion lists. Brutinel was certainly not shy about his virtues and never failed to remind his protectors – Sifton and Hughes until 1916 and Byng and Currie thereafter – how the Canadian war effort would be well served if only people listened to him.[11] This kind of competition between peers and currying of favour among the powerful fuelled personal differences.

But let us return to the first two points mentioned above. Brutinel is now recognized as the principal promoter of applying machine gun batteries to produce indirect fire as a means of preventing the enemy from using its advanced positions. The Canadians and the British developed a technique, somewhat like artillery but without its range, for showering a hail of bullets on the enemy's advanced trenches and particularly on communication trenches perpendicular to the front. McNaughton believed the use of machine guns and gunners, a fairly scarce resource in the 1914 to 1918 period, was a waste and that howitzers would do just as well if not better at lower cost. History would prove McNaughton right on this point.[12] Had Brutinel done no more than support the technique of indirect fire, McNaughton's scorn would have been justified. But Brutinel was an innovator in other fields as well.

Another obvious innovation for which Brutinel is known is the armoured car. He was most likely inspired in this area by the various achievements of European automobile manufacturers, such as Charron, Girardot, and Voigt from France and Daimler from Germany.[13] Brutinel was not an inventor, but, given his insatiable curiosity, he perfected equipment and put it in the hands of Canadian soldiers.

It is particularly worth remembering that, starting in August 1914, Brutinel became an active defender of the use of machine guns in a conflict for which Canadians had yet to mobilize. Rare are the officers who have shown such foresight, and it was the great slaughters of the fall of 1914 that would similarly open the eyes of British generals. (At the start of the war, armies of the British Empire were only issued two machine guns per battalion!)[14]

The question arises of how Brutinel had managed to learn so much about machine guns by the summer of 1914. As mentioned earlier, he only had a secondary school education, had served no more than a couple of years as a non-commissioned officer in the French army, and, at best, had taken a training course for non-commissioned officers identified for commissioning from the ranks. Before 1914 he had never commanded a unit larger than a squadron and had not studied tactics in a military college in either France or Canada. (He was not a member of the Non-Permanent Militia in 1914.) Furthermore, he would not have had the opportunity to study in England during the months of "phoney war" experienced by the Motorized Brigade before its transfer to France. However, the evidence shows he knew a great deal about the tactics of modern weaponry when he joined the Canadian Militia, whether in terms of the importance of using motorized forces, the volume of fire produced by machine guns to support rifle companies, logistics, or communications of mobile columns.

The only indication Brutinel gives us on the origins of his tactical ideas comes from the account he prepared for the CBC in 1962. He stated he had taken his conception of modern warfare from a study of the 1904-1905 Russo-Japanese War. The Japanese actually invented indirect fire and used it to assault a Russian trench on March 13, 1905.[15] Brutinel admitted that many of his tactical ideas were merely modernized versions of those developed by the Japanese.[16] But he went no further in his remarks. To learn more, we would have to look at military writers of the time, as did Brutinel himself.

Two writers involved in analyzing the Russo-Japanese War, who were widely read at the time but are now forgotten, foreshadowed Brutinel's ideas. The first was British Major R.V.K. Applin. In a book on machine gun tactics first published in 1909, Applin discussed the theory of indirect fire at great length.[17] Furthermore, Applin clearly exposed the utility of machine guns in a host of other tactical situations. This work essentially incorporates the doctrine that would be developed by the War Office in February 1917! It seems as if it would take more than the two years in which hundreds of thousands of its men were mowed down by machine gun fire for the British to finally discover what one of their officers had wisely proposed in 1909.

In another chapter of his handbook, Applin proposed a method of using advanced cavalry by once again evoking the Japanese experience. He concurred in this area with the other author from whom Brutinel probably drew his inspiration – General Négrier. Négrier was one of the most important French theoreticians prior to 1914 and undoubtedly one of the most widely read. He wrote for a conservative publication, the highly prestigious *Revue des Deux Mondes*, that served as a forum for members of the military who wanted to debate issues of the times.

Despite its numerical inferiority and its lack of a tradition in the field, the Japanese cavalry proved superior to its Russian counterpart, particularly while reconnoitring in force, attacking communications, and in battles with opposing cavalry. According to Négrier, this is because the Japanese used their cavalry logically, which meant like a troop for which firepower is the essential means of action: firepower delivered to the desired spot with a speed that can only be provided by mounted men. The Japanese cavalry actually fought like the infantry, but because of its mobility it could accomplish in-depth missions.

Négrier's conclusion is paradoxical. He believed that with modern weaponry – that is with the magazine rifle, the machine gun, and the quick-firing gun – it would be impossible to hold ambush positions indefinitely. "Only mobility escapes destruction," he insisted. Based on his studies of Japanese methods, Négrier concluded that Western cavalries should be reorganized. More than ever, he felt that they should become elite arms led by selected men.[18] Numerous texts by Brutinel, the CBC transcripts, and Brutinel's 1914 letters to Sifton, gave the impression that he drew on Négrier's writing. Furthermore, during the war, Brutinel met with Major Applin, who assisted in the preparation of tactical pamphlets for the War Office. In fact, a photo taken in 1916 or early 1917 shows Applin observing tests conducted by Brutinel in the Camiers region.[19]

Brutinel's experience in the French Army as a Drill-Sergeant, as a fencing master, and as a self-taught student, combined with his sense of initiative, would help make him one of the key players in providing a body of instruction to the Canadian contingent. While training the Motorized Brigade in Ottawa during the fall of 1914, he prepared a small handbook to offer basic instruction on the use of machine guns. In addition to familiarizing the reader with this weapon, the guide served two other purposes. One was to inculcate the notion of combined arms combat, in which infantrymen, machine gunners, artillery, cavalry, and armoured vehicles worked in co-operation with each other. The other was to develop what he called the "credo" of the machine gunners: "It was explained that the Infantry, being the only element able under all battle circumstances to physically take and hold a position, it follows that every other component part of the Army is subservient to the Infantry. Consequently, all arms, services and specialties must be animated by the same purpose, i.e. to help the Infantry in every way, up to and including self sacrifice."[20]

Brutinel preferred that the recruits who presented themselves to him in Ottawa had knowledge about mechanics and, if possible, handling machine guns.[21] He could be demanding, undoubtedly possessing a special affinity for the technique himself. That is why he never hesitated to suggest making mechanical modifications to the Colt machine gun that would suffer so many failures. And at the request of General Alderson, predecessor of Byng and Currie, he supervised modifications to the tripods for all Vickers to be delivered to the 1st Canadian Division.[22]

Upon arriving in England with the first contingent of the Canadian Army Expeditionary Force (CEF), Brutinel purged his unit of officers and men whom he judged incompetent, particularly those imposed on him by his political patrons in exchange for their favours. Thus, nearly twenty percent of the authorized strength of the Motorized Brigade would be sent back.[23] The brigade was an elite unit in the spirit of its founder, and Brutinel, with his refined airs, knew how to turn implacable when he felt it necessary. Similarly, Brutinel had little patience for misbehaviour; at least during the first few months of the war his concept of discipline was very basic. He insisted that the uniform should be worn with dignity at all times and despised officers in particular and soldiers in general who showed a weakness for alcohol.[24]

When the 1st Division moved from England to France, Brutinel and the Motorized Brigade found themselves unemployed. He languished on British soil until June 1916. In fact, even after their transfer to France, the armoured vehicles did not prove their utility until the German offensive of March 1918. In the meantime, while remaining frustrated at being unable to lead the armoured vehicles into combat, Brutinel organized the Canadian Machine Gun Corps. Although it was only officially formed in October 1917, independent companies of machine gunners from each battalion were under the supervision of the CEF machine gun service staff officer, who was Brutinel. Having become responsible for administering instruction to several thousand men, Brutinel was promoted to Brigadier General in March 1918.

Furthermore, until Vimy Brutinel was involved almost full-time teaching machine gunners. This is how he summarized his first year of experience in England:

> Since the early days at Bustard [headquarters of the 1st Canadian Division in Salisbury Plain in 1914] I have been responsible for the training of M.G. Officers, N.C.O.s of the M.G. detachment of the 1st Can. Division. Naturally the high class of the men I have in the Brigade [in this case, the armoured vehicle unit] has rendered it possible. In that capacity alone I think you will agree with me that we have proved our usefulness. Machine Guns are coming into their own now – <u>after a year</u> – and Machine Gun companies are being formed, except for the matter of transport.... The principles are the same as those which preside at the organization of the Brigade.[25]

One of the essential points of combined arms co-operation he emphasized in teaching machine gunners was the need to closely follow the howitzers and set up machine gun nests flanking the areas conquered by the infantry in order to break up the relentless German counterattacks.[26] It was no easy task to convince machine gunners to transport their heavy equipment to the front lines, often in the presence of the enemy.

Most instructional schools were shared with the British, and co-operation with them was not always easy. Brutinel had to fight to impose certain of the tactical concepts for which the Canadian Forces would be subsequently known. However, it is unclear to what extent Brutinel and his officers were involved in designing the curricula for machine gunners; in drafting the tactical notes prepared by the brigades, the divisions, the corps, and the armies of the British Empire; or in preparing the tactical brochures published by the War Office. But his role seems to have been decisive, to judge by a few indications. These include the tactical notes left in the archives of the CEF, few of which were signed, but many of which came from Brutinel's unit; various testimonials from British officers, including Brutinel's counterpart in the British machine gun corps, G.M. Lindsay; and an interesting file of correspondence drafted in Brutinel's hand. All of this suggests Brutinel exercised intense intellectual activity fuelled by his experience on a front he frequently visited, and his tactics were communicated to machine gunner schools by officers who had been won over to his ideas.[27]

The final innovation with which the name Brutinel is associated is a synopsis of the preceding ones. It involved an alliance of firepower, mobility, and combined arms combat for in-depth operations. This meant an armoured column, an elite force designed to follow-up on a breakthrough. Although the Allied armies had taken the trouble of applying a systematic method to break through a powerfully fortified continuous front, following up on a breakthrough before the enemy was able to reorganize remained a weakness that would not really be resolved until 1939 to 1940, and then by the Germans. But the solution could already be envisaged by the late summer of 1918 in Brutinel's Independent Force and in other similar armoured columns organized by the Canadians and the British. It should be recalled that tanks were penetration engines at the time, and their poor speed and handling made them unsatisfactory for any use behind enemy lines.

These independent forces were commanded by Brutinel on the Canadian side and by Colonel Lindsay on the British side. Neither force was fully satisfactory,[28] essentially because they lacked all-terrain capabilities. It was difficult for the armoured vehicles and armoured lorries of that time to operate off road. Nonetheless, in the words of one of the greatest specialists of tactical history, British writer Paddy Griffith, these armoured columns represented "a milestone in conceptual development" as important as the establishment of the British Tank Corps.[29] Significantly, in the conclusion of his book on the British Expeditionary Force (BEF) for the years 1916 to 1918, Griffith cites three great innovators. One belonged to the Australian and New Zealand Army Corp (ANZAC), one to the Canadians, and one to the British. These were, respectively, Australian General John Mosher, General Brutinel, and Colonel J.F.C. Fuller.[30] Griffith cites Brutinel and not Lindsay because his research in the British archives, particularly in the Lindsay collection, demonstrates that the real innovator in the use of machine guns in the British Empire since 1914, was the Canadian, and not the British, officer.

The full benefit of this intellectual activity and teaching became truly apparent in preparing the assault against the Vimy Crest in April 1917, in the fierce resistance by Canadian machine gunners to the German advance in March 1918, and ultimately in the counteroffensive leading to the Allied victory in the summer and fall of 1918. In addition to the inherent benefits of mobility yielded by Brutinel's armoured vehicles, the density of mobile communications equipment – such as motorcycle messengers and the cumbersome wireless telegraph trucks – provided valuable service during the last battles in which the front ceased to be fixed. Thanks to Brutinel's foresight which, since at least May 1916, had seen the addition of numerous motorcyclists, the Motorized Brigade, and the Machine Gun Corps were able to fairly effectively complete the missions they had been assigned.

Unfortunately, a well-developed corps spirit, an acute sense of duty, and tactical efficiency often resulted in high losses. For a period of about one hundred days of offensive operations from August to October 1918, the Canadian Machine General Corps (CMGC) lost 2,339 men, while the Artillery lost 1,881.[31] For the duration of the war, Colonel Nicholson calculated that the number of deaths of the Canadian army reached nearly 9 percent of the total forces. In the Machine Gun Corps, this rate reached some 36 percent – or four times higher than that of the army as a whole[32] – obvious proof, were any needed, of the excellence of Brutinel's units under fire.

After the war, with his business neglected for five years and his financial situation compromised, Brutinel returned to France where he rapidly rebuilt his wealth. In 1939, too old to return to active duty, he still provided conspicuous service by facilitating the escape of General Vanier during the collapse of France in June 1940.[33] His property, castle, and vineyards were strategically located in the southwest of France, near the Spanish border, and could serve as relay stations and hiding spots as part of an escape network. Furthermore, his business permitted him to move about without arousing suspicion. He thus hosted an escape network for the French Resistance starting in 1941 (the Marcus network), extending from Bordeaux to Toulouse to the Basque and Spanish borders. Although the Gestapo had asked the French police to keep Brutinel under surveillance because of his Canadian military past, Brutinel was not really worried. He most likely benefited from the complicity of various Vichy officials in avoiding the Germans.[34]

It was previously mentioned that Brutinel kept ties with his former Commander-in-Chief, General Currie from 1919 to 1930. He also maintained correspondence until the end of his life with many of his subordinates,[35] including H.T. Logan (1952-1963), Mark Marshall (1956-1964), and F.F. and Larry Worthington (1956-1964). He also made three trips to Canada to participate in activities of the CMGC veterans association, the last time being in September 1958,[36] when his health began to decline. Although Brutinel had made mistakes as commander of the Motorized Brigade and the Machine Gun Corps, these continuing relationships were evidence that not everyone held a grudge.

What made Brutinel an effective military leader? In accordance with the military historian, John Keegan's categories,[37] leadership of a military chief is based on the following imperatives:

> i. The imperative of forming alliances: the ability of a military chief to be surrounded by people who are respected for their various military talents and who serve as relays to the mass of soldiers.

> ii. The imperative of effectively issuing commands: the ability to explain orders verbally or in writing and to inspire a confidence that success will result from following such orders.

> iii. The imperative of sanction: the ability to use the authority to punish conferred by the chain of command,

only applying this power when absolutely necessary and never employing it in an arbitrary manner or against the will of the majority.

iv. The imperative of example: the ability of leaders who expect orders to be obeyed – including orders that could result in death – to show they know how to take risks and, also, to show empathy for the troops. For Keegan, this was the most important imperative.

v. The imperative of action: the need for the leader to remain constantly in control of and in touch with the troops in the field, to be informed and thus act wisely. This entails overcoming any distance between troops and their leader that may be created by the use of staff to keep the leader informed.

It can be concluded that Brutinel possessed the qualities of an effective leader because of the warm exchanges between Brutinel and his former subordinates (i), his skill in preparing written orders and training his men (ii), his blunt manner in dealing with incompetents (iii), his empathy for men still alive after the war (iv), and his delight in supporting organizational and conceptual innovations and in getting results in the field (v).

Endnotes

Chapter 3

1. Translated from the original French.
2. Many issues in Brutinel's life are still unclear. However, we can refer to biographical notes by his son Pierre Brutinel and by Dominique Baylaucq, a distant relative. They are in the possession of Mr. Baylaucq from whom the author obtained a copy. D. Baylaucq is a resident of Pau, France.
3. On this period in the life of Foch, see the brilliant essay of Lieutenant Colonel T.M. Hunter, "Marshal Foch: a study in leadership," Ottawa, Army Historical Section, 1961, Chap. II.
4. Letter from R. Brutinel to L. Worthington, April 28, 1964, National Archives of Canada, A.E. Powley collection, MG 30, E333, Vol. 3.
5. See Yves Tremblay, "Raymond Brutinel et la guerre de mouvement," in Roch Legault and Jean Lamarre, *La Première Guerre mondiale et le Canada: contributions sociomilitaires québécoises* (Montreal: Éditions du Méridien, 1999), 195-224. In contrast with what I had written in this chapter, Brutinel was born in 1882 and not in 1872. D. Baylaucq was kind enough to send a copy of his birth certificate, which we gratefully acknowledge.
6. H.T. Logan and M.R. Levey, *History of the Canadian Machine Gun Corps*, typed manuscript, Ottawa, 1919, 3 volumes; C. S. Grafton, *The Canadian "Emma Gees": A history of the Canadian Machine Gun Corps* (London, Ontario: Hunter Printing, 1938), 218; Larry Worthington, *Amid the Guns Below: The Story of the Canadian Corps* (Toronto: McClelland and Stewart, 1965), 236.
7. The transcriptions appear in the Powley collection, *op. cit.* See also Y. Tremblay, "Brutinel et la guerre de mouvement," 201, n. 11.
8. This correspondence appears in the National Archives Collection, hearinafter NAC, A.W. Currie collection, MG 30, E100, Vol. 3, File 6.
9. McNaughton's version appears in his biography: John Swettenham, *McNaughton, Volume I: 1887-1939* (Toronto: The Ryerson Press, 1968), 150-153 and 166. While McNaughton took pleasure in ridiculing Brutinel publicly, Brutinel studiously ignored his rival.

10. Ibid., 99-100; for Brutinel, see the transcriptions cited above.

11. See the correspondence to Clifford Sifton that was very revealing of Brutinel's failings.

12. On the issue of the best use for machine guns, which was then a fairly new weapon, see Bill Rawling, "Technology in Search of a Role: The Machine Gun and the CEF in the First World War," *Material History Review/Revue d'histoire de la culture matérielle*, 42, Fall 1995, 87-100.

13. See B.T. White and John Wood, *Tanks and armoured fighting vehicles 1900 to 1918* (London: Blanford Press, 1982), 199.

14. Bill Rawling, *Surviving Trench Warfare: Technology and the Canadian Corps, 1914-1918* (Toronto: University of Toronto Press, 1994), 18.

15. Roger Ford, *The Grim Reaper: Machine-Gun and Machine-Gunners in Action* (London: Sidgwick & Jackson, 1995), 81-84.

16. R. Brutinel, in NAC, Powley collection, transcriptions of tapes two and seven.

17. R.V.K. Applin, *Machine-Gun Tactics* (3rd ed.; London: Hugh Rees, 1915), vii-194.

18. General de Négrier, "Quelques enseignements de la guerre russo-japonaise," *Revue des Deux mondes*, January 15, 1906, 295-333.

19. R. Brutinel, in NAC, Powley collection, transcription of tape eleven; the photo was graciously sent to the Directorate of History and Heritage, hereinafter DHH by D. Baylaucq.

20. R. Brutinel, in NAC, Powley collection, transcription of tape four. With rare exception, Brutinel always wrote in English with regard to his Canadian affairs.

21. This may be observed in the service offer by W.H. Key Jones of 7 September, 1914 (NAC, Sifton collection).

22. NAC, Sifton collection, letter from Brutinel to Sifton written in Bristol and dated 24 January 1915; numerous memos concerning maintenance of the Colt in his file of correspondence for the fall of 1915. The original of this file is in the possession of D. Baylaucq. On deficiencies of the Colt compared to the Vickers, see B. Rawling, "Technology in search of a role: the machine gun and the CEF in the First World War," *passim*.

23. Y. Tremblay, "Raymond Brutinel et la guerre de mouvement," 205.

24. NAC, Sifton collection, letter from Brutinel to Sifton, 12 November 1914.

25. NAC, Sifton collection, letter from Brutinel to Sifton, 6 November 1915. Brutinel underlines. Also see the letter of 8 March 1915 in

which Brutinel expresses his frustration at having been left in England with the depots.

26. A.M.J. Hyatt, *General Sir Arthur Currie: A Military Biography* (Toronto and Ottawa: University of Toronto Press and Canadian War Museum, 1987), 121. Brutinel never stopped emphasizing this point. For an early example, see his file of correspondence for the fall of 1915.

27. Y. Tremblay, "Raymond Brutinel et la guerre de mouvement," *passim*; file of correspondence for the fall of 1915.

28. In general, see B. Rawling, "Technology in Search of a Role," *passim*; for a virulent criticism, see Desmond Morton and J.L. Granatstein, *Marching to Armageddon: Canadians and the Great War 1914-1919* (Toronto: Lester & Orpen Dennys, 1989), 221-222.

29. Paddy Griffith, *Battle Tactics of the Western Front: The British Army's Art of Attack 1916-18* (New Haven, Conn.: Yale University Press, 1994), 129.

30. Ibid., 192.

31. B. Rawling, "Technology in Search of a Role," 98.

32. C.W.L. Nicholson, *Le Corps expéditionnaire canadien 1914-1919* (Ottawa: The Queen's Printer, 1963), 580; C. S. Grafton, *The Canadian "Emma Gees,"* 214. Grafton states there were 5,777 deaths for some 16,000 members of the CMGC.

33. See Robert Speaight, *Georges P. Vanier: soldat, diplomate et gouverneur général* (Montreal: Fides, 1972), 215-219.

34. NAC, A. E. Powley collection, Vol. 3, letter from Brutinel to L. Worthington, April 28, 1964; three laissez-passers for the Resistance and the FFI, one signed Rémy, are in the possession of D. Baylaucq, who sent copies of them to the DHH; one-page biographical note by his son Pierre.

35. Copies were graciously sent to the DHH by D. Baylaucq.

36. *The Legionary*, August 1958.

37. John Keegan, *The Mask of Command: A Study in Generalship* (London: Pimlico, 1999), Conclusion.

FORGED IN FIRE

THE WORLD WAR II
EXPERIENCE

CHAPTER 4

THE GENERALSHIP OF ANDREW MCNAUGHTON: A STUDY IN FAILURE

Bill Rawling

T
HE study of generalship is fraught with peril. Opinions differ widely as to what distinguishes a superior from an inferior general. Some analysts still insist on the importance of "leading from the front" while others prefer to emphasize the qualities taught in business management schools. There is also much room for subjectivity, so that, regardless of the amount of evidence one gathers to support a case, it is still possible to be accused of having got it all wrong. Studying an individual such as Andrew McNaughton especially brings such a dilemma to the fore. Until the end of his days in the mid-1960s, McNaughton felt that he had done a good job as commander of the Canadian Division (later Corps, later Army) overseas from 1939 to 1943. But he was fired in the latter year by policy makers who emphatically insisted he was unfit for the task. A study of his generalship may not resolve the controversy, but it may provide a means of studying the role a general officer plays in a military institution and, more specifically, the role he (now she as well) may play in a Canadian military institution.

Before the outbreak of the Second World War McNaughton's career had been solid; he had known more success than failure. As a counter-battery staff officer for the Canadian Corps in the First World War, he had helped adopt techniques which made artillery more effective in such battles as Vimy and Amiens, and even those who criticized him later in life praised his technical abilities. His posting as Chief of the General Staff from 1929 to 1935 was more controversial, especially given his seeming willingness to sacrifice the Royal Canadian Navy in order to guarantee funding for the Army and Air Force. His main contribution to waiting out the Great Depression was more controversial still, consisting in setting up camps where unemployed young men could find work, food, shelter, and 20 cents a day in "allowance." As he himself explained in a 1966 interview, "Like everything else of that sort you can get away with it for just so long." Politically there was bound to be a reaction. In 1935, the reaction set in with a vengeance. The term "slave camps" was created by people who afterwards were Liberal ministers of the crown.

Some of the camps' residents organized a "March on Ottawa" which ended in a battle between themselves and government officers in Regina. It was not McNaughton's best moment.

His next assignment was as President of the National Research Council from 1935, and according to his successor, C.J. Mackenzie, "His four years at the Research Council would be the most tranquil period of his life and the most happy."[1] The atmosphere was certainly more collegial than one where relief camps were described as "slave camps," and, for McNaughton, dealing with technical and scientific issues was more satisfying emotionally than navigating the hazardous shoals of politics. In another 1966 interview, Lieutenant-General Elliott Roger opined that McNaughton "had a most inquisitive-type mind, particularly in the scientific direction and nothing gave him greater pleasure than to be working with the scientists, investigating new ideas, and even leading them on into what was necessary for further development of scientific military equipment."[2] In 1942, three years after leaving the National Research Council to command military formations overseas, his technical abilities were still recognized. The High Commissioner for Australia, also a member of Britain's War Cabinet, asked the General if he would "take over direction of Technical Development work for the three Services under the British Government." McNaughton declined, explaining that he considered himself "responsible to the people of Canada for the Canadian Army Overseas and felt that he should remain with it."[3] It was not a wise choice.

That McNaughton never lost his interest in the technological and scientific has been well documented by dozens of examples, but limited space only allows for one in this study. McNaughton was appointed General Officer Commanding (GOC) 1st Canadian Infantry Division soon after the outbreak of war. The formation was still in England when France fell in May 1940, bringing the issue of the defence of the British Isles front and centre. Since it was impossible to put an iron ring around the entire country, light forces were placed on the coast, with larger formations prepared to counter-attack any enemy attempts to create a bridgehead. That meant that certain facilities, such as airfields, would undoubtedly fall into German hands, at least initially, forcing defenders to destroy them before withdrawing. As McNaughton later related, "I went to talk with all the engineers of the command, this was done at the request of home forces to explain what could be done for preparing all the fields for demolition without actually blowing them." The idea was to make advanced preparations with explosive-filled pipes pushed under critical facilities. "We could make them useless and we didn't have to do it unless the necessity arose and we could be perfectly confident ... these things were not going to destroy the airdromes unless it was needed."[4]

After he was relieved of command, such a focus on technical issues would be seized upon as evidence of McNaughton's poor generalship. Colonel A.S. Price, in a 1966 interview, said, "I think that it is a fair criticism that he did pay an awful lot of attention to details that were not within the province of a GOC, details that should have been handled by his staff, because he was terribly interested and because he was very good at it."[5] General Guy Simonds, who commanded various formations in the field, including 2nd Canadian Corps in the Normandy Campaign, spoke in like manner, suggesting that "General McNaughton tended to be so absorbed in the technical and equipment and organizational problems that to my mind he definitely neglected the operational aspects,"[6] a serious accusation to level at a formation commander.

This accusation needs to be studied more closely because although after his dismissal McNaughton was criticized for spending more time on technical issues than he should have, it is just as certain that he also focussed on other matters. When he was Chief of the General Staff in the early 1930s, for example, a topic of much of his writing was the education of young officers. As Brigadier R.J. Orde put it, "He encouraged young lads to study. There is no question of that. And he studied himself. McNaughton was undoubtedly the first CGS that really engendered an atmosphere of 'Well, this is a professional job and let us make the best we can of it.'"[7] As McNaughton himself remembered decades later:

> Of course there was another thing too that had run through the militia in the old days; anybody who got into the militia, whether he was good or not, automatically went up more or less on the time scale. If he lasted in the militia he went up. You found units being commanded by people without regard to their education. Now, education, and it is not a snobbery attitude, if a man is educated, he is usually adaptable and if a man is adaptable, he can be trained to fit a rising condition and to make his proper contribution, but if a man has not been through the discipline of a proper education, it does not much matter whether it is Arts or Science, if he has not been processed and had to show

his adaptability, he is a menace in the Army because the conditions that you face are almost certain to be different to what we thought they might be and what had been used in building up the Army.[8]

To put it more succinctly – The most important ingredient in your officer corps is a broadly educated corps.

Another aspect of leadership McNaughton found occasion to stress was the need to take care of one's troops, an issue that was perhaps at its most prominent in the early days of the war when units and formations were being mobilized with only the barest minimum resources – or less. McNaughton recounted:

> For example, I remember going down to one of the units in Nova Scotia and discovering to my horror that this unit had been called out and it was accommodated in an old curling rink and all where the ice panels had been they had merely scooped the ice out and thrown straw down for these recruits to sleep on; but they had no blankets and nobody had bought blankets for them. They didn't even have underwear and certainly they did not have boots, all of which were procurable in the public market if people were willing to spend money, and there was an unawareness on the part of the staffs down there, right from the DOC [District Officer Commanding] downwards, of what his responsibilities in this sort of thing were and that they had to be discharged. Of course it did not take long, with a fresh report to the Minister, with Quartermaster general and others and adjutant general sitting there, until this thing was shaken loose and these things were corrected.[9]

Quite clearly, making friends was not part of his view of what constituted generalship.

Later, after more equipment had been made available and the division moved to England, McNaughton revisited the issue of "taking care of the troops" from another direction when he, his staff, and officers had to maintain morale at a time when soldiers had nothing to do but train:

> You see, one of the things in England was a psychological position to keep the interest of the troops up in this enforced period while we were getting equipment, and so they had to invent all sorts of things of a ceremonial character which did not require very much material or anything of that sort but something which would keep these people interested, and so it was with that purpose in mind, to keep the interest up, that on my first visit with His Majesty that I suggested that we might put some of the regiments of which either he or the Queen were Colonels-in-Chief, to take those regiments and put them on guard duty at the Palace, which was very well received and of course did a tremendous lot for morale.[10]

Similarly, after relating how the hoist at a brewery had been used to suspend an oil drum so it could be dropped on a German tank in case of invasion, McNaughton admitted that "Nobody landed so it was never used but one of the great things was it caused a good deal of hilarity among the troops, you see. You are halfway through if you can get people to laugh and this was part of the business."[11]

McNaughton's beliefs concerning such issues as officer education and soldier morale undoubtedly derived from his battlefield doctrine, the philosophy he expected to apply when it came time to put those officers and soldiers to the ultimate test. An important aspect, in his mind, was initiative, as exemplified by his discussion of Lord Gort's decision, in May 1940, to refuse to obey an order to continue attacking advancing German columns. According to McNaughton, "he was labouring at the time, labouring under this overriding instruction that he was to keep on striking to the southeast which, of course, if he had continued, we would have lost the war." But a commander needed to use his initiative on occasion. In this case, "he used the right responsibility for a commander on the spot to appreciate the situation and to take the appropriate action to see that his forces were not extinguished despite the fact that the people in London who did not know the full situation were still urging him along the lines of an entirely impossible course." Instead of continuing the attack, Gort used the 5th and 50th Divisions to plug a gap between British and Belgian forces.[12]

Nor was initiative to be limited to field marshals and generals, especially in the period following the Fall of France when formations in England were still being organized and equipped. Should the enemy effect a landing, McNaughton said:

> The first thing that became obvious was that the speed into action was the criterion which was of the greatest importance, and having regard to the roads and so on, it became obvious to me that we had to organize primarily on a battalion basis. The battalion commander became the linchpin of the whole thing. From the central place he would get his general instructions and, mind you, they had to be very general, that there had been a landing at somebody's beach and their people are shored and your mission is, the first thing is to go hell-for-leather and knock them out.[13]

Put another way, "We had lieutenant-colonels and knew their men and these battalions had means of cooking and feeding and there was a command organization there that, through the brigades and so on, that we could control it even if we were decentralized."[14]

To test doctrine and train officers and troops required rehearsals – Canadian units and formations taking to the field from time to time to be put through their paces – though McNaughton's glee when describing the chaos that sometimes accompanied such exercises must have been disturbing to many of his colleagues. Describing manoeuvres that had taken place soon after the formation of the Canadian Corps at Easter 1942, for example, he stated bluntly:

> Those exercises were very useful because they failed. [One officer] got into the most God-awful confusion. We had not had a chance really to have our drivers trained and we had not our staff officers trained in the art of handling mechanized forces, motorized forces. We did not know about the kind of road spaces we had to use and all that sort of thing and we got this whole division into one God-awful mess, I have never seen the like of it. It took three days to get them disentangled... It was the finest thing we ever had and it let these fellows know that they just had to get their noses down in the ground and learn the art of movement, particularly the art of being able to move lorries at night.[15]

As early as 1940, such experiences had already led McNaughton to write to Ottawa that "development of new tactics which differ radically from old requires that Divisional Commanders be selected from men having current experience."[16] This statement proved to be an ominous foreshadowing of events. Issues like officer education, troop morale, and tactics were common to all armies, but a Canadian general faced another task which made his job different in kind from those of his colleagues in American or British formations – he acted as his army's representative vis-à-vis higher headquarters, such as the office of the Chief of the Imperial General Staff. The result was that an officer who might be seen as competent in purely military fields could, potentially, become a target for removal for being disruptive in carrying out his representative duties. Whether that applied in McNaughton's case is an issue best left for later in this study, but certainly the task of speaking for 1st Canadian Division, 1st Canadian Corps, and First Canadian Army in succession often placed the General in awkward situations. Sir Alan Brooke, whom McNaughton had known in the First World War and who had risen to the position of Chief of the Imperial General Staff (CIGS), thought McNaughton was "over-exact in his interpretation of his charter as to how Canadian forces were to be employed and under what conditions of independence." According to Alan Brooke's biographer, the CIGS "complained that they [the Canadians] were the most difficult to deal with in that respect. He ascribed this largely to McNaughton." On one occasion, he even went so far as to refer to the Canadian general's "warped outlook."[17]

McNaughton had a different view, of course. In September 1942, for instance, he met with the CIGS to complain about not being informed of Allied Forces intentions: "I told General Alan Brooke that I was under some considerable embarrassment through the lack of stability in plans for operations in which the Cdn Army had been invited to participate. My particular present trouble was in connection with the postponement of 'Round-Up' and the institution of 'Torch' and other schemes of which so far I had only the vaguest particulars."[18] "Round-up" was the nickname given for the build-up towards an invasion of northwest Europe, with First Canadian Army part of the initial assault, while "Torch" referred to upcoming landings in North Africa. If the latter were carried out, the Canadians would be without a major operation to contribute to for some time.

In his discussions with Alan Brooke, McNaughton was most adamant on the need to be informed of such developments. First

Canadian Army had expended much effort building up its personnel for "Round-up":

> Then suddenly, and without warning, a change of plan had been made, which had not been communicated to me until later and then had only been casually and incidentally indicated through a conversation I had had with C-in-C [Commander-in-Chief] Home Forces, on other subjects.
>
> The matter might have been very serious in my relations with my Government and in its effects on the confidence of the Canadian Government in the direction of the war by the UK War Cabinet. In fact, very grave questions of Cdn policy had been involved, which might have had most serious effects on our war effort. I suggested that it was most unwise to leave that sort of condition to chance and yet, while I did not wish to interject myself into the British direction of the war (as I had all I could undertake in getting the Cdn Army ready for a particular theatre of operations) nevertheless, I thought I must have more complete and more timely information of plans as they developed, so that I could adjust our course to the requirements of the situation and avoid needless waste, effort, or political repercussions which might be critical.[19]

According to notes taken by McNaughton's personal assistant, Alan Brooke agreed with the need to keep information flowing to the Canadian general, but noted that he himself was not yet certain of what Roosevelt and Churchill intended.

The matter was clarified later when the President and Prime Minister agreed to the landings in North Africa, forcing a re-allocation of shipping away from the build-up for an invasion of northwest Europe. In November 1942, McNaughton had another of his frequent meetings with Alan Brooke to discuss the impact on First Canadian Army:

> I told General Alan Brooke that while I, perhaps naturally, thought that Canada's contribution could be most effective if given in the form of a Canadian Army substantially self-

contained, yet the thing which weighed most with me was that the contribution should be the maximum towards winning the war and that if this, having regard to time and place, required the use of individual divisions separately or even the breaking up of divisions then I was prepared to consider any proposition on its merits and to report thereon to Canada.[20]

Alan Brooke mentioned several possibilities which might call for part of First Canadian Army, such as Italy or the Canary Islands (Operation Tonic), and, in a report to Canada, McNaughton mentioned the two, as well as possible attacks against U-boat bases and a return to northwest Europe after 1 August 1943, as "the tasks in front of us for which we should organize. The War Office have no present thought of employing Cdn units or formations on operations elsewhere."[21]

Should the reader conclude that McNaughton, in his representative capacity, was willing to be flexible on certain issues pertaining to First Canadian Army, it must be noted that the Canadian general reserved to himself and himself alone the decision as to whether to be flexible or not. In July 1942, in a discussion with Vincent Massey, Canada's High Commissioner to the United Kingdom, he pointedly stated that:

> He [McNaughton] could not divorce himself from the responsibility to the Cdn Government for the proper employment of Cdn troops in Home Forces or in a BEF [British Expeditionary Force], and that he must, therefore, have not only full power to place these forces into or out of operational control as he saw fit, but also must have full control himself over the interior administration, including training equipment, organization and discipline of the Cdn forces. As an example of the importance of his having this control, he referred to the pressure from the War Office for the Cdn Army to follow the new British divisional organization, and that he was able successfully to resist this and retain our previous organization.... It was mentioned that under existing regulations it is mandatory for the Canadian forces to be placed in combination with the British as soon as they go to the Continent, and General McNaughton stated that he might ask the Cdn Government to rescind this order.[22]

His approach was thus more akin to the bluntness of an army officer than the reasoned argument of a diplomat.

Still, though McNaughton took his responsibility for First Canadian Army very seriously, in keeping with his emphasis on the importance of initiative, he was willing to delegate that responsibility to subordinates whom the fortunes of war might place in command of Canadian formations in distant lands. The best example of this approach followed the decision to send 1st Canadian Infantry Division to take part in unnamed operations (most likely against the Canary Islands) in January 1943. In discussions with Alan Brooke, McNaughton stated for the record "that he had every confidence in the GOC 1st Cdn Div and that he felt sure that he would be able to keep out of difficulties and to function correctly within the constitutional arrangements for a mixed force."[23]

The operation never came to pass, however. When McNaughton was advised in April 1943 that a staff had been formed for the Supreme Commander (eventually Eisenhower was chosen) responsible for the return to northwest Europe, he said that he had "made it clear to General Morgan," the Chief of Staff to the Supreme Allied Commander (or COSSAC), that he was quite ready to accept operational direction from General Paget as Commander of the Army Group of which First Canadian Army would be a part, "but that all concerned should clearly understand his responsibilities to the Cdn War Cabinet as Senior Combatant Officer Cdn Army Overseas." General McNaughton had said that these responsibilities made it necessary for him to have direct access where necessary to the "fountain head" (e.g., CIGS). General Morgan "fully agreed."[24]

McNaughton thus considered himself to be something of a plenipotentiary. But the Canadian government reserved certain decisions to itself, and reality came knocking in the form of the Chief of the Imperial General Staff in April 1943. Alan Brooke advised that the chances of a cross-Channel attack anytime during 1943 "was now very small" and that, "in view of the insistent requests made by the Minister of National Defence and CGS, Canada," Churchill had directed him "that Cdn participation in the next operation was to be arranged." The campaign in question was "Husky," the invasion of Sicily. Alan Brooke "then invited General McNaughton to agree to the participation of one Canadian infantry division and one Cdn tank brigade and certain ancillary units in a proposed operation based on Tunisia against Sicily. He described the plans for this operation in some detail. He said that the British 3rd Division and other units which would be displaced would be very disappointed and he indicated that his Staff at the War Office were against the change, and he said that the matter must be arranged within the next two days if it was to proceed." The Government of Mackenzie King having made its wishes known, the Canadian General authorized the commencement of preparations and training and chose 1st Canadian Infantry Division (under command of Major-General H.L.N. Salmon) and 1st Canadian Army Tank Brigade (under command of Brigadier R.A. Wyman) for the task.[25]

Now aware of the political situation in Canada, McNaughton saw fit to remind National Defence Headquarters that if further formations were sent out of England, "it will end the conception on which we have been proceeding, namely that Canada's contribution to the war can best be through her own army."[26] In fact, British plans in June called for the return of the Canadians from the Mediterranean to the United Kingdom in time for the cross-Channel attack, but there were no guarantees.[27] Once again policy makers in Canada determined events in England, however. In a July discussion between McNaughton, Morgan, and Canada's Chief of the General Staff Ken Stuart, the latter delivered Ottawa's message on "the importance of Cdn division gaining battle experience, and he said that if further operations are to be conducted in the Mediterranean it was the view of the Cdn Government that an additional div and a Corps Headquarters should be provided." They could be returned to the United Kingdom in time for a cross-Channel attack. But more importantly, "General Stuart spoke of the anxiety, both Governmental and public, which would be occasioned by a further period of inactivity by the Cdn Forces in the UK."[28] A few days later, he added that "he favoured building up Cdn Forces in Africa to a Corps, by exchanging Cdn division for British, even if there was no certainty that they could be brought back. He said that if this were done, HQ First Cdn Army as an operational command would be redundant and that it might therefore be advisable to combine HQ First Cdn Army and CMHQ [Canadian Military Headquarters in London] to administer all Cdn Forces in European and North African theatres."[29] If such a turn of events came to pass, McNaughton would no longer have an operational command, a situation that no doubt coloured subsequent events.

For example, with the meeting still ongoing, McNaughton replied to Stuart's comments with a memorandum stating that "Canada would be glad to raise our contingent in North Africa [actually Sicily by this time] to a Corps of appropriate composition," but that "we would continue to go on the basis that the Cdn contingent in North Africa would return to the Cdn Army in the UK before the date set for a major offensive on the Continent." According to the General's personal assistant, neither Stuart nor Minister of Defence J.L. Ralston, who was present at the meeting, agreed to the latter part of the memo.[30] McNaughton was headed towards a confrontation with his own government, one made obvious in a conversation with Ralston on 9 August, where the General made so bold as to accuse his own minister of manipulation. "I told the Minister that I thought that as a result of the statements he had made, and the suggestive suppositions he had advanced, it could now be taken as a foregone conclusion that Cdn Army would be dissipated." Ralston denied the accusation, insisting that he merely sought battle experience for Canadian troops. But McNaughton repeated the charge and later said, "If the Cdn Government decided upon dispersion, then I thought it would be wise for them to put someone in control who believed in it. I certainly did not, and did not wish the responsibility."[31]

That was not all, for at the same meeting in the course of a discussion about the need for Canadian commanders to have battle experience, which McNaughton lacked, McNaughton suggested that he would be glad to develop the commander of 1st Canadian Corps, Lieutenant-General H.D.G. Crerar, through battle experience so that Crerar could take his place as commander of First Canadian Army. McNaughton insisted that "the important thing for Canada at the end of the war was to have her Army together under command of a Canadian."[32] (Unknown to McNaughton, concerns about battle experience had come up earlier that day in a discussion between Ralston and Alan Brooke.) In early November, when the issue came up again, McNaughton told Ralston that he believed he would be one of the two army commanders in the Anglo-Canadian army group to invade northwest Europe, but he said so unaware of discussions in other circles. For on 6 November 1943, J.L. Ralston, the Minister of Defence, met with Alan Brooke who advised that "McNaughton's flair was for mechanics rather than men, and that instinctively he [McNaughton] was inclined to go about examining vehicles and guns, shock absorbers and mechanical contrivances rather than getting to know the capabilities of his commanders. He mentioned that an Army Commander should know thoroughly his Div and Brigade Commanders and Battalion COs who might likely be fitted for higher commands and he doubted if McNaughton did. His time was so taken up with weapon development."[33]

As we have seen, this was not entirely the case, but since McNaughton's interest in the scientific and technological has long been cited as a reason for his dismissal, a few words of clarity are necessary. When the CIGS mentioned McNaughton's technical work, was it really a major issue or simply a symptom of what he perceived as the Canadian General's negligence in properly preparing himself for battle? Some illumination might be provided by Ralston's account of his conversation with Lieutenant-General Bernard Paget, Commander of Home Forces slated to take charge of the Anglo-Canadian army group. (That position would, in the event, go to Bernard Law Montgomery.) Paget, in a meeting two days following the one with Alan Brooke, stated that "he felt he could not accept McNaughton in the field ... he expressed great admiration for and appreciation of his cooperation but felt he had been under too great a strain to last as Army Commander in the field.... He spoke of his trying to do two jobs, one as Army Commander and another in connection with administration of Canadian matters generally. It was too much. And then he had done a lot of work on technical matters."[34] The last comment thus came as something of an afterthought.

Far more important than the General's scientific leanings in putting doubts in the minds of Alan Brooke and Paget was a March 1943 exercise called Spartan. In his post-exercise comments, Paget was highly critical – if somewhat circumspect. "Higher commanders cannot and must not attempt to deal with the minute-to-minute details of the current battle," he wrote. He then noted how "frequent changes of plan at a late hour had severe repercussions on the operations," before citing three specific examples relating to McNaughton's performance.[35] The CIGS was even more critical. According to an insightful article, "McNaughton and Exercise Spartan," by John Nelson Rickard, after a 7 March visit to First Canadian Army Headquarters, Alan Brooke wrote in his diary that the Canadian was "quite incompetent to command an army!" and "He does not know how to begin to cope with the job and was tying up his force into the most awful muddle."[36] Rickard points out that Alan Brooke had only spent an hour visiting with McNaughton and his staff, and as with other exercises, the commander of the First Canadian Army felt much had been learned from the disaster, but it is important to note that the CIGS' opinion of the Canadian General had been formed long before the events of November 1943. According to Rickard's article, McNaughton's greatest mistake was attempting to pass one corps through another at night, leading to a horrific traffic jam.

Though Alan Brooke was shocked, it is interesting to relate that Sir

Basil Liddell-Hart, British historian and commentator on tactics, saw nothing wrong with McNaughton's concept,[37] so the CIGS' reaction was not universal. In fact, when interviewed in 1966, Liddell-Hart said: "Whether McNaughton would have proved an effective Commander in the field may be questionable, and is a question that can never be settled, but he was certainly a soldier of outstanding vision and ability who grasped the conditions of modern war earlier and more fully than most others."[38]

Still, McNaughton clearly did not have the confidence of the CIGS – nor of many others – a fact J.L. Granatstein has encapsulated in excellent form in his study, *The Generals*. Citing Alan Brooke's diary, he notes how on 18 June 1943, the Chief of the Imperial General Staff wrote that Crerar "is very unhappy about Andy McNaughton who is ... undoubtedly quite unsuitable to command an Army. I only wish I could find some job I could remove him to but that is not easy." On 5 July it was Stuart who came to visit Brooke. "Apparently he realises McNaughton is unsuitable to command the Canadian Army! We discussed possible ways of eliminating him; not an easy job!" Finally, on 3 August, it was Ralston's turn, the Minister of Defence discusses "how we are to get rid of McNaughton as an Army Commander. No easy problem."[39]

With such doubts surrounding McNaughton's ability to lead First Canadian Army, there could be little doubt as to the outcome. It should be mentioned here, however, that as these discussions were underway no one had broached the issue to the General in question. Paget noted at an 8 November meeting that he had not stated his opinions of McNaughton to the man himself because he did not want to interfere with the Canadian's relationship with his government. According to Ralston, Stuart joked that "you have given us a dirty deal in going on as if McNaughton would command the show." However, the British General insisted it was up to Canadian authorities to communicate bad news to their commanders. Such indeed took place that very day, in an interview that the Minister of Defence described as "the most painful I have had since I took over the Department. I was deeply sorry for him and admired the quiet soldierly way he discussed the prospect of losing what to him must have been the height of his ambition and the fruition of over four years of ceaseless faithful, untiring effort."[40] This seemed a dignified end to what must have been a very difficult process, but it was not over yet.

Given that neither Alan Brooke, nor Paget, nor others in the British high command had advised him of any lack of confidence in his ability to command First Canadian Army, McNaughton concluded that his removal had been engineered by the Minister of Defence because of his resistance to sending a corps to Italy and hence breaking up the very formation for which he was responsible. The result was that McNaughton went over the minister's head in a cable to Prime Minister Mackenzie King, which began with its own justification: "You will recall ... when I was first appointed to Command 1 Cdn Div and later reaffirmed on the occasion of my last visit to Canada now nearly two years ago that if any very serious matter arose I was to communicate to you direct." McNaughton wrote that he had not made use of that privilege, but felt the need at this time because "I have lost all confidence in Ralston and I must say that I can no longer remain in command of First Cdn Army responsible to any government of which he is a member." According to the General, the crux of the matter was: "The situation we have to face is that a Minister of the Crown on whom I have every right to rely for support comes here and by suggestions and suppositions casts doubt in the minds of senior officers of another country with whom I have to work as to my fitness. Then takes their silence or partial replies as assent to the view he has implied. Then comes to me and no doubt to others also and imputes his suggestions to them as a positive statement of their opinion." McNaughton's anger then exploded with the statement: "I would say Mr. Prime Minister that quite apart from the question of the support which a Minister of National Defence owes I think to a Cdn Army Comd I regard Ralston's action as one of the meanest and most despicable of my whole experience and this is not the first time he has acted in this way to cause me very great anxiety for the welfare of the Cdn Army."[41] A copy was sent to Ralston.

Historically, the telegram is crucially important in that it may well have coloured the opinions of all those involved, and even affected their memories of the years leading up to McNaughton's dismissal. The General, himself infuriated at loss of command (which came to him as a complete surprise), then infuriated others with his communication to Mackenzie King. For the rest of his life McNaughton believed that he had been a victim of political manoeuvring on the part of Ralston, a belief his biographer, John Swettenham, perpetuated in his three-volume study of the General's life. There has thus been much anger on both sides of the issue.

Given such a state of affairs, any conclusion would be an over-generalization, but perhaps there are a few simple lessons to be learned from the General's career nonetheless. McNaughton saw the role of an army commander as multi-faceted: he had to see to the education and training of his officers and troops, he had to ensure they were well-equipped and supplied, and he had to keep an eye towards maintaining morale. Alan Brooke, the policy maker most responsible for his dismissal, would not have disagreed, though he himself tended to de-emphasize the need to supervise research and development. But McNaughton also felt the role of a Canadian commander was to represent his formations – aggressively – vis-à-vis Allied Forces, including the higher headquarters under which those formations would operate. With this Alan Brooke did not agree. The tragedy in the Canadian general's case was where he undoubtedly failed: an important task for any commander is to prepare himself or herself to lead a formation in battle, preferably by getting combat experience. On that we can all agree, and it is on that score that General A.G.L. McNaughton, commander of First Canadian Army in 1942 and 1943, fell short.

ENDNOTES

CHAPTER 4

1. National Archives of Canada, hereinafter NAC, MG 31, E42, v.3, Interview transcript, Andrew McNaughton – Canadian, 1966, General McNaughton, 11.
2. Ibid., Lieutenant-General Elliott Rodger, 14.
3. NAC, MG 30, E133, v.248, War Diary Jul 42, 9.
4. NAC, MG 31, E42, v.3, Interview transcript, McNaughton and the First and Second World Wars, File 2, Session 2, Tape 5, 8-9.
5. NAC, MG 31, E42, v.3, Interview transcript, Andrew McNaughton – Canadian, 1966, Colonel A.S. Price, 15.
6. Ibid., General Guy Simonds, 15.
7. Ibid., Brigadier R.J. Orde, 6.
8. NAC, MG 31, E42, v.3, Interview transcript, McNaughton and the First and Second World Wars, File 1, Session 1, 15.
9. Ibid., Tape 3, 6.
10. Ibid., Tape 4, 9.
11. NAC, MG 31, E42, v.3, Interview transcript, McNaughton and the First and Second World Wars, File 2, Session 3, Tape 4, 7.
12. Ibid., Session 2, Tape 4, 3.
13. Ibid., Session 3, Tape 4, 3.
14. Ibid., Session 2, Tape 5, 7.
15. Ibid., Session 3, Tape 4, 1-2.
16. NAC, MG 30, E133, v.248, War Diary 1940, Massey to External, 29 Jun 40.
17. David Fraser, *Alan Brooke* (London, 1982), 188-189.
18. NAC, MG 30, E133, v.248, War Diary Sep 42, McNaughton Memo 20 Sep 42.
19. Ibid.
20. NAC, MG 30, E133, v.249, War Diary Nov 42, McNaughton Memo, 20 Nov 42.
21. Ibid., Canmilitary to Defensor, 21 Nov 42.
22. NAC, MG 30, E133, v.248, War Diary Jul 42.

23. NAC, MG 30, E133, v.249, War Diary Jan 43, Appx G, Memo of Conversation Alan Brooke- McN, 6 Jan 43.
24. Ibid., Appx X, Memo of Conference, 13 Apr 43.
25. Ibid., Appx PP, Memo of Discussion McNaughton-Brooke, 23 Apr 43.
26. Ibid., Appx R, McNaughton to Stuart, 6 May 43.
27. NAC, MG 30, E133, v.250, War Diary Jun 43, Appx R, Memo of Conversation McNaughton-Paget, 17 Jun 43; Memo of a Discussion McNaughton-Kennedy, DMO, 19 Jun 43.
28. Ibid., Appx U, Memo of Conversation McNaughton-Stuart-Morgan, 27 Jul 43.
29. Ibid., Appx X, Memo of a Discussion Ralston-McNaughton-Stuart, 29 Jul 43.
30. Ibid.
31. NAC, MG 30, E133, v.250, War Diary Aug 43, Appx F, Conversation McNaughton-Ralston-Stuart, 5 Aug 43.
32. Ibid.
33. NAC, MG 27, III, B II, Ralston Paprers, v.51, McNaughton, Lt-Gen A.G.L. – Diary and documents, 1943-44, 6 Nov 43.
34. Ibid.
35. Directorate of History and Heritage, 545.003 (D1) GHQ Exercise Spartan, Comments by Commander-in-Chief Home Forces, 13.
36. John Nelson Rickard, "The Test of Command: McNaughton and Exercise Spartan, 4-12 March 1943," *Canadian Military History* (Summer, 1999), 28.
37. Ibid., 34.
38. NAC, MG 31, E42, v.3, Interview transcript, Andrew McNaughton – Canadian, 1966, Basil Liddell-Hart, 18.
39. J.L. Granatstein, *The Generals: The Canadian Army's Senior Commanders in the Second World War* (Toronto, 1993), 75.
40. NAC, MG 27, III, B II, Ralston Papers, v.51, McNaughton, Lt-Gen A.G.L. – Diary and documents, 1943-44, 8 Nov 43.
41. NAC, MG 27, III, B II, Ralston Papers, v.51, McNaughton, Lt-Gen A.G.L. – Minister's Notes, Lists, and Documents, 1943, McNaughton to King, 10 Nov 43.

CHAPTER 5

IN THE SHADOW OF THE CORPS:
HISTORIOGRAPHY, GENERALSHIP,
AND HARRY CRERAR

Dean F. Oliver[1]

H.D.G. Crerar, Commander of the First Canadian Army during the climactic struggles of 1944 to 1945 in northwest Europe, is Canadian military history's most famous nobody. Unlike Sir Arthur Currie, who led the Canadian Corps from June 1917 to the end of the First World War (though not, as Canadian media commentators regularly insist, at Vimy Ridge)[2] and whose pear-shaped profile is Canada's best-known military figure, Crerar is largely an historical non-entity. Unlike General G.G. Simonds, his stiff-upper-lipped corps commander and sometime stand-in as army commander, Crerar is also frequently deemed suspect among Canada's Second World War generals. Simonds hated him, especially after Crerar failed to recommend him for post-war promotion to Chief of the General Staff.[3] British Field Marshal Sir Bernard Law Montgomery thought him far inferior to Simonds as an army commander, and many of his contemporaries thought him flawed in myriad ways: as an inveterate schemer perhaps, or a political climber whose penchant for administration, procedure, and bureaucratic nicety was counterproductive on the modern battlefield and the antithesis of modern leadership.

Major-General Chris Vokes, who commanded an infantry division under Crerar in Italy, loathed his superior's old-fashioned adherence to paperwork and administration. "I felt, militarily, having just been separated from my competent British superiors, as though I was in the position of a boy whose loving mother had just died and who is then put under the control of a cold-hearted and ignorant stepmother. I didn't like it." Crerar, Vokes concluded, "stood for shining buttons and all that chickenshit."[4]

History books, especially high school and university textbooks, regularly ignore Crerar. The third edition of *Nation*, authored in 1990 by a six-person team including military historians J.L. Granatstein and David J. Bercuson, mentions him in a single sentence; Currie appears on several pages, with numerous references, including a paragraph-long career synopsis. Ramsay Cook's chapter on the 1900-1945 period in Craig Brown's best-selling edited work, *The Illustrated History of Canada* (1991 edition), leaves out Crerar altogether. There are, to be sure, works that treat with equal disdain or disinterest military affairs and personalities in either of Canada's wars, like the second volume of Alvin Finkel, Margaret Conrad, and Veronica Strong-Boag's *History of the Canadian Peoples* (1993), which, in its determination to redress history's alleged imbalances, leaves out both generals and virtually all the battles in which they fought.[5] Where the literature does deem fit to incline an ear towards the faint echo of guns and trumpets, it is a near-certainty that Crerar will fare poorly in comparison to his First World War predecessor. The same is true, for the most part, of works that pick more carefully through the embers of Canada's Second World War experience or those that survey more broadly the country's military history. As Bercuson and Granatstein noted in the *Dictionary of Canadian Military History* (1992), Crerar's reputation, "highest during the war, has now been almost entirely superceded by that of [G.G.] Simonds."[6] Bothwell, Drummond, and English offer a rare balanced portrayal, one drawn mainly from Stacey's post-war memoir.[7] Currie, finally, has had several enthusiastic biographers; Crerar has none, except for Paul Dickson's 1993 doctoral dissertation which remains, at present, unpublished.[8]

Explaining such discrepancies in the treatment accorded Canada's most senior Second World War general is, at one level, a less than taxing pursuit. In character and circumstance, Crerar, a Hamilton, Ontario, native and Royal Military College graduate (1909), appears decidedly underprivileged when weighed against the rotund but likeable former teacher and militiaman, Currie. In addition, Crerar's reputation, especially in his relations with senior British and American officers, suffered through comparison with some of his more self-consciously prototypical peers. For example, unlike Crerar, Simonds was a natural fit for the mother country's aristocratic officer caste (a cultural artifact the existence of which Simonds nevertheless sought vigorously to deny)[9] in ways that the bureaucratic, nationalistic Crerar was not.

As well, there was a "battlefield gap" between the circumstances contributing to the Currie legend and those that continue to deny Crerar similar acclaim. There was no Vimy Ridge or Amiens in First Canadian Army's trek from Normandy to Germany in 1944-45. The efforts of historian Terry Copp notwithstanding – whose insistence that an ill-considered infatuation with all things German has skewed Western scholars' understanding of Allied accomplishments in Normandy – accounts of the fighting from D-Day to Germany's surrender frequently emit a self-deprecating, apologetic tone. As Copp concluded in his history of the Fifth Canadian Infantry Brigade, "the evidence confirms my belief that historians have greatly underrated the achievements of the Allied combat troops who inflicted a series of defeats on the German army and thereby played a major role in the liberation of the people of North-West Europe."[10]

In the consensus to which Copp has here responded, it is almost as though Allied military planners, and the personnel they commanded, succeeded in spite of themselves. There are numerous variations on this theme, notably the deceptively simple argument proposed by John Ellis that the Allies prevailed through sheer weight of numbers and precious little else.[11] Such tautological vulgarities are nothing new in the history of writing on war. The longevity of the argument that attributes the North's success in the American Civil War to quantitative causes alone is a classic example of the genre, however quickly it falls apart on closer examination.[12] But in the case of Crerar, Canada, and Normandy, such arguments seem to have survived their encounter with memoir, counter-revisionism, and good sense more or less intact.

Crerar's infamy, or the faint praise with which he is equally well damned, was solidified in recent years largely by a single influential volume: John English's The Canadian Army and the Normandy Campaign.[13] The muted aspersions of earlier scholars, including the writings of official historian, Colonel C.P. Stacey, had secured a firm foundation for posterity's monument to his supposed mediocrity, but to modern officer candidates and university students English's work is pre-eminent. As Copp noted in November 1998, "English's book quickly became the new standard interpretation of the Canadian army's experience in the Second World War."[14] While neither Stacey nor English, as Copp pointed out, proposed a definition of failure or success – implying simply that failure could be implied wherever all of one's objectives were not achieved – Stacey at least painted a more balanced portrait of Crerar than his successor. Describing in his memoirs a remark to a reporter that Crerar "seems to me the sort of man who would never make a bad mistake," a comment that later appeared in abbreviated form on the cover of Time magazine, the historian later reflected on his lapse in judgement with a member of the press. "Looking back," wrote Stacey, "I don't think my off-the-cuff opinion of Crerar was far wrong. He was not brilliant, as McNaughton was, but his judgment was far better than McNaughton's. I think it can be said, in retrospect, that Harry really never did make a bad mistake, whereas Andy made a great many. And men who don't make bad mistakes are very useful in war."[15] English, in contrast, repeatedly emphasizes Crerar's lack of field command experience, his pedantic orientation, and "silver spoon career,"[16] and he retells at some length an anecdote from Vokes on the inappropriateness of Crerar's First World War artillery mentality to the conduct of modern war. English accepts frequently and without critique Montgomery's damaging opinions of Crerar, elevating the army group commander to something approaching a sainted status, the all-knowing military muse whose assessments of lesser Canadians are, one assumes, acceptable *sans* comment or qualification.

Dickson's work on this subject is not definitive – few works are – but it is convincing, reinforcing the more favourable components of Stacey's after-the-fact summation. Dickson points to a Crerar whose expertise lay not so much in battlefield prowess, though even here he remained highly competent, as in his shrewd understanding of the dual demands of politics and generalship deriving from his peculiar politico-military appointment. Always explaining his actions in terms of the good of the armed forces *and* the state,[17] Crerar also propounded regularly on the political demands of his position, first as Chief of the General Staff early in the war and later as the commander of First Canadian Army. Dickson argued in his thesis that Crerar relied on common sense, discipline, good morale, and knowledge, which integrated his pre-war experience, education, and training with subsequent actions and operations. This was also in accord with Crerar's scholarly and political interest in international affairs, the balance of power, and their potential effects on Canada and its armed forces. By the late 1930s, Crerar's earlier advocacy of strengthened imperial defence ties had given way to a more overtly nationalist posture – a "broad national perspective," according to Dickson – but one adumbrated nevertheless by the same overweening ambition recognized by Granatstein, Stacey, and other scholars, as well as contemporaries like Simonds and Vokes. This national perspective, argued Dickson, was the necessary context for any assessment of Canada's senior wartime general and the professional context in which he worked. As W. Denis Whitaker and Shelagh Whitaker had noted in their assessment of Crerar's leadership during Operation Veritable, the General's position rendered him susceptible to legislative, governmental, and British military pressure, but "few commanders were as qualified to handle an operation of such complexity – and precariousness" as Crerar.[18]

This was high praise from a duo otherwise inclined to a healthy skepticism concerning Canada's senior wartime command, and Granatstein's collective work on Canada's Second World War generals makes more or less the same point, offering fulsome praise for the few who, in the face of crisis, rose substantially above the inadequacies of the many. In his delightfully sub-titled chapter on Crerar, "Ambition Realized," Granatstein offers a positive appraisal:

> Harry Crerar had shaped the Canadian army. He built up its overseas headquarters, gave it an efficient training organization in Canada, and began the process of turning the 1 Canadian Corps into an effective military organization. In Northwest Europe he led the army effectively and cautiously, and he represented Canada with care and circumspection in Allied councils. He more than merited the honours he received.[19] [However, his concluding comments on Crerar are ambiguous and grudgingly offered] Crerar had learned much about command and politics during the first three years of war, and he was temperamentally much better fitted than McNaughton to lead a national contingent in a huge Allied army. Crerar was no Montgomery, no Patton, but despite his overweening ambition and his cravings for rank and personal power, he was a competent soldier in a good, middle-ground Canadian way.[20]

In this respect, Crerar's status and the ambiguity attached to assessments of him reflect a broader disjunction between the depictions of the First and Second World Wars in Canadian historiography. More than a function of battlefield success, this anomaly instead, one suspects, derives from the primacy in Canada's wartime history of a discourse informed by national politics and, in recent decades, by sub-national social, cultural, and identity dynamics. Domestic politics, or national unity, is the background for almost all major interpretations of Canada's wartime experience. This process, especially the nature of French-English relations, the Quebec question, religious discord, linguistic politics, regionalism, and the coming together of these in each conflict over the divisive question of compulsory overseas service, has in large part determined the place in posterity for the wartime governments of Sir Robert Borden and W.L.M. King; it has also helped determine, or so it appears, the historical footprint of their senior generals. Curiously, both liberal nationalist scholars in the old mould and revisionists of more recent methodological vintage have played to the same tune: in the first case, they helped establish the criteria and context in which political leadership would be judged, and in the second, they helped restack the academic deck to help ensure that, through not-so-benign neglect, it stayed that way.

There is no straight line between domestic politics and military interpretation, but at the confluence of domestic politics and interpretive vision lie intriguing possibilities. Short-changing, even inadvertently, both the experience of war and, especially, the experiences of Second World War veterans, may have harnessed both popular and scholarly perceptions of Canada's crusades to a panorama of interpretive vignettes of great breadth but questionable depth. A few have already been called into question by recent scholars such as Terry Copp and veteran George Blackburn;[21] others await judgement with remarkable staying power. The cumulative effects of such optical imprecision have been both dramatic and ironic. Thus, the sordid and brutalizing First World War is said to have witnessed the flowering of Canadian military talent, and this with solid biographies of only one Canadian general, Currie. The moral clarity deriving from the struggle against Hitler, on the other hand, was waged allegedly by a caste conspicuous only by its shortage of talent, but this conclusion too comes without biographies, solid or otherwise, of most of the senior military figures. Such ironies cry out for emphasis: Canada's First World War generals, even the British ones like Byng, escaped for the most part denunciations of their military professionalism. Their Second World War successors, who incurred roughly 25 percent fewer fatal casualties in a far longer struggle, are derided, often explicitly, as uninspired and incapable, with one or two notable exceptions. Overall, they are deemed unworthy of Currie's successful mantra.

The Canadian Corps, in helping to defeat the Kaiser's powerful but arguably unexceptional military, is likewise held up as a paragon of military excellence, the shock army of the British Empire according to one recent account. However, First Canadian Army and its counterparts at sea and in the air during the Second World War, despite helping to defeat Hitler's military machine which was possibly the finest European military of the twentieth century, have been found wanting by two generations of armchair strategists. Myths attaching to the generals and their national military establishments likewise gravitate, inevitably, towards the men and women under their command.

The grounds for comparison between the sea and air wars in the two struggles are less firm than for land operations, if only because of Canada's comparatively small First World War naval service and the fact that most Canadian fliers served in British formations after 1914. But even here indiscreet questions lurk. The Royal Canadian Navy fought a losing struggle against Germany's submarines for most of the Second World War; poorly equipped, it was the inadequately trained junior partner of larger and better-armed British and, later, American fleets. The Royal Canadian Air Force's largest strike formation in the air war against occupied Europe, Number 6 Bomber Group, likewise fared badly for many months after its formation, incurring catastrophic casualties; nonetheless, its fliers, ground crew, and commanders eventually learned the rudiments of strategic bombing technique. This muted praise and occasional disdain, proffered by academic scholarship on the efforts of Canada's Second World War commanders, is slightly at odds with the favourable treatment usually accorded the country's political leadership and with the praise frequently reserved, especially in the populist-attuned media, for the military's rank and file. Canada's fighting forces, it seems, avoided the leadership of donkeys in the first war only to follow tragically an entire herd in the second.

The comparison spills over into the political, the social, and the economic as well. The First World War left Canada victorious but bled white, astonished at its own successes and appalled at the cost – human, financial, and political. The Second World War left the country successful but urbane, imbued with the quiet confidence of a nation that has faced its demons and stared them down. The First World War may have forged the conditions for the fulfillment of constitutional independence afterwards, but its benefits were dearly bought; the second confirmed sovereignty's permanence but this time with righteous certainty and nowhere near the same level of domestic political turbulence.

None of this pseudo-consensus is uncontested – on King's leadership travails alone a small library has been written – yet it is omnipresent. Broad brush strokes notwithstanding, there is a marvellous juxtaposition that attends most comparisons of Canada's wars under Borden and King, at home and abroad. There is no need to rehabilitate here Borden's tattered image to appreciate the incongruity of it: a successful and skilled war leader whose sins in the name of peace helped lay the foundations for Canadian political independence and military victory, whose failings are at least as attributable to the period's vengeful politics – and to the views of their latter-day expositors – as to any objective assessment of his admittedly flawed character. He has been tagged by scholarly convention as one of Canada's least able prime ministers. On the other hand, a paunchy spiritualist reviled by the troops and by their generals, whose opportunism and occasional ruthlessness were the objects of fear and loathing even among Liberals, is held up to posterity as the quintessence of Canadian political acumen.

This crudely caricatures the differences of people and place, war and warriors, between the two conflicts, yet it also highlights the oddities in a scholarship that has lionized the first war's soldiers but the second war's politicians. Borden's political cronies and the vast majority of those generals and admirals who fought Hitler are remembered, where they are remembered at all, with almost rancid indifference, a point to which Crerar's carefully attenuated memorials so obviously attest.

No doubt Crerar's post-war espousal of conscription and his forthright arguments in favour of military preparedness against the day when global peace would lapse once more placed him somewhat outside the pro-Quebec, anti-conscription, Liberal political machine that continued to be re-elected for a decade after 1945. In so doing, Crerar might have moved himself onto the country's military historical margins. As he had noted throughout the war and immediately afterwards, the precarious position of the Western democracies early in the struggle had been due in no small part to their having been unprepared militarily for the onset of war. For example, in December 1945 as demobilization continued its frantic pace, Crerar noted that armaments "are the effect, not the cause," of international "illness." He maintained forcefully that "the peace-loving democracies must always be prepared in a military sense, to defeat sudden attempts by other nations – less susceptible to the steadying influence of an informed public opinion – to settle grievances by aggressive action."[22] International preparedness was indeed a watchword in the immediate post-war period, but it was only a small leap to advocating the form of compulsory military service that alone was likely to secure the level of readiness Crerar endorsed.

It is also tempting to see in the disjuncture between successful commander and public ignominy a weakness in the Canadian literature's ability to fully come to grips with the implications of modern warfare for generals and political leaders in Canada's peculiarly exposed, multi-tasked appointments. They had to do more than simply win battles: the larger issues of national unity, sovereignty, and alliance politics had to be addressed. As such, Canada's military and political leadership – past and present – should be judged in this light. Furthermore, as Wavell noted in 1941, during the conflict in which, according to consensus, Crerar would largely fail to excel, tactics and battlefield performance in the age of modern warfare occurred largely outside the purview of the commanding general. Administration and logistics, on the other hand, even in the opinion of the ancient Greek, Socrates, whose view Wavell quotes in support of the point, are the essence of command, the essential prerequisite without attention to which battlefield exertions will likely fail to secure the desired result.[23] It is certainly possible to exaggerate this point, but Crerar's critics, with no clearer delineation of the terms of debate, can just as surely lean in the opposite direction. English's derogatory comments on Crerar's directives to his senior formation commanders on 22 July 1944, that "all told they remain more revealing of a commander who never had an original idea of his own than they were stimulating," remain marvellously pithy but inconclusive and suspiciously one-sided. Others too (including, most notably, Vokes) indicted Crerar's artillery predisposition in commenting upon his pre-modern tactical tendencies, but, in light of the poor showing of Allied armour in Normandy until after Falaise, it is in some sense counterintuitive to rest altogether smugly on that lamp-post. There are, in short, more sides to an assessment of Canadian generalship than that which senior British officers might care to advance. Even here, it might be said, the results are more ambiguous than later-day Pattons would have us believe: Montgomery and Crerar got along well through much of the war. Monty, for example, commented favourably on Crerar's command abilities in early 1942.[24]

This suggests less the proper basis for leadership instruction in our modern service academies – as armchair critics point out, administration and logistics already prosper perhaps at the expense of strategy and war fighting – than the value to be derived from a more careful reconsideration of the historical (and historiographical) benchmarks by which generalship and its ultimate political effects have heretofore been defined. Such considerations, or rather reconsiderations, rest at least as much in the realm of national political history (and contemporary politics) as they do in the province of military history. Most critically, perhaps, among the offending quartet of "traditional" academic historical pursuits – political, military, diplomatic, and economic – political history has been all but annihilated in the post-modern university, relinquishing its curriculum slots to a breathtaking, if spasmodic, assemblage of social, gender, labour, and regional course offerings that ignore, often gleefully, the patterns of national historical development etched out by their grey-haired professorial predecessors. The result, in part, has been the arrested development of political historiography and, inadvertently, the impoverishment of opinion on the critical questions of civil-military relations, command, leadership, grand strategy, national interests, and wartime high politics that are relevant to a thorough assessment of Harry Crerar and his time. J.L. Granatstein's seminal *Canada's War*, for example, an essential volume on the Mackenzie King Government's conduct of the Second World War, is now a quarter century old with no equivalent successor; C.P. Stacey's weighty *Arms, Men and Governments*, the starting point for all serious work on the period, appeared five years before that, in 1970.[25] Dickson's doctoral dissertation updates both in substantial ways, but a quarter century between revisions is an astonishingly long gap. As Granatstein inferred in his best-selling and controversial 1998 pot boiler, *Who Killed Canadian History?*, in the "battle" between old and new historians, "the old was swept away almost completely."

> The new historians effectively and efficiently took over Canadian history, setting up new journals or assuming control of the old. They ascended to the presidencies of the scholarly associations and set up specialized associations of their own, driving out all those who did not follow the mandated approach. They rewarded themselves with the prizes and fellowships that were under the control of historians – though they did less well with awards that were controlled by more broadly based organizations. They took over the hiring processes in their departments, thus guaranteeing that they could replicate themselves at will, and they trained graduate students to do the kind of work they preached and practiced. They freely denounced the political historians as second-rate, teaching unimportant subjects and publishing shoddy work.[26]

One beneficiary of political history's defeat in the academies has been the federal civil service, whose policy directorates, crown corporations, and strategic analysis cells have hired numerous masters and doctoral students from the university system, but this strengthening of the government's policy-making apparatus has come partly at the expense of published scholarship and original research. Brilliant work continues to be completed at schools like the University of New Brunswick, Wilfrid Laurier University, and the University of Calgary, but all too frequently at the Masters (M.A.) level only, there being few post-secondary outlets for doctoral students in political history and related fields, including military studies.

It is utterly fanciful to assume that a revitalized national history, even if it were possible, would rehabilitate Harry Crerar, whether in the indexes of the next generation of standard texts or in the comparative opinions of the professional scholars who wait eagerly to dismiss them. That is hardly the point of thinking wistfully in this vein. But a revitalized political-military genre, along with more detailed attention to the meaning of "modern" or even "post-modern" generalship, might at least help place Crerar more properly in the context of his time. No revisionist will likely succeed in making Crerar a more attractive or less ambitious personality, character traits on which scholars remain almost unanimously insistent, and none will make him, like Liddell Hart did with Rome's Scipio Africanus, "greater than Napoleon" (or even Currie). But they may help rescue somewhat Crerar's personal military reputation and, by implication, that of the army he so successfully led in Canada's greatest military endeavour. To say that the requirements of high command in modern coalition warfare render fungible the tenets by which generalship, broadly defined, must be judged, would be too fine point, and possibly disingenuous too: critics, like Montgomery or the historian, John English, comment appropriately enough on Crerar's command shortcomings even as, perhaps, they bestow insufficient praise. (Crerar's performance during Operation Veritable is an example.)

But they may miss the mark as well. As Dickson and, to a lesser extent, Granatstein make clear, a more balanced appraisal suggests, distastefully perhaps, that Crerar's professionalism fit well with the peculiar requirements of his post. It might not be an early occurrence of the "heroic" versus "post-heroic" form of generalship discussed by Edward Luttwak and others, but it is at least a telling commentary on the evolution of command in the Canadian context. Moreover, and in addition to whatever expository value might be derived from this qualifier, to take Copp's conclusion but to argue it in reverse, a reconsideration of the battlefield performance of Canadian troops against their German opponents must, of necessity, involve a similar reconsideration of their commanders, and not just at the battalion and brigade levels. Crerar was builder, administrator, liaison officer, chairman of the board, and more, all the while fulfilling both operational and political roles with great competence.[27] He led a complex, multinational army on the offensive to victory against a well prepared, resilient, and battled-tested foe. These ought to count for more in our reckoning of the man and the troops he led.

We should not discount the importance of battlefield competence. But equally, we should not accept that somewhat nationalist, avowedly revisionist hypothesis that is represented by the currently fashionable journalistic sleight of hand that sells copy even as it distorts reality: to propose, on the slightest of pretexts, that the military would get along famously (composed as it is of men and women fine and true), were it not for the encrustation of blinkered, self-serving, and frequently corrupt officers up the Army chain of command under whom these fine service personnel are forced to serve. It is too clever by half and intellectually unsustainable to boot. First World War Minister of Militia and Defence Sam Hughes and many of today's honourary colonels might readily consent to such militia-enhancing snobbery, but analytical and logical perspective ought properly to lead in the other direction. Granatstein's conclusion, though criticized by some for being too soft on the generals thus perhaps strikes the right note in acknowledging failure but highlighting accomplishment, thereby linking Canadian victories with, deservedly, those who orchestrated them.

In the modern context, tainted indelibly by the Somalia affair and the media muck-raking that accompanied it, a besieged military establishment and defence department showed themselves poorly prepared to make the kinds of linkages and, where necessary, distinctions demanded by such subtlety. Ambushed repeatedly by the evidence of bad practice, indifferent leadership, and occasional dishonesty within its own ranks, the military's senior leadership breathed life into controversy by a hyper-sensitive response that frequently alienated otherwise supportive members of the defence community. That neither the department nor its senior leadership was guilty of even a fraction of the misdemeanours ascribed to them became a moot point in what can only be classed as a media circus. The debate, however, at least helped set the terms, in unexpected ways, for a broader inquiry into questions of leadership and command. Harry Crerar might be an unsuspecting beneficiary of this revival, or – at least – he might prove its unsuspecting goat. But the former possibility is surely the more intriguing. Like Ulysses S. Grant, the

Union army's victorious but decidedly unheroic, perhaps even anti-heroic, commander in the last campaigns of the American Civil War, Crerar might yet come to assume more comfortably a peculiarly double-edged mantra: he was no Currie, it will continue to be argued, but he might well have been Canada's first modern general, and not an altogether bad one at that.

ENDNOTES

CHAPTER 5

1. The views expressed in this paper are my own and in no way reflect the position of the Canadian War Museum.
2. The repeated error, by both anchors and reporters alike, was a running discomfort during the ceremonies attending the repatriation of Canada's Unknown Soldier in May 2000.
3. On this, see especially C.P. Stacey, *A Date with History: Memoirs of a Canadian Historian* (Ottawa: Deneau, 1983), 233-5.
4. Chris Vokes with John P. Maclean, *Vokes: My Story* (Ottawa: Gallery Books, 1985), 152.
5. *History of the Canadian Peoples,* Volume II: *1867 to the Present* (Toronto: Copp Clark, 1993). For a vituperative commentary on such works, see J.L. Granatstein, "Canadian History Textbooks and the Wars," *Canadian Military History* 3/1, Spring 1994, 123-4. Finkel, in a similarly uncompromising vein, later penned *Our Lives: Canada After 1945* (Toronto: James Lorimer, 1997), another wildly selective diatribe masquerading as "new" history.
6. David J. Bercuson and J.L. Granatstein, *Dictionary of Canadian Military History* (Toronto: Oxford University Press, 1992), 55-56.
7. Robert Bothwell, Ian Drummond, and John English, *Canada, 1900-1945* (Toronto: University of Toronto Press, 1987), 342-3.
8. Paul Douglas Dickson, "The Limits of Professionalism: General H.D.G. Crerar and the Canadian Army, 1914-1944," (unpublished PhD thesis, University of Guelph, 1993).
9. See, for example, G.G. Simonds, "Commentary and Observations," in Hector J. Massey, ed., *The Canadian Military: A Profile* (Toronto: Copp Clark, 1972), 273-5, where Simonds states flatly that the British Army's alleged class system is a "myth."
10. Terry Copp, *The Brigade: The Fifth Canadian Infantry Brigade, 1939-1945* (Stoney Creek, Ont.: Fortress Publications, 1992), 200.
11. John Ellis, *Brute Force: Allied Strategy and Tactics in the Second World War* (London: Andre Deutsch, 1990).
12. See, for example, Gary W. Gallagher, "Blueprint for Victory: Northern

Strategy and Military Policy," in James M. McPherson and William J. Cooper, Jr., eds., *Writing the Civil War: The Quest to Understand* (Columbia: University of South Carolina Press, 1998), 8-35.

13. John A. English, *The Canadian Army and the Normandy Campaign: A Study of Failure in High Command* (New York: Praeger, 1991).

14. Terry Copp, "From the Editor," *Canadian Military History* 7/4, Autumn 1998, 2.

15. Stacey, *A Date with History*, 112.

16. English, *The Canadian Army and the Normandy Campaign*, 183.

17. Dickson, "The Limits of Professionalism," 475.

18. Dennis Whitaker, *Rhineland: The Battle to End the War* (Toronto: Stoddart, 1989), 32.

19. Ibid., 115.

20. J.L. Granatstein, *The Generals: The Canadian Army's Senior Generals in the Second World War*, (Toronto: Stoddart, 1993), 263.

21. Blackburn has published three volumes of war memoirs. See especially *The Guns of Normandy: A Soldier's Eye View, France 1944* (Toronto: McClelland & Stewart, 1995).

22. General H.D.G. Crerar, "Some Thoughts on Peace and War," address to the Canadian Club of Montreal, 5 December 1945, 2 and 4.

23. Sir Archibald Wavell, *Generals and Generalship: The Lee Knowles Lectures, 1939* (Toronto: Macmillan, 1941), 1-10.

24. Granatstein, *The Generals*, 101-2.

25. J.L. Granatstein, *Canada's War: The Politics of the Mackenzie King Government, 1939-1945* (Toronto: Oxford University Press, 1975); and C.P. Stacey, *Arms, Men and Governments: The War Policies of Canada, 1939-1945* (Ottawa: Queen's Printer, 1970).

26. J.L. Granatstein, *Who Killed Canadian History?* (Toronto: HarperCollins, 1998), 58-9. For a spirited rebuttal to this, see A.B. McKillop, "Who Killed Canadian History?: A View from the Trenches," *Canadian Historical Review* 80/2, 1999. The *Canadian Historical Review*, one of the academic outlets criticized by Granatstein, reviewed his book in the March 1999 issue, but also published two blistering rejoinders, McKillop's and another by Bryan D. Palmer, "Of Silences and Trenches: A Dissident View of Granatstein's Meaning," 80/4, 1999.

27. This is Dickson's convincing thesis.

Chapter 6

General Guy Simonds:
The Commander as Tragic Hero

Lieutentant-Colonel Roman Johann Jarymowycz

Est Modus in Rebus
Horace[1]

I do not express the above view with the object of directing criticism on officers ... but as a matter of historical record, when this operation can be examined in all its aspects, I feel under an obligation to express my frank opinion.
Lieutenant-General G.G. Simonds,
GOC Canadian Forces
in the Netherlands, 21 January 1946

G UY Granville Simonds is the tragic hero – at once revered and condemned. His many admirers tend to rationalize his failures, while his great successes are diminished by the even greater success of Allied counterparts. Although Simonds' 2nd Canadian Corps closed the Falaise Gap, trapping two German armies, its accomplishment was abridged by the fact that it did not close it *according to schedule*. The acquisition of Operation Maneuver by his armoured corps (the first corps in 21st Army Group to achieve breakout) was overshadowed by American armoured divisions successively appearing in Rennes, Le Mans, Chartres, and Paris.

Simonds is the complex general – a tortured intellect, the *almost* brilliant commander, unforgiving of incompetence yet unable to correct his own failure; esteemed by foreigners, despised by his own high command; respected by the ranks yet not beloved; frustrated by those he depended on, then clandestinely betrayed by pedestrian conspirators. With the exception of O'Connor, who had the cup of victory dashed from his lips by long-range tank fire during Operation Goodwood, he remains the only corps commander bequeathed the opportunity and the tools to elevate a tactical victory to a strategic triumph.

Simonds' enthusiasm for Montgomery led him to turn his back on McNaughton and initiate a hatred in Crerar that nearly cost him command and certainly forever banned him from the halls of power in Ottawa. Simonds inspired extremes in both the military and military historians: General Chris Vokes considered him "the finest Canadian general we ever had" but added that as "a leader of men" he wasn't worth "a pinch of coonshit."[2] James Eayrs included Simonds in his list of commanders "who might be described (as intellectual soldiers) without inaccuracy and without insult." C.P. Stacey, while pitiless in his assessment of Canadian regimental officers in Normandy, forgave the senior commanders: "Canadian generalship [did] not suffer by comparison with that of the other Allies engaged." In the case of Guy Simonds, he was not only correct, but may have been too tempered.

Simonds was born in England, but his formal education was all Canadian. Indeed, he was bilingual. At the Royal Military College (RMC) he was the best equestrian in his class, joined the Horse Artillery, and played a great deal of polo; his regimental commander was Lieutenant-Colonel H.D.G. Crerar. By the time he joined the RMC faculty, he had completed his professional military education including the Staff College in Kingston in 1935, where the course director was Lieutenant-Colonel Ken Stuart, and Camberley, which he completed in 1936 with Charles Foulkes and Rod Keller. He returned to RMC in 1938 as an instructor in tactics, strategy, and international affairs. "The most noticeable feature were his eyes – blue, penetrating and observant. He was of average height."[3]

It was at the British Staff College that Simonds was first schooled in "the importance of the Breakin Battle,"[4] and it gave him a taste for the military art. He demonstrated his new-found confidence by attacking the opinions of a senior officer and veteran, Lieutenant-Colonel E.L.M. Burns, who had written an article in *Canadian Defence Quarterly* (CDQ) suggesting that "the assault must be carried out by tanks; not by infantry, or even infantry with tank assistance" ("A Division That Can Attack"). Simonds wrote an article that was also published by CDQ ("An Army that Can Attack – A Division that Can Defend") and promptly instigated the only bona fide debate regarding mechanization in pre-war Canada. Simonds echoed the opinions of the British military establishment against the Fulleresque all-tank "torrent of armour." Burns, without tank experience, nevertheless sympathized with the Royal Tank Corps and saw armour as the arm of decision – arguing in a further CDQ article that tanks required their own standard division ("Where do the Tanks Belong?"). Simonds' CDQ rebuttal ("What Price Assault without Support?") reviewed cost and made a pitch for more artillery.[5] His position regarding armour supported the "infantry tank" school as a handmaiden to infantry, in essence arguing for General Headquarters tank battalions, allotted to divisions only as required: "In the war 1914-18 massed artillery and surprise was the formula for successful attack ... given sufficient support the range and endurance of tanks may enable them to convert a 'breakin' into a 'breakthrough'.... Air bombing may develop to the stage where massed air craft ... can provide a sustained bombardment."[6]

This exchange was a mere bagatelle in an era when the cavalries of Europe and North America were fighting for their doctrinal survival. Mechanization first triumphed in Germany and the Soviet Union where tanks, built by workers and controlled by officers who owed their survival to despotic leaders, were exactly what Stalin and Hitler wanted. The West did not produce armoured formations until well after Blitzkrieg devoured Poland. Both the British 1st Armoured Division and the French *Divisions Cuirassées* did not appear until just before the 1940 campaign. The creation of an American Armored Force required a palace revolt against Major-General John K. Herr, Chief of Cavalry, led by Adna Romanza Chaffee. Yankee Armored Divisions did not appear until after Pearl Harbor.

The literary debate between Burns and Simonds may be dismissed as a footnote in Canadian military history – a bun fight between a Sapper and a Gunner over the best type of division the Empire required – if it were not for the distinct opinions presented. Burns, sentenced to command the 5th Armoured in the rocky terrain of Italy, did no harm: Montgomery's welcome to him ("You're useless to me – totally useless."[7]) referred more to the rationality of deploying a tank division in Italy than to Burns' tactical skills. Simonds, conversely, was to carry his pre-war philosophy into the dangerous Panther-prowled plains below Caen, where his uncompromising approach to battle would be costly.

Military England 1940

When war was declared, Simonds briefly took command of 1 Royal Canadian Horse Artillery (RCHA) at Aldershot then sailed for England as a member of General Staff. He was rated "cool and resourceful" in organizing the evacuation of Canadian troops from France. Simonds' British background proved an asset. His natural ability and keen eye for detail ensured he continued to fit into the future plans of the Canadian High Command and the approval of Whitehall's generals. He was soon posted as acting Brigadier at the Canadian Corps Headquarters. This was the first time he was at close proximity to Montgomery.

As an RMC cadet he was nicknamed "the Wegimental Wabbit" because of his lisp. As a member of the Directing Staff he exhibited an upper class aloofness and was dubbed "the Count" for "his immaculate turn-out and haughty demeanor."[8] Yet once back in Britain, he quickly became one of the boys.[9] He ensured that Bernard Montgomery's new South East Army doctrine was adopted throughout the Canadian Corps. Simonds' enthusiasm and efficiency did not go unnoticed. Montgomery wrote to Crerar, temporarily replacing McNaughton as commander, Canadian Corps: "You have a first class BGS [Brigadier, General Staff] in Simonds; I would like you to tell him I thought he was very good."[10] This may have been the spark that lit a growing resentment. When Montgomery requested having Simonds on his staff, "Crerar strongly opposed his appointment, disapproved of him being there [working for Montgomery] developing antipathy between Simonds and his former battery commander."[11]

After a series of staff appointments and a four-month stint as Commander, 1st Canadian Brigade, Simonds was sent into the Mediterranean Theatre to observe British professionalism first hand. He visited Lieutenant-General Sir Brian Horrocks' 10th British Corps in Tunisia in March 1943, where his quick grasp of the essential elements in North African operations made him stand out: "Monty was very impressed. He was the best officer who ever visited us in the desert."[12] Within a month Simonds was promoted to Major-General and named to command 2nd Canadian Division. Montgomery's opinion must have been a contributing factor because a subsequent evaluation of Simonds by Canadians was less enthusiastic: "Most outstanding officer but not a leader of the type that will secure the devotion of his followers. Similar in characteristics to General Burns and would give his best service as a high staff officer."[13] This likely would have sentenced Simonds to the dustbin of history if not for the tragic plane crash that killed Major-General H.L.N. Salmon as he flew to take over the 1st Canadian Infantry Division, designated part of the Sicily invasion force. It was "the greatest break of his career."[14] Simonds inherited Salmon's Division, assuring that at 39 he would be the youngest Canadian general to lead Canadian troops into action and the first to acquire contemporary operational experience.

Italy

Simonds easily fit into the 8th Army's style. As an American historian observed: "The British believed there was only one way to fight, and that was the British way. Far too easily they ascribed incapacity or mediocrity to troops who were non-British. Far too often they mistrusted people who, like the Canadians, except Guy Simonds, lacked an Oxford accent."[15] Grouped in 30th British Corps under General Sir Oliver Leese, Simonds led three brigades and his own armour – the Three Rivers Regiment into Sicily on 10 July 1943.

Simonds soon distinguished himself, drew praise from Montgomery and Leese, and was cited for a Distinguished Service Order (DSO): "great boldness and efficiency ... he is an inspiring example to his Division – by his frequent visits to the forward areas – where under bomb, shell and mortar fire he carries out his reconnaissance."[16] As Commandant he proved an unforgiving critic: "His tendency to tell his brigade commanders how to execute their missions did cause some friction.... He tended to over-control his subordinate commanders, not only telling them what to do but often, how to do it."[17] Simonds also had a nasty streak – his tactless treatment of Brigadier Howard Graham eventually forced Montgomery to interfere.[18]

A revealing glimpse into Simonds' character was his refusal to see his commander, General Andy McNaughton, who was subsequently kept out of Italy and away from Canadian troops until 20 August. Montgomery felt that "Simonds who was just beginning to find his feet ... should not be distracted." When he was advised of McNaughton's intended visit Simonds is said to have replied, "For God's sake keep him away."[19] This was a curious display of loyalty. His "lessons learned" portfolio grew quickly, particularly after the unsuccessful attack against Nissoria on 23 July which read like a horoscope for Operation Totalize: communication failure, scrubbed missions by the Air Force bombers, uncoordinated artillery support, unsupported battalion actions, and a heavy cost to supporting armour.[20] Simonds blamed "failure in communications." These essentials were to plague him again in August 1944.

Nonetheless, by mid-summer Montgomery strongly recommended him as the next dauphin: "I know of no other Canadian other than Guy Simonds in whom I would have confidence as a corps commander."[21] To broaden his repertoire, Simonds was given command of 5th Armoured Division. It has been suggested that the three months during which Simonds commanded the armoured division were wasted. Simonds' only experience as Panzer leader came when his 11th Brigade, led by its new commander, George Kitching, took a crack at German paratroopers in Arielli on 17 January 1944. Kitching's men were determined to show 1st Canadian Division veterans how to handle *Fallschirmjägers*. Despite good artillery support, the Brigade was soundly trounced by the 1st Parachute Division.[22] The supporting tanks from a non-divisional outfit, 1 Canadian Armoured Brigade (CAB), were timidly dispensed in parsimonious packets. Kitching made a point of blaming 1st Armoured Brigade's inactivity ("lack of vital support from the tanks") on its commanding officer, Brigadier Robert Wyman, who was to later serve both Kitching and Simonds in Normandy. Wyman ordered his tanks not to get "into too much of a dog fight." Kitching later snorted: "Had I known that tanks were not expendable but infantry were, I would never have agreed to put in the attack."[23]

Although the logic of infantry preceding armour in rough terrain is sound, it does little for confidence in all-arms co-operation. The riflemen of an armoured division must think and act as *Panzergrenadiers*. One problem was training. Despite being at war since 1939, "We were novices … my Brigade had not been able to train with tanks,"[24] Kitching later wrote. The other problem was leadership. Wyman was allowed to dawdle in Italy and did not become any more aggressive in France, where he successively wasted every opportunity 2 CAB was offered to perform as an *armoured force*. That was Simonds' fault – he had plenty of time to deal with Wyman both in the Mediterranean and before Operation Overlord. The commander of a tank formation is both conductor and Master of Fox Hounds (MFH). It is his job, like the Whippers-In of the Hunt, to get his brigadiers, colonels, and tanks to follow the scent. During his inaugural ride with armour as MFH, Simonds was content to patiently *observe* – a trait that would follow him like a pestilence to Normandy.

As Simonds' operational experience grew and his star rose, it became evident that he was head and shoulders above competing corps commanders, indeed, above designated Army commanders. This inspired jealousy. The "Captain Kirk Incident" should be dismissed for the silly spat it was if not for the lasting grudge and dark passions it stirred in Crerar. The incident was a trifle: Simonds brusquely tore a strip off a young officer named Kirk who he discovered inside his private caravan. The officer was on a mission from Crerar who wanted a command caravan for himself and sent the officer to measure Simonds' caravan. The subsequent correspondence, typed in tight single spaced lines on legal sized paper is impressive – considering there was a war going on – staggering, really.[25] The pique that took hold of Crerar spawned schemes that, even in the becalmed balance of historical reflection, can be only termed evil. Crerar determined to get Simonds.

His stalking was at once noticed by the victim, who correctly assessed Crerar's intent: "Your letter reinforces the feeling that you are looking for an opportunity to 'take a crack' at me." Simonds asked to be relieved if he no longer had Crerar's confidence.[26] Despite his protests of good faith, Crerar, aware that Simonds was his designated replacement as corps commander, now schemed to prove Simonds insane. He first wrote to Montgomery, feigning concern over Simonds' health: "through increased rank and responsibilities, he might go 'off the deep end' very disastrously indeed."[27] He then attempted to covertly dispatch psychiatrists from 1st Canadian Army to visit Simonds' headquarters and clandestinely observe him under stress.[28]

Montgomery bluntly checked Crerar's attempts to undermine his protégé: "Simonds is a first class officer ... you have no one else with his experience."[29] Unmoved, Crerar created an incriminating file against Simonds and sent it to Ken Stuart in London for inclusion in Army records, much like a computer virus poised to destroy whenever triggered:

> I am sending by safe hands the attached copies of communications and memoranda I consider that you should be informed as to the present and potential problem of Simonds.... I arranged a meeting, under most confidential arrangements with Van Nostrand and my DDMS, McCusker, to obtain from the "medicals" their technical advice on the fitness of Simonds continuing in command, or of assuming still higher responsibilities, in view of his mental condition.... It is "background" to be locked up for now, but to be read over again at some future time when the further employment of this brilliant, comparatively young, man comes up for consideration.[30]

Crerar's resentment would grow during the Normandy campaign, fuelled by self-incrimination for his own inferiority. It was the stuff of Shakespearean drama, nay, tragedy.

COMMANDER 2ND CANADIAN CORPS

Lieutenant-General G.G. Simonds CBE, DSO, was 41 when he took over 2nd Canadian Corps. He was considered "handsome with even features, dark hair, dark moustache; he had a good sense of humour, did not swear, rarely drank," but was "hard to get to know ... if he had a confidant it was his Corps G1, Murphy." Those who knew him suggest he was "really quite shy."[31] Simonds arrived in London in late January and "hit his troops like a khaki tornado." He directed immediate introduction of the Chief of Staff system at Corps HQ[32] – a brigadier who co-ordinates all activity and reports for his boss. This left Simonds free to visit and assess; "his steely blue eyes kept searching for weakness."[33] Each senior officer apprehensively awaited the interview, hoping to be told: "You're staying."

Simonds hastily decided to release Major-General F.F. Worthington – the Canadian Chaffee. The General may not have demonstrated the skills to command an army or an infantry corps, but he was Canada's first and only legitimate tank general and certainly the only officer of his rank to have any idea of what an armoured division did.[34] Simonds' decision to replace him with Kitching, an infantry officer with no experience with armour, not even at the regimental level, was to backfire. In hindsight, Worthington would not have done any worse than Kitching[35] or Maczek and, given his personal style, it could be argued he might have done better in a situation that required spontaneous, dynamic action.

Simonds considered age far too important a factor: "A man is never too young for a job, but he may well be too old, for age reduces speed of mental and physical reaction. If an officer is fit to command a unit at twenty-five, he will be twice as good in command as he will be at thirty-five ... Experience is only useful insofar as it represents knowledge. acquired or knowledge confirmed by practical application."[36] As Maczek, Wood, and Grow were to demonstrate during the Normandy breakout battles, style and leadership figured more than youth and vitality. Despite the ruthlessness of Simonds' exacting preparation, he never actually exercised his corps and Kitching was never able to exercise his division. Time was against them; Tactical Exercises Without Troops (TEWTs) would have to do.[37]

D-Day, the Western Allies' most impressive display of a strategic offensive, successfully deposited two armies in France. Eisenhower permitted Montgomery to direct Supreme Headquarters Allied Expeditionary Force's (SHAEF) ground forces and patiently awaited the relentless expansion of the beachhead into Brittany, the Loire, and eventually the Seine. Simonds' corps was activated on 11 July. Its mission was to expand the Caen sector, the best tank country in Normandy, and to draw to itself and contain the maximum number of German divisions in order to permit an American breakout along the western flank through the *bocage* and the rough terrain of the *suisse normande*. The logic of this strategy was not challenged.

The SHAEF Art of War

> *I have introduced many divisions into their first battles –*
> *Canadian, British, American and Polish and I am*
> *convinced that no amount of training can compensate*
> *for actual battle experience.*
> Lieutenant-General G.G. Simonds,
> 21 January1946

Although he cut his teeth in Italy, it was in France, during the "Norman Summer" that Simonds learned the Operational Art. The importance of Normandy in Simonds' career was such that it was to overshadow everything else he accomplished. His campaigns in Holland and the Rhineland, though memorable and valiant actions, were strategic footnotes to the campaigns in Europe. Simonds' arrival in Normandy coincided with Montgomery's attempt to pre-empt Bradley and test the eastern flank of the beachhead. Operation Goodwood (18 to 21 July 1944) was launched, supported by every technique for a strategic breakout that the Allies owned.

The summer of 1944 marked an interesting transition in the Allied Operational Art. The British had been fighting since 1939, yet had not developed a métier to match the Germans or their Russian allies' skills. The standard for British, hence Canadian, *war fighting* doctrine was based on the *set piece battle*, El Alamein – England's only strategic land victory of the war. Essentially it held all the nuances of the Operational Art at its most complex level – the orchestration and embellishment of simple components: outnumber the enemy, choke off his supplies, wear him down through air attack, and *attrition* versus his centre of gravity – hit him where he is strongest. The essence of Blitzkrieg, the "panzer division as tool box," had been reluctantly recognized and only partially imitated. The German army's practice of *Auftragstaktik* (mission directed tactics) and *Kampfgruppen* (*KG*: ad hoc, all-arms battle groups) was regarded as a sort of Germanic cultural approach to war – which it was.

Despite its tactical excellence, the British Army was second rate technically and operationally. An American Major-General wrote that "the British officer seems to know very little about defense, liaison, contact between units and mutually supporting units. He covers his ignorance by a studied nonchalance and indifference."[38] Learning from the enemy or from their own Allies appeared to conflict with British military culture: "The British character is naturally not inquisitive enough and individual officers and soldiers tend to shirk inquiring into matters which they consider the business of other people."[39]

Montgomery's system was pedantic: careful phase lines, sequential objectives, and a mysterious, inconsistent philosophy of control. In Normandy, the Montgomery approach both encouraged doctrinal separatism and interfered at the tactical level. Supposedly orchestrating an Allied symphony, he permitted Bradley, to an extent Crerar, and, specifically, Simonds, to fight as they chose. When frustrated, he was not above directing the movement of a single division, as demonstrated with Maczek's 1st Polish Armoured during the closing of the Falaise Gap.

While the *Stavka* planned complete strategic offensives in the east, Eisenhower permitted Montgomery to conduct the western ground war as Mage. Once ashore, Allied strategic doctrine was improvised – an ongoing experiment in creative problem solving. One of the leading lights, indeed the only operational star, to emerge from Normandy was Guy Simonds. His first battle was to be fought in the wings of Operation Goodwood's grand stage. As he watched the air bombardment and armoured advance from the high ground west of the Orne, the sight of burning British tanks made a lasting impression. Simonds' decision was immediate: "When my turn comes, we will do it at night."[40]

Second Canadian Corps' performance during Operation Atlantic (the Canadian portion of Operation Goodwood) gave some cause for worry: disjointed brigade advances featured unsupported battalion attacks and a frugal distribution of armour. Although at one point Simonds' troops had taken Verrières ridge (whose northeast spur is more famous as Bourguébus ridge, one of the key objectives in Operation Goodwood), they were thrown off by a series of armoured counterattacks. A rout was prevented when Simonds personally co-ordinated a new *fireplan* and ordered the Black Watch to counterattack and restore order. Determined fighting continued on the Canadian front well after Operation

Goodwood had been abandoned by Montgomery – 2nd Canadian Division receiving the continued attention of no less than three Panzer divisions' *Kampfgruppen*.[41] Judging by the 2nd Canadian Corps war diary and radio logs, Simonds appears to have taken little notice. He was already secluded, planning the first all-Canadian corps offensive in Normandy – Operation Spring.

Operation SPRING – 25 July:
Neither Holding Action nor Breakout

Operation Goodwood's failure had dramatically elevated the importance of Bradley's coming offensive. There is little doubt Montgomery had greatly disappointed Eisenhower, and there was growing opposition within SHAEF, headed by the Tedder's RAF band: "The visit of General Marshall on 24 July must have been his worse moment – Marshall was quite prepared to unseat him because of slow progress."[42] As a direct result, Montgomery fattened up Simonds' corps with two complete armoured divisions (the 7th "Desert Rats" and The Guards Armoured) as a *force de chasse* should Operation Spring penetrate its opponents' defences.

To understand Operation Spring's importance in the great scheme of things it must be appreciated that it was the doppelganger to Operation Cobra – this double offensive on 25 July was as close as Montgomery ever came to matching the scope of the Soviet Operational Art. Operation Spring was allegedly bait. Simonds later complained to Stacey that he had been forced to conduct a "holding attack" – in fact Operation Spring had the potential to do much more.[43]

Simonds' opposite number, who was to frustrate him in his next three offensives, was SS General Sepp Dietrich, "a soldier's soldier," an original member of the *Leibstandarte* and fresh from operational victories against Zhukov (at Kharkov in the winter of 1943) and Montgomery (in Operations Epsom, Windsor, and Goodwood). Despite Dietrich's tactical trumps, Montgomery was winning the battle of *attrition*. Most panzer divisions shared front line duties with infantry formations; there was only the smallest operational reserve. Those Panzers that were available had been committed to, or were heading towards, the busiest and most dangerous sector in Normandy – Simonds' front line.

Across the Normandy front near St. Lo, General Bradley had two field forces ready: General Courtney Hodges' 1st Army, with two heavy armoured divisions, and General George S. Patton Jr.'s 3rd Army, with four tank divisions ready to romp through Brittany and the Loire once American infantry slashed their way through the *bocage*. However, getting through thousands of fiercely defended farm fields, each fortified by medieval hedgerows, would take time and blood. Simonds faced no *bocage*. In fact, the area south of Caen presented the best possible opportunity to break out and cut off the bulk of Hitler's armies in the European Theatre of Operations. And it was because of this that Simonds faced the highest concentration of German armour yet seen on the western front – more Panzer divisions than were present at either assault at Operation Zitadelle: 1st SS *Leibstandarte* Adolf Hitler, 2nd (Vienna) Panzer Division, 9th SS *Höhenstauffen*, 10th SS *Frundsberg,*and 12th SS Hitler *Jugend* supported by the entire compliment of Tiger and *JagdPanther* battalions in France. Immediately outside Caen waited the well dug-in 272nd Infantry Division backed up by the combined artillery resources of the above units and augmented by two *Nebelwerfer* (multiple rocket launchers) brigades.[44] Should Simonds break through, the war in western Europe was virtually over; should Simonds succeed in "writing down" these armoured units – magnetizing them to the Caen front – then Bradley's success was assured. Simonds did neither.

Notwithstanding Dietrich's Panzer superiority, German defences were stretched thin, and local counterattacks comprised tank platoons or reduced companies. The Tigers fought at longest range and waited on the reverse slope under the constant attention of Typhoon attacks. Operational reserves were limited to the 9th SS Panzer (south of May-sur-Orne) and 116th Panzer (in the Falaise area) and jealously guarded by Field Marshal Hans Gunther von Kluge, commander of Hitler's armies in France. Dietrich's corps reserve was a *Kampfgruppe* from 2nd Panzer. Second Corps, with two and a half tank divisions, a surfeit of artillery, two infantry divisions, and total air superiority had at least a better than even chance of *fixing* von Kluge's Panzer's to its sector.

Simonds' solution to German webbed defence and superior tanks was to attack at night in a carefully written operation that prescribed three infantry phases and a fourth, exploitation phase for armour. It was an original, albeit risky, scheme. The initial assault surprised the Germans, but Canadian inexperience with night actions led to confusion and wasted the advantage. Had Operation Spring improved on Operation Atlantic and demonstrated a degree of mutual support within the brigades, had both divisional commanders demonstrated a modicum of talent, Simonds' first phase might have worked. He ought to have held Verrières by morning, inviting Dietrich to throw his Panzers at him through a rain of artillery (three Army Groups Royal Artillery [AGRA] and eight field regiments), seventeen-pounder and Typhoon strikes. But there was little opportunity for *Auftragstaktik* at any level – Simonds' score assigned specific roles for each battalion. The intermediate commanders, fearing to experiment with the corps directive, were reduced to cheerleaders and interested observers. In the end, so was Simonds.[45]

The tactical battle was soon a shambles: companies lost, battalions hung out to fend for themselves, the entire Black Watch destroyed in under twenty minutes, and tank support reduced to hors d'oeuvre sized stings. Simonds moved through his cacophony of command like the reluctant conductor, hoping the orchestra would get it together and play to his revised score. He left the podium to visit the brass, the tympani, and the winds – gravely urging each to do its best. He argued with Foulkes, ignored Keller, and tolerantly waited for his savaged infantry to sort things out, while two British armoured divisions were lying in the valley before Verrières, their engines ticking over, their guns silent.

Simonds watched his battalions slaughtered piecemeal, seemingly helpless to interfere. He then ordered spent units back into suicidal attacks and instigated mutiny: two veteran battalion commanders and an experienced brigadier openly refused to follow orders.[46] "It was perfectly clear that the attack should have been called off at a very early stage.... Instead the Corps commander was pressing the divisional commander and he was pressing us to get on with an attack which we knew was almost hopeless."[47] Historian Terry Copp asked, "Why did Simonds fail to see the light?" One reason may be that, although he had an artist's soul, he did not have the artist's touch: *Fingerspitzengefühl* – a sixth sense for the tempo of the battle, an instinctive understanding of the symphony of war. Finally, disheartened, he cancelled Operation Spring after watching it grind to a halt. Stearns recalling the effects on Simonds said that tears came to his eyes on one occasion when, once again, he was asked to put forth a holding attack: attrition was never any part of his strategy. In the end Operation Spring had become "an unmitigated tactical debacle and Simonds was obviously deeply upset."[48] But not for long.

On the other side of the ridge, Dietrich, who had *Fingerspitzengefühl* and realized by midday that Simonds was hesitant to use his armour, convinced von Kluge to release two KGs from the *Höhenstauffen*, and promptly counterattacked the single Canadian success, Verrières village.

By nightfall 1st SS Panzer Korps presented von Kluge with "a complete defensive victory – *Hierbei hatte der Feind höhe bultige Verluste* [The enemy took high bloody casualties]."[49] Next to Dieppe, Operation Spring rated as the Army's darkest day in France. Popular opinion continues to argue that it was a necessary part of the campaign strategy: US VII Corps breakout was made possible by these holding attacks. In fact, the Panzers were already drawn to Caen by Operation Goodwood. The advent of Operation Cobra and particularly Operation Spring's failure to "fix" the armour to east of the Orne ensured that, by the end of July, most of the *Panzerwaffe* had trekked west toward Bradley.[50] As feared, Operation Cobra was slowed by terrain and Montgomery's third venture, Operation Bluecoat – sending General Miles Dempsey into the *bocage* near Caumont with six divisions (three of them armoured) – also foundered. Both offensives were tormented by the Panzer divisions that should have been *written down* by Operation Spring. Montgomery was not pleased, and Simonds was told to try again.[51]

Operation TOTALIZE 8th August 44: Smelling a Breakthrough

> *Crerar simply did not know as much as Simonds, which in effect left the 2nd Corps commander without any of the usual counsel, help, and coercion that he might have received from an army headquarters.*
> *He could not have been more alone.*
> John A. English,
> *A Study of Failure in High Command*

Operation Totalize has been studied as a corps attack, but a review of the battle suggests a different interpretation. Operation Totalize was Montgomery's second serious effort to breakout south of Caen and the 1st Canadian Army was mightily reinforced: two armoured divisions, two armoured brigades, three motorized infantry divisions, and a cornucopia of artillery and tactical air. To support his *Panzerarmee* Simonds was given the hallmark of a SHAEF principal effort, *heavy bombers* – the Russians overwhelmed with artillery and armour, the western Allies bombed.

Totalize should be properly seen for what it was: a *strategic offensive*. Presenting the resources of the USAAF to Crerar's Army illustrates both the importance of the operation and the deference given Simonds – since it was clear to Montgomery who would create the plan of attack. "Crerar leaned on Simonds all the time. I don't think he ever issued an important order without consulting Simonds, and most of those orders were inspired by Simonds.... Monty was in direct personal contact with Simonds more often than Crerar was."[52] The Army commander prepared for Operation Totalize by dumping the operation into Simonds' lap, then agonizing about the outcome. "Harry Crerar is fighting his first battle.... He is desperately anxious ... he worries himself all day. I go and see him a lot and calm him down." Simonds agreed: "To be quite honest, Crerar has no grip of the situation."[53]

The Russian High Command, already critical of Operation Goodwood's failure, would have been interested in the state of the Allied Operational Art – SHAEF's next major offensive would be planned and executed by a Canadian corps commander.[54] Simonds was determined to find a way through Dietrich's defences: "A characteristic of Guy Simonds was that when he had real problems on his hands he would withdraw for hours on end during which time he would remain in his caravan or room.... He would avoid contact with anyone, unless it was urgent, until he had reached a solution.... He had great powers of concentration."[55] Simonds was very enthusiastic about his (indeed, any Canadian general's) first opportunity to use an entire armoured corps; "[he] wanted to shoot the works."[56]

Simonds wore the tanker's black beret more likely as a frank replication of the Montgomery style rather than a melancholy tribute to 5th Armoured Division.[57] His demonstrative alliance with tanks belied the fact he little understood the arm that was to contribute most to his legend yet cause him most distress. Simonds' legendary anxiety about armour is well illustrated by his confrontation with Brigadier G.R. Bradbrooke (5th Armoured Brigade) who challenged his new commander during a TEWT in Italy. Simonds insisted the brigade wait for the artillery to catch up. "'Brad' disagreed strongly with this policy and went on to commit 'hari-kari' by saying, 'Why should I wait for another 24 guns when I've got over 150 of them in my tanks. I don't need the artillery to shoot me on to anything and I can get there quite well myself'.... The atmosphere became instantly electric. Guy Simonds was an artillery man and to a 'gunner' this was heresy of the worst kind."[58] Bradbrooke was fired.

Simonds' solution for Operation Totalize was a variation of Operation Spring: "Several Division comds sat in a circle under the pine trees (all being much older than GGS and some had desert sand in their ears) to whom he opened, 'Gentlemen, we will do this attack at night with armour.' Their jaws dropped noticeably."[59] The plan required a penetration in darkness by two tank brigades (2 CAB and 33 British Armoured Brigade [BAB]) in columns packed tighter than the Guards at Waterloo. Once German mines and defenders were flailed into submission, Simonds planned to insert his armoured gauntlet: George Kitching's 4th Armoured and Major General Stanislaw Maczek's 1st Polish Division. There was grumbling from the various commanders: "My Division was given a frontage of only 1000 yards … no room to maneuver."[60] Simonds then planned for this procession to halt and await the arrival of American strategic bombers. Simonds schemed to obliterate a second *Hauptkampfline* (defence line) held by the 1 SS *LAH* – at least that is what he determined based on his understanding of Canadian intelligence reports and Ultra fragments. (He was the only Allied Corps Commander to have access to Ultra.)[61] Simonds decided "two 'break in' operations are required."[62] Unfortunately, despite some marvellous work prior to Operation Spring, this time Canadian Corps Intelligence was wrong in its assessment of the enemy. By the time they got it right, Operation Totalize planning was too far advanced for Simonds to stop. Besides, the bomber attack was big league stuff and could make Operation Totalize a *slam-dunk*. The very last intelligence summaries were even more promising; the bulk of German Panzers had been accounted for by Operation Bluecoat or discovered moving to attack Bradley's flank at Mortain (begun 6 August at Hitler's command and resumed 8 August – the same day as Operation Totalize) This left one Panzer division facing Simonds, the rather tired and depleted 12th SS *Hitlerjugend*.

The 12HJ was masked by a newly arrived 89th Division, which, despite a low number of infantry, still had most of its artillery and antitank resources. A night attack with two tank brigades was against all armoured doctrine and the results were near predictable – save for one aspect: Simonds broke through! He was the only corps commander to achieve a decisive corps level penetration of a German defence line in Normandy – von Kluge exclaimed, "A breakthrough has occurred south of Caen, such as we have never seen."[63]

Unfortunately the breakthrough was halted to await the heavy bombers; Simonds was trapped by the air attack's five hour "go/no go" clause. Simonds was concerned that he could not bring up his AGRAs. (Infantry were still mucking out German strong points from proposed gun positions in his rear areas). He decided, "It would have taken time to turn off this second planned attack [bombing by US B-17s] ... felt he had no choice but to halt short of the second bomb line even though the Germans would have time to regroup ... and continue with the original plan."[64] This permitted the 12 SS commander, General Kurt Meyer, to organize a counterattack and prepare a hasty antitank line. Simonds had been trapped by his own plan and his tendency to be "overcautious; as a result we lost the momentum of the attack, the very thing General Crerar had warned against ... General Meyer said it was like stopping to water the horses in the middle of a cavalry charge."[65]

There were many reasons for Operation Totalize's failure. One is the dependence on heavy bombers which, instead of blasting the enemy, committed fratricide by pummelling Simonds' front line. In typical fashion he immediately said, "From now on it will be the RAF." Another difficulty was the loss of control by brigade and division commanders: "General Simonds felt that the lack of communication, liaison, wireless, from formation to formation ... had more to do than anything else with the failure of the armour to get on as planned." "Leadership and failure to 'get cracking' when the opportunities were there were the reasons Operation Totalize ground to a halt."[66] There were other problems.

Despite Simonds' exhortations to press on through the night, he was ignored as tank regiments returned to Laagers at dusk – as they had been trained to do in England by officers following British desert doctrine.[67] At a time when Dietrich was thinking by the seat of his pants, dragging reserves out of von Kluge, and organizing a second line of defence, Simonds' direction mostly comprised of stern admonitions to "Get cracking!" sent by wireless. Kitching, Maczek, and their brigadiers needed to be pulled up by the scruff of their necks and shown what to do. Simonds, as composer, may be forgiven for not having enough virtuosos in the pit, but, as captain, Simonds must be held accountable for his inability to inspire or direct. Nonetheless, foreign and most Canadian historians have exonerated him. Chester Wilmot describes him as, "the radical innovator, forever seeking new solutions, Simonds' originality was strikingly evident in the plan he devised for this operation [Totalize] ... the revolutionary nature of the plan and the incalculable scope of the opportunity fired the enthusiasm of the troops and their commanders ... There is little doubt that, if the armoured Divisions had been more experienced and aggressive, the Canadian offensive would have been completely successful."[68] Simonds inadvertently predicted his woes when he set down 2nd Corps Operational Policy before the invasion: "Complicated, involved plans seldom succeed."[69]

OPERATION TRACTABLE 14 AUGUST:
THE SECOND BREAKOUT ATTACK

What looked good to [Simonds'] precise engineering
mind on paper seldom worked in practice once the
human element was added.
Major General Harry Foster, *Meeting of Generals*

By mid-August Bradley's 12th Army Group had begun its breakout, sending Wood south and Grow west into Brittany; however, 21st Army Group floundered, with Dempsey still struggling around Vire while Crerar left Simonds nose to nose with Dietrich well north of Falaise. Montgomery was determined to effect some sort of operational manoeuvre – trapping von Kluge by reaching Trun seemed the best bet. He again selected 2nd Canadian Corps. Simonds once more was presented with the breakthrough problem.

Simonds' next breakout plan has drawn harsh criticism from normally polite quarters, "The result was a scheme few coffee-table strategists would use, even in desperation."[70] Other opinions were more balanced: "The reality is that no Allied armoured formation, British, American, Polish or Canadian, proved capable of breaking through organized German defenses during the entire campaign in Northwest Europe without the assistance of the most elaborate air and artillery support. Tractable, like Goodwood and Totalize, had lost momentum once that support was no longer available."[71]

Simonds expanded upon Operation Totalize: more bombers, tighter packages of tanks, and this time he would go by day. "Each armoured brigade had about 150 tanks drawn up in three ranks of about 50 in each rank and only fifteen yards between tanks. Each of the two blocks of 150 tanks, represented a solid phalanx of armour about 1000 yards wide and 200 yards deep … move in daylight behind a wide smoke screen."[72] Operation Tractable's start was no better than Operation Totalize's. This time it was the RAF that shattered Canadian front lines while determined German rearguards checked any hope of blitzing through to Falaise.

Kitching's division was a particular disappointment and Simonds turned to Maczek, who he did not particularly like, and even contemplated taking away all the tanks from the Poles after their lacklustre performance on 8 August. He was to be pleasantly surprised. Maczek quickly crossed the Dives, and in a textbook demonstration of manoeuvre warfare, formed *groupment tactiques,* headed for Chambois, and closed the Falaise Gap!

Simonds, although he was never comfortable with mission driven tactics, let him range free. Then, as the Germans savaged Maczek's precarious shoulder on the Gap, he directed Kitching into Trun and ordered 4 Canadian Armoured Division (CAD) to rescue the Poles. Kitching indignantly refused: "To hell with them. They have run out of food and ammunition because of the inefficiency of their organization; our people have been fighting just as hard but we managed to keep up our supply system." Kitching may have been technically correct – but a corps commander will always select tactical results over an efficiently managed system that follows the rules but fails to produce victory. Kitching missed the key point – but then it was not a point of doctrine that was common to the Canadian Army in 1944. Maczek's natural sense of *Auftragstaktik* permitted him to manoeuvre even in the most tank unfriendly terrain and seize the Army, indeed, Theatre objective. The pursuit battle, for that is what Operation Tractable became, demanded that an armoured commander ignore his flanks and strike for the political, the psychological prize. It is to Simonds' credit that he gave Maczek his reins and did not interfere.[73] When Simonds visited Maczek's tactical HQ and was informed that Kitching had not advanced, he sacked him. "He had decided to replace me as Commander of the 4th Armoured Division and Harry Foster would take over from me that evening,"[74] Kitching wrote. Kitching's subsequent rebuttal included references to "too many changes in orders over a period of ten days … very heavy casualties." He was partly right but the blame lay elsewhere.

The confusion was Montgomery's doing; he faced the bitter prospects that, as Bradley's armour ranged far and wide, Normandy was becoming an all-American show. Torn between the covert desire to achieve some kind of flashy grand finale, that would give him credit for the greatest victory of the war, and his main job, to direct the operations of both 21st and 12th Army Groups, he fell short. At first he had 12th Army Group range into Brittany, well away from the Falaise front. When Dempsey and Crerar failed to deliver, Montgomery called Bradley back. There were no fewer than five different operational instructions regarding a technical corps level operation to capture Falaise and close the pocket:

On August 4, he assigned the place to Crerar, on August 6 to Dempsey, on August 11 to Crerar or

Dempsey, on August 13, to Dempsey, and finally on August 14, to Crerar. His inconsistency on Falaise paralleled his lack of firm decision on how to trap the Germans in Normandy.[75]

The "there-I've-given-my-orders-nothing-to-do-but-go-to-bed" style that is the Montgomery legend emerged as a fumbling, indecisive control that, in the end, became a race with Bradley as 21st Army Group pressed Simonds to close the gap.

Critics may suggest Simonds' hold on manoeuvre warfare was apprehensive and he had to pry his own fingers away from the radio. For example, he insisted on regular corps conferences in the middle of a manoeuvre battle – 2nd Canadian Corps concept of *Auftragstaktik* was still very mired within *Befehlstaktik* (command directed tactics). The concept of the *Glubokii Boi* – Tukhachevsky's "deep battle"– required a sixth sense and boldness. Maczek had it while Kitching did not. Dynamic operational manoeuvre produced spectacular results: von Kluge recalled, "The news that an American armored Division [Wood's 4th] was in Rennes [eighty miles southwest of Falaise] had a shattering effect, like a bomb burst, upon us."[76]

POST FACTUM

Kitching later argued that his division's slow progress was due to the long delay in dispatching Robert Moncel to replace Brigadier Leslie Booth who had been killed at the onset of Operation Tractable. "He [Simonds] grumbled of Booth's colossal gall getting himself killed at the head of his Brigade instead of staying back where he belonged."[77] Given the standards displayed by Simonds' tank commanders during Operation Totalize, Booth's attempt to rediscover *Fingerspitzengefühl* across the Laison should have been applauded. Both Simonds and Kitching ended up wasting time securing a replacement, the prepubescent Moncel, rather than driving forward themselves and getting their *Schwerpunct* into Falaise. Simonds admitted that sacking Kitching was "the most difficult thing he had ever had to do."[78] This is a peculiar comment given the realities of his operations:

> Corps commanders cannot afford the indulgence of emotional involvement with their subordinates'

hardships. Simonds's sacking of Kitching showed his capacity to be a "good butcher," a quality lacking in some senior officers who are, in consequence, badly served by their "friends."[79]

Simonds is often accused of being dictatorial, suffocating, and unforgiving. Yet in battle he tended to effect that all too British tendency to leave his commanders alone, even when it was clear nothing good was happening. There is that fine line between *Auftragstaktik* – an analysis of changing situations that *requires* disobedience of orders as long as they respect the *commander's intent* – and the essence of *Fingerspitzengefühl* – an intuitive gift that grasps the moment and secures triumph from chaos. Simonds did not have it; the closest he came was Operation Atlantic, and that was to save his command. In the offensive he often appeared lost; it took Maczek to lead him by the nose to victory. His solution to the 4 CAD's inability to deal with manoeuvre was to dump Kitching. Simonds' flaw was not that of Crerar (and Foulkes), who preferred the map and telephones of a command centre. In fact, the opposite was true. It was noted that "he is frequently well up in advance of the Division HQs. This really burns them up." Simonds was brave and Spartan, "Our tactical headquarters was set up near Ifs in an open field – two vehicles against a fence. Only other occupant ... was a dead cow."[80] Yet he was not capable of impromptu tactical solutions or inspiration. Simonds' frustrations occurred because he was a tortured soul, an incomplete prodigy. He had the vision but not the warrior's skill.

After his own success, Simonds turned his attention toward his corp's performance. He was unforgiving: of the nine brigadiers, six were decapitated, and of twenty-four infantry battalion commanding officers, fourteen lost command because they were unsuitable.[81]

THE LONG LEFT FLANK: THE SCHELDT, THE RHINELAND, AND VICTORY

Simonds continued to battle the German Army in Holland and the Rhineland. He and his staff became the consummate Montgomery-approved professionals, but his master left him in a soggy purgatory, doomed to suffer the agonies of bloody but secondary campaigns. His reputation had flourished in the golden wheat fields of Normandy; Simonds now waded through polders and floods in the wings of the Allied stage. He still had flashes of creative genius – his amphibious cum heavy bomber attacks on Walcheren Island (fortified by "some of the strongest defences in the world"[82]) have won both criticism and commendation:

> Simonds has been greatly praised for his decision to "sink" Walcheren, and for making full use of the amphibious capacity of the Allied Forces.... Equally, Operation Switchback, at least in its original, simultaneous-attacks form, was a superb example of Simonds's capacity for creating an innovative plan.[83]

Simonds, years ahead of his time, advocated *joint operations*:

> I consider it would be quite wrong to make no preparations ... to be faced at some later time with the necessity of having to improvise at very short notice. I am strongly of the opinion that the necessary military and naval forces should now be earmarked, married up and trained against the contingency that they might be required.[84]

As the European war drew to a close, it was Simonds who represented the acme of Canadian generalship and professionalism. He did not suspect that, as he mopped up German divisions and concentrated on saving the Dutch from famine, the Crerar virus was doing its work.

At the end of the war it was Foulkes, not Simonds, who left Europe to dominate the post-war Canadian Army. Foulkes' concern over the blinding effects of Simonds' star was such that it was successfully conspired to keep Simonds away from Canada for a further five years.[85] Canada's "greatest soldier" was kept in virtual exile, despite efforts on his behalf by Montgomery who said that "the treatment Simonds received, however, was almost cruel."[86] He was not sent for until 1949, returning to take command of the National Defense College in Fort Frontenac – just down the Rideau from Ottawa but safely distant from the Department of National Defence.[87] When Simonds was finally given command of the Army in 1951, he was to discover that Foulkes still controlled him as the newly created Chairman, Chiefs of Staff – directing inter-service operational and strategic planning. As head of the Army, "Simonds advocated peacetime conscription and close ties with Britain, criticizing the Government for seeking a closer military relationship with the US."[88] If Simonds left a legacy it was one that reflected both British and Canadian interpretations of the Operational Art. The Canadian military has been praised for the ability to sift through both British and American styles, blow off the chaff, and adopt what makes sense. This perhaps is the essence of the Canadian way of war.

Simonds influence on the Canadian military culture endured throughout the Cold War era, even within a unified *tri service* force.[89] The Simonds spirit was exorcised in 1997, when the National Defense College was closed in Fort Frontenac and the Army Junior Staff College, across the parade square, replaced the Oxfordian style of its syndicate rooms with a series of cybernetic teaching stations.

As chairman of the board, Simonds was bohemian in his daring, exhibiting a readiness to take risks coupled with the clear understanding it carried total responsibility – Operations Spring, Totalize, and Tractable were *his* plans, *his* appreciations, *his* solutions. This type of leadership is now unfashionable. Today's operational planning is staff driven – a military *soviet* massages the plan via a myriad of decision matrixes, trigger lines, and presents the commander a list of stock options and recommended trades.

Simonds' operational planning procedure was no different from the modern approaches taught in staff colleges. The key difference, and important in the understanding of the Canadian military culture, is that it centred on the commander. This was the way of Simonds, Foster, Hoffmeister, Rockingham, and Vokes. It was not the way of Crerar and Foulkes. As Simonds directed the Staff College and curriculum, it may be that the Simonds *prinzip* shaped the Canadian officer class toward the end of the century. Whether it has survived at the turn of the millennium is debatable. The Canadian military culture, once predominantly influenced and modeled after the British system, has become increasingly predisposed to American military philosophy and method. The Simonds era was further corrupted by Reagan's *AirLand Battle* – it certainly terminated after the Gulf War.

English states that "within the Canadian military system Simonds was, and remains, almost *sui generis* [one of a kind]. Though by no means perfect, he was, as Montgomery so clearly perceived, the best of the lot."[90] His book's title suggests culpability but, although most Canadian generals are found guilty of not winning efficiently, Simonds is excluded, indeed elevated. This may be too generous. Brereton Greenhous differed completely: "The trouble is Simonds was not very good either – in fact, he was poor by any objective standards."[91] Greenhous' argument against *firepower at the expense of manoeuvre* overlooks that nasty secret that plagued all commanders from Patton at Metz to Schwartzkopf at *Desert Shield*: attrition precedes manoeuvre. Simonds became the recognized expert.

Once Simonds broke through, his armoured divisions, as so elegantly demonstrated by Maczek, would manoeuvre with style. The trick was to get them past the *dogfight* – *breakout* phases into von Kluge's rear areas. This Simonds wrestled with and solved as creatively as he dared. His inability to dominate a fluid battle and his frustrations at directing tanks may have been due to his training. Canadian battlefield doctrine was controlled by what Greenhous calls the "unholy alliance" of "the artillery generals" – McNaughton, Crerar, and Simonds. Stephen Harris refers to the "gunner-dominated Canadian Army ... unable to develop its own doctrine to foster genuine all-arms cooperation and movement, remained overly dependent on the artillery to shoot everybody else forward."[92]

The Canadian situation is not unique; the American Armored Force's attempts to create a *Panzerwaffe* for the European Theatre was hamstrung by General Leslie McNair, George Marshal's "maker of armies" – a committed artillerist. His concept of manoeuvre warfare echoed that of another gunner from the Great War, Général Jean-Baptiste Estienne, who noted, "*le char est très délicat*" – McNair's theory of modern war rested on the *Tank Destroyer* (TD), a mobile gun. The Americans were saddled with the billion-dollar tank destroyer programme that included the status of a separate arm, corps schools, and no less than four production series of TDs. One result of his enthusiastic pursuit of the TD fad resulted in the American armoured force landing in Normandy with five tank divisions, not the dozen it demanded.

Another curiosity is, when given an opportunity for strategic offensive, how much Simonds relied on strategic bombers – which go over once and, as events proved, often miss. It was not so much a gunner mentality as the inability to direct the *groupment tactique* in its various forms (balanced with, or without, infantry) that frustrated Simonds. This is not a matter of corps background – the Western Allies' pre-eminent manoeuvre generals were not necessarily cavalry or armour. John S. Wood was a gunner, Bruce C. Clark an engineer, and B.M Hoffmeister, perhaps Canada's best armoured commander, was an infantry officer. Simonds may have been too influenced by his mentor, Montgomery, who introduced the strategic bomber as tactical artillery to his army commanders. This resulted in an air force summer that, in Simonds' case, extended into the fall and the Scheldt: "The Army having been drugged with bombs, it is going to be a difficult process to cure the drug addicts."[93]

The key difference between the two North American armies that did battle in Europe was that the Americans conducted the Louisiana Maneuvers and developed a homegrown doctrine – "As we maneuver in Louisiana, so shall we fight."[94] Canadian armour trained in the confines of England where they were forbidden to cross farmland. Louisiana gave the American Armored Corps a tank *métier*; England taught Canadian squadron commanders troop tactics modeled after the western desert. The final American product was sent to a finishing school in North Africa, while the Canadian armoured force – per capita the most mechanized of the Allied armies – arrived in Normandy having not completed a single operational or tactical exercise with its new corps commander or division commander. A previous Canadian tank experience with German arms lay rusting on the rocky beaches of Dieppe. That Simonds managed anything out of this force is commendable – that he was not really capable of handling this arm is lamentable.

The Canadian Army has always been too small to be comfortable with great generals. Canadians like their heroes larger than life, but on skates. Simonds' passion for the Operational Art and militarism was an embarrassment in an army that has always been more comfortable with managers. Yet it is within his passion that one finds Simonds the tragic hero, the gifted composer who cannot conduct. Simonds did not have the *Fingerspitzengefühl* to communicate either the cadence of battle or stir warrior's hearts. He wrote opus after opus but didn't have the left hand to bring his orchestra to full crescendo.

Perhaps Simonds' final legacy may well be the single sharp précis written by Stephen Harris: "Much favoured by Field Marshal Montgomery for his ruthless and offensive spirit."[95] In the end, English will be the more quoted: Simonds remains *sui generis*, not simply because he stood out among *Canadian* corps commanders, but because he was both unique and outstanding amongst Allied corps commanders.

Simonds must be judged not with Haislip or Horrocks – great *corps* commanders all – but rated against Hodges, Dempsey, and Patton – the West's great *army* commanders. A Simonds success meant de facto, an end to the Western Front, the only opportunity the Canadian Armoured Corps, indeed, the Canadian Army, received to effect a strategic decision in the war.

It is time to both stop apologizing for Simonds or attempting to minimize his errors. In the great scheme of things that was the

Normandy campaign, his defeats were grave and seen as such by the Allies. His ultimate closing of the gap not only rescued Montgomery's career but also encouraged Bradley to finally allow his tank commanders to manoeuvre and head east to Paris. Bradley's inability to conduct mobile operations and his uninspired conservatism has been lambasted and admitted to: He said, "the fault was mine alone." Yet it does not detract from his stature. The same should be true of Simonds.

While the delay and miscues in getting to Falaise make Simonds apparently less capable than Patton, the latter's indecision and bungling in Lorraine, particularly at Metz, gives both, particularly Simonds, more room to manoeuvre in military history. That 2nd Canadian Corps did not capitalize on its opportunities and appear in Argentan, then Paris, before Patton is unfortunate, and the reasons must be laid at Simonds' feet. However, the laurels of the Normandy Campaign must also be placed before Simonds. Operation Totalize in the end was not Vimy. But had Simonds succeeded, there would be required a second monument – this time on Verrières ridge.

ENDNOTES
CHAPTER 6

1. "There is a middle course in things."
2. General C. Vokes interview with Tony Foster, quoted in J.L. Granatstein, *The Generals* (Toronto: Stoddart, 1993), 159.
3. Major-General George Kitching, *Mud and Green Fields – The Memoirs of Major General George Kitching* (Langley: Battleline, 1986), 118.
4. W.E.J. Hutchinson, "Test of a Corps Commander: Lieutenant-General Guy Granville Simonds Normandy – 1944" (unpublished thesis, University of Victoria, 1982), 82.
5. Lieutenant-Colonel E.L.M. Burns, "A Division That Can Attack," *Canadian Defence Quarterly*, 3 April 1938, 282-298 (Cited hereafter as *CDQ*); Captain G.G. Simonds, "An Army that Can Attack – A Division that Can Defend." CDQ, 4 July 1938, 413-417. Lieutenant-Colonel E.L.M. Burns "Where do the Tanks Belong?" *CDQ*, 1 October 1938, 28-31, and Captain G.G. Simonds, "What Price Assault without Support?" *CDQ*, 2 January 1939, 142-147.
6. Simonds, *CDQ*, 2 January 1939. Burns' earlier articles "The Mechanization of Cavalry" *CDQ*, April 1924 and "A Step to Mechanization," CDQ, April 1934 made him the only active Canadian "apostle of mobility."
7. Montgomery's welcome to Burns in 1944. Montgomery "then made the very negative and rather dismaying pronouncement: 'There is no role for an armoured Division in Italy!'" E.L.M. Burns, *General Mud* (Toronto: Clarke, Irwin, 1970), 123.
8. Hutchinson, 81.
9. Ibid., 40.
10. National Archives (NAC), RG24 Crerar Papers: Montgomery to Crerar, 6 April 1942.
11. Hutchinson, 106.
12. Ibid., 111.
13. Ken Stuart's evaluation of Simonds as GOC 2nd Canadian Division. NAC, MG 27 Volume 54, Ralston Papers, File: "Officers

Overseas – Personal Evaluations."

14. Hutchinson, 113.
15. Martin Blumenson, *The Battle of the Generals – The Untold Story of the Falaise Pocket – The Campaign that Should Have Won the War* (New York: William Morrow, 1993), 269.
16. Crerar Papers: Letter Monty to Crerar, 23 July 1943.
17. Hutchinson, 146, 122.
18. Stephen Brooks, ed., *Montgomery and the Eighth Army* (London: 1991), 247.
19. Hutchinson 133.
20. G.W.L. Nicholson, *The Canadians in Italy, Volume II, The Official History of the Canadian Army in the Second World War,* (Ottawa: Queen's Printer, 1957), 122-124.
21. DND Directorate of History and Heritage (DHH); Crerar Papers Volume 3. Montgomery to General Alexander, 29 June 1943.
22. Nicholson, 364-371; Kitching 186-189.
23. Kitching, 189 and, Letter from Kitching quoted by, D.G. Dancocks, *The D Day Dodgers – The Canadians in Italy, 1943-1945* (Toronto: McClelland & Stewart, 1991), 212.
24. Kitching, 189.
25. DHH; NAC, MG 30 E 157, Crerar Papers Volume 3. See also Granatstein 161; J.A. English, *The Canadian Army and the Normandy Campaign – A Study of Failure in High Command* (New York: Praeger, 1991), 186.
26. DHH File 86/544. Correspondence: Simonds to Crerar, 15 December 1943, also, Hutchinson, 141.
27. DHH File 86/544. Crerar to Montgomery 17 December 1943.
28. Dominick Graham, *The Price of Command: A Biography of General Guy Simonds* (Toronto: Stoddart, 1993), 119-122, and Hutchinson, 142.
29. DHH MG 30 157 Crerar correspondence.
30. Crerar Papers, 21 December 1943, and 13 January 1944. Brigadier General Dennis Whitaker, although hesitating to take sides suggested that Crerar was better suited to command an army than Simonds. "Simonds saw things only from a military point of view, "his friend of many years, Major-General H.A. Sparling, remarked. "He didn't recognize that the political side had problems too." Quoted by Dennis Whitaker, interview with Major-General H.A. Sparling: W. D. and S. Whitaker, *The Tug of War* (Toronto: Stoddart, 1984), 74.
31. Correspondence between Captain Marshal Stearns and Dr. R.H. Roy

during the preparation of Professor Roy's work: *1944: The Canadians in Normandy* (Ottawa: Macmillan, 1984); documents provided by Dr. Roy, 1990 (Cited hereafter as Stearns) letter, 27 April 1981.

32. In Normandy Simonds "split his mess into A mess (Operational Staff) and B mess (support) this caused resentment" Stearns, letter, 27 April 1981.

33. Hutchinson, 147.

34. Worthington was born in Scotland but a graduate of the University of California. As a young man he volunteered to join General Pershing's US Expeditionary force and chased Poncho Villa through Mexico. He fought as a mercenary in revolutions in Nicaragua, Mexico and Chile. Worthington had won both the Military Medal and the Military Cross twice. By 1944, he was a legend in the Armored Corps: "As stern a believer in the striking power of an armored Division as Martel of England, de Gaulle of France, General Worthington is known throughout the land as the 'Father' of the Canadian Armd Corps." NAC, RG 24 17446. Camp Borden, Canadian Armored School Journal, *The Tank*, May 1944.

35. Stuart's evaluation of Worthington in 1942 (as he took over 4th Armd Division) "Aggressive, with reputation as fearless fighter. Not a good disciplinarian.... Allows interest to be absorbed in too many matters outside his command ... Consider present command too high for his abilities. Good personality." Worthington continued to command 4 CAD until Simonds forced him out. NAC, Ralston Papers. "Officer Overseas – Personal Evaluations."

36. NAC, RG24 10925 239 C3 (D9) Simonds letter to 2 Canadian Corps "Essential Qualities in the Leader," 19 February 1944.

37. "Among all the brigadiers and more senior ranks in the Canadian Army at the outset of the Second World War, there was not one who in two decades had even exercised a complete battalion in field manoeuvres!" Reginald Roy, *1944 The Canadians in Normandy* (Ottawa: Macmillan, 1984), 319.

38. Major-General Harmon, letter to Lieutenant-General Mark W. Clark, 29 September 1943, Harmon continued: "Our officers [US Army] are fundamentally better grounded in tactics than I have ever seen in any British officer." The Ernest Nason Harmon Papers; US Army Military History Institute, Carlisle, Penn (Cited hereafter as MHI).

39. *The Tactical Handling of the Armored Division,* "Cooperation with other Arms", HM War Office February 1943.

40. Stearns, letter, 23 March 1981. See NAC, RG24 10808 *2 CDN Corps*

Operation Instruction Number 2 Operation Spring, 16 July 1944. Instructions to 2 Cdn Armd Bde (less one regiment but facing "tank country" at last) limited it to a vague support role and one specific task: "Establish firm base." Initial Corps orders actually allocated individual tank squadrons to brigades for specific infantry battalion tasks.

41. See: Jarymowycz, "Radley Walters Defence of St Andre, 20-21 July 1944" also, "Der Gegenangriff vor Verrières: German Counterattacks during Operation Spring: 25-26 July 1944", *Canadian Military History*, Vol 2, Nr 1, Spring 1993, 74-93. For Spring plans see NAC, RG24 War Diary II Canadian Corps: "Operation Instruction Number Three Operation Spring", July 44 and, NAC, RG24 14046 Log, 2nd Cdn Armoured Brigade, July 44.

42. "Colonel Dawney has recorded that this was one of the few occasions when Montgomery was visibly worried." Alun Chalfort, *Montgomery of Alamein* (New York: Athenaeum, 1976), 244. See: Carlo D'Este, *Decision in Normandy* (New York: Harper, 1983); Alister Horne, *Monty, The Lonely Leader, 1944-1945* (New York: Harper, 1994.)

43. This was later challenged by Foulkes who regarded Spring "as a breakthrough operation with prospects of success." He went on to chide Simonds for attempting "to blame the inefficiency of our troops for our misfortunes." CP Stacey, *A Date with History* (Ottawa: Deneau, 1983), 174-178.

44. *Abendmeldung 25.8.44. Kriegstagebuch des Panzer-Armeeoberkommando 5 10.6.44-8.8.44.* RH19 IX/M.

45. See: NAC, RG 24 10808, "2 Cdn Corps Operation Instruction Number Three Operation Spring," 245, July 1944. Spring broke up 2 CAB between 2nd and 3rd CID, leaving one regiment in reserve. His instructions to 7th and Gds Armd Divs clearly establish a breakout plan with specific objectives south, area Cintheaux. Simonds did not hold an "Orders Group" for Spring. Corps instructions, on four typed pages, were sent to Divisions by dispatch rider.

46. This combat refusal ended the careers of three distinguished commanding officers: Lieutenant-Colonel C. Petch of the North Nova Scotia Highlanders, Lieutenant-Colonel C.H. Christiansen of the Stormont Dundas and Glengarry Highlanders and their commander Brigadier-General D.G. Cunningham who confronted General Keller and openly challenged Simonds' orders. Interview, Brig D.G. Cunningham, (Kingston, Ontario: 1989). See also:

English 249-251. Simonds defended his actions and invited criticism from 9th Brigade officers. When challenged he replied: "Men are fired in war because they think they need only make a partial commitment. In war you are fully committed." Quoted by Dennis Whitaker, interview with Brigadier J.M. Rockingham: Whitaker 79. This explains Simonds' philosophy of subordinate command but does not explain Spring's premature break-off.

47. Brigadier W.J. Megill, quoted in, Terry Copp, *The Brigade – The Fifth Canadian Infantry Brigade, 1939-1945* (Stoney Creek: Fortress, 1992), 85. Megill argued with Foulkes about the plan but was made to understand that the divisional plans "originated with Simonds." Interview, Brigadier WJ Megill (Kingston, Ontario: 1990).

48. English, 230, 249. In post war reflection Simonds defended his plan for Spring and stated the defeat was the fault of junior commanders: "The whole plan was fully discussed with and approved by General Dempsey GOC in C Second Army (under which 2 Canadian Corps was operation) before and after the operation.... That we failed ... and that we suffered what were, in my opinion, excessive casualties was due to a series of mistakes and errors of judgement in minor tactics." DHH 24/Reports 1/3 Lieutenant-General G.G. Simonds "Attack by RHC – Operation Spring," 21 January 1946, 5.

49. RH19 IX/M. *Morgenmeldung 26.7. 44 Kriegstagebuch des Panzer-Armeeoberkommando 5 10.6.44-8.8.44.*

50. RH19 IX/20, Box 2. *Heeres Gruppe B Meldungen und Unterlagen Ia von der Zeit 1.7.44 – 31.8.44.Meldung 26.7.44: "Abge sehen von einigen schwächeren Vorstössen im Bereich des I.SS-Pz.Korps und eines stärkeren Angriffs auf Verrieres verhielt sich Feind während des ganzen Tages ruhig.* [Apart from a few minor advances in the sector of 1st SS Pz Corps and an important attack on Verrieres the enemy keeps a low profile during the whole day.]" See also, DHH SGR II 264 Folder 34, "Situation Reports by German Army Commanders in Normandy May 15: October 11, 1944"; *Weekly Report, July 24-30, 1944* and, *Weekly Report, July 31-August 7, 1944.*

51. "Two things were uppermost in Guy Simonds' mind on that day. (25 July) First we had to find some way of getting the assaulting infantry through the forward enemy defenses without their having to take such heavy casualties and second, he must get rid of General Charles Foulkes who, in his opinion, did not have the right qualities to command our 2nd Division ... on at least three

occasions Guy Simonds confided to me he was going to get rid of Charles Foulkes. I can only assume that General Crerar must have intervened...." Stearns, see also, Kitching, 206.

52. Stearns.

53. Alanbrooke Papers, 14/29, Montgomery to Brooke, 9 August 1944, quoted in J.L. Granatstein, *The Generals*, 111; and Simonds, quoted in Whitaker 403.

54. "When senior Russian Army Officers visited us when our Headquarters was still west of Caen and asking what the enemy strength opposite us was compared to our own. When we told them and that we were going to attack they were greatly surprised." Stearns, letter, 27 April 1981; they had just visited Bradley's HQ (13-26 July) where wags cracked: "Look, the Russians have broken through to St. Lo!" Party comprised: Major-General I. Skliarov, Major-General. V.A. Vasiliev, Colonel V. Gorbatov and Rear-Admiral N. Kharlamov. See: The Colonel Chester B. Hansen Papers; Hanson Diary "Brad Plans for Cobra" entry week 16-25 Jul 44. MHI and, RG24 10808 WD.2 Canadian Corps, 27 July 1944.

55. Kitching, 177. Simonds' conundrum, the great Normandy tactics test was, "In Essence the problem is how to get the armour through the enemy gun screen to sufficient depth to disrupt the German anti-tank gun and mortar defence, in country highly suited to the tactics of the latter combination." NAC, RG24 2 Cdn Corps WD "Planning Operation Totalize, Appreciation by Corps Commander." 1 August 1944.

56. Interview, Dr. R.H. Roy and Captain Marshal Stearns (Toronto, Ontario: 14 July 1982).

57. "Simonds drove about in a Buick with two RCMP motorcyclists, closer to the front he made use of a [Staghound] converted armoured car, his staff was one engineer and two signalers ... [Simonds] wore a beret because of his armoured car...." Stearns interview.

58. Kitching, 183.

59. General Elliot Rodger, letter to Graham, quoted in *The Price of Command* 148. Also: NAC, RG24 10808 "Corps Comd's 'O' GP 281000B July 1944." Simonds emphasized: "Drive on whenever there is a gap. NO "waiting for George." Don't expect battle to go quite to plan."

60. Kitching, 210. See RG 24 2 Cdn Corps WD "Planning Operation Totalize" Section IV, Para C. *The Corps Plan* – in essence, "to

attack under cover of darkness after a preliminary action by heavy bombers."

61. G2 SHAEF Internal Memo "List of Recipients of Ultra" The Richard Collins Papers (G2 SHAEF) August 1944. US Army Military History Institute, Carlisle (Hereafter cited as MHI) and, SRH-023 "Reports by US Army ULTRA Representatives with Army Field Commands in the ETO" MHI. Also, Stearns, 14 July 1982. "Simonds knew of Ultra information ... critical of Americans overuse of Ultra." Notes from interview Dr. R.H. Roy and Captain Marshal Stearns, (Toronto, Ontario: 14 July 1982). See also: RG24 10844 Insums No 37-38 and, Simonds' "Planning Operation Totalize, Appreciation by Corps Commander." 1 August 1944.

62. Stearns, letter, 23 March 1981.

63. Von Kluge to SS General P. Hausser, 1845 hrs, 8 August 1944. Telephone Log, *Kreigstagebuch des Panzer-Armeeoberkommando 5 10.6.44-8.8.44.* RH19 IX/M, translation in ETHINT, MHI.

64. Stearns, letter, 23 March 1981.

65. Kitching, 210-211.

66. "General Simonds had a constant complaint, and had voiced it several times, that our contact with the Air Force was too remote." Stearns, letters, 23 March 1981 and, 27 April 1981 and, Simonds to Stearns, letter, 23 March 1981.

67. Kitching, harassed by Simonds to "get cracking" went forward to sort out what must be termed combat refusal and to his surprise found Brigadier Booth (4 CAB) asleep in his tank. Kitching, 213. See RG24 WD 4th Cdn Armd Div Operation Totalize, 8-9 Aug 44 and 1 Pol Armd Div *Operational Report, C.O. 1 Polish Armd Div – Fighting During The Period From 7-12 Aug 44,* "After all day fighting, the armd regts set out for the night bivouac," 2.

68. Chester Wilmot, *The Struggle for Europe* (London: Collins, 1952), 417-419. British armour expert K.J. Macksey wrote: "His educated approach to battle made use of every possible modern aide [Simonds "invented" the modern APC by creating Kangaroos from Priest chasis] to help reduce casualties and still achieve striking penetrations of the enemy line. No Canadian field commander had greater experience or required more respect from friend or foe." Major K.J. Macksey, "The Canadian at War," *The Readers Digest,* Montreal, 1969, 487.

69. RG 24 WD 2 Canadian Corps, GSO 1, "Operational Policy." 17 February 1944. While prepared to distribute tanks in squadron

poackets, Simonds stressed that: "the weight of artillery support must **NOT** be divided [emphasis by Simonds]," 3.

70. J.L. Granatstein and Desmond Morton, *Bloody Victory* (Toronto: Lester & Orpen Dennys, 1984), 173.

71. Terry Copp and Robert Vogel, *Maple Leaf Route: Falaise* (Alma: Maple Leaf Route, 1983), 116.

72. Kitching, 216. See, RG 24 2 Cdn Corps Instructions for Tractable, also: 2 CAB "An Account of Operations by 2 Cdn Armd Bde in France 14-16 Aug 44." Simonds' plan shows touches of cavalry style – he attaches 7th Recce Regt (3rd Div) under command to 2 CAB with 2 sqns Flais, sqn AVREs and det RCE bulldozers. This nicely solved "the recce question" and permitted momentum beyond the Laison. The big problem was the Laison, which proved to be a tank obstacle – another Intelligence failure by 2 Corps G2.

73. See Kitching, Maczek, *Avec Mes Blindes*, and, RG24 2nd Cdn Corps War Diary/1st Polish Armd Div War Diary, 15-31 August 1944. See Maczek, *Operational Report*, Part 2: "Report on Fighting During the Period 12 August to 22 August 1944."

74. Kitching, 226.

75. Martin Blumenson, *The Battle of the Generals. The Untold Story of the Falaise Pocket – The Campaign that Should Have Won World War II* (New York: William Morrow and Company, Inc, 1993), 217.

76. European Theatre Intelligence Studies 1945 (hereafter cited as ETHINT), von Kluge, ETHINT 67 3. MHI.

77. Lieutenant-Colonel John Proctor, quoted by Tony Foster, *Meeting of Generals* (Toronto: Methuen, 1986), 381.

78. Stearns, letter, 27 April 1981.

79. Graham, 168.

80. Stearns, also see: J.L. Granatstein, *The Generals*, 173.

81. Stacey, Victory Campaign 275, see: Crerar Papers, "Personal and Secret to Simonds 29 August 1944 re 'Demotion of Commanding Offrs.'" Crerar finally noticed the number of artillery officers in command positions. In his instructions to Simonds regarding the replacement for A/Brig Ganong, Crerar wrote: "to be replaced by a suitable nominee (<u>not</u> a Gunner officer)." Crerar underlined the last line.

82. "Experience in Normandy and the Channel Ports suggests that if it had been possible to deal direct with Air Chief Marshal Harris the bomber effort at Walcheren might have been heavier and lives might have been saved." Stacey 407 and 411.

83. Terry Copp and Robert Vogel, *Maple Leaf Route: Scheldt* (Alma: Maple Leaf Route, 1985), 137. See also, Jeffery Williams, *The Long Left Flank* (Toronto: Stoddart, 1988). For an important study of the senior Canadian Army staff in the European campaign, see: Lieutenant-Colonel John A. Macdonald, *In Search of Veritable* (unpublished thesis RMC, 1996.)

84. Simonds writing of the Scheldt operations, quoted in Stacey, 370.

85. DHH. Simonds correspondence with Foulkes; Foulkes correspondence Min Def 1947-1950. Simonds was seconded to the Imperial Defence College where he held the position of chief instructor ("A signal honour for a Canadian" – Steven Harris).

86. Granatstein 176. See: DHH. Correspondance Montgomery to Foulkes, 12 September 1947: "Guy Simonds has done us very well over here, and I feel he should not be discarded and have to retire."

87. Simonds' written concerns about his career were immediately denied by Foulkes to Simonds 27 January 1950 "Foulkes assures Simonds 'there was certainly no intrigue or lack of frankness in this approach to your problem [Simonds' prolonged exile in England and denial to what most considered his logical appointment as Chief of General Staff].'"

88. Dr. Stephen Harris, notes on General Simonds, interview DHH (Ottawa: 1996).

89. "Between 1939 and 1951 the army's prewar pomp and colour had been bleached to a utilitarian gray.... Simonds, on the other hand, understood the importance of smart uniforms, efficiently run and colourful messes, bands, protocol.... He looked like an advertisement for his own policies." Graham, 285.

90. English, 307.

91. Brereton Greenhous, reviewing English's book, quoted by Dominick Graham, 281 and interview, Ottawa, 26 June 2000.

92. Stephen Harris, review of English for *The Journal of Soviet Military Studies*, 2 April 1992.

93. Air Marshal Tedder, commenting on yet another *bombers-as-artillery* scheme: Simonds' attack against Walcheren Island, October 1944. Tedder's protest against this "misuse" of strategic airpower began at Goodwood. See: Lord Tedder, *With Prejudice* (London: Cassell, 1966), 606.

94. Crittenberger Papers, MHI.

95. Stephen Harris, "Guy Granville Simonds," *The Canadian Encyclopedia Second Edition, Volume II* (Edmonton: Hurtig, 1988), 2005.

CHAPTER 7
E.L.M. BURNS:
CANADA'S INTELLECTUAL GENERAL

Lieutenant-Colonel Bernd Horn and Michel Wyczynski

War is not a static science; it is a dynamic art; improvements in attack and defence succeed each other continuously. Unless we are constantly thinking how we can overcome the enemy's latest technique, we will never win battles. So it is the duty of all of us to think about these things, and contribute what we can.
E.L.M. Burns, 1943[1]

THESE words were more than just mere musings to the intellectual Lieutenant-General E.L.M. Burns. They represented a philosophy by which he lived. Burns continuously studied and actively debated contemporary issues in military art and science. Having experienced the carnage of the First World War, he was committed to ensuring that the blunders perpetrated on the muddy battlefields in France and Belgium were not repeated. "The tactical problem," according to Burns, "always has been and is fire and movement whether the former is a stone, an arrow, a bullet, or a bomb, and whether the latter is accomplished on foot, on an elephant, in a tank or in an airplane."[2] True to his premise that it is the "duty of all" to "contribute what we can," Burns turned his impressive intellect to the challenge. Throughout the interwar years he attempted to instigate, through his prolific writing in forums such as the *American Mercury* and the *Canadian Defence Quarterly* (*CDQ*), the modernization of the Canadian Army. His arguments, however, fell largely on deaf ears. Economic and political constraints in Canada, as well as a large degree of institutional conservatism within the military, relegated his arguments strictly to the conceptual. Nevertheless, he proceeded to "contribute" what he could. As both a staff officer and a formation commander in World War II, he continued to apply his experience and knowledge in an effort to drag the Canadian Army into the age of modern warfare.

In many ways Burns was an anomaly. He was one of the rare generals who combined experience with both disciplined intellectual development and thought. Burns was once described as "the brain that marches like a soldier."[3] Although remembered more for his lack of command presence, cold personality, and aloof manner, Burns' contribution to the Canadian Army, specifically in the fields of doctrine, training, and scientific development, was significant. He represented an avant-garde philosophy that promoted professional discourse, debate, and progressive thought. "The real danger of insubordination," believed Burns, "comes when officers and men no longer understand one another, when men are not allowed to speak of what they know to be wrong, or to have their views heard."[4] In the end, Lieutenant-General E.L.M. Burns can be considered as Canada's pre-eminent, if not only, intellectual general.[5]

Eedson Louis Millard Burns was born in Westmount, Quebec in June 1897. He was educated at the exclusive Lower Canada College in Montreal. In 1913, at 16, he enlisted in the Militia, in the 17th Hussars. A year later, Burns was accepted at the Royal Military College (RMC) in Kingston. His formal studies, however, did not last long. In June 1915, upon turning 18, he took a commission in the Royal Canadian Engineers (RCE) with the intention of actively joining the war effort. One year later, after training in Canada for nine months, Lieutenant Burns deployed overseas, eventually going to France as a signal officer in the 11th Canadian Infantry Brigade, 4th Division, in August 1916. Twice wounded in action, Burns received the Military Cross for his gallant actions in personally laying and repairing signal cable under heavy fire at the Somme. Following the armistice, he was employed as a Staff Captain in the 12th Infantry Brigade. At the age of 21, he was the youngest Staff Captain in the Army. In 1920, Burns enrolled in the Permanent Force where he held various staff appointments in different headquarters and did a tour as an instructor in military engineering at RMC.[6] Burns' intellectual brilliance was demonstrated on one of these assignments. As a general staff officer with the Geographical Section at National Defence Headquarters (NDHQ) in Ottawa his experimentation with aerial mapping eventually led to a process by which extremely accurate maps could be made from aerial photos. The significance of his work was such that it was adopted by Britain for military mapping and became known as the Modified British Grid System.[7]

Scientific experimentation was not the only indication of Burns' active intellect. His World War I experience ingrained in him a lasting memory of the "will-sapping effect of struggling through mud, living in mud, for days on end." No one who struggled through it, he later recalled, will ever forget it.[8] According to Burns, the mud and the effect of bad weather negated the ability to effectively execute offensive operations. Put simply, nothing could move. Surprise and decisiveness of action were nearly impossible to achieve. And so, Burns' wartime service entrenched in his thinking a belief in the necessity for mobility and speed, specifically in the form of mechanization, as the key to modern warfare.

In keeping with his philosophy, he began to share his ideas by writing, particularly on the topic of mechanization and the character of modern war. Undeniably, his thoughts were heavily influenced by the work of J.F.C. Fuller who was both a soldier and military theorist. To appreciate Burns' views, one must first understand Fuller. J.F.C. Fuller was a strong advocate of the tank and by the end of the war stressed the use of armoured vehicles en masse. In the spring of 1918, then Colonel (later Major-General) Fuller wrote a memorandum entitled "Strategical Paralysis as the Object of Decisive Attack." The title was later changed to "Plan 1919." At the heart of Fuller's idea was the premise that "the fighting power of an army lies in its organisation, which can either be destroyed by wearing it down or by rendering it inoperative." The first option entails attritional warfare or "body warfare." The latter, insisted Fuller, was achieved by rendering inoperative the enemy's power of command or "brain warfare."[9] He arrived at this conclusion through his observations of the German Michael Offensive on 21 March 1918. Sitting on top of Mont St. Quentin, near Peronne, France, Fuller watched the retreat of British troops. Answering his own question of why they were withdrawing, he realized that the deep German penetration of the Allied lines had paralyzed command. Specifically, the Germans had severed the command and control and logistics between the Allied rear (headquarters) and the front line (combat troops). This in turn created a state of "strategic paralysis" in the Allied armies.[10] Thus, the "mystery" of modern warfare was revealed. Fuller later explained the secret of the offensive:

> It was to employ mobility as a psychological weapon: not to kill but to move; not to move to kill but to move to terrify, to bewilder, to perplex, to cause consternation, doubt and confusion in the rear of the enemy, which rumour would magnify until panic became monstrous. In short its aim was to paralyse not only the enemy's command but also his government, and paralysation would be in direct proportion to velocity. To paraphrase Danton: "Speed, and still more speed, and always speed" was the secret.[11]

The young Captain Burns absorbed the ideas of J.F.C. Fuller as well as others, such as British Captain B.H. Liddell Hart. Well aware of the axiom that "soldiers always prepare for the last war" and surrounded by the stagnation of military thought and doctrine in the aftermath of the Great War, Burns argued for the modernization of the Canadian Army. To Burns this initially meant motorization and, eventually, mechanization. (The cost and technological immaturity of the tank made immediate mechanization inconceivable even to Burns.) In his article, "The Mechanization of Cavalry," written in 1924, he argued that "modern war is a war of machines, and progress in the art will be along mechanistic lines; cavalry must follow the trend or be lost."[12] Burns insisted that the traditional horse-bound cavalry must give up their chargers and instead become an even more "mobile arm" by adopting a "machine" which could carry four or five men, including the driver. In addition, the vehicle would mount a Lewis machine gun with all-around traverse. Burns' conceptual vehicle had no armour because he felt that it would rely on its speed for safety. "The cavalry machine," reasoned Burns, "would be for reconnaissance, rapid transport of the fire power of its crew, the more open varieties of offensive action – encounters when neither side would be organized for attack or defence, and speed essential for success."[13] His attempts at "contributing" were not welcomed by many of his brethren officers. Burns sardonically recounted that the sentries at the Royal Canadian Dragoons garrison were told to bayonet him on sight.[14]

Burns realized mobility and speed were key. He also demonstrated an innate comprehension of Fuller's concept of "Deep Battle," namely the strategic psychological dislocation of command and control of an enemy's army. In his 1932 *Canadian Defence Quarterly* prize winning essay on the "Protection of the Rearward Services and Headquarters in Modern War," he hammered home this point as well as the need for modernization. Burns believed that ultimately armoured fighting vehicles would become the dominant force on the battlefield. As such, "the fighting power of a modern army would be affected sooner and more dangerously by the cutting off of its petrol than by the cutting off of its food or ammunition. Lack of motor fuel means immediate immobility."[15] As a result, Burns emphasized the threat of "mosquito attacks" by what Fuller described as "motor-guerillas."[16] Burns explained that "the main armies move at the rate of the marching man or horse, while the communications may be attacked by armoured fighting vehicles moving nearly a hundred miles in a day, or by aeroplanes moving a hundred miles in an hour."[17]

Despite his best efforts, Major Burns still remained a seemingly lone voice in the wilderness. To his credit he remained unrelenting. In 1935, he wrote "A Step Towards Modernization," in which he attacked the military's "pedestrian imagination."[18] Burns ridiculed the fact that the average Canadian citizen, given the task of travelling from one location to another fifteen miles distant on a road, would undoubtedly take a "motor-car." Yet, he pointed out, if that average Canadian belonged to the Militia he would ignore the "revolution in transport" and tacitly assume that "except as regards the carrying of stores, we are still in the horse and buggy days."[19] Burns challenged this out-dated doctrine and philosophy. He asserted that "there is one prophecy about future warfare that can be made with assurance, it is that mechanical transport in all its forms will be used to the greatest possible extent to give mobility to the fighting troops." Instead, "we are thinking about the operations of war in terms of mobility of the foot-soldier," he lamented, "[at] 2 1/2 miles per hour."[20]

By the mid-1930s his writing emphasized the wide scale offensive applicability of motorized troops. Burns explained that in the future "swarms of 'motor guerillas'" would infest "all portions of the theatre of war." Furthermore, he assigned to them a myriad of roles which included: reconnaissance, picketing of bridges and tactical points, delaying the advance of an invading force, offensive operations against the enemy's motorized forces, and the seizure of strategically important areas. Although aware of the economic and political constraints, Burns criticized the fact that the Army had no armoured fighting vehicles. "It means," he warned, "that in Canada, we have no soldier trained in the operation of what responsible military opinion recognizes as the potentially most powerful arm of the service – and what is even more serious, *no officer trained in the command of this arm*."[21]

Burns' experience combined with his study of military art and science led him to believe that the Army's reluctance to abandon its outdated doctrine would prove to be costly. "I would submit," he commented, "that, unless we are resigned to the Canadian land defence forces being merely lines of communication, or third line troops – to being forever a kind of 'sedentary militia' – we must remedy this defect in our training and equipment." He ominously added, "A 2 1/2 mile an hour soldier in a 60 mile an hour age is an anachronism. And nothing can be so costly as a military anachronism."[22]

Burns was unremitting in his attempts to awaken the Canadian Army to the modern age. In 1937, he reasoned that "units of the various arms must be grouped together in formations in such proportions that in co-operation they will be able to exercise the greatest total effect." He repeatedly asserted that "the more mobile a given force is, the greater will be its fighting efficiency."[23] The following year his articles demonstrated an evident evolution in his concept of mechanization. Reports emanating from the Spanish Civil War indicated that tank technology had matured and that they could be used on a daily basis for weeks on end without mechanical failure.[24] With this evident technological advancement Burns took his belief in mechanization a step further. In a seminal article in the *CDQ* entitled, "A Division That Can Attack," Burns focused on the need for "medium tanks." He dismissed his earlier predilection for armoured cars on the premise that light and medium tanks would soon make them obsolete. More importantly, Burns attacked the notion that tanks be employed as a "shock tank force geared to the limited pace of infantry." Instead, he argued that the medium tank, which represented the best compromise between "the conflicting demands of armour protection, speed, steadiness and fire-power," become the principal engine of assault, with the infantry providing the role of fire support and consolidation. "A tank assault," insisted Burns, "will have far greater chance of achieving real success than an infantry assault, or an infantry-cum-tank assault, because it moves much faster, is less dependent on artillery fire, and is immune to the weapons with which the bulk of enemy troops are armed."[25] Burns stated that the Canadian Army must be designed to overcome a "hypothetical" enemy whose organization and equipment conformed to the most modern standards. He further concluded that the standard division should consist of one armoured and two infantry brigades so as to have "real assaulting power, so that the advantages conferred by mobility could be reaped."[26]

The dissertation put forward by Burns was on a level equal to that of other international military theorists such as Fuller and Liddell Hart. His comprehension of mechanization and the character of modern war was innovative, accurate – and controversial. Captain G.G. Simonds picked up the gauntlet in what has since been labelled "the absolute high point of interwar military thinking in Canada."[27] Simonds contested the rationality of Burns' balanced division that was "capable of taking the offensive under its own steam." He countered that it was wasteful to disperse tanks among all divisions, but, rather, they should be maintained centrally as an army commander's reserve. To Simonds, the division was designed to hold a defensive position, and the army now represented the balanced formation of all arms. He believed that, should the division be required to attack, then the army commander would assign the necessary supporting arms. "A division that can attack," insisted Simonds, "is not wanted."[28]

Burns' superior understanding of modern war became evident in his rebuttal. "In rapidly-moving warfare," he explained, "when a division may have to advance, attack, retire, defend and guard in various directions in the space of a few days, it will be extremely difficult for a higher commander to distribute and redistribute his 'offensive' weapons in time to meet the needs of the changing situations."[29] Burns' comprehension of human behaviour and the complexities of all arms co-operation also led him to believe that tanks, infantry and artillery could only truly co-operate if they were trained together and given the proper orders. Here, he realized, was a fundamental flaw in Simonds' highly centralized option. "Unless he [commander] is responsible for their organisation and training," declared Burns, "he will not, as a rule, regard the tanks as one of his normal tools of war, and will not become really familiar with their capabilities, and learn how to use them effectively in conjunction with the other arms which are essential to their success."[30] Burns concluded by contemptuously dismissing the "insidious" notion that the British Army's task in the future would be defensive. "One of the surest ways to repeat the failures of those days [World War I]," he asserted, "is to retain as the normal basic formation of the British Army a division which is incapable of attacking with its own resources."[31]

Like many, Simonds was unconvinced. Similarly, like the majority of others he was unable to make the conceptual leap to the modern age. "In the war 1914-18," wrote Simonds as a counter to Burns' latest argument, "*massed artillery and surprise* was the formula for successful attack. Given those two conditions and the 'break-in' succeeded whether tanks or infantry were the main assaulting arm."[32] The written debate soon became inconsequential. The German conquest of Poland in September of 1939, and the subsequent conquest of Europe in the spring of 1940, graphically demonstrated the requirements of the new age of warfare. It is easy, with the benefit of hindsight, to criticize and denigrate the apparent ignorance of those that disregarded and resisted outright the calls for mechanization in the interwar years. However, this serves no useful purpose. Of greater importance is the recognition of the prescience of individuals, such as Burns, who were able to translate their wartime experience and conceptual understanding of the theory of modern war into concrete ideas which would later be validated.

Burns' ability to conceptualize the tactical utilization of men, equipment, and ground, and their application to modern war through the filter of experience, professional knowledge, and intellect, did not cease once his ideas were proven by events. He continually attempted to stay abreast of the latest developments. During the German invasion of the Low Countries in April and May 1940, Burns' mental agility combined with his appreciation of the concept of "Deep Battle" allowed him to quickly realize the significance of the successful utilization of German Fallschirmjäger (paratroopers). They revealed for him a viable tool to strike at an enemy's command and logistical facilities in the rear areas. "The successes obtained by the Germans with air-borne troops," Burns insisted, "seem to show that this will become a regular method of warfare."[33]

The subsequent parachute scare that erupted in Europe in the aftermath of the German aerial onslaught further strengthened Burns' belief. By the early summer of 1940, the German Fallschirmjäger, by virtue of their stunning accomplishments, were quickly perceived by the military and general public as invincible. This created a wave of paranoia that infected the still unoccupied territories in Europe as well as in Britain.[34] This chaotic and desperate environment deeply influenced Colonel Burns. In July 1940, he returned to Canada and was appointed Assistant Deputy Chief of the General Staff. As such, the Chief of the General Staff (CGS) tasked him with various special assignments concerning the organization and development of Canada's Army. Burns' fertile mind now set to work on modernizing the Canadian Army. Based on his understanding of "Deep Battle" and his comprehension of modern warfare, he was convinced that parachute troops were "no longer just a stunt," but rather, because of their mobility, an important element of any modern army.[35]

It was not the novelty of a new "weapon" that impressed Burns. "We hope to turn to the offensive against Germany some day," he explained, "and it appears that full advantage must be taken of all forms of mobility in carrying out operations."[36] Unquestionably, to Burns paratroopers represented mobility and offensive power. Airborne forces also personified a modern army. He argued passionately that the establishment of airborne forces "would be a step toward a 'quality' army, and would show that we were actually doing something to create a force with offensive capabilities."[37] And so, on 13 August 1940, he submitted his first proposal for the establishment of a Canadian airborne capability to Colonel J.C. Murchie, the Director of Military Operations in NDHQ. Murchie flatly dismissed the idea. Within the next three months, Burns submitted two additional memorandums to Major-General Harry Crerar, the CGS. However, the idea was consistently turned down. Once again, Burns was ahead of his time. It would take the German conquest of the Mediterranean Island of Crete in May 1941, by Fallschirmjäger, to finally convince the Allies of the merits of airborne forces. In July 1942, almost two years after Colonel Burns' initiative, NDHQ finally established the 1st Canadian Parachute Battalion.

Despite the eventual success of his efforts at establishing a Canadian airborne force, Burns was no longer in NDHQ to savour it. By the spring of 1941, he was promoted to Brigadier and posted overseas to a staff position in 1st Canadian Corps. In February 1942, he took command of 4th Canadian Armoured Brigade. As a brigade commander, he continued in his attempt to master the dynamic art and science of war. Burns consistently studied the enemy's tactics, applied his experience and intellect, and attempted to translate it into useable information for his subordinates and the Army at large.[38]

This quickly became evident. As the Canadian High Command worked feverishly to raise a modern mechanized force, Burns perceived that valuable training time had been lost. More importantly, he believed that the current leadership did not possess the required experience or skills to develop and implement the new doctrine. Officership, according to Burns, particularly at the most senior levels, necessitated both a sound understanding of the theory of modern war as well as combat experience. "Very few of the commanders and senior staff officers of this army," noted a concerned Burns, "had war experience, and none of them would have the experience in the current war."[39] Exacerbating this problem was the urgent need for "new blood" at all levels of command – firstly, those individuals who could embrace and understand the new doctrine of modern war and, secondly, those who possessed the energy and zeal to implement it. But, "new blood" invariably meant lack of combat experience.

To solve this problem, Burns recommended that field officers and units be deployed to North Africa "to gain experience" and provide "war-proven officers" capable of leading "expanded forces."[40] He believed that this exposure would provide all ranks with invaluable current tactical experience and, more importantly, command and leadership confidence. Combat would also allow new vehicles and equipment to be tested in a modern setting against the seasoned German Army tactics and weaponry. Burns considered this proposed deployment crucial for gaining much needed battlefield exposure which, in turn, would be instrumental in providing information that could be used in developing modern unit and officer training programs.

The Canadian High Command dismissed the recommendation due to the administrative complications it would entail. The issue of national command always remained at the forefront of Canadian military consideration. Nonetheless, Burns quickly proffered alternate methods of educating and training the Officer Corps and modernizing the Canadian Army. First, in an effort to accelerate the development of new modern war fighting doctrine, he insisted that all veteran officers revisit their past experiences, examine lessons learned, and see how pertinent information could be culled. Second, he encouraged the gathering and analysis of tactical data used by the enemy during recent campaigns. He felt this material could be immediately incorporated into the Army's new training programs.

It seems paradoxical that Burns, particularly in light of his advocacy for modernization, would place so much emphasis on the re-examination of World War I experiences. However, his rationale was sound. He believed there were principles of war which were inviolate. In his memoirs, he criticized the overall poor planning process used in the Dieppe Raid fiasco. "Those who planned the operation," he wrote, "did not need to go back far into history to inform themselves about the risk or possible course of events."[41] Burns deplored the fact that the responsible commanders did not consult official histories and personal accounts. He knew that they contained valuables lessons that could substantially accelerate and improve the planning process of future operations.

Burns' continuing study of the art and science of war enabled him to juxtapose past tactics and events against those currently used, thus revealing lessons that should simply not be ignored. As a formation commander in Italy in 1943, Burns felt that "the conclusions forced upon me in the last three months are that we have locally, at least, and temporarily, I hope, completed the tactical circle and reached the place.... where we discovered ourselves to be just twenty-five years ago.... The truth of the matter is there never has been, or will be, anything really new in tactics."[42] According to Burns, it was all a question of fire and movement. The main tactical flaw in the 11th Brigade actions in the Arielle River operations in 1943, he noted, was in the attempt to dislodge well-entrenched combat proven German forces from fortified positions. "World War I should have taught the lesson," insisted Burns, "that attacks on a narrow front enabled the enemy to concentrate his artillery fire against them, and so were seldom-if-ever-successful."[43] Through his numerous addresses and papers Burns constantly sought every opportunity to heighten the awareness of his staff and other audiences to the importance of using personal experiences and observations to avoid repeating mistakes. "With the modern edition of the problems which face us in the 1 Cdn Div and Cdn Corps of the last war before us, it is worth while to extract every ounce of value we can out of those muddy, bloody last war experiences."[44] He also observed that a certain arrogance or perhaps ignorance reigned in the upper sanctum of the Senior Command when it came to studying and applying military theory and the lessons of the past. "There was a certain disposition [by Canadian commanders] to assume," commented Burns, "that the history of modern warfare had begun on July 10, 1943, and that only the lessons learned after that date had any relevance."[45]

Undaunted, Burns continued to write numerous innovative military articles, attempting to incorporate newly acquired information with the anticipated requirements of the new mechanized warfare. Burns wanted his writings to trigger a wave of progressive modern military thought and accelerate the implementation of a logical and sound offensive doctrine. It appeared, however, that few officers reacted to his writing or, for that matter, even understood war as a "dynamic art and science" in the same manner as Burns.

This shortcoming of others underlines Burns' strength. It provided him with the ability to translate theory into practice and develop efficient modern training initiatives. His interest in training and ways to continually enhance and modernize it was reinforced by his unshakeable World War I reminiscence – the image of a hapless young soldier desperately clutching his unfired rifle during the battle of Vimy Ridge. At that time Burns asked him why he did not shoot. The poorly trained soldier answered that he had not fired his rifle since his arrival in France. The rage Burns felt at that moment remained with him, and he vowed never to allow men to be sent into battle without proper training to become "merely moving targets to be shot down by a better-trained enemy."[46]

And so, Burns worked hard at improving what he felt to be outdated training programs, exercises, and equipment. He realized that this directly affected the soldiers' performance. He noticed that they displayed a disturbing lack of initiative, interest, and motivation. His emphasis, therefore, was on securing modern vehicles and equipment, so that his men would not be placed in a predicament where they would have to fight and learn at the same time.[47] Furthermore, to instil a more progressive proactive mindset, Burns insisted that elements such as imagination and realism be employed during exercises to continually challenge, motivate, and test personnel. "Boredom, discouragement and apathy," warned Burns, "are the great enemies." He added, "we must fight them, and help others to fight them."[48]

Time, however, was often the greatest constraint. Despite his prolific writing and continual warnings throughout the interwar years and after, Burns' chain of command appeared to ignore the changing nature of warfare, as well as the lessons of the past. The Canadian Army now had to make up for lost time. Burns' emphasis on modern training techniques in 1941 was but his latest contribution. "When the day comes," asserted Burns, "it will be useless to wish for the skill, the knowledge and the fortitude that we only acquire by hard work during the time of our training."[49]

But Burns' active mind and intellect were not simply limited to the question of training soldiers in the new forms of mechanized warfare. He also turned his attention to the improvement of Canadian Armoured corps doctrine. Burns long ago realized that the key to success in offensive operations was the rapid, co-ordinated execution of battle-drills through firepower and movement. He understood that standardized tactics and doctrine were necessary to ensure an effective armoured Corps, much less a modern army capable of combined arms operations. To his great frustration, nothing of substance existed. Realizing the Canadian reliance on British doctrine, he criticized the British High Command's inability "to make up their collective mind how the tank arm should be used, and what kind of a tank should be designed to fit the use."[50] Furthermore, Burns became increasingly concerned by his own superiors' slavish adherence to the British model and lack of foresight and understanding of mechanized warfare. Burns' decided that if directives, guidelines, and policy did not come from above, then he would develop his own to temporarily fill the critical doctrinal void.

Once again, Burns used his writings to bring forward essential tactical information that would benefit all and optimally encourage further doctrinal initiatives. For example, while commanding the 4th Canadian Armoured Brigade in Canada, he prepared a series of papers in which he developed and established combined arms drills as well as tactical and technical operational principles.[51] His elaboration of "tank versus tank" tactics stemmed from his understanding of the imperative to develop unit and sub-unit standard operating procedures. As a result, he provided his armoured crews with what can be considered as the forerunner of the Canadian Armoured Corps doctrine.[52]

But Burns understood that the neophyte Canadian Army required every possible assistance to ensure it was ready for the new, modern methods of war. Therefore, he emphasized that it was essential that his officers learn to evaluate each tactical situation using similar criteria to ensure that they made the best possible decisions. It was, in a crude form, artificial experience to help guide decision making in the chaos of battle. Typical of Burns, he combined the intellectual with the technical. He analyzed all the armoured vehicles' characteristics, their strengths and weaknesses, in order to deploy the appropriate vehicle and required support units for any given task. In characteristic Burns fashion, no detail, however insignificant, was left to chance.

Burns took the preparation of his subordinates even further. In accordance with his belief in a comprehensive lessons-learned process, he prepared briefs, discussions, and meetings to educate and inform all his officers on the most recent battlefield and doctrinal advancements. He encouraged the testing of experimental techniques to assist soldiers and officers to anticipate and develop potential reactions to various possible tactical situations. Burns insisted that all new tactical information be disseminated to all rank and file.

Through these developments, Burns attempted to demonstrate that it was not necessary to rely on – or wait for – British instruction or doctrine. He firmly believed that the ongoing historical, doctrinal, and subservient mind frame which reigned in the Canadian Army had to be broken. If not, he argued, it would be difficult to develop combat leaders capable of offensive action in the genre of warfare that they would be exposed to in Europe.

Burns' contribution did not cease with the improvement of training techniques and philosophy. Concurrently, he proceeded to evaluate and explore innovative options that would enhance the armoured units' rate of advance. His belief, theoretically in any case, that speed was core to modern offensive operations, remained central to his philosophy of modern war. During a series of exercises, Burns observed that the armoured units' initial thrust and progress were repeatedly slowed down by terrain, obstacles, and rear delaying tactics, hence weakening their role. In order to increase the effectiveness of armour, Burns turned to technological advancements that he had assisted in pioneering during the interwar years. In a series of letters exchanged between Burns and the

Royal Canadian Artillery Headquarters, First Canadian Army, the question of using "high oblique photos" to increase effectiveness and offensive capability of the Army was examined. Burns asserted that the high oblique photographs "taken successively with the axis of the camera along the direction of advance, gives a very good idea of the country ahead and covers considerable distances in advance."[53] Although, in the end, his suggestion was not adopted, Burns' innovative attempt at applying new technology to increase the ability to maintain rapid offensive operations by providing up to date and timely information is commendable.

Even when occupied in combat operations, Burns continued to contribute what he could to the understanding of the dynamic art and science of war and the improvement of the Canadian Army's effectiveness. His focus on lessons learned and their promulgation was evident in his writings analyzing the weaknesses in the breakthrough and pursuit phases of his summer operations in Italy in 1944. His papers, "The Set Piece Attack from the Breakthrough of the Hitler Line, 6 July 1944" and "The Pursuit from Melfa to Agani, 16 July 1944,"[54] brought forward recommendations in assessing the enemy's new defensive tactics, the use of various weapons, and the swift crossing of natural obstacles. He also examined the policy on in-theatre deployments, methods of enhancing front line co-ordination between units, and tactical procedures to accelerate pursuit. Not surprisingly, he also emphasized the need for efficient traffic control strategies to facilitate the rapid deployment of units in the combat zone.

This level of detail is not surprising. In his memoirs, Burns acknowledged that his attitude and meticulous attention to detail during the planning of operations caused his subordinates to think that he was fundamentally pessimistic. "However, my habit of mind," he explained, "is generally to think of misfortune which can happen.... In short, I tried to leave nothing to luck, although of course I didn't succeed in eliminating all mischief."[55] Burns was a creature of his own experience. His recollections of combat and the First World War, combined with his study of the theory of war, particularly mechanization, instilled in him the requirement for detailed planning to ensure the offensive did not become mired in immobility. A paradox emerges. Theoretically, Burns understood that in combat "bold action-taking risks which in other circumstances might be reckless – is essential for success."[56] However, rightly or wrongly, his immediate superior castigated him for his formation's slow advance. Burns' British commanders strongly felt that he lacked command presence and was unable to inspire fighting troops. This criticism was largely supported by Burns' Canadian superiors and subordinates as well.[57] A Canadian Brigadier would later describe Burns as, "an example of a good man in the wrong appointment."[58]

Whatever Burns' command ability may have been, his intellect, unconventional thinking, and refusal to be limited by traditional and stifling – albeit popularly accepted – attitudes, single him out as an exceptional individual. His inquiring mind was evident in his paper *What is Tank Country?* This effort was drafted as a direct rebuttal to General Bernard Montgomery's conservative opinion that there was no role for an armoured division in Italy. Not surprisingly, Burns presented a different perspective. He argued exactly the opposite and presented innovative ways to use armour in the Italian Theatre. Careful manoeuvring, skilful driving, and the assistance of engineers, he insisted, could open up avenues of approach that were previously inaccessible to armoured vehicles, ultimately enhancing the elements of surprise and aggressive advance: "The more difficult the tank going," Burns concluded, "the better the tank country, so long as the tanks can get through."[59] This latest debate was just another case of Burns demonstrating his progressive thinking and continual exploration for original new ideas to maximize offensive action and the proficiency of the Canadian Army.

His persistent and dogged pursuit of the Army's doctrinal improvement and modernization continued unabated to the end of the war. In October 1944, he wrote "Notes on Tactical Methods," in which he argued an old theme, namely the use of leading armour elements to generate an offensive push deep enough into the enemy's rear so as to disorganize his withdrawal and ability to employ delaying tactics. More importantly, Burns wanted the paper to ensure "a sound and common tactical doctrine on these matters in the 1 Cdn Corps, which will render co-operation and combined attacks easier." Burns reiterated another old truth, specifically that attention to doctrine and lessons learned were sadly lacking. He wrote, "that neither principle nor the methods discussed are new, but there have been failures to apply them, which have limited our success."[60] It appears that many of Burns' fellow officers emphasized experiential development rather than a less costly focus on a balance of experience, education, and training. In early November 1944, Burns was sacked as the Commander of 1st Canadian Corps. He was subsequently appointed Officer-in-Charge and General Officer-in-Charge, Canadian Section, General Headquarters, 1st Echelon, 21st Army Group and ended the war as a Staff Officer.

With the cessation of hostilities, Burns moved on to a series of varied careers which included employment in the immediate post-war period, 1945 to 1946, as the Director General of Rehabilitation in Veterans Affairs, and later, between 1950 and 1954, as the Deputy Minister of the same Department. In 1954, he was seconded to the Department of External Affairs and lent to the United Nations where he was the Chief of Staff of the UN Truce Supervisory Organization for two years. From 1956 to 1958, he was appointed as the Commander of the United Nations Emergency Forces in Egypt. Two years later, from 1960-1968, he was the advisor to the Canadian government on Disarmament. His final career was as a Professor of Strategic Studies, from 1972-1975, at Carleton University in Ottawa. Throughout these years and varied employments, Burns held true to his philosophy of "contributing what one could." In the introduction to *Memoirs of Two World Wars, General Mud*, Burns, ever the intellectual, revealed his motivation for his continued writing. "No Canadian general," he explained, "who had command in the field has left memoirs.... There is this gap in which what might be called Canadiana. I offer this book in hope it may do something to fill it."[61] This leitmotiv was evident in his seven books[62] and numerous articles. As an officer and a scholar, he considered it his duty to share his acquired knowledge and experiences so that one day they could benefit future generations of Canadian military officers.

"Smiling Sunray" as he was pejoratively called by his men may not be remembered in the annals of Canadian military history as a dynamic combat commander. However, his efforts at promoting military discussion and study for the purposes of the development, both intellectual and operational, of the Canadian Army, as well as its modernization, should not be forgotten. To Burns, war was truly a dynamic art and science. To understand and attempt to master it, he believed, required intellectual investigation and debate in addition to experience. His penetrating intellect and "avant-garde" thinking, combined with his prolific writing, have left an indelible record which easily establishes Lieutenant-General E.L.M. Burns as one of Canada's best, if not only, intellectual generals.

ENDNOTES
CHAPTER 7

1. National Archives of Canada (hereinafter NAC), MG 31, G6, E.L.M. Burns Fonds, Vol. 9, File – Articles, Papers, Speeches, "Notes for Lecture Delivered to Offrs of CACRUs at Blackdown, 29 Dec 43," 9.
2. NAC, MG 31, G6, Vol. 1, File - WWII GOC 1-0, GOC's Personal File, OPS 1 Cdn Corps, 5.
3. NAC, MG 31, G6, Vol. 1, File – Veterans Affairs – MGen Burns, "Meet 'Tommy' Burns – A Soldier's Soldier," by N. Gregor Guthrie.
4. NAC, MG 31, G6, Vol. 1, File – WWII GOC 1-0, GOC's Personal File, OPS 1 Cdn Corps, 2.
5. The American sociologist Morris Janowitz makes a distinction between an intellectual officer and a military intellectual. Janowitz explains that the former is the soldier who brings an intellectual dimension to his job. His intellectual quality is held in check by the needs of the profession. The latter, according to Janowitz, is distinctly different. Although a professional soldier, his attachments and identifications are primarily with intellectuals and with intellectual activities. Morris Janowitz, *The Professional Soldier – A Social and Political Portrait* (New York: Free Press, 1971), 431. Although Burns fashioned himself to be an intellectual officer, others viewed him as a military intellectual. Peers, subordinates, and historians over-whelmingly described him as a "staff officer by nature, not a field commander." See J.L. Granatstein, *The Generals* (Toronto: Stoddart Publishing, 1993), 143; and Daniel G. Dancocks, *The D-Day Dodgers* (Toronto: McClelland & Stewart Inc, 1991), 384-385.
6. For further details see Lieutenant-General E.L.M. Burns, *General Mud* (Toronto: Clarke, Irwin & Company Ltd, 1970), 1, 84-96; Granatstein, 117-120; and NAC, MG 31, G6, Vol. 1, File – Veterans Affairs – MGen Burns, "Meet 'Tommy' Burns – A Soldier's Soldier."
7. NAC, MG 31, G6, Vol. 9, File – Articles, Papers, Speeches – U, "The Use of High Oblique Air Photos in Armoured Force Operations"; and Vol. 1, File – Veterans Affairs – MGen Burns, "Meet 'Tommy'

Burns – A Soldier's Soldier." In 1939, Burns was awarded the Order of the British Empire for this work.

8. Burns, *General Mud*, 18, 25.
9. Major-General J.F.C. Fuller, *The Conduct of War 1789-1961* (London: Eyre & Spottiswoode, 1961), 243; and Burns, *General Mud,* 60-61.
10. A.J. Trythall, *Boney Fuller: The Intellectual General 1878-1966* (London: Cassell, 1977), 60; Brian Holden Reid, *J.F.C. Fuller Military Thinker* (Basingstoke: Macmillan, 1987), 49-51; and Field Marshal, F.M. Lord Carver, *The Apostles of Mobility: The Theory & Practise of Armoured Warfare* (London: Weidenfeld & Nicolson, 1979), 40.
11. Fuller, 256-257.
12. Captain E.L.M. Burns, "The Mechanization of Cavalry," *The Canadian Defence Quarterly* (hereafter *CDQ*), Vol. 1, No. 3, 7.
13. Ibid., 5. At this juncture Burns felt that the "present service tank is a weapon for the overcoming of organized, thick, machine-gun resistance, and is not adapted for reconnaissance, holding ground, pursuit, or the functions of cavalry generally.
14. Burns, *General Mud*, 89.
15. Major E.L.M. Burns, "1932 Prize Essay – Protection of the Rearward Services and Headquarters in Modern War," *CDQ*, Vol. 10, No. 3, April 1933, 298.
16. Carver, 40; and Burns, "1932 Prize Essay," 305.
17. Burns, "1932 Prize Essay," 296. Burns asserted that "operations against the rear by a force of medium tanks will be a major threat to an army; probably the most dangerous which it will have to meet, and in the final analysis can only be countered by operations of the defending armoured force."
18. Major E.L.M. Burns, "A Step Toward Modernization," *CDQ*, Vol. XII, No.3, April 1935, 298.
19. Ibid., 298.
20. Ibid., 298.
21. Ibid., 305. Italics are his.
22. Ibid., 305.
23. Lieutenant-Colonel E.L.M. Burns, "The Theory of Military Organisation," *CDQ*, Vol. XIV, No. 3, April 1937, 328-329.
24. NAC, MG 31, G6, Vol. 9, File: Articles, Papers, Speeches – U, "Tank or Anti-Tank? Does the Spanish War Show Which is Superior?" by Major Sieberg (translation of an article appearing in the *Militar-Wochenblatt* of 11 Feb 38). During the First World War tanks were considered capable of going into battle only two to three times.

25. Lieutenant-Colonel E.L.M. Burns, "A Division That Can Attack," *CDQ*, Vol. XV, No. 3, April 1938, 291.
26. Ibid., 298.
27. Granatstein, 125.
28. Captain G.G. Simonds, "An Army that can Attack – a Division that Can Defend," *CDQ*, Vol. XV, No. 4, July 1938, 417.
29. Lieutenant-Colonel E.L.M. Burns, "Where Do The Tanks Belong?" *CDQ*, Vol. XVI, No. 1, October 1938, 30.
30. Ibid., 30.
31. Ibid., 30.
32. Captain G.G. Simonds, "What Price Assault Without Support?" *CDQ*, Vol. XVI, No. 1, October 1938, 147. Italics are his.
33. NAC, RG 24, Vol. 12260, File: 1 Para Tps/1, Memo Burns to CGS, 12 November 1940, 1.
34. Captain F.O. Miksche, *Paratroops* (London: Faber and Faber Ltd, 1942), 38-39. See also Callum MacDonald, *The Lost Battle* (New York: The Free Press, 1993), 38.
35. NAC, RG 24, Vol. 12260, File: 1 Para Tps/1, Memo Burns to CGS, 12 November 1940, 1.
36. Ibid., 1.
37. Ibid., 2.
38. During World War II Burns held the following appointments: General Staff Officer, 1st Grade, Canadian Military Headquarters, London, England, 17 October 1939 – 19 May 1940; General Staff Officer, 1st Grade, 2nd Canadian Division, 29 May 1940 – 5 August 1940; Assistant Deputy Chief of Staff, 6 August 1940 – 9 April 1941; Brigadier General Staff, 1st Canadian Corps, 10 April 1941 – 6 August 1941; Officer Administrating Canadian Armour Corps Centre, 27 August 1941 – 1 February 1942; Commander 4th Canadian Armoured Brigade, 2 February 1942 – 5 May 1943; General Officer Commanding 2nd Canadian Division, 6 May 1943 – 10 January 1944; General Officer Commanding 5th Canadian Armoured Division, 30 January 1944 –19 March 1944; General Officer Commanding 1st Canadian Corps, 20 March 1944 – 5 November 1944; Officer-in-Charge, Canadian Section, Section, General Headquarters, 1st Echelon, 21st Army Group, 5 December 1944 – 26 February 1945 and General Officer-in-Charge, Canadian Section, General Headquarters, 1st Echelon, 21st Army Group, 27 February 1945 – 5 September 1945.
39. Burns, *General Mud, 106.*

40. Ibid., 107.
41. Ibid., 115.
42. NAC, MG 31, G6, Vol. 1, File – WWII GOC 1-0 GOC=s Personal File, OPS 1 Cdn Corps, Address on Principles of Effect Fire Support in the 'Break-in Battle' by the Commander, 1 Cdn Corps, 11 February 1944, 5.
43. Burns, *General Mud*, 126.
44. NAC, MG 31, G6, Vol. 1, File – WWII GOC 1-0 GOC=s Personal File, OPS 1 Cdn Corps, Address on Principles.
45. Burns, *General Mud*, 133.
46. Ibid., 42; Later as General Officer Commanding 2nd Division, 6 May 1943 to 10 January 1944, Burns noted that the theoretical weapons training sessions were not followed up by range practice. To rectify this situation, small arms ranges were built and Burns himself took part in firing range exercises, 118.
47. When the Brigade arrived in England during the summer of 1942, it was noted that they were in a "somewhat more advance state of training than earlier armoured formations, mainly because of respectable numbers of tanks from Canadian production were now available in Canada for training use." Colonel C.P. Stacey, *Six Years of War, The Army in Canada, Britain and The Pacific, Official History of the Canadian Army in The Second World War*, Vol. 1 (Ottawa: DND, 1957), 247.
48. NAC, RG 24, Vol. 18215, War Diary, A8, CAC(8), Training Centre, Colonel E.L.M. Burns, "Give the Troops a Break," *The Tank-Canada*, Camp Borden, Ontario, December-January 1941-1942, No.1, Vol. 1, 3.
49. Ibid.
50. Burns, *General Mud*, 111.
51. NAC, RG 24, Vol. 14050, War Diary, 4th Armoured Brigade, File 950, Appendix D, "Discussion Tank vs Tank Tactics," 31 May 1942, Frame 762, Microfilm reel T-10, 656.
52. Ibid., File 950, Appendix K, "Principles of Tanks vs Tanks Tactics," 7 August 1942, Frames 864 - 870, Microfilm reel T-10, 656.
53. NAC, MG 31, G6, Vol. 9, File: Articles, Papers and Speeches – U. Letter from HQ, RCA, First Canadian Army to General Burns, 11 November 1942.
54. Burns, *General Mud*, 164, The Set "Set Piece" Attack, Lessons From The Breakthrough of the Hitler Line, 6 July 1944; and NAC, RG 24, Vol. 13686, War Diary, HQ 1st Canadian Corps, "G" Branch, The Pursuit from Melfa to Anagni, 16 July 1944, Frames 1601-1603,

Microfilm reel T-7113.

55. Burns, *General Mud,* 113.

56. NAC, RG 24, Vol. 13686, War Diary, HQ, 1st Cdn Corps, "G" Branch, Frames 1601- 1603, Microfilm reel T-7113.

57. Burns' difficult character earned him the reputation of being a "dour intellectual." In mid-1943, an evaluation report prepared for the attention of the Minister of Defence described Burns as follows: "Exceptionally high qualifications but not a leader. Difficult man to approach, cold and sarcastic. Will never secure devotion of his followers. Has probably one of the best brains in the Army and whilst he leads his Division successfully, he would give greater service as a high staff officer." NAC, MG 27, III, B11, J.L. Ralston Papers, Vol. 54, File: Officer Assessment, n.d. (mid-1943). See also Granatstein, 133-143; and Dancocks, 289-290, and 384-386.

58. Granatstein, 43.

59. NAC, MG 31, G6, Vol. 1, File: WWII, GOC 1-0, GOC's Personal file, Reports and Lessons from Operations, What is Tank Country?, 30 September 1944.

60. Ibid., Notes on Tactical Methods, 5 October 1944.

61. Burns, *General Mud,* xii.

62. Ibid., xii.

CHAPTER 8

REAR-ADMIRAL L.W. MURRAY
AND THE BATTLE OF THE ATLANTIC:
THE PROFESSIONAL WHO LED CANADA'S
CITIZEN SAILORS

Roger Sarty

A GOOD case could be made that Canada became a significant naval power on 24 May 1941. On that day the British Admiralty accepted the suggestion of Naval Service Headquarters (NSHQ) in Ottawa that a Canadian officer should be appointed to command a new transatlantic escort force that was to be established at St. John's, Newfoundland. In acceding to the Canadian request, the British Admiralty named L.W. Murray, at that time a Commodore,[1] as most suitable for the command. "[I]t would give us great confidence," signalled Admiral Sir Dudley Pound, First Sea Lord at the British Admiralty, to Rear-Admiral Percy Nelles, chief of the Canadian naval staff, "if you saw your way to selecting him."[2] Pound, in agreeing to the request for a Canadian commander, was making a notable gesture. The Canadians, in urging one of their own, were under the impression that the force would mostly be made up of Canadian ships.[3] That may have been the original British intention,[4] but within days further analysis of force requirements made it clear that the Newfoundland Escort Force would have to be on a large scale – as many as eighty warships – of which more than half were to be British.[5]

Murray succeeded in the Newfoundland command. He kept in very close personal touch with the men who served at sea, and they performed far better than anyone could have expected in the face of challenges from the enemy and also from Allied policy that relentlessly grew during Murray's tenure at St. John's. Fittingly, on 30 April 1943, after Murray had moved to the larger naval command at Halifax, he became Commander-in-Chief, Canadian Northwest Atlantic. This was a new appointment created by the Allied supreme command, and it recognized Canada's capacity to control trade defence operations in the western Atlantic, a vast ocean area off Canada's east coast. Murray thus became the only Canadian to lead an Allied theatre of war.

The assignment of a Canadian officer to senior commands in the main Maritime theatre of the war was a remarkable achievement for a navy that had scarcely existed in 1939.[6] On mobilization for war in September 1939 – scarcely twenty months before the creation of the Newfoundland Escort Force – the Royal Canadian Navy (RCN) had only six seagoing warships and 3,500 personnel, including reserves. The corps of regular officers was tiny, numbering hardly more than fifty in the executive, that is non-engineering, branch.[7] The Navy, in other words, had to draw its senior leadership from a small pool of talent, so small that it would have been unsurprising if the Royal Navy (RN) had been unable to have confidence in any of its members for a task as demanding as command of the Newfoundland Escort Force.

The Navy's history was short and troubled. Founded only in 1910, its first dozen years had been scarred by political controversy, which reflected widespread doubts among the few citizens who gave the matter much thought as to whether Canada really needed a navy at all. During the 1920s the Government had slashed the regular force to a cadre intended only for instruction of the reserves, the cheapest form of naval development. Sustained – but very modest – expansion had begun only in the mid 1930s, too late to enlarge the pool of senior leaders in time for the Second World War. What saved the professional cadre of the RCN from stagnation in these depressing circumstances was the service's intimate link with the Royal Navy, on which the RCN, like the new Royal Australian Navy, was modelled, and of which the dominions' navies really formed overseas divisions.

Murray's career traced the major developments in the Canadian Navy from its earliest days.[8] As a military professional his outlook and skills reflected both the difficult circumstances of the embryonic Canadian service, and the extraordinary opportunities afforded by the service's close ties to the Royal Navy. He was born at Granton, on Pictou Harbour on Nova Scotia's north shore, on 22 June 1896. His father managed the piers at Granton and later at nearby Pictou Landing where colliers were loaded with coal from the Pictou County mining district. Having spent the whole of his youth near ships and the sea, the teen-aged Murray was attracted by the new navy. He sat a competitive examination and won a place in the first class of the Royal Naval College of Canada at Halifax, which he joined upon its opening in January 1911. When he graduated in 1913 (third in his class), the RCN's ships, the former RN cruisers HMCS *Niobe* and HMCS *Rainbow,* had been laid up as a result of political debates over the very existence of the

Navy. Murray and his classmates therefore went to Britain for a year's training as midshipmen in Royal Navy cruisers.

In August 1914, when the First World war broke out, Murray was taking further courses at the naval college in Halifax. During the conflict he participated as a midshipmen and junior officer in all phases of the challenges the Canadian and British navies faced in protecting the heavy sea trade from North America. Britain depended upon this trade for the sustenance of its war effort and the health of its domestic economy.[9] Initially he served in HMCS *Niobe*, Canada's east coast cruiser, which was hastily prepared for sea with a crew that was partly Royal Navy and partly Royal Canadian Navy to patrol off New York; these patrols aimed to interdict German trade from the neutral United States and block German attempts to operate cruisers from US ports. In April 1915, Murray moved to HMCS *Margaret*, a Canadian government customs patrol steamer that the Navy commissioned and armed in an emergency effort to guard the Gulf of St. Lawrence against a new enemy menace – submarine attacks on merchant shipping. In 1916, he joined the cruiser HMS *Leviathan*, flagship of the North America and West Indies station, which the Royal Navy had revived to protect north Atlantic shipping. In 1917, Murray had the chance to work with the admiral's staff on the *Leviathan* in organizing the first transatlantic merchant ship convoys from North America to the United Kingdom, the measure that proved the most effective defence against submarines. The United States having entered the war in April of that year, the cruiser frequently visited Chesapeake Bay so that the British commander-in-chief could work with the US Navy Department in co-ordinating the sailing of convoys from Canadian and American ports.

The appointment of Canada's young professional officers to major British warships like *Leviathan* was a conscious policy designed to give them wider experience than was available in the Canadian service which, from 1915, was mostly limited to the operation of small coastal auxiliary anti-submarine vessels. Merchant seamen, commissioned as reservists, and retired Royal Navy officers, who were resident in Canada or willing to come out from the UK and other parts of the empire, looked after these tasks.

In early 1918, Murray, now qualified as a lieutenant, joined HMS *Agincourt*, a modern battleship that formed part of the Royal Navy's Grand Fleet. The ship was based in the northern United Kingdom, ready to sortie into the North Sea in the event that the main German High Seas fleet ventured out of its ports. Murray thus had a chance to develop his skills in a great ship in the most powerful battle fleet the world had seen. He also witnessed the result of Britain's Maritime dominance: the surrender of the German fleet at Firth of Forth in Scotland in November 1918.

With Canadian naval policy again in flux, Murray, like the other young Canadian officers, remained in the United Kingdom after the armistice. He continued training for his specialist's qualification as a navigator and served in other major Royal Navy warships until 1920, when he returned to Canada as the navigating officer in the cruiser *Aurora*. The Royal Navy transferred this ship to the RCN as part of an endeavour to revive the Canadian service along the lines originally intended in 1910. Government cutbacks in 1922, however, forced the RCN to get rid of the cruiser, retain only two destroyers (one for each coast), and emphasize the development of reserve forces that in a future war could man auxiliary patrol vessels like HMCS *Margaret* to carry out basic harbour and coastal defence duties. The Royal Naval College of Canada was closed and entries into the regular force officer cadre virtually ceased, other than to fill specific vacancies within the tiny establishment.

One advantage the small officer cadre had was mentoring by Commodore Walter Hose, who was professional head of the Navy from 1920 to 1933. Hose, a former Royal Navy officer who had transferred to the RCN in 1912 because of boredom with his slow-moving career,[10] was sensitive to the need for variety and challenge to develop promising young officers. He sought out in the Royal Navy the best training and employment opportunities for his people. Murray spent fully a third of his career from 1922 to 1939 on specialist courses, then progressively more advanced staff courses at RN establishments, and honed his knowledge with appointments in British warships and at the Admiralty. Between these tours, Murray, of whom Hose had an extremely high opinion, commanded one of the modern Canadian destroyers from 1932 to 1934. From 1934 to 1936 he served as senior officer of the establishments at Halifax, where, among other things, he ran summer training programmes for the reserves, thus becoming familiar with those organizations.

In January 1939, Murray became Director of Naval Operations and Training at Naval Service Headquarters in Ottawa, the number two billet on the staff under Nelles, who had succeeded Hose as chief of the naval staff. Nelles was absent, taking his son for medical treatment in the United States, when on 21 August warnings of potential war began to arrive from

Britain. Murray, therefore, had to initiate precautionary mobilization measures pending Nelles' return on the 23 August.[11] Thereafter Murray was the principle co-ordinator of staff action, as recognized by the change in the title of his appointment seven days later to Deputy Chief of the Naval Staff. The actions required were complex and far-ranging, including the appointment and transportation of retired Canadian and British naval officers resident in Canada who had registered for war service and were desperately needed to augment the minuscule pool of qualified officers for staff and command positions in Ottawa and on both coasts. They also included the introduction of shipping intelligence reporting to Ottawa from all Canadian and United States ports, the exercise of government control over the movements of Canadian merchant shipping, and mobilization of the reserves. These steps were also delicate, requiring close consultation with the Government. The Prime Minister had promised that the country would not enter a war until the Canadian Parliament had been consulted, an assertion of nationhood that delayed Canada's declaration of war on Germany until 10 September, a week after that of Great Britain. In any event, it proved to be mainly a matter of form. King obtained the agreement of his cabinet colleagues in an emergency meeting on 24 August that the Government should recommend participation in the war, and in the meantime, take precautions in lockstep with the British Government.[12] This by no means had been a foregone conclusion from August 21 to 23, when Murray had been in charge of the initial measures.

The naval effort that emerged from the naval staff's deliberations during the early weeks of the war was imaginative and ambitious, through not greatly different from the role the RCN had played in the First World War as a coastal waters force. The surface threats were German cruisers and armoured ships that were few in number but were long-range, fast, and very powerful. The submarine threat, as confirmed by the destruction of an unarmed British liner on the day of Britain's entry into the war, was "sink on sight" attacks on merchant shipping. Submarines could most readily locate and attack shipping in coastal waters. Therefore the role of the RCN's destroyers was to provide escort for the first two days, or four hundred miles, of passage as merchant ship convoys sailed from Halifax.

The Government approved a large-scale construction programme of auxiliaries, some ninety corvette and bangor class coastal escorts and minesweepers, the maximum number that they considered Canadian industry capable of producing in a two-year programme. When auxiliaries were completed, they would be manned by the reserves, giving them a much greater capability in the coastal and harbour defence role than they had with the assortment of civil government steamers and converted trawlers that were available during the first months of mobilization. In addition, the Government approved the naval staff's recommendation that two large tribal class destroyers should be built on Canadian order in England in the expectation that, when these vessels were completed within two years, the service would have a sufficiently large body of experienced personnel to man and operate these ships in the main fighting theatre in European waters. This expansion programme, together with the ongoing convoy, harbour control, and coastal defence operations, stretched the service to foreseeable limits because of the shortage of qualified officers and specialists and the shortcomings of Canada's depression-wracked industry.

Nevertheless, pressure on the Navy increased exponentially with Germany's offensive in the west in the spring of 1940. Norway was conquered in April and then France and the Low Countries in May and June respectively. Britain lost its major ally, and the German forces were now within close striking distance of the British Isles; the German submarine force quickly moved to French ports, and thus gained a great advantage in attacking the transatlantic shipping upon which Britain was now utterly dependent. In response to British pleas for help, the RCN sent four of its seven destroyers (the seventh had been purchased from the Royal Navy shortly after the outbreak of war), which, given the needs for periodic refits, left only one or two for operations in Canadian waters. During the fall of 1940, Britain obtained fifty over-age destroyers from the still neutral United States. In exchange the Americans gained access to large military base sites among British possessions in the western hemisphere, including Newfoundland – which was still separate from Canada, had lost its self-governing status, and reverted to being a British dependency. Short of trained manpower, the Royal Navy asked the RCN for help in crewing the ships. The RCN took over six (and later a seventh)ships and assigned the four most capable to operations in British waters in January 1941. At the same time ten corvettes that were being built in Canada on British account were completed. At the Admiralty's request, the RCN provided crews that sailed the vessels to Britain and then began to operate them there. The ex-US destroyers and the corvettes absorbed nearly two thousand trained seamen – the pool of qualified people the RCN had been depending upon to man its own large fleet of corvettes and bangors when they were completed in 1941.[13] At the same time, Britain's own urgent new needs for equipment prevented the shipment to Canada of many items that were needed to outfit the new Canadian ships.

The crisis in Western Europe transformed not only Canada's war effort but also its relations with the United States. Aside from a brief period of co-operation during the last eighteen months of the First World War, there had never been military ties between the two countries. With Britain apparently on the verge of collapse and Canada and its waters constituting the main route for attacks on North America by the Axis powers, the United States took a great interest in Canadian defence. In August 1940, Canada's prime minister, William Lyon Mackenzie King, and the US president, Franklin Delano Roosevelt, established the Permanent Joint Board on Defence (PJBD). This panel of military officers and senior civilian officials from both countries was to study and recommend to their respective governments joint measures required for the security of North America. Murray participated in secret military staff talks in Washington that laid the basis for King and Roosevelt's meeting, and he then became the Canadian naval representative on the permanent joint board. His main responsibility was to make arrangements whereby the RCN further developed its bases so that the US fleet could operate in northern waters in the event of a major Axis attack, but he also had to work out the operational details of agreements that protected Canadian sovereignty without unduly hampering the effectiveness of the US fleet. The US Navy would not exercise control at Canadian bases and would not assume command over Canadian Forces except in the extreme contingency of a British collapse.[14]

Murray, like other combat arms officers, was anxious to escape staff work. He was delighted in October 1940 to get the RCN's senior seagoing command, Commodore Commanding Halifax Force, flying his flag in the destroyer HMCS *Assiniboine*. In January 1941, he crossed the Atlantic in *Assiniboine* with yet another new appointment, Commodore Commanding Canadian Ships and Establishments in the United Kingdom, to take charge of the augmented RCN force operating in British waters.

Murray quickly discovered that the days of seagoing command in the war against the U-boats were over. The Canadian ships were operating as part of an enormous organization which supplied some one hundred and fifty escorts[15] for convoys that sailed from and arrived at ports all along the west coast of the British Isles according to

171

complex, interlocking schedules. Consulting with Admiral Sir Percy Noble, Commander in Chief of Western Approaches, the principal British command in the Battle of the Atlantic and one of Murray's former commanding officers, Murray realized he would have to move ashore. He opened his office at the Canadian High Commission in London, close by the Admiralty, the only place where he could obtain full information on the movements of Canadian ships and personnel.[16]

The Battle of the Atlantic was undergoing a transformation in early 1941. Strengthened anti-submarine escorts for convoys in the waters off Britain, to which the Canadian ships were contributing, were driving the U-boats to hunt further and further out in the Atlantic. In order to solve the problem of finding convoys in the open ocean (the greatest protection offered by convoys was the fact that a large convoy is little easier to locate at sea than a single ship), the submarines were operating in groups in extended patrol lines or checker-boards. When a U-boat sighted a convoy, it transmitted a report to U-boat headquarters in France, which directed all other U-boats in the vicinity to the contact. The submarines then attacked en masse, at night, and on the surface. In the darkness, the small conning towers of the U-boats were all but invisible to the lookouts on the merchant ships and escorts, and the submarines could take full advantage of their fast surface speed to make multiple attacks. Over the winter of 1940-1941, to counter these tactics the British concentrated all available escorts to provide strong anti-submarine screens as far as Iceland, then, in mid-April, to 35 degrees west longitude, about two-thirds of the way towards Greenland from Iceland. They hoped that diverse routing in the wide-open central ocean would throw the U-boats off the scent.[17] The Admiralty was reluctant to adopt full end-to-end anti-submarine escort because many of the destroyers lacked the necessary range, and that would leave the job to the corvettes. These vessels had superbly long endurance and were immensely seaworthy, but they were designed for coastal work; the motion of their small hulls in heavy seas and the crowded conditions in their living spaces raised grave concerns that the crews would be too exhausted to achieve anything. The vessels were also too slow to outrun a U-boat on the surface, and their fighting equipment was the most basic: an asdic set (as sonar was known in the British Commonwealth navies), depth charges, a single four-inch gun, and some machine guns and light anti-aircraft weapons. There were, furthermore, only enough corvettes to provide a screen of four for most convoys,[18] merely a token force given experience in the eastern

Atlantic which showed that twelve escorts, including two or more destroyers, were essential for effective defence.

When on 20 May a U-boat patrol line caught convoy HX 126 from Halifax at 41 degrees west, south of Greenland, before the anti-submarine escort had joined, the Admiralty had no choice but to implement end-to-end escort. The western gap would be filled by a force based at St. John's that would join UK-bound convoys off Newfoundland and take them as far as Iceland, where the escorts would refuel and pick up a westbound convoy. The Iceland route was inefficient, a long diversion from the direct route to the UK into severe Arctic weather conditions, but there was no choice given the limited range of the destroyers that were critical to the defence. The Royal Navy could supply only about half of the sixty escorts immediately required to provide a minimally effective defence, and counted upon the RCN to provide the remainder. The Admiralty released the eighteen Canadian ships operating in British waters for this duty. The rest would have to come from the additional corvettes that were now coming out of Canadian shipyards in growing numbers. The Canadian force would mostly be a very raw one. The four ex-US destroyers and ten corvettes that had crossed to the UK had required a good deal of additional training under expert British instructors, even though their crews included the best qualified people available in the rapidly expanding Canadian service. The ships also needed dockyard attention because overcrowded yards and shortages of equipment had precluded completion of the work in Canada. When the four ex-US destroyers and ten corvettes came to Newfoundland in the spring of 1941, they had just begun regular operations and were still novice ships by any standards. Of the new corvettes coming from Canada, only the first seven, which arrived at St. John's at the end of May, had had "workup" training to familiarize the inexperienced crews with their vessels, basic ship manoeuvring, and convoy escort tactics.

The intention was that these first seven corvettes, and all of those to follow, would have at least some weeks of training cruises and local defence patrols to prepare them for the savage Atlantic crossing.[19] It was not to be. Intelligence that the U-boats were deploying still further west to pick up convoys in the funnel of traffic south of Cape Race and track them back across the Atlantic, forced the immediate assignment of the RCN corvettes to the Iceland run.[20] Murray was at that time undergoing briefings at Western Approaches Headquarters in Liverpool, England. He then flew to Ottawa for further instructions before flying to Newfoundland and arriving at St. John's on 13 June 1941.[21]

About the only certainty in Murray's job was the need to precisely orchestrate extremely complex, inter-related, and wide-ranging tasks in the face of myriad uncertainties and gaps in resources. Aside from the few ships present in port or on missions to rescue survivors from steamers that had been sunk by the U-boats closing Newfoundland, he had only a general idea of what ships were under his command and where they were. Some ships had been delayed in Iceland or Britain by unexpected defects: the teething troubles of newly built corvettes and wear on the old British and ex-US destroyers that formed much of the escort fleet. Other escorts at sea with westbound convoys had been diverted far to the south as a result of the further movement of the U-boat concentration off Newfoundland, south of Cape Race; they would go to Halifax rather than St. John's with resulting delays in their availability to Murray.[22] Yet it was Murray who had the responsibility of ensuring that sufficient numbers of escorts of the right type were available at the right place at the right time. The link-up of eastbound convoys with the Newfoundland escorts was proving to be very challenging as well. The main convoy from Halifax and joiner groups of merchantmen from Sydney and Newfoundland had to be brought together at sea with the Newfoundland mid-ocean escort, often in near zero visibility in the heavy fogs that hung over the Grand Banks during the spring and fall. Ultimately the success of these evolutions depended upon the escorts on the scene. But the inadequate communications and navigation equipment and inexperienced personnel in many of the Canadian warships left them unable to do much more than look out for themselves, much to the frustration of the people in the capable senior Canadian and British escorts, who found themselves having to coach the junior warships in their groups while also shepherding the merchant vessels into position.

A British destroyer depot ship and its experienced personnel provided essential support at St. John's. Otherwise, however, that port was bereft of naval operating facilities. These were being built on a large scale in a joint Canadian-British enterprise. However, the need to secure the approval of two governments and that of the Newfoundland government, together with the shortage of experienced construction personnel and many essential materials in Newfoundland, required Murray's close personal attention to overcome bottlenecks. The result was to deny his people essential facilities. It was a problem that would demand Murray's attention and that of his successors until the end of the war.

Unknown to any but the most senior Royal Navy commanders and the inner sanctum of the British intelligence service, code-breakers at the

Government Code and Cypher School had finally, in the spring of 1941, cracked the German Enigma encryption system and were able to intercept and read U-boat radio traffic. The Admiralty was, therefore, able to route all convoys clear of the U-boat patrols in the north Atlantic. In the case of the one convoy escorted by the Newfoundland force that the Germans intercepted, decrypt intelligence gave enough warning that Western Approaches was able to provide timely reinforcements; the encounter was slightly in favour of the British, who sank two submarines in exchange for the loss of five merchant vessels, a rate of exchange highly unfavourable to the U-boat force.

In terms of daily operational pressure, however, there was no respite for Murray's command. The British had to divert escorts to the runs to Gibraltar and west Africa, where the convoys were virtually unprotected against the U-boats which began to concentrate against them in the wake of the failures in the north Atlantic.[23] Thus, the Newfoundland Escort Force ran at a strength of only about fifty escorts – two thirds of the them Canadian – rather than the sixty or more that had been originally planned as the minimum number that could carry out the job. Most of the missing ships were British destroyers, the most capable convoy escorts; the gap was being filled by Canadian corvettes, which, as a result, had no time to complete their training or receive proper dockyard attention.[24]

There was apparent relief for the Newfoundland force on the near horizon, but it proved to be illusory. During the summer of 1941, President Roosevelt was preparing to commit the US Navy to escort convoys between Newfoundland and Iceland to relieve the British. It was initially intended that at least a portion of the Canadian escorts in the Newfoundland command be reassigned for service in European waters and on the routes to the Mediterranean and Africa. At the end of August, the Admiralty adjusted the convoy schedules in anticipation of early US assistance. One result was to increase the sailing frequency of slow convoys. These, because they crawled at a speed of only six to seven knots (less than half the speed of a surfaced U-boat), were especially vulnerable to attack. In a ghastly coincidence, there were delays in the decryption of German radio traffic at precisely the time that strengthened British defences in the eastern Atlantic drove a strong U-boat concentration towards the coast of Greenland. There, far from any reinforcement, slow convoy SC 42 ran into the pack on 9 September. Because of the increased demands placed on the Newfoundland Escort Force by the new convoy organization, the sixty-seven merchant ships were escorted by only four warships, all Canadian. There was only one destroyer, HMCS *Skeena*, and three corvettes, one of which, HMCS *Kenogami*, had been in commission for just over two months and was on its first ocean crossing.

During the forty-two hours from 9 September until British reinforcements from Iceland arrived on 11 September, the RCN held the ring alone in the face of ten U-boats. Despite the impossible odds and depressingly heavy losses – eleven ships – the Canadian ships were tenacious and effective throughout the battle. The U-boat records confirm that the escorts kept good station and responded aggressively to any trace of the enemy, thereby blocking attacks or persuading U-boats not to linger for a second shot.[25] Notably, in a running battle, where the escorts had little chance to make sustained pursuits, they damaged one U-boat, *U-85*, severely enough to force it to abandon the fight and destroyed another.

The action that sank *U-501* was the product of desperate measures that would have only ever been attempted by a command that was as hard pressed as the Newfoundland Escort Force. On 4 September, Commander J.D. Prentice, RCN, commanding officer of HMCS *Chambly* noted the early indications in British estimates of U-boat locations of the movement of submarines to the west of Iceland. Prentice was a Canadian who had served in the Royal Navy, retired in British Columbia, and then come out for service on mobilization. An extremely aggressive officer with a superb sense of tactics, he had trained the first group of seven RCN corvettes and then come to Newfoundland, ostensibly to continue to conduct sea training of newly arrived ships. He had been frustrated in this task by the need to constantly push vessels into service. Now he proposed that he take his own ship, together with the recently arrived HMCS *Moosejaw*, for a training cruise in the central ocean where the two corvettes could assist in the event that the U-boats west of Iceland made contract with a convoy. Murray instantly approved the scheme,[26] even though it ran the risk of hurling an entirely inexperienced crew – many members became seasick the moment *Moosejaw* left harbour – into some of the most demanding conditions in the world.

The corvettes arrived ahead of SC 42 on the night of 10 September, just as *U-501* was closing. Prentice, who had mastered the art of the quick depth charge attack, blew the crash diving submarine to the surface, and the two corvettes then closed to ram and pour gunfire into the stricken U-boat. This action could just as well have ended in disaster. At the end of the voyage, *Moosejaw*'s young commanding officer went straight into hospital for extended treatment of severe stomach illness brought on by the exhaustion and stress resulting from the burden he had carried in operating his ship with almost no other fully trained person on board. The responsibility for the operation was Murray's, and it reflected the spirit of the Newfoundland Escort Force under his command.

After the SC 42 battle, the pressure on the command became even more intense. It was obviously necessary to greatly increase the strength of the escort with each slow convoy. In theory this should have been readily possible because the US Navy joined escort operations starting 16 September. What the Admiralty did not realize, as it urged the augmentation, was that the main burden fell on the Canadians. Fleet Admiral E.J. King, USN, Commander in Chief, US Atlantic Fleet, did not believe his force could manage anything more than the escort of fast convoys. King, who now controlled convoy operations west of Iceland, including those of the Newfoundland Escort Force, pressed the Canadians to take all responsibility for the slow convoys that now constituted fully half of the transatlantic convoys. NSHQ warned Murray that his forces would probably prove inadequate for the task. However, there was little hope of getting him additional destroyers – his most critical shortage – or any other experienced ships because the whole point of the US Navy's participation had been to allow the Royal Navy to withdraw its forces to the eastern Atlantic.[27] Murray did the only thing that he could: he continued to push recently commissioned corvettes newly arrived from minimal sea training programmes at Halifax and Sydney directly into the slow convoy schedule.

Murray attacked NSHQ and the command at Halifax for the inadequate support he was receiving, in letters so scorching – he referred to the officers at Halifax who controlled appointments of seagoing personnel as "pirates" – that they created or exacerbated tensions in his relations with other senior officers.[28] Murray's intense commitment to his mission, however, instantly won the confidence of Admiral King and his staff.[29] This was no small achievement. King was a bitter Anglophobe who especially mistrusted the Royal Navy. When, in October 1941, King delegated control over the north Atlantic convoys to Rear-Admiral A.L Bristol, USN, who flew his flag at the new US naval base at Argentia, Newfoundland, the initial favourable impression Murray had made laid the basis for a solid and friendly working relationship. As Murray later recalled:

Admiral Bristol was a very excellent person to work under.... He spoke English very well and understood the British Navy. He spoke English with an American accent when America's interests were involved of course, but it was a great honour to serve under someone who was so understanding. Well of course, one thing he did understand was that we'd been doing this for two years now and his people had no experience whatever, so his method of taking command was to send first his Operations Staff Officer, followed by various other junior officers to my offices in Newfoundland, as liaison for a week at a time, and from there they carried on.[30]

At sea, the nightmare that had begun with SC 42 continued. German shipyards were now delivering additional U-boats to the north Atlantic, most of them with carefully trained crews. The larger number of submarines on patrol, together with delays in breaking the German radio codes, was making it difficult for shore commands to route convoys clear of danger, and the slow moving SC convoys were most at risk. On 18 and 19 September, three submarines in contact with SC 44 sank the corvette HMCS *Levis*, the first Canadian warship to be lost to enemy action, and four merchant ships.

In the early morning darkness of 15 October, a drama began to unfold around SC 48 on the grand scale of the SC 42 battle. Frantic efforts by shore authorities to steer the convoy clear of a large U-boat concentration at mid-ocean failed when *U-553* made contact and sank two ships. The convoy was virtually undefended because of the strain on the resources of Newfoundland Escort Force. The assigned escort included a destroyer and seven corvettes. The destroyer, HMCS *Columbia*, was "short leg," and, as part of the desperate measures to provide coverage at mid-ocean, had sailed after the convoy at economical speed (nearly twice that of the ponderous slow merchant ships) as SC 48 neared known danger areas. Wild weather and the repeated evasive changes in course by the convoy, however, made it impossible for *Columbia* to find its charges. Meanwhile, three of the corvettes, all of them on their first ocean crossing, lost the convoy as it made radical turns in darkness amidst the heavy seas. *Columbia*, however, persisted in its search for four days, further and further out into the Atlantic even as its fuel expenditure began to reach the limits for safe return to harbour. The destroyer was thus able to home on the radio reports from SC 48 of *U-553*'s initial attacks, and raced towards the convoy, nearing its position at mid-day on 15 October. The approaching destroyer sighted *U-553* on the surface and drove the U-boat under with well-executed suppression tactics. There was no time for a prolonged hunt to sink the submarine given the vulnerability of the thinly escorted convoy to other U-boats that were known to be in the area. Quietly creeping up on the U-boat to get as close as possible before it saw the threat and dived, *Columbia* had delivered a snap depth charge attack over the diving swirl, shaking the boat sufficiently to persuade it to keep submerged, thereby preventing the submarine from renewed pursuit. *U-553* was unable to attack again for another thirty-six hours,[31] although another U-boat, *U-568*, sank a merchant ship on the night of the 15th.

Next day, 16 October, five US destroyers, two British destroyers, two British corvettes, and two Canadian corvettes reinforced the escort, but this large concentration of ships was unable to mount a defence that was much more effective than that of the small escort for SC 42. During the night of 16-17 October, five U-boats sank six merchantmen, the corvette HMCS *Gladiolus*, and severely damaged the destroyer USS *Kearny*. The German success was partly the result of many of the reinforcing ships not arriving until the attacks were underway in the middle of the night, making it difficult to co-ordinate the defence, not least because of communications failures between the Commonwealth ships and the inexperienced US ships. The greatest problem, however, was the crawling pace of the slow convoy, which allowed the Germans ample time to penetrate past the escorts and carefully aim their torpedoes.

German records show that the escorts made only two counterattacks that night where the target was a U-boat and not a false contact. One of these attacks was by HMCS *Pictou*, a corvette that was on return passage from another mission in the vicinity and had voluntarily joined the beleaguered convoy. *Pictou* sighted *U-568* moving on the surface after that submarine put a torpedo into USS *Kearny*. *Pictou* made a dogged pursuit of the speeding submarine, forced it under, and delivered a depth charge attack that was "fairly well placed" in the words of the submarine commander. *U-568* did not rejoin the battle.[32]

Pictou's was a notable performance, for the commanding officer, Lieutenant A.G.S. Griffin, was a volunteer reservist who had received his commission only fourteen months before, and he had been in command for only seven weeks. The ship had had the misfortune of two commanding officers who had not worked out since its commissioning in April, 1941. Griffin, an inexperienced first lieutenant, had been elevated to command as a result of Murray's personal intervention. Griffin's memory of the interview gives a glimpse of Murray's command style:

> The Commodore, very quiet-spoken but direct ... asked me about my background and questioned me in some detail about the state of morale in the ship, bearing in mind the experience of having had two commanding officers come and go within only a few weeks. I reported favourably but added how keen we all were to get going.... In retrospect I thought his eyes lighted up at this statement, and he talked for several minutes about keenness and offensive spirit being the two essential ingredients of not only an efficient, but a happy ship. Finally he said: "Well, Griffin, my main purpose in having you come and see me today was to tell you that while the difficulties in finding suitable commanding officers are, as you know, prodigious, your ship has top priority. But you may have to wait another week or two at least. So keep up the good work."
>
> At this, on a wild impulse, I ... said, "Sir, let me take her." He ... said, even more gently, but with great emphasis, "By jove, I will." Then quickly added: "I'm taking a big chance on you and you must not let me down." I could only answer, "Sir, I will do my best."[33]

Griffin, as a member of the Royal Canadian Naval Volunteer Reserve, the class of the reserves for those who had no professional marine experience before entering the Navy, represented the majority of the people the service had to depend upon. The expansion in 1940 had absorbed all of the more experienced personnel, mostly former merchant mariners who had been enrolled in the Royal Canadian Naval Reserve. Griffin's appointment to command had been an enormous leap of faith on Murray's part, which is striking for a professional whose career had been shaped by the high standards of the Royal Navy.

The creditable performance of the Canadian warships in the SC 48 battle was all the more noteworthy because, at that very time, Murray's staff was warning him that the pressure on the Newfoundland-based ship had become unendurable. The policy of rushing newly commissioned corvettes to sea without proper work-up training and with only a handful of experienced personnel on board had reached its limit. Even the best of the veteran ships had lost their edge through withdrawals of key personnel for the new ships, and all were suffering from exhaustion from the gruelling schedule. Murray passed these warnings to headquarters with his own characteristically emphatic comments, which showed profound understanding of the human side of the war at sea. He singled out the example of HMCS *Orillia*, one of the seasoned corvettes, that had been drained by the posting of its best personnel and by over-employment:

> Lieutenant W.E.S. BRIGGS, R.C.N.R. (Temp.) is one of the more intelligent, experienced and trustworthy of those now commanding H.M.C. Corvettes....
>
> I fear, however, that after return from the present escort service he may be unfit for further duty at sea ... if indeed he is able to complete the voyage.
>
> With a Sub-Lieutenant, R.C.N.V.R. (Temp.) Of two months sea experience as Senior Watchkeeper, backed up by a Sub-Lieutenant, R.C.N.V.R. (Temp.) With no sea experience ... it will be necessary for the Commanding Officer to spend on the bridge as much of every 24 hours as his constitution will stand.
>
> This, coupled with the necessity of acting as Executive Officer of the ship, A/S Control Officer, Gunnery Officer and cypher staff, is more than the best constitution can be expected to support over a period of 28 days, with only a short break of a few hours in harbour in the middle....
>
> We are asking a lot of the morale of an inexperienced crew, to expect them to be happy, and remain fighting fit and aggressive, in a ship in which they know their safety from marine accident alone, and not from any action of the enemy, depends upon the ability of the Captains to remain awake.
>
> It should also be remembered that this fortitude is being expected from men who have seen gasoline tankers disintegrate in five seconds, less than half a mile away from them, and who have also been through

the harrowing experience of seeing men with little lights on their shoulders bobbing up and down in the water and shouting for help....

Only the desperate operational situation which exists off our coast at the present time persuaded me to allow "ORILLIA" [to] proceed ... She is quite unfitted to meet the enemy, and in no other Service would a unit be placed in the firing line before the officers had mastered the use of their weapon. She has been allowed to proceed, however, because her presence will fill a gap in the A/S [anti-submarine] screen visible to the enemy, and her presence may result in saving the lives of many merchant seamen, in which case the sacrifice of the health of one Commanding Officer would be justified.[34]

Headquarters responded in December 1941 with a new scheme for extended workups and employment in coastal duties during a "shakedown" period for newly commissioned ships. By that time the western north Atlantic had been free of U-boat concentrations since early November, as a result of the German high command's decision that the submarines had to interdict Allied supply lines to and within the Mediterranean. However, the Newfoundland command had little respite. Savage winter weather drove many escorts into refit thus increasing pressure on the remainder, and the new training scheme fell by the wayside in the face of a new U-boat assault in the west.

Following the United States' entry into the war, Hitler finally agreed to the inshore assault on North America that Admiral Karl Doenitz, Commander in Chief, U-boats, had long urged. The assault commenced on 12 January 1942. Of the fourteen submarines assigned to Canadian and Newfoundland waters, half hovered off the Avalon Peninsula and the south coast of Newfoundland and began to take a heavy toll of independently routed merchant ships. Within four days, Murray's command started to run local convoys between ports in Newfoundland and the mainland; this was part of the quick response by the RCN that soon brought the Germans to shift the weight of their attack south into unprotected (and more clement) US waters. By the end of the month, twelve escorts had completed a total of nineteen coastal runs, a large new commitment that had to be continued until war's end. [35] That was just the first of the increasing pressures. The Americans now faced a war on two oceans. They were forced to withdraw all but a handful of their escorts from the north Atlantic convoys because they had to escort large numbers of troop convoys in both parts of the world to deploy their land and air forces overseas. Since the main thrust of the U-boats was now overwhelmingly in the western Atlantic, the Royal Navy was able to redeploy escort groups back to Newfoundland to fill the gap, but strains on British resources caused delays and shortfalls in meeting schedules, resulting in a further strain on Murray's command.[36] That strain grew worse throughout the summer as both the British and Canadian transatlantic escort forces had to be thinned out to provide ships for the comprehensive coastal convoy system in the western Atlantic, Caribbean, and Gulf of Mexico.

The effective defences in the west brought the U-boats once again to concentrate in the central ocean during the summer and fall of 1942. The U-boat fleet, with nearly two hundred submarines, was nearly twice as large as it had been in 1941 and, because the Germans had upgraded their cypher machine, the Allies had lost the ability to read the U-boat signals. Yet, because of the new commitments in the western Atlantic, the Newfoundland-based escort groups were once again sailing with only four to six escorts. Nevertheless, Murray's groups achieved what historian Marc Milner termed an "acceptable rate of exchange,"[37] sinking a total of four U-boats while holding losses of merchantmen to acceptable levels during the battles of July through September 1942. In September, just as Murray was leaving St. John's to take up the much larger Atlantic Coast command at Halifax, the Americans expressed concern about the poor state of maintenance of the hard-driven Canadian ships. Characteristically frank, Murray replied, "With the plea from all sides for more and more escorts, ships have been sent to sea as soon as officers could be trained to handle them, and maintenance has taken second place in the training programme." One reason why Murray was optimistic for the future was that "a new type of Corvette Commanding Officer is slowly coming to the fore – the Naval trained R.C.N.V.R. Officer."[38] In such high level professional correspondence, this was a ringing endorsement of Canada's citizen-sailors.

During the fall and winter of 1942, losses to convoys began to skyrocket, bringing searching inquiries into all aspects of the Battle of the Atlantic by the Anglo-American supreme command. The problems of the RCN's rag-tag mid-ocean force came in for close analysis and criticism by Allied experts. This scrutiny also included the anomalous situation whereby Canada was providing nearly half of the north

Atlantic escorts (thirty-eight based at Halifax and thirty-four at St. John's),[39] and a substantial portion of the Maritime aviation support (nine "bomber-reconnaissance" squadrons),[40] but was subordinate to US commands that had only a handful of ships and aircraft deployed. Part of the rationalization of command structures was the creation of the Canadian Northwest Atlantic (CNA) theatre, embracing the waters from south of Nova Scotia to the Arctic and extending seaward to east of Newfoundland. On 30 April 1943, Rear-Admiral Murray received the new appointment Commander-in-Chief, CNA, with control over the Newfoundland-based escorts, as well as those operating from Halifax, and all Canadian and US anti-submarine aviation that operated from bases in Canada and Newfoundland.

Murray initially did not fully grasp how centralized the direction of Atlantic operations had become. He refused to move from his headquarters in the dockyard to the new and greatly expanded combined services operations centre at the RCAF's Eastern Air Command Headquarters, where he and his staff could directly co-ordinate air and sea operations. He explained to Admiral Nelles that his first duty was to be immediately on hand to support his escort captains and ensure effective co-ordination with the merchant navy.[41] Yet once he finally did move to the new facility in the summer of 1943, his instincts for the offensive soon grasped the possibilities.[42] High grade intelligence, much of it based on renewed and almost instant reading of German submarine traffic by US and British code-breakers, was now being rapidly fed from Washington and London to analysts at Naval Service Headquarters in Ottawa; from there it was transmitted to the combined operations centre at Halifax in the form of readily usable predictions of U-boat tracks. After some reconnaissance missions in late 1943 and early 1944, the U-boats, having been defeated in the mid-ocean campaign, once again pushed into Canadian waters. By the summer of 1944, there were five U-boats on station at a time, a scale that matched the inshore offensive of 1942. This effort continued undiminished until the end of the war in May 1945. The submarines were now assisted by the snorkel breathing tube that allowed them to cruise submerged almost indefinitely and thereby deny the Allied Forces the sighting and radar contacts on the surfaced submarines that had been the basis of Allied counter-measures. Murray's headquarters organized extended hunts along the predicted U-boat courses by surface escorts and aircraft that succeeded in so effectively harassing the submarines that they achieved few sinkings in Canadian and Newfoundland waters. Murray's command, moreover, achieved these results with limited resources. To support the Normandy invasion and the campaign to liberate northwest Europe, the RCN shouldered the whole of the burden of north Atlantic escort during the first part of 1944, thereby freeing British groups for service in European waters, and also sent many of the best Canadian groups to that theatre. Murray, because of the heavy demands on his forces for escort of shipping, never had more than two Canadian support groups ("hunter-killer" in US parlance) for offensive searches in his immense theatre.[43]

Even as two U-boats still on patrol in Canadian waters surfaced and surrendered to the Canadian Forces on 10 and 11 May 1945, Murray's career was destroyed. When word of the victory in Europe reached Halifax on 7 May, rioting had broken out and continued the next day. A naval officer and a naval rating died and the city centre was heavily vandalized. Naval personnel were in the forefront of the trouble, and Murray accepted responsibility. On 12 May 1945, the Government temporarily relieved Murray from his command and then retired him with effect from 14 March 1946. In the meantime, a royal commission had concluded that the riots were the result of the failure of Murray's command to maintain discipline.

Perhaps two years before, when Murray had so strongly resisted moving to Eastern Air Command headquarters some two miles from the dockyard, he had feared he would lose the personal touch that was the hallmark of his leadership. Yet the situation in Halifax demanded a great deal more than the influence of a single strong personality. Robert Caldwell has recently argued that the city, as the Navy's principal base, was the stress point for most of the many corners that were cut and things not done in the unheralded expansion of the Navy from 3,500 personnel and six seagoing warships, in 1939, to nearly 100,000 personnel and over 250 seagoing warships by 1945. Base development at Halifax had, from the very beginning, lagged far behind fleet expansion. The city was almost immediately overcrowded as a result of the demands of all three military services and the exponential increase in merchant shipping sustained by the port. In May 1945, there were some 18,000 naval personnel in the establishments at Halifax, many of them poorly housed and many of them transients in manning depots where there was not the cohesion and discipline of a normal ship's company.[44]

In 1954, a British author published an account of Vice-Admiral Sir Max Horton's command of the British forces in the battle of the Atlantic during the latter part of the war.[45] Horton took over in November 1942, one of the blackest periods in the battle, but at a time when greatly increased resources were becoming available that would turn the tide against the U-boats in May 1943. Murray wrote to the British *Royal United Service Institution Journal* to protest that the author gave too little credit to Horton's predecessors in the British Western Approaches command, Admiral Sir Martin Dunbar-Nasmith (1939-41) and especially Admiral Sir Percy Noble (1941-1942). He wrote:

> From this book the uniformed reader ... will, most certainly, not be made to realize that, under the inspiration and guidance of these two former Commanders-in-Chief, the escort forces then available, though extended to their uttermost limits, managed, by sheer guts and will power, to hold the ring against the U-boats for upwards of three years....
>
> Only one who has been intimately connected with this problem can fully realize the frustrations of the "build-up" period. Every available ship was, and had to be, committed to the front line. There was no reserve. Gaps in the ranks caused by enemy action, or by weather damage, had to be filled, or left unfilled....
>
> Health frequently had to be sacrificed to grim necessity, and morale had to be sustained by the inspiration and leadership provided by the Commanders-in-Chief, coupled with the realization throughout all ranks that the organization was good, that they were never called upon to do anything that was not directly to the point, and that their ships and equipment were being used to the fullest possible advantage.[46]

Murray, perhaps subconsciously, was also describing his own contribution.

ENDNOTES

CHAPTER 8

1. Murray was promoted rear-admiral with effect from 2 December 1941.
2. Admiralty to CNS [chief of the naval staff] Canada, 1520B/24 May 1941, "Personal from First Sea Lord," Ottawa, National Archives of Canada [NAC], RG 24, vol. 3892, NSS 1033-6-1, part 1.
3. NSHQ [Naval Service Headquarters] to Admiralty, 2108Z/21 May 1941.
4. Admiralty to Admiral Commanding Western Approaches et al, message in three parts, 1909B/1920B/1939B/23 May 1941.
5. Commander-in-Chief, Western Approaches to NSHQ, 1707B/31 May 1941.
6. The overview of the history of the Royal Canadian Navy and the Battle of the Atlantic in this chapter draws principally on two pioneering works by Marc Milner, *North Atlantic Run: The Royal Canadian Navy and the Battle for the Convoys* (Toronto: University of Toronto Press, 1985); *The U-Boat Hunters: the Royal Canadian Navy and the Offensive against Germany's Submarines* (Toronto: University of Toronto Press, 1994); and Roger Sarty, *Canada and the Battle of the Atlantic* (Montreal: Art Global and the Department of National Defence, 1998).
7. William Reaveley Glover, "Officer Training and the Quest for Operational Efficiency in the Royal Canadian Navy 1939-1945" (PhD thesis, University of London, 1998), 30.
8. The best account of Murray's career is the transcript of an interview W.A.B. Douglas conducted with the Admiral in 1970, and the Admiral's comments in Murray to Douglas, 23 October 1970, National Defence Headquarters, Directorate of History and Heritage [DHH], biography files, L.W. Murray. James M. Cameron, *Murray The Martyred Admiral* (Hantsport, NS: Lancelot Press, 1980), largely based on these sources, is hagiography, but adds some information.
9. Gilbert Norman Tucker, *The Naval Service of Canada: Its Official History*, Vol. I: *Origins and Early Years* (Ottawa: King's Printer,

1952), chapter 11; Michael L. Hadley and Roger Sarty, *Tin-Pots and Pirate Ships: Canadian Naval Forces and German Sea Raiders 1880-1918* (Montreal and Kingston: McGill-Queen's University Press, 1991).

10. Hadley and Sarty, *Tin-Pots*, 71-2.

11. Nelles diary, 22-3 August 1939, DHH, biography files, P.W. Nelles.

12. Mackenzie King diary, 24 August 1939, NAC, William Lyon Mackenzie King papers, MG 26 J13.

13. Glover, "Officer Training," chapters 3-4.

14. David R. Murray, ed. *Documents on Canadian External Relations, 1939-1941:* Vol. 8, Part II (Ottawa: Department of External Affairs, 1976), 163-83; Chief of the Naval Staff and Minister of National Defence for Naval Services, "Operational Plan of Royal Canadian Navy to implement Joint Canadian-United States Basic Defence Plan, 1940," 17 December 1940, NAC, RG 24, vol. 11129, file "Joint Defence Plan 1940."

15. *Defeat of the Enemy Attack on Shipping 1939-1945: A Study of Policy and Operations.* Vol. 1B: *(Plans and Table)* (Naval Staff History Second World War)(London: Admiralty, 1957), plan 55.

16. Murray to Naval Secretary, DND, 27 March 1941, NAC, RG 24, vol. 5632, NS 30-26-2.

17. Admiralty to Flag Officer Commanding 3rd Battle Squadron et al, signal 1936/15 April 1941, NAC, RG 24, vol. 3972, NSS 1048-48-1 part 6.

18. Director of anti-submarine warfare to assistant chief of the naval staff (F), 27 March 1941, Kew, England, Public Record Office [PRO], ADM 199/935.

19. Jones to Commanding Officer Atlatnic Coast [COAC], "H.M.C. CORVETTES – DISPOSITION," 19 May 1941, NAC, RG 24, vol. 6797, NSS 8375-330.

20. Keate, nd, "The Royal Canadian Navy in Newfoundland, 1940-1944," pp. 9-11, DHH, NHS 8000, "HMCS Avalon (Base)."

21. CCCS to NSHQ, 1012B/28 May 1941, DHH, NHS 8440-70 Newfoundland Escort Force; Commodore Commanding Newfoundland, report of proceedings for June 1941, DHH, NSS 1000-5-20, part 1.

22. Ibid.; see also DHH 88/1 mfm, reel 5, files for OB 331, OB 332, OB 333, OB 334.

23. Admiralty to NSHQ, 1612B/12 [July 1941], NAC, RG 24, vol. 11941, "15 Group 11-Organisation."

24. Captain (D) Newfoundland, "Organisation of the Newfoundland Escort Force," 27 July 1941, DHH, NHS 8440-70 "Newfoundland Escort Force"; CCNF war diary, July 1941, DHH, NSS 1000-5-20, part 1.
25. Translations of logs, 9-11 September 1941, of *U-81*, *U-82*, *U-84*, *U-85*, *U-202*, *U-207*, *U-432*, *U-433*, *U-652* by Jan Drent, DHH 83/665.
26. Captain (D) Newfoundland to CCNF, "Secret Hand Message," 1733Z/4 September 1941, CCNF to Captain (D) Newfoundland, "Secret Hand Message," 1856/4 September 1941, staff officer (operations) to Chambly, nd, CCNF to Chambly, Moose Jaw, 1858/4 September 1941, DHH, A.F. Pickard papers, 80/125, file 7.
27. Reid to Murray, "Most Secret and Personal," 25 August 1941, NAC, RG 24 Acc 83-4/167, vol. 218, NSS 1400-WPL 51.
28. For example, Murray to Naval Secretary, 14 August 1941, NAC, RG 24, vol. 11929, file 00-220-3-6 and Murray to Reid, "Personal and Most Secret," 15 October 1941, NAC, RG 24, vol. 11979, file 51-15 (quoted).
29. Arkansas to Commander-in-chief, US Atlantic Fleet [Cinclant], 0030/11 September 1941, file 1-20 September 1941, Washington, National Archives and Record Administration [NARA], RG 313, Entry NHC 69, file 1-20 September 1941, messages to Cinclant, box 1.
30. Murray interview, p 42.
31. Davis to Commander-in-chief Western Approaches, "Report of Attack on U Boat by H.M.C.S. *Columbia* on 15th October, 1941," 18 October 1941, PRO, ADM 199/1130; *U-553* log, 15-16 October 1941, translation by Jan Drent, DHH 83/665.
32. Griffin, "Report of attack on submarine by H.M.C.S. *Pictou*," 17 October 1941, PRO, ADM 199/1130; *U-568* log, 17 October 1941, translation by Jan Drent, DHH 83/665.
33. Anthony Griffin, "A Naval Officer's War: Episode Two," *Starshell*, Vol. 7, Summer 1999, 13.
34. Murray to Naval Secretary, Naval Service Headquarters, "Relief of trained officers and men from H.M.C. Ships of the N.E.F.," 6 November 1941, NAC, RG 24, vol. 11929, file 00-220-3-6.
35. Flag Officer Newfoundland, "Operational Report January, 1942," DHH, NSS 1000-5-20 part 1.
36. For example, Commander in Chief United States Atlantic Fleet, "Administrative History of the U.S. Atlantic Fleet in World War II. Vol. II: Commander Task Force Twenty-Four," 1946, U.S. Naval Historical Center microfilm, 128.

37. Milner, *North Atlantic Run*, 129.

38. Murray to Secretary, Naval Board, 10 November 1942, NARA, RG 313 Red, CTF 24, Confidential, 1942, box 8810, file A3-1.

39. Plans Division, NSHQ, "History of North Atlantic Convoy Escort Organization and Canadian Participation Therein, September, 1939 to April, 1943," 1 May 1943, DHH, 81/520/1650-1 "Plans."

40. W.A.B. Douglas, *The Creation of a National Air Force: The Official History of the Royal Canadian Air Force*, Vol. II (Toronto: University of Toronto Press and the Department of National Defence, 1986), 376.

41. Murray to Nelles, 30 November 1942, DHH 193.009(D14).

42. See, for example, Murray to commander Task Force 24, 8 April 1942, NARA, RG 313 Red, Commander-in-Chief Atlantic Fleet, 1942, Secret, box 163, file A16-3(AS) which makes an early proposal to use intelligence estimates of U-boat courses for air searches.

43. Douglas, *Creation of a National Air Force*, chapters 16-17; see also Roger Sarty, "Ultra, Air Power, and the Second Battle of the St. Lawrence, 1944" in *To Die Gallantly: The Battle of the Atlantic*, Timothy J. Runyan and Jan M. Copes, eds. (Boulder, Colorado: Westview Press, 1994), 186-209.

44. R.H. Caldwell, "The VE Day Riots in Halifax, 7-8 May 1945" *The Northern Mariner*, X (January 2000), 3-20.

45. W.S. Chalmers, *Max Horton and the Western Approaches: A Biography of Admiral Sir Max Kennedy Horton, G.C.B., D.S.O.* (London: Hodder and Stoughton, 1954).

46. Rear-Admiral L.W. Murray (Retd.), "Max Horton and the Western Approaches: A Comment," *Royal United Service Institution Journal*, (May 1955), 280-1.

THE POST-WAR WORLD

General Sir Sam Hughes stepping off a torpedo boat on the coast of France
on his way to visit the Front, August 1916.

General Sir Arthur Currie (left) with Field Marshal Sir Douglas Haig,
February 1918.

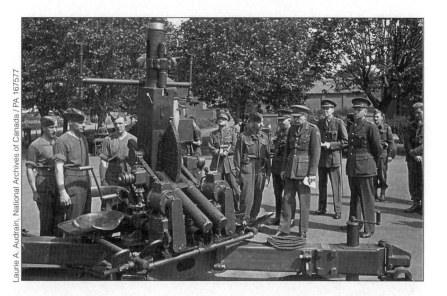

Inspection of an anti-aircraft gun of the Royal Canadian Artillery by
General A.G.L. McNaughton, Colchester, England, 9 July 1941.

General A.G.L. McNaughton addressing personnel of the
Royal Canadian Scottish Regiment, Sicily, August 1943.

General H.D.G. Crerar, 1943.

General H.D.G. Crerar (left) and Lieutenant-General E.L.M. Burns in Italy, 1944.

General Sir Bernard Montgomery imparts final words to
Lieutenant-General G.G. Simonds (standing beside jeep) prior to leaving
2nd Canadian Corps Headquarters, France, 24 July 1944.

Lieutenant-General Guy Simonds observes the Canadian Grenadier Guards
crossing the Seine River, Elboeuf, France, 28 August 1944.

Field Marshall Montgomery (left) with General Crerar,
Cleve, Germany, 23 February 1945.

Winston Churchill overlooking the Rhine Crossing, vicinity of Krannenburg,
Germany, 4 March 1944. He is accompanied by (left to right)
General Crerar, Lieutenant-General Simonds, Field Marshal Alan Brooke,
and Field Marshal Montgomery.

General Foulkes (right) and Lieutenant-General Murchie near the tail of a
German submarine, Ljmuiden, Netherlands, 25 May 1945.

Rear-Admiral L.W. Murray (extreme left) presenting awards to crew members of H.M.C.S. St. Croix, which sank the German submarine U-90, 24 July 1942, St. John's Newfoundland.

Vice-Admiral H.T.W. Grant (left) handing over the post of Chief of the Naval Staff to Vice-Admiral E.R. Mainguy, Ottawa, Ontario, 1 December 1951.

Air Marshall Wilfred Curtis, Chief of Air Staff, climbing out of an F82 aircraft during Exercise Sweetbriar, 23 February 1950.

Air Marshall Roy Slemon, Chief of Air Staff, being checked out on a CF-100 aircraft at RCAF Station Uplands.

Lieutenant-Colonel J.A. Dextraze, Commanding Officer,
2nd Battalion Royal 22e Regiment,
Korea, 9 November 1951.

Lieutenant-General Allard, Commander Force Mobile Command, inspects a
guard of honour composed of men of 4 RCHA on his arrival at
Camp Petawawa, Ontario, to formally accept its inclusion into
Mobile Command, 14 March 1966.

Brigadier-General Lewis MacKenzie (second from left)
at the Sarajevo Airport, 1992.

Brigadier-General Romeo Dallaire (left) and Argentinean Major Miguel Martin (Desk Officer in New York) in discussion with members of the Organization of African Unity (OAU) observer group and a rebel brigade commander (camouflage jacket), Rwanda, August 1994.

General John de Chastelain, Chief of the Defence Staff, in Visoko, Bosnia Hercegovina, December 1994.

CHAPTER 9

VICE-ADMIRAL HAROLD GRANT:
FATHER OF THE POST-WAR ROYAL CANADIAN NAVY

Captain (N) Wilfred G.D. Lund

VICE-ADMIRAL Harold Taylor Wood Grant, CBE, DSO, CD, took command of the Royal Canadian Navy (RCN) as the fifth Chief of the Naval Staff (CNS) on 1 September 1947 when it was at its lowest ebb of the post-war period. His predecessor, Vice-Admiral Howard Emerson ("Rastus") Reid, had essentially been given a caretaker appointment. Reid had never aspired to be CNS and accepted the office reluctantly upon the sudden death in 1946 of the incumbent, Vice-Admiral G.C. Jones. He had agreed to stay on only until the end of the transitional period of the "interim force." This was a period of drift characterized by an ill-defined defence policy and financial stringency. Grant was the natural successor to Jones, and his appointment brought renewed energy, confidence, and a presence to the office. Most importantly, he brought strong leadership, decisiveness, and a sense of direction.[1] In the eyes of the pre-war RCN cohort he was a hero. To junior staff officers at Naval Service Headquarters (NSHQ) Vice-Admiral Grant was "a gentleman, considerate, a cheerful presence with soft manner of speaking and understanding of junior officers."[2] He was looked up to and respected by all who served under him.

Grant faced the daunting task of rebuilding the peacetime Canadian Navy into an effective force with recruits from a society and for a nation that had both been transformed substantially by the Second World War. During his four year tenure, he would adopt Anti-Submarine Warfare (ASW) as the Navy's primary role and inaugurate the construction of a new fleet of Canadian designed destroyer escorts. These decisions set the course for a rapid expansion of the Navy to meet the challenges of the Cold War and large commitments to the North Atlantic Treaty Organization (NATO). Grant also had to overcome severe personnel problems and reorient the administrative and cultural structure of the Navy to meet the demand for change. With these accomplishments, Vice-Admiral Harold Grant became the father of the modern post-war Royal Canadian Navy.

Harold Grant was born in Halifax in 1899, the youngest of six children. His father, the Honourable MacCallum Grant, owned a thriving fishing and shipping business and was a powerful force in the Halifax business community and society. Young Harold was brought up in the conservative Scots-Presbyterian tradition of loyalty, hard work, and self-reliance and, as in many Nova Scotia families, a strong affection for the British connection.[3] The Grants were members of the Halifax aristocracy, and their stately residence, "Armdale," possessed spacious gardens and a sweeping view of the Northwest Arm, which was their playground. The Grant boys learned to love the sea and became accomplished sailors. MacCallum Grant, a great admirer of the German system of education, took the entire family to Germany for two years where the boys studied at Heidelberg College.[4] The family returned to Halifax in 1911. Canada had established the Canadian Naval Service in 1910, and Harold's elder brother, John, joined the first term of cadets at the new Royal Naval College of Canada (RNCC), located in the Halifax dockyard. Harold Grant joined the fourth term at RNCC in 1914, the same year that his father was appointed to be the Lieutenant Governor of Nova Scotia.[5]

Harold became imbued, as was Leonard Murray and all who attended the RNCC, with the traditions of the Royal Navy (RN) and its credo of service above personal consideration. He came under the influence of the remarkable mentor, Commander Nixon, who encouraged a strong sense of camaraderie in the cadets. As a result, an enduring loyalty to graduates of the RNCC would be a notable characteristic throughout Grant's career. Grant, small and frail as a boy, was often ill as a cadet but bright, quick-witted, and determined. The RNCC journal, *Sea Breezes,* reported that Grant was "perhaps the finest example of what grit and will can do."[6] "Character and determination" appear frequently in performance reports by his commanding officers.[7] He passed out of the RNCC with a first-class certificate in 1917 and continued his training as a midshipman in RN "big ships" until the end of World War I. He saw no action.

Between the wars, Harold Grant's career followed the standard pattern for RCN officers. He took his specialist navigation and staff training with the Royal Navy. Sea experience was obtained in both RCN and RN ships, which included four years in British battleships.[8] He also served in staff positions at Naval Service Headquarters (NSHQ) as Director of Plans and, later, the Naval Reserves. With the RN, he gained valuable experience in charge of ships' movements on the staff of the Commander-in-Chief, Atlantic Fleet. While Grant impressed the Royal Navy as a determined, hard-working and loyal officer, he was rated only as an above average performer. However, in his own navy, both Leonard Murray and G.C. Jones considered Grant worthy of accelerated promotion and he made Commander in 1935, ahead of some of his seniors.[9]

By this time his leadership ability and confidence were well developed. Harold Grant had acquired a reputation as a solid professional officer and a gentleman of modesty and humour. Physically, he developed into a strong man who excelled in sports. He handled both officers and men easily and was very popular socially. His connections as one of the Haligonian aristocracy enabled him to move in the right social circles wherever he served. Grant enjoyed a fun time, a good party, and could be counted on to lead the "run ashore." Some stories became legend, such as receiving the "Displeasure of the Department" as a reprimand for harassing a honeymooning couple at a hotel in Chester, Nova Scotia.[10] The new bride turned out to be the secretary to the Deputy Minister of Defence. This incident merely added to his growing reputation. Grant married Christine Mitchell of Halifax who became a universal favourite with both his contemporaries and juniors as an elegant and charming hostess and lady.[11] However, Grant's decisiveness could be over-bearing and on one occasion earned him a caution from the Chief of Naval Staff, Percy Nelles, who thought his rapid promotion may have gone to his head.[12] That notwithstanding, Nelles sent him in command of HMCS *Skeena* in 1938. He was appointed ashore as the Chief of Staff to Captain Reid, Commanding Officer Atlantic Coast, shortly after war was declared.

Grant served with exceptional distinction during the war and emerged as one of Canada's most decorated naval officers.[13] He was promoted to Captain in 1940 and appointed to NSHQ in the critical position of Director of Naval Personnel, where he supervised the initial rapid wartime expansion of the Navy. In 1942, his was the cautionary voice that recommended checking growth in order to consolidate training. He was overruled, owing to the critical need for escorts.[14] Grant was Captain (D) in St. John's, Newfoundland, for barely six months when appointed to command the older Royal Navy cruiser HMS *Diomede* in March 1943. This appointment had been arranged with the British Admiralty by the CNS, Vice-Admiral Nelles, who wanted to give RCN officers experience in command of "big ships," anticipating the eventual acquisition of cruisers by Canada. Three months later, Grant was re-appointed from *Diomede* to the command of the HMS *Enterprise*. On 28 December 1943, *Enterprise* and HMS *Glasgow* engaged in a spirited gun action against a force of eleven enemy destroyers, of which three were sunk and others damaged.[15] For this victory, Grant was awarded the Distinguished Service Order (DSO), an achievement doubly unique in the annals of the RCN in that it was immediate and while in command of an RN cruiser. This is the stuff of which legends are made.

Enterprise also participated in the D-Day landing operations where Grant earned a Mentioned in Dispatches (MID) for leading the assault force to "Utah Beach" and bombardment operations. Grant was in action again on 25 June 1944 in a bombardment of Cherbourg, where *Enterprise* engaged enemy shore batteries at close range in support of US Army ground forces. In the intense exchange of fire with large calibre enemy guns, he was wounded. For meritorious service in this engagement, Grant was awarded the American Bronze Star Medal by the Government of the United States. Common in all his citations for gallantry is mention of Grant's "exemplary leadership and aggressive determination." In early 1945, he was commissioned, assumed command of the cruiser HMCS *Ontario* for the Canadian Navy, and took the ship to the Pacific, but was too late to see action. His final wartime distinction was an appointment as a Commander of the Military Division of the Most Excellent Order of the British Empire (CBE) for "exceptionally competent seamanship and gallantry at sea, and administrative ability ashore."[16] His accomplishments made Harold Grant a hero in the eyes of his juniors, such as Harry DeWolf and Ken Dyer, but his illustrious war record is little known by Canadians because it was achieved in command of Royal Naval units.

Grant became a pivotal figure in building the post-war Navy. He was appointed in February 1946 to NSHQ as Chief of Administration Services and Supply (CNAS) as a Rear-Admiral. This was nominally the position of comptroller but filled by an officer of the executive branch who was also a member of the Naval Board. He was the second most senior officer to the CNS, Vice-Admiral Reid, and would succeed him. Grant was pragmatic and had a powerful influence on policy, but he also had ingrained ideas resulting from his pre-war RN training and orientation. Rear-Admiral Tony Storrs commented that Harold Grant "was very emotionally oriented toward the Royal Navy and very much inclined to the imperial idea."[17] Grant, initially, also exhibited a preference for promoting pre-war regular officers of "pure laine" antecedents over officers from a reservist entry. Also, He was of the old school that believed naval officers did not need formal staff training.

However, as a true professional Grant was open to change, sometimes radical, if he could be persuaded that it was in the best interests of the RCN or that it just made good sense.[18] But on occasion, Grant had to be directed by the Minister of National Defence to implement policies that Grant opposed as not being good for the RCN. He readily embraced the new commitments to NATO and the ASW role for the RCN. He was particularly vigorous in his efforts to improve professional opportunities, conditions of service, and welfare for the sailors and their families. Rear-Admiral Storrs believed that Grant made the difficult transition to an American orientation during his tenure as CNS, which had decisive long-term consequences for the Royal Canadian Navy.[19] This was particularly evident in Grant's decisions to sustain naval aviation, to introduce USN standards of habitability in ships, and to adopt USN tactical doctrine and communications procedures.

In short, Vice-Admiral Grant was faced with the Herculean challenge of rebuilding the Navy. He told the National Defence College, "the size of the Fleet including ships in reserve is hopelessly inadequate to meet the most modest commitment of the Naval role."[20] The active fleet was reduced to a skeleton force of eight partially manned ships in commission. Only the carrier, HMCS *Warrior*, had a full peacetime complement. Plans for a balanced fleet based on two carrier groups, one for either coast, had been abandoned owing to cost.[21] The authorized complement of the "interim force" navy was 7,500 officers and men, 25 percent below the nominal ceiling of 10,000. The number on strength in 1947, was actually 6,814 and wastage was outstripping gains.[22] Morale was low and plummeting. The Defence Minister, Brooke Claxton, was reticent on the issue of increased pay and other improvements to conditions of service, such as more dependent housing for married men.[23] In this pre-Cold War intermission, Claxton's strategic policy relegated the Navy to an ASW training role. Moreover, the RCN lacked a clear mission in defence of North America, as had been identified for the other two services. An increasing concern for Grant was the impact of the government's integration policies on the traditional organization and structure of the Navy. The Navy itself was pursuing a rather ill-defined general purpose training programme, owing to the instability caused by personnel restrictions, a burgeoning training load, and uncertainty in funding. Grant's task was daunting.

Poor conditions of service and inadequate provision for the welfare of sailors and their dependents were so serious that achieving improvement became Vice-Admiral Grant's first priority. The main problems were poor pay and accommodations on board and ashore. He directed his Vice-Chief of the Naval Staff, Rear-Admiral Frank Houghton, to conduct an extensive study of the spectrum of personnel problems. The result was a comprehensive memorandum by Houghton entitled, "The Morale of the Navy."[24] It was based on staff reports from the fleet and contained twenty-six major recommendations aimed at improving training, morale, and conditions of service. These addressed the major complaints, such as inadequate pay and accommodation, but also pointed to the poor wartime training of junior officers and senior non-commissioned officers in the administration and care of their men that resulted in poor leadership and ineffectiveness of the divisional system.

"The Morale of the Navy" indicated how worried senior officers were about the personnel situation and their determination to find solutions. The document is an interesting admixture, reflecting the old pre-war RCN paternalism, on the one hand, but also a recognition of the need for change towards a navy better suited to Canadian circumstances, on the other. There is in "The Morale of the Navy" a substantial understanding that new conditions existed in the Navy as well as in Canadian society, and that the one must replicate the other as far as the service could allow. There is also an admission that the Navy had got into bad habits during the war, and this was having a telling effect on discipline and morale. Demonstrating a radical shift in thinking, the document suggested that the United States Navy provided the model for the post-war RCN.

"The Morale of the Navy" stands as a seminal document that provided a blueprint for implementing a progressive personnel policy in the post-war RCN. Recommendations included substantial changes to bring the Navy more in line with Canadian society. Initiatives to improve morale were establishing welfare committees in ships and revitalizing the divisional system.[25] Major recommendations to improve conditions of service were: increased pay, more accommodation for married and single men ashore, assisted travel leave for single men, income tax relief, improved habitability in ships, and comprehensive leadership and divisional training for junior officers and senior rates. Vice-Admiral Grant formally submitted the Navy's morale concerns with his recommendations to the Minister of National Defence, Brooke Claxton, in October 1947.[26] The problem was that many of the recommendations required increased government funding that was not forthcoming. The consequence was continued under-manning of ships that created instability, low morale, and unrest. Regardless, under the direction of the Naval Board, many of the major recommendations were being prepared for implementation or in train when a series of "incidents" occurred on board RCN ships in 1949 that led to an investigation called the Mainguy inquiry. The point is that Grant was fully apprised of the RCN's personnel problems in 1947, brought them to the attention of his political masters, and took initiatives within his power to correct them. His extensive remedial programme has never been acknowledged.[27]

In 1948, Grant commissioned Commodore Adrian Hope, a term mate from the RNCC, to conduct a follow-up survey of conditions in the fleet. Hope's interviews largely confirmed Houghton's conclusions but put a human face on the problems.[28] Hope's major proposals pertained to reorganization of the rank and trade structure to properly classify and compensate sailors for their technical naval skills. The Navy's problem was that a Claxton policy to integrate the forces' trade structure was based on a civilian industrial model that fit the Army and RCAF but did not recognize traditional naval trades. Vice-Admiral Grant considered this to be an injustice of the highest order, one having a severe effect on morale in the RCN. He was very aggressive on this issue and told Claxton that as a consequence, "the experienced and good Executive [Seaman] Petty Officer is leaving the Navy because there is no incentive to remain. He is irreplaceable and as a result the efficiency of our ships as a fighting unit [sic] is being dangerously undermined."[29]

This issue set the tone for a confrontational relationship with Claxton. Grant also opposed Claxton's initiative to create tri-service colleges to train officers of the three services. Grant argued, correctly as history would prove, that Claxton's Canadian Service Colleges scheme would provide neither adequately trained nor sufficient officers to satisfy the RCN's requirements. Claxton had already concluded, through his previous dealings with Vice-Admiral Reid, that the senior naval officers were "an extra ordinarily homogeneous group" and spoke with one voice in opposing his integration policies.[30] Claxton, the ardent nationalist, formed the opinion that this highly conservative group was out of step with Canadian society, and this notion prejudiced him against his senior naval advisers. It certainly reinforced his belief that an integrated officer training plan was needed to bring the naval officer corps into the Canadian mainstream. Grant was uncompromising and fought much more aggressively than Reid for the Navy. Significantly, after his retirement, Harold Grant confided that failure to seek compromise with Claxton on certain issues was unproductive for the RCN, and if he had to do it again he would proceed differently.[31]

In retrospect, Grant's opposition to some aspects of administrative integration was entirely justified. Claxton was a micro-manager whose schemes produced an unworkable committee system that eventually created gridlock at National Defence Headquarters (NDHQ). Moreover, Claxton's initiative – to achieve symmetry in the rank structure of the three services to facilitate financial accounting – forced the RCN to adopt two new non-commissioned ranks that were not required and that resulted in severe dislocation and disharmony on board ships. The simultaneous promotion of every senior leading seaman in the Navy to fill the new rank of petty officer second class created a leadership vacuum in the junior ratings messes that led to trouble in 1949. The Mainguy inquiry concluded that lack of supervision at the junior level was a contributory factor in causing the incidents and observed that "the revised rating structure [was] an unfortunate and reprehensible error."[32]

It is evident that by the beginning of 1948, Grant had checked the drift that characterized Reid's tenure and was forging ahead on a broad front. He advised a meeting of senior officers that the RCN would adopt the ASW role and directed that plans be drawn up for a new anti-submarine destroyer escort to be built in Canada.[33] The ship was to meet North American standards and habitability and be modelled on the USN. United States Naval tactical doctrine and signals publications were to be adopted by the RCN with provision to retain the RN system in some circumstances. Ships were to implement welfare committees that would allow free discussion by non-commissioned ranks of issues pertaining to morale and welfare on board. Grant was progressive in accepting staff recommendations to adapt the organization of both Naval Service Headquarters and branch functional structures to the new administrative and technical environment that was developing. The Naval Board began to meet weekly and took on a more businesslike atmosphere. The Naval Board also pursued the objective of devolving more responsibilities to the commands. This included the principle of establishing a separate command to administer the naval divisions.[34]

Vice-Admiral Grant also approved the creation of new branches to develop and consolidate the new skills and emerging technology needed by the post-war Navy. The TAS (Torpedo/Anti-Submarine), Electrical and Ordnance Branches were approved in November 1947. A most significant step in deciding the future character of the RCN was the creation, under Grant, of a Supply Branch on the USN model in conjunction with a decision to adopt the USN system for supply and material management.[35] He also approved the establishment of the Naval Secretariat Branch responsible for administration. The existing supply system was an inefficient adaptation of the RN model with responsibility split between the Vice Chief of the Naval Staff (VCNS) and the Chief of Naval Technical Services (CNTS). Grant accepted arguments from staff officers that adopting the USN model would achieve greater efficiency, North American orientation, and a superior uniformed personnel structure.[36] Grant was persuaded, Rear-Admiral Charles Dillon recalled, on the strength of the benefits for the RCN.[37]

While improving conditions of services to make the RCN an attractive career would reap benefits in the long term, Grant had to manage the Navy to ensure its survival in the short term. His problem was not a shortage of ships but of trained personnel. The Navy was actually five times larger than before the war, but the majority of personnel were wartime volunteers whose training had been indifferent and who lacked any depth of experience. Moreover, as Vice-Admiral Harry DeWolf observed, the best "hostilities only" personnel had gone back to civilian life, and the quality of many who transferred to the regular force was mediocre.[38] Grant's personal preference was that the RCN should rebuild from scratch, but the dye was cast when he became CNS.[39]

Wastage was cutting into gains, and there were insufficient personnel available to man the minimum number of ships to execute basic training requirements. Rear-Admiral Houghton reported to CNS that "the Navy as presently constituted is far too small even for its modest role as a nucleus for expansion in an emergency."[40] He persuaded Grant that the complement of the Navy had to be increased. Grant, therefore, made persistent representation to the Defence Minister and won a concession from the Government in October 1948 to allow the RCN to recruit to a ceiling of 9,047 personnel.[41] This decision coincided with the announcement of the government decision to undertake the St. Laurent class programme for the construction of seven anti-submarine escort vessels.[42] This favourable decision was influenced as much by the Berlin blockade as by Grant's persuasive efforts.[43] The blockade inaugurated the Cold War and led directly to the establishment of NATO. To meet projected expansion, the RCN reopened HMCS *Cornwallis* in 1949, as its new entry recruit training centre, and also commissioned HMCS *Shearwater* as its operational and training base for naval aviation.

The initiatives taken by Vice-Admiral Grant to improve conditions of service and morale either lacked government financial support or could not be implemented swiftly enough to quell growing unrest in the fleet and avert incidents of mass insubordination. Vigorous efforts had failed to make a significant dent in the backlog of trainees, and instability prevailed.[44] The situation was exacerbated owing to new manning commitments required to commission HMCS *Shearwater* and HMCS *Cornwallis*.[45] In spite of these challenges, an ambitious operational training programme, reminiscent of the pre-war era, was planned. A major spring exercise entailed the transit of the Panama Canal by West Coast ships to join East Coast ships for a joint exercise with the RN's America and West Indies Squadron in the Caribbean. The Pacific Squadron was comprised of *Ontario, Athabaskan* (II), *Crescent,* and *Antigonish,* and the Atlantic Squadron of *Magnificent, Nootka,* and *Haida.* The Pacific Squadron sailed from Esquimalt on 28 January 1949 without *Crescent,* which was being despatched instead to China on a special mission. Incidents of mass insubordination occurred on board three of the ships within the period of one month – 26 February on *Athabaskan* (II) at Manzanillo, 15 March on *Crescent* at Nanking, and 20 March on *Magnificent,* the carrier, in the Caribbean.[46]

There was a known environment of discontent in the fleet; a similar "incident," essentially a work stoppage, had occurred on board HMCS *Ontario* in 1947. It had been handled by removing the Executive Officer who was the object of the men's complaints. The Navy mishandled the *Ontario* incident by removing the Executive Officer and not punishing the perpetrators. This set a precedent. This new series of incidents caught the Navy completely by surprise and sent shock waves through NSHQ and the Government. The *Crescent* incident was reported in a Vancouver paper, making political intervention inevitable. Grant had previously warned Claxton of the possibility of paid agents operating in the fleet, and now a fear of subversive activity gained hold.[47] A commission of inquiry was appointed by Claxton to flush this out and determine the circumstances that prompted these demonstrations of mass insubordination. Vice-Admiral Grant wanted it to be an internal inquiry, but Claxton believed that it must be public. Upon Grant's insistence, the president of a three-man commission was Rear-Admiral Rollo Mainguy. Claxton selected the two civilian commissioners, Leonard Brockington and Louis Audette, both personal acquaintances and lawyers. Audette tried unsuccessfully to persuade Claxton that the commission should be composed entirely of civilians.[48] Audette had been a Royal Canadian Navy Volunteer Reserve (RCNVR) officer during the war and commanded two ships during the Battle of the Atlantic. He had a personal agenda based on his dislike of certain officers of the pre-war RCN cohort, particularly Vice-Admiral Grant. Audette became a self-proclaimed champion of rights for the lower deck and critic of the traditional hierarchical structure of the Navy.

The Mainguy inquiry, as it became known, was a seminal experience for the RCN. The objective of the inquiry was to find out and report to the Minister what had happened on the occasion of the incidents. Based on its conclusions, the inquiry was to make recommendations to improve conditions of service, relations between officers and men, and the method for the ventilation of grievances in the RCN. At the inquiry another concern became apparent: the Canadianization of the Navy through the adoption of symbols and the repatriation of training from the RN, particularly of officers.

The inquiry received evidence in confidence from 238 witnesses after a broad invitation to appear or submit written briefs was extended to the fleet.[49] Vice-Admiral Grant spent an entire morning giving evidence before the inquiry. His testimony fills fifty typed pages and covers the full spectrum of issues.[50] He opened his testimony stating, "I think that this is probably one of the best things that could have happened to the Navy and it is probably just as well it happened now."[51] He went on to say that the action taken in removing the Executive Officer after the incident in *Ontario* was a mistake that provided a pattern for subsequent incidents, and he accepted his responsibility for his part in that decision. What emerges from a fair and balanced reading of all Grant's evidence is a profile of a knowledgeable and highly professional naval chief who was exceptionally well-informed of all the Navy's problems and deeply concerned for the future and welfare of the RCN. Moreover, Grant had plans, either in place or underway, to correct deficiencies and to improve the men's welfare and conditions of service. We also see a CNS who was very conservative, reactionary, hard-nosed, vocal, and highly opposed to initiatives that he believed were not in the best interests of the RCN.

He believed that the Navy had expanded far too quickly after the war, approximately 600 percent, in order to retain its share of the defence budget. In doing so, the Navy had outstripped its resources in its ability to train both officers and men and had taken in many poorly equipped wartime volunteers to fill the complement.[52] Grant stated that, "These fellows have all the guts in the world, but they never had any training to condition their minds for service in peacetime, which is pretty onerous and certainly entails sacrifices in family life and probably finances far beyond that which is accepted by the ordinary fellow ashore, particularly in the post-war period when business is booming."[53] The CNS told the commissioners that fiscal restraint by government and opposition and red tape from bureaucrats had prevented the Naval Board from implementing a large agenda designed to improve conditions of service and alleviate the plight of naval families.

However, Grant's blunt testimony to the Board of Commission was not examined in an objective way by everyone. Following the lead of commission member Louis Audette, historians have seized narrowly upon Grant's angry response to a blatantly provocative line of questioning involving the use of distinctively Canadian symbols on naval uniforms that Audette himself admitted later was a mistake.[54] Grant's comments that the sailors could sew "Canada badges on the seats of their trousers" and that "Canada makes enough damn noise in this world without doing anything about it" permitted Audette to accentuate the negative and later portray Grant as vulgar, anachronistic, and unpatriotic. Examining the context, it is evident that the basis for Grant's rancour stemmed from the infamous incident where the Canadian government under Mackenzie King gave the sailors the opportunity to vote themselves out of the war in the Pacific.[55] The ship's company of HMCS *Uganda*, Canada's only warship to see action in the Pacific theatre, voted three to one not to volunteer for further combat duty.[56] Volunteer reservists made up most of the negative majority. In mid-July 1945, *Uganda* left American, British, and Australian naval ships facing Japanese kamikaze attacks and sailed for home. The disgrace of deserting brothers in arms thoroughly rankled the pre-war RCN professionals and was never forgotten by officers like Rear-Admiral Bill Landymore, who was *Uganda's* Gunnery Officer.[57] The debacle was fresh in Grant's mind in 1949.

Grant, who was compelled to conduct a similar vote on the *Ontario* but achieved a different result, implied that this government policy reflected a laissez-faire attitude endemic in society that was at the root of the problem in teaching young Canadian sailors to accept discipline and to do their duty. He stated, "I cannot see how any person serving at sea today dare put up the word 'Canada' until he is fit or has shown himself fit to man a ship and take responsibility."[58] Grant was in fact arguing vociferously for pride in country, ethical behaviour, and professionalism. It is hardly surprising that he expected the Navy he commanded to meet his own high standards. Harold Grant was respected because he would not demand of others what he did not demand of himself. On the other hand, Audette believed the right to wear Canadian symbols had been won by the RCNVR sailors in the Battle of the Atlantic where, as William Pugsley wrote, the corvettes and men who sailed them "somehow stood for Canada."[59] There was merit on both sides.

Grant indicated before the inquiry that he would consider an initiative on Canada badges if it came from the fleet but that it had not been an issue. Heretofore, poor pay, accommodation, and conditions of service had formed the basis of complaints. Subsequently, Audette felt compelled to attack Grant after his death and was selective in the evidence used for his case. He did not differentiate between Grant's professional competence and insensitivity to what today would be called "political correctness." Audette promoted the illusion of an archaic, inept, and poorly educated hierarchy that, by inference, condemned out of hand all senior Canadian naval officers and Grant in particular. Less rigorous historians have been seduced by the Audette version so that Grant's powerful leadership and immense contribution to the development of the post-war RCN have received neither the attention nor merit they deserve.

The findings and recommendations of the Mainguy Report were far reaching. As stated, many issues had been previously identified by the RCN, and remedial action was either in train or planned and awaiting funding. Great emphasis was placed on the revitalization of the divisional system, proper divisional training for officers and senior non-commissioned officers, and implementation of welfare committees in every ship. The thrust towards Canadianization of the Navy, as included in the report, was not against the British emphasis on leadership, the Nelsonian tradition, but rather the style and execution. The British style of leadership reflected the national culture and was based on the class system, where officers were considered a distinct class from the men. This artificial separation with its inherent paternalism was contrary to the mores of Canadian society, and the commissioners said it had no place in the RCN. The affectation was not found to be widespread. However, enough officers from both regular and reserve entries affected English accents and notions of artificial superiority to make this a major irritant with Canadian sailors and university educated technical officers who joined during the war. The report strongly recommended that all officers receive a broad liberal education to the degree level in order to equip them intellectually and philosophically for the leadership of young sailors drawn from Canadian society. The practicality of this recommendation was not discussed.

Vice-Admiral Grant took no issue with any recommendations to improve leadership training, conditions of service, or welfare. These, in the main, reinforced existing initiatives. As Rear-Admiral Harry DeWolf stated before the inquiry, the regulations were in place and only needed to be followed.[60] The RCN was not broken; it only needed adjustments. The Naval Board moved quickly to expand divisional training at *Cornwallis* to be mandatory for all junior officers and to include courses for senior ratings. More difficult for Grant was the issue of Canada badges and painting Canadian maple leafs on the funnels of ships. He procrastinated, and Claxton simply directed him to get on with it.[61] Grant, realizing further opposition was unproductive, did just that and never looked back. There were more important things to do.

The issue of officer education was critical because Grant believed that if the early education of naval officers was not the responsibility of the RCN then the character of the naval profession and the culture itself would fundamentally change. The recommendation of the Mainguy Report pertaining to officer education, by chance or design, gave weight to Claxton's Canadian Service Colleges scheme, where cadets of the three services would be trained together to the degree level. This became the Regular Officer Training Plan (ROTP). Grant had no alternative on this issue because Claxton was adamant and the Navy could not afford a separate naval college in any case. History would show the ROTP was unable to meet the officer production requirements for any service. All had to rely on supplementary direct entry and commissioning from the ranks (CFR) plans to make up numbers. In the RCN's case, the Venture Plan was introduced in 1954 and, in fact, the largest proportion of officers was commissioned from the ranks.

Rear-Admiral Tony Storrs observed, "The Mainguy Report was good and the result excellent. It turned out to be beneficially cathartic. It exposed a lot and got it out of our systems and really gave us a clear identity."[62] Subsequently, the Mainguy Report featured in every divisional course taught in *Cornwallis*. It became a kind of Magna Carta for the lower deck; every junior officer and senior rate has since been instructed that the modern divisional system of the Royal Canadian Navy was established upon its recommendations. The implications were that the RCN had a new attitude toward the divisional system and that the cultivation of officer-man relations was of primary importance. The men of the lower deck clearly benefited from this important episode in the history of the RCN. Grant, however, was equally adamant that naval recruits should be purged of the liberal excesses of Canadian society and taught loyalty and obedience. To accomplish this, the intense recruit training and indoctrination period at *Cornwallis* was extended to twenty-one weeks.

Whether the Mainguy Report was needed to accomplish these reforms or whether they would have occurred in the normal course of events is a moot point. The evidence is conclusive that the RCN was already making improvements in many areas. However, there is no doubt the Mainguy Report accelerated needed change and created an environment for a Canadian identity to emerge. Significantly, the report gave the Navy little leverage to obtain increased funding for improvements in conditions of service. This materialized only with the crisis created by the invasion of South Korea. It may be argued that Claxton was more interested in the optics of adopting Canada badges and red maple leafs on funnels, which satisfied his nationalist inclinations, than correcting the root personnel problems caused by underfunding.

During October 1949, at the same time that the Mainguy Report was released, Vice-Admiral Grant was engaged in a campaign that would decide the future composition of the fleet. The issue was the necessity of naval aviation to the RCN. Despite the fact it consumed 25 percent of the Navy's budget and had significant teething problems, Grant had become convinced of the need for naval aviation and argued that carrier-borne aircraft were fundamental to the RCN fulfilling its role of convoy protection against threats from both enemy submarines and aircraft.[63] Grant embarked on a public relations campaign to muster support for naval aviation. His timing was opportune because the Soviets had exploded their first atomic bomb the month before. This had raised public concern over the deteriorating world situation and focused government attention.

He consolidated the position of the carrier by committing the RCN's existing fleet to NATO's ASW force in the first meeting of North Atlantic Regional Planning Group (NAORPG), which was held in Washington that October.[64] Grant stated that Canada wished to concentrate on the "organization, control and protection of convoys."[65] This would prove to be a critical initiative, not only for consolidating the position of naval aviation but also in determining the role, composition, and disposition of the Canadian fleet and personnel requirements until the end of the Cold War. Rear-Admiral Storrs remarked retrospectively, "NATO came as a great relief, clarified much of our uncertainty of purpose and gave us [the RCN] a clear role."[66]

The issue over the future of naval aviation came to a head in March 1950, in the Chiefs of Staff Committee (COSC), when Air Marshall Wilf Curtis, Chief of the Air Staff, openly opposed Grant on naval aviation and the RCN's proposal to acquire seventy-five Avenger aircraft from the USN for ASW.[67] Curtis, with support from the Minister of Finance, D.C. Abbott, was attempting to establish RCAF control of everything that flew. As unanimity could not be reached in the committee, Grant demanded a vote. General Charles Foulkes, acting as chairman, gained agreement to submit the issue to Claxton, where Grant won his case, thereby saving naval aviation and the Avenger purchase.[68] Thereafter, naval aviation was accepted by the Government as having a key role to play in "the immediate defence of Canada" and "anti-submarine warfare."[69] The RCN went on to build its NATO contribution around the carrier *Magnificent,* which was subsequently replaced by the updated *Bonaventure.* The RCN Task Group of *The Bonnie* and the new St. Laurent destroyer escorts subsequently became a very effective force, highly respected in NATO.

The decision on the concept of design and construction of the St. Laurent class destroyer escorts was one of Grant's crowning achievements because it advanced the RCN's operational capability, habitability, and technology. While the naval uniform remained British (with "Canada badges"), the design of the new anti-submarine escort was uniquely Canadian and become the recognized hallmark of the RCN. The new St. Laurent class ships required significant changes in the Navy's personnel structure as well as training to operate and maintain its advanced ship's systems. Constructor Captain "Rolly" Baker was borrowed from the RN to head the project.[70] Baker, "untrammelled by the constraints of the Royal Corps of Constructors," pirated the design of the new RN Type 12 A/S frigate, incorporating its main features into the RCN design, including the British Type Y-100 propulsion system.[71] However, many aspects of the design were "radically altered" to incorporate many Canadian ideas and requirements. These included a concept of habitability derived from the USN and based on experiments on HMCS *Sioux,* initiated by Grant. The electrical system was designed to USN Bureau of Ships (BuShips) specifications and American radars; communications systems and Gunar fire control were installed. The St. Laurents and variants would add immeasurably to the growing national identity of the RCN.

In the face of challenges and setbacks, Vice-Admiral Grant had pressed hard to establish a degree of operational preparedness and efficiency in the fleet. He anticipated that naval forces would be needed to meet contingencies in the unstable post-war world. In 1948, Grant told the National Defence College that the Navy must, in peacetime, be prepared for international "police duties" and be "available at immediate notice to visit the scene of tension or disorder without deviating noticeably from normal routine."[72] Operational training of fully manned destroyers began in 1950, an accomplishment that required a huge combined effort by NSHQ and the ships. Grant's leadership and determination through a difficult transition period was decisive. His drive to succeed was contagious and became the RCN's sustaining strength. This "can-do" spirit was one characteristic that the Mainguy Report referred to as being "overwhelmingly right" with the Navy. "Can-do" would become synonymous with the Royal Canadian Navy in the NATO fleet. Grant's decision to stretch resources to the limit to maintain a core of operational ships had a definite purpose and produced enormous dividends. The RCN was able to dispatch three destroyers to Korea within two weeks of the order. It was months before the other two services could respond.

The "sickly season," where parsimony was the norm, ended abruptly for the RCN on 25 June 1950 when the Korean conflict erupted.[73] On 30 June 1950, Vice-Admiral Grant directed Rear-Admiral DeWolf, Commanding Officer Pacific Coast, to sail the destroyers *Cayuga, Sioux,* and *Athabaskan* to the Far East on 5 July 1950.[74] The destroyers were stored and ammunitioned for war; personnel were scrounged from other ships and *Naden* barracks to bring them up to wartime complement. Task Group 214.4, under the command of Captain J.V. Brock, sailed on schedule for Japan. On 14 July 1950, the three ships were placed by NSHQ under the operational control of American General Douglas MacArthur, who commanded the United Nations' forces. After a brief and uncertain five years of peace, the RCN was at war as part of a United Nations' coalition force.[75] On arrival in Sasebo, Japan, they joined Task Force 96.5 under the command of Rear-Admiral Hartman, USN. NSHQ arranged that the USN would provide logistic support for RCN ships serving in Korea. Close co-operation with the USN would further weaken the traditional British connection.

The Korean commitment marked the beginning of a period of rapid expansion for the RCN, similar to that experienced during World War II, with all the attendant difficulties and pitfalls. The fear was that

Korea was the beginning of a Communist expansion that would soon spread to Europe. Claxton directed the chiefs of staff to accelerate completion of plans to achieve a war-ready state.[76] He also asked for proposals to improve war-fighting capability and for increased ceilings and estimates.[77] A naval personnel strength of 13,440 was subsequently authorized. Grant proposed a fleet strength of twenty-six operational ships to be attained by 1953.[78] He also requested authorization to build all seven St. Laurents and pressed to increase Canada's shipbuilding capacity.[79] NATO was estimated to be 260 ASW vessels short. When the NATO Military Cooperation Committee (MCC) met in Washington in October 1950, Grant committed the RCN to providing "as many A/S escorts as possible."[80] At this juncture, the RCN's commitment to NATO became virtually open-ended and governed naval policy for the next twenty years. Within a year, the Naval Staff was planning for a ceiling of 21,000 to be reached by 1954.

Vice-Admiral Harold Grant, the Chief of the Naval Staff from 1947 to 1951, was very much a transitional figure whose hard-driving Nova Scotian Presbyterian character could be misconstrued as that of a hide-bound British traditionalist. He was determined and inflexible on points of principle and fought to retain those things he believed to be essential to the continuing existence of the RCN. To his naval colleagues, he was a hero whose wartime exploits in command of RN cruisers established the standard of professional excellence for RCN officers to emulate.[81] He provided strong effective leadership with humour during the often chaotic times the Navy experienced in the late 1940s. The RCN weathered the storm of the incidents that resulted in the Mainguy inquiry and fiscal restraint under Grant. The RCN did not emerge with a new identity in spite of Harold Grant because it gained symbols, "Canada badges" and maple leafs. A new identity, rooted in professionalism and closer association with the USN, was already emerging across the spectrum of naval activity, and most of its necessary components were being put in place before the incidents. The Mainguy Report merely accelerated the process and accentuated the qualitative aspects.

HMCS *St. Laurent* was launched on 30 November 1951. Vice-Admiral Harold Grant retired as CNS the following day. The launching of "Sally" was the physical and material expression of the new Royal Canadian Navy. This was a key component of Grant's broad strategic plan to establish the post-war ASW specialization of the RCN and part of his great legacy to the Navy he loved and served faithfully. The RCN continued to develop its new identity and expand very much on the course that Grant laid out. His successors as CNS to 1964, Mainguy, DeWolf, and Rayner, followed it with no appreciable deviation. Vice-Admiral Grant died in 1965 at the young age of sixty-six. The war and devotion to duty had taken its toll. Harry DeWolf called Harold Grant "a unique Canadian" and "the best CNS we ever had."[82] To these accolades should be added, "Father of the Post-war Royal Canadian Navy."

ENDNOTES

CHAPTER 9

1. Vice-Admiral H.G. DeWolf, interview by the author, tape recording, (Ottawa, Ontario: 1 November 1994). Vice-Admiral K.L. Dyer, interview by the author, tape recording, (Ottawa, Ontario: 3 November 1994).
2. Rear-Admiral R.W. Timbrell interview by the author, tape recording, (Halifax, Nova Scotia: 2 May 2000). Timbrell was Staff Officer (TAS) at NSHQ for two years during Grant's tenure as CNS.
3. DeWolf interview.
4. Nancy Braithwaite (daughter of John Grant) interview by the author, (Salt Spring Island, BC).
5. R.E. Bidwell, "Eight Cadets, 1914," *Sea Breezes,* Vol. 1 No. 4, December 1917, 6.
6. Ibid., 6.
7. Vice-Admiral H.T.W. Grant, S.206 Performance Evaluation Reports, Grant File, Directorate of History and Heritage (henceforth referred to as DHH).
8. Vice-Admiral H.T.W. Grant, Certificate of Service, Vice-Admiral Grant file, DHH.
9. Vice-Admiral H.T.W. Grant, S.206 Performance Evaluation Reports by Jones (9/2/31) and Murray (24/11/32), Grant File, DHH.
10. Grant was leading a lively party of naval officers and RMC cadets on "a run ashore" in Chester. The harassment took the form of placing a ladder against the building and climbing up and scaring the couple. This prank was in response to a thumping on the floor by the couple to quiet Grant and his mates who were partying noisily in the room below. Commander Victor Brodeur was dispatched from NSHQ to investigate after the secretary phoned her boss complaining of the antics of some drunken naval officers. Rear-Admiral H.N. Lay, *Memoirs of a Mariner* (Stittsville: 1982), 56.
11. Dyer interview and L.C. Audette, interview by the author, tape recording, (Ottawa, Ontario: 2 November 1994). Audette was one of

Grant's strongest critics but had nothing but praise and admiration for Mrs. Grant.

12. Vice-Admiral H.T.W. Grant, S.206 Performance Evaluation Reports by Nelles (10/6/36), Grant file, DHH.

13. The other celebrated hero was Vice-Admiral Harry DeWolf who won the DSC in addition to the CBE and DSO. Grant was considered by DeWolf and others to be in a class by himself. DeWolf interview by the author.

14. Marc Milner, *North Atlantic Run* (Toronto: 1985), 124.

15. M.J. Whitley, *Destroyer!: German Destroyers in World War II* (London: 1983), 192-199 for details of the engagement.

16. Grant file, DHH.

17. Rear-Admiral A.H.G. Storrs, interview by the author, tape recording, (Victoria, BC: 20 June 1995).

18. Rear-Admiral C.J. Dillon, interview by the author, tape recording, (Victoria, BC: 6 October 1994).

19. Storrs interview.

20. Vice-Admiral H.T.W. Grant, "Future Strategic Role of Naval Forces," Lecture to the National Defence College, 15 February 1948, Vice-Admiral Grant file, DHH.

21. J.F.K. Kealy, "The Development of the Canadian Navy, 1945-67," SGR II 223, DHH, 3.

22. 4000-100/14, Press release, 7 November 1951, Vice-Admiral. Grant file, DHH.

23. David Bercuson, *True Patriot: The Life of Brooke Claxton, 1898-1960* (Toronto: 1993), 177.

24. VCNS to CNS, "The Morale of the Navy," memo, 29 September 1947, National Archives of Canada (NAC), RG 24 Acc 83-84/167, Vol. 1596, NSS 4490-1, Pt. 1, "Morale and Service Conditions 1947-50." Houghton called the memo a "collation" of issues. The staff papers used as sources are contained in the file.

25. The RN had recently introduced Welfare Committees and they had been established informally in some Canadian ships during the war.

26. CNS to the Minister, memo, 8 October 1947, NAC, RG 24 Acc 83-84/167, Vol. 1596, NSS 4490-1, Pt. 1, "Morale and Service Conditions 1947-50."

27. "The Morale of the Navy" covers much of the same ground as the "Mainguy Report" and predates it by two years. This provides conclusive evidence that the RCN hierarchy had a grasp of the

problems respecting conditions of service that contributed to low morale and were taking measures to eliminate them.

28. Acting Commander Hope to CNS, "Morale, Welfare and Trade Grouping in the Royal Canadian Navy," 12 January 1948, NAC, RG 24 Acc 83-84/167, Vol. 1596, NSS 4490-1, Pt. 1, "Morale and Service Conditions 1947-50."

29. CNS to MND, memo, 5 February 1948.

30. Claxton Papers, NAC, MG 32, Vol. 221, "Memoirs," 869.

31. Vice-Admiral D.S. Boyle interview by the author, tape recording, (Ottawa, ON: 1 February 2000).

32. Report on certain "Incidents" which occurred on board H.M.C.S *Athabaskan, Crescent* and *Manificent* and on other matters concerning The Royal Canadian Navy, (October 1949), 16. Referred to hereafter as the "Mainguy Report."

33. Minutes Fourth Senior Officers' Meeting, 26-27 November 1947, NAC, RG 24 Acc 83-84/167, Box 143, NSS 1279-118, Vol. l, Naval Committees-Senior Officers' Meetings.

34. Naval Board Minutes, 258-1, 8 September 1948, DHH. Abbreviated henceforth NBM.

35. NBM 279-4, 15 February 1949 and NBM 289-1&2, 1 June 1948.

36. NBM 279-4, 15 February 1949. The staff officers were Captain(S) Rupert Wright and Commander(S) Charles Dillon, both "Supply Officers." Their arguments were substantiated by a study of the RCN system conducted by Commander (SC) M. A. Peel, USN Supply Corps.

37. Dillon interview.

38. DeWolf interview.

39. Grant evidence, "Audette Papers," NAC, MG 31, E 18, Vol. 4, file 14.

40. Ibid.

41. PC 84/4994 amending PC 3/3144 of 6 August 1947 and PC 122/5111 of 12 December 1947 to allow the RCN to recruit 1399 officers and 7648 men - total of 9047.

42. For background on the St. Laurent Programme and decision see, J.H.W. Knox, "An Engineer's Outline of RCN History: Part II," in *The RCN in Retrospect*, ed. J. Boutilier (Vancouver: 1982), 317-333, and S. Mathwin Davis, "The St. Laurent Decision: Genesis of a Canadian Fleet," in *The RCN in Transition*, ed. W.A.B. Douglas (Vancouver: 1988), 209-232.

43. NBM 256-1, 21 June 1948. When the blockade began Claxton directed that all three services look at emergency planning and

propose implementation procedures.

44. NSec, memo, "Employment Programme 1 October 1948 to 31 March 1949", 19 July 1948 NAC, RG 24 Acc 83-84/167, Box 455, NSS 1650-26, Vol. 2, Operations and Plans.

45. Naval Staff, "Brief on the Proposed Employment of HMC Ships for Fiscal Year 1949-1950," November 1948, NAC, RG 24 Acc 83-84/167, Box 455, NSS 1650-26, Vol. 2, Operations and Plans.

46. See the "Mainguy Report", 6-25, for a full description of the incidents and facts and causes relating to them. Also, Louis Audette's, "Board of Investigation ... Brief of the Evidence" in the "Audette Papers", NAC, MG 31, E 18, Vol. 1, file 5. The brief is Audette's independent submission. The other civilian commissioner, Leonard Brockington, drafted the final report drawing heavily on Audette's brief.

47. CNS to the Minister, memo, 8 October 1947, 2.

48. Audette interview.

49. Witnesses were told that their evidence would be non-attributable and destroyed by burning. Audette saved copies of the evidence and all documentation pertaining to the inquiry and later gave it to the National Archives of Canada.

50. Grant evidence, "Audette Papers," Vol. 4, file 14, 3462-3512.

51. Ibid., 3462.

52. Ibid., 3467-3468.

53. Ibid.

54. Audette, "The Lower Deck and the Mainguy Report of 1949," in *The RCN in Retrospect*, 247, and Audette interview.

55. Grant evidence, "Audette Papers," 3496.

56. Ron Armstrong, "The ship that left the war," *Times Colonist*, 13 August 1995, M1. See also Bill Rawlings, "Lonely Ambassador: HMCS *Uganda* and the War in the Pacific," *The Northern Mariner*, VIII, No. 1 January 1998, 39-63.

57. Rear-Admiral W.M. Landymore, interview by the author, tape recording, 7 July 1997, Lawrencetown, Nova Scotia. Landymore still has nothing but the greatest disdain for the mainly RCNVR personnel who voted against remaining in combat. It remained a burning issue long after the war.

58. Grant evidence, "Audette Papers," 3497.

59. William Pugsley quoted in Harbron, "The Royal Canadian Navy At Peace, 1945 - 1955: The Uncertain Heritage," *Queen's Quarterly*, Vol. LXXIII, No.3, Autumn 1966, 9.

60. DeWolf evidence, "Audette Papers," Vol. 4, file 12.

61. Claxton, "Autobiography," NBM 284-8, 6 April 1949; NBM 308-2, 12 January 1950; NBM 309-2, 20 January 1950; NBM 310, 23 January 1950.

62. Storrs interview.

63. Vice-Admiral Grant, Speech to the Defence Services Institute of London, Ontario, 14 October 1949, Grant file, DHH. Grant was influenced by Admiral Halsey, the USN carrier admiral. His decision was later reinforced when he visited Korea and General MacArthur told him, "the success of the Inchon landing was due to Naval gunfire and carrier-borne aviation, which provided 100% of the support." NBM 334-1a, 25 October 1950.

64. Joel J. Sokolsky, "Canada and the Cold War at Sea, 1945-68," *Royal Canadian Navy in Transition*, 213-214. The RCN Force Requirements for protecting sea lines of communication built around the carrier and naval aviation were developed under Ministerial direction and passed by the Naval Board in September, 1948. NBMs 256-1 and 259-5 Basic RCN Plan (Plan "B"). NAORPG became SACLANT after it was decided that an American admiral would permanently hold the position. The RCN supported the choice of an American for Supreme Commander Atlantic against the RN's bid to hold the position and their nominee, Admiral Louis Mountbatten. This indicated the extent that the RCN had moved into the USN sphere of influence.

65. Joel Sokolsky, "The US, Canada and the Cold War in the North Atlantic: The Early Years", paper presented to the Canadian Political Science Association, May 1981, 30-31.

66. Davis to Douglas, 21 March 1984, enclosure "The DDE Decision Process - Involvement of Cdr/Capt AHG Storrs," Rear-Admiral Storrs file, DHH.

67. Colonel R.L. Raymont, "Development of Canadian Defence Policy," November 1979, 87/47, DHH, 83-84.

68. Authors of popular histories on Canadian naval aviation have generally inaccurately portrayed the role of Grant. The truth is that without the tenacity and support of Grant, the carrier and naval aviation would have gone in 1950. See for example Stuart Soward, *Hands to Flying Stations: A Re-collective History of Canadian Naval Aviation*, Vol. 1, (Victoria: 1995), 139-140, 173-174.

69. Department of National Defence, *Canada's Defence Programme*, 1951-52, (Ottawa: King's Printer, 1951), 7.

70. Captain Baker, in Rear-Admiral Storrs' opinion, designed the St. Laurent class by himself.

71. Minutes Seventh Senior Officers' Meeting, 2-3 February 1950, NAC, RG 24 Acc 83-84/167, Box 143, NSS 1279-118, Vol. 2, Naval Committees-Senior Officers' Meetings. The meeting was held to discuss the new ship design and conversion of *Algonquin* to an anti-submarine escort.

72. Vice-Admiral Grant, "Future Strategic Role of Naval Forces," Lecture to the National Defence College, 15 February 1948. Grant's strategic thought reflected the emerging nature of the Cold War and was entirely consistent with Canada's foreign policy.

73. Tony German used "sickly season" as the title of his chapter on the period of fiscal restraint and personnel problems in *The Sea Is At Her Gates: The History of the Royal Canadian Navy* (Toronto: 1987). He takes literary licence with a naval toast that actually refers to opportunities for promotion.

74. CANAVHED TO CANFLAGPAC 2030Z/30 JUNE 50, Operations Korea, 1650-239/187, DHH.

75. T. Thorgrimsson and E.C. Russell, *Canadian Naval Operations in Korean Waters, 1950-1955* (Ottawa: 1965) is the official history.

76. NBM Special Meeting, 21 July 1950. Claxton's directive was dated 20 July 1950, and the COSC proposals were entitled "Accelerated Defence Programme" and dated 2 August 1950.

77. Sec.COSC to CGS, CNS, CAS, 31 July 1950, NAC, RG 24 Acc 83-84/167, Box 1392, NSS 4100-1, Vol. 3, Complements General.

78. The initial target was twenty-six ships consisting of one carrier, two cruisers, one A/S escort, nine destroyers, five frigates, seven minesweeepers and one icebreaker. This was increased in the final submission to Claxton by one destroyer and one frigate.

79. CNS to MND, memo, "Accelerated Defence Programme, Accelerated Shipbuilding Programme," 31 July 1950, Claxton Papers, Vol. 94, Folder Accelerated Defence Programme.

80. DeWolf interview. Rear-Admiral DeWolf had become VCNS and accompanied Grant to this meeting.

81. DeWolf and Dyer interviews.

82. DeWolf interview.

CHAPTER 10

GENERAL CHARLES FOULKES:
A PRIMER ON HOW TO BE CDS

Sean M. Maloney

THE Cold War was unlike the two other world wars of the twentieth century. Soldiers trained to fight, technology steadily advanced, and military forces remained in-being and at high levels of readiness to deter the eradication of life on this planet through the mass use of thermonuclear weapons. There were "brush fire wars" which could erupt into nuclear conflagration at any time. Men occupied deep underground bunkers and watched radar screens every day, every week, every month, every year, waiting for signs of enemy attack. Ships constantly patrolled at sea looking for nuclear-armed submarines off Canada's coasts. The Cold War defence system had to be maintained in "peacetime" which placed strains on how the Government of Canada went about its business of balancing domestic and international political interests. Generalship and the art of the Admiral had to adapt to meet these conditions: the pre-eminent Canadian Cold Warrior was General Charles Foulkes, Chief of the General Staff from 1945 to 1951 and then Chairman of the Canadian Chiefs of Staff Committee from 1951 to 1960.

Charles Foulkes is an enigma to those seeking to understand the formulation and implementation of Canadian national security policy in the 1950s. Negative rumours and the lack of a substantial personal paper collection have deterred detailed examination of his critical role in this endeavour and his *modus operandi*. Careful examination of available information, however, provides us with a much more round and detailed view of the man and his leadership abilities, particularly during the period of maximum danger to world peace in the early part of the Cold War. What is often overlooked is the fact that Charles Foulkes was in a position to provide unprecedented continuity through three governments – two Liberal and one Conservative – over the span of fifteen years. It was Charles Foulkes who added the muscles and organs to the skeletal Canadian and NATO national security structure which was in part generated by the efforts of the Secretary of State for External Affairs Lester B. "Mike" Pearson and Minister of National Defence Brooke Claxton.

It is disturbing to discover that personal and ill-informed opinion has been allowed to replace considered thought and analysis of Charles Foulkes. This can be attributed to several factors. One is that Foulkes was unpopular, particularly amongst his peers, and in the small Canadian Army this had long term effects on personal relationships. He has been described as "dour, short, pudgy [and] unapproachable." C.P. Stacey privately referred to him as a "cold fish."[1] Foulkes was essentially an introverted person (his favourite sport was fishing) in an army full of men who thrived on tactical and operational action, but had little appreciation of the larger aspects of strategy and Canada's place in the world. Unlike E.L.M. Burns, who wrote books and published in *American Mercury*, Foulkes unfortunately did not allow his intellectual attributes to blossom in the early years of his career. Indeed, Foulkes has been described as a "know-it-all" and a "conniving sonofabitch,"[2] a "pedestrian" and "ruthless character,"[3] "pleasant but unimpressive, restrained and thin-skinned," and "not endowed with any great amount of brains."[4] Anyone looking for information on Charles Foulkes is immediately confronted with this opprobrium.[5] The exception is James Eayrs, who thought that Foulkes was "nothing if not wily."[6]

A second factor contributing to Foulkes negative reputation involves the very public "Simonds Cult" in the post-war Canadian Army, which overrode the more obscure Foulkes who did not hunt out the limelight. There was a fair amount of uproar in the Army when, in 1945, the 42-year old Foulkes was appointed by the Government to be Chief of the General Staff (CGS). There were many people within the Army who felt that Guy Simonds should have been CGS. Simonds was a popular and aggressive field officer and had been "anointed" by Sir Bernard Law Montgomery as the only competent Canadian division or corps commander. There was a perception that Simonds had been treated unfairly by the Government and the CGS, General J.C. Murchie, since Simonds' war record appeared at the time to be more impressive than Foulkes'. When Simonds finally became CGS in 1951, he was in a position to augment his image within the Army, while Foulkes laboured in relative obscurity (within Army circles) at the highest levels of national security policy formulation.[7]

Foulkes' reputation was also dimmed by the fact that the bulk of his work was conducted within the highest and most secretive levels of government, which prevented public appreciation of such activities. This was even more so within NATO, whose secretariat tended to stamp everything Cosmic Top Secret.

Foulkes' military operational background was varied but not undistinguished. Unlike Andy McNaughton or some other Canadian generals of the Second World War, Foulkes was not a First World War veteran. He was a University of Western Ontario graduate with an LLD and was commissioned as an officer with the Royal Canadian Regiment in 1926. In terms of military education, Foulkes completed Staff College at Camberley in 1938, just in time for the war. He then commanded an infantry battalion (1941), then a brigade (1943), then a division (1944), and finally 1st Canadian Corps (1945). He was, for a time, Brigadier General Staff, First Canadian Army.

The specific effects of this background on Foulkes and his conduct as CGS and Chairman of the Chiefs of Staff Committee (COSC) must be inferred since there is a lack of detailed documentary evidence. As a peacetime soldier in the 1920s and 1930s, Foulkes would have been intimately aware of how unprepared Canada and the Canadian Army were to fight the Second World War. His Camberley experience, coupled with the contacts he would have made operating alongside British commanders in Italy and northwest Europe, would certainly have contributed to a certain amount of wariness when dealing with larger coalition partners and, after Dieppe, quite possibly would have produced some concern about the misuse of Canadian troops. Finally, in his capacity as commander of 1st Canadian Corps, he had direct contact with the American coalition partners and their methods of operation.

INTEREST AND INNOVATION

When Foulkes was appointed CGS in August 1945, he was confronted with a New World order not unlike that of the 1990s. The old order was destroyed, the new one was chaotic. (The Cold War stalemate did not develop immediately.) Boundaries were being redrawn, and the UN was thrust upon the world stage as the solution to all security issues. Ethnic cleansing would swing into full force in the Indo-Pakistan dispute and in Palestine. The question as to the specific role of weapons of mass destruction in warfare was under serious discussion.

Though keen to examine Canada's place in the new world order of 1945, Foulkes was immediately tasked with the demobilization of Canada's wartime armed forces. This did not totally prevent him from thinking ahead. He kept abreast of the developing world situation, but noted internally that it was difficult for Canada to do so. The CGS was firmly convinced that technological advantage was critical in any future war and, most importantly, that keeping ahead of potential opponents' technological capabilities had to be done in the most economical and expeditious fashion possible, particularly in the Atomic Age. Foulkes and C.J. Mackenzie, the man in charge of the National Research Council of Canada (NRC), both proposed that a special body of scientific advisors and analysts be formed to support the three armed services so that Canada "would not be caught unprepared." This body, called the Defence Research Board (DRB), was created in 1945 but was only formally authourized in 1947.[8]

There was serious opposition from the RCAF, which not only opposed the creation of a "fourth service," but also opposed the appointment of Omond McKillop Solandt as the head of DRB. Foulkes had specifically selected Solandt for the position and, as a result, had to use a variety of methods, some of which probably involved end runs around the RCAF by talking with Brooke Claxton, the Minister of National Defence. In the end, Canada got its DRB, due primarily to Foulkes' efforts.[9]

Foulkes was also a vocal champion of what became known as the American-British-Canadian (ABC) standardization and exchange bodies. This tied in with the Defence Research Board in that the DRB co-operated with its allied counterparts in the exchange of all forms of technical and scientific information, including operations research and development. Canada could contribute significantly in these areas and could then reap the benefits from allied developments in a fair exchange.[10]

Related to this were the ABC intelligence sharing relationships. Foulkes believed that Canada had to have an "in" with the allies so that Canadian interests could be exerted and protected. In his view, "whether aggressive or pacific, a nation will pursue its national policies and defend its national interests with success only if the leaders are thoroughly informed.... Any nation not so well informed may well forfeit the influence which its position warrants in world affairs."[11] It is clear that Foulkes was interested in intelligence relationships and that they played a key role in his Cold War vision of the Canadian national security establishment. Partially on Foulkes' recommendation, the Government eventually established the Joint Intelligence Board and the Joint Intelligence Committee specifically to carry out these functions.[12]

It is clear that there is an emerging pattern and that Foulkes is a key player in its formulation. This relates to the concept of saliency. Canada cannot, for political and demographic reasons, provide large standing conventional forces in the same manner as the United States or the

United Kingdom. On the other hand, Canada cannot allow her Armed Forces to be misused by such partners as was done in the Second World War in such instances as the Dieppe and Hong Kong fiascos. To be salient in a coalition, Canada must bring something unique to the table to make up for the lack of mass. Foulkes was essentially refuting Stalin's aside that "quantity has a quality all of its own." Canada could provide technologically advanced forces to a coalition fight. Canada could collect and analyze strategic intelligence and trade it for other information. Canada could foster technological and scientific innovation and use it to deal for other things. The objective was to have Canadian interests protected with the projection of Canadian power under Canadian control while, at the same time, working with a coalition and deriving the attendant benefits from it.[13]

It is not surprising, then, that Foulkes was intimately involved with the debates over NATO's military structure from very early on. The CGS noted that those at the political level, particularly Pearson and St. Laurent, had their hands full sorting out Article 2 of the North Atlantic Treaty and were relatively uninterested in the shape and form of how the treaty would actually be implemented. In effect, NATO organization was an amalgam of the existing Western Union Defence Organization (WUDO), the Permanent Joint Board on Defence (PJBD), and its affiliated but secret Military Co-operation Committee (MCC). Foulkes observed the back and forth debate between the British and the Americans as to who would exert command and control over what territory if war broke out. During the course of these 1948 and 1949 discussions, Foulkes proposed a solution.[14]

The Foulkes' plan, accepted by NATO in 1949, involved the creation of several Regional Planning Groups (RPG): Canada-US, North Atlantic Ocean, and then three for Europe – Western, Northern, and Southern. Each RPG was to have a political committee and a defence planning committee made up of those NATO members pledging standing deterrent forces in-being to the regional areas controlled by each RPG. Foulkes saw the RPG system as an interim step until a full-time NATO commander could be appointed to handle peacetime defence planning for the Northern, Western, and Southern RPGs. This occurred in 1951 when General Eisenhower was appointed Supreme Allied Commander, Europe. The North Atlantic Ocean Regional Planning Group eventually became Supreme Allied Commander Atlantic (SACLANT) while the Canada-US RPG was the NATO version of the PJBD/MCC and was the grandfather of the North American Air Defence Command (NORAD).[15]

The complexity of NATO politics and defence planning meant that Canada had to develop a more sophisticated approach towards Canadian representation. As a result of Foulkes', as well as Claxton's, prompting, the St. Laurent Government created a new position in 1951: the Chairman of the Chiefs of Staff Committee. The Chairman was set above the three service chiefs as an impartial broker and also served as Canada's representative to NATO's Military Committee. Foulkes was appointed to this position.

Foulkes comes across in all of these cases as an insightful thinker and as a man ready to back revolutionary organizational ideas, something risky in the face of the isolationist impulses inherent to the Mackenzie King Government of the day. There is no doubt that all cases (DRB, ABC, and NATO) were team efforts. However, it is difficult to see how this important national security matrix would have been established and maintained over time without Charles Foulkes.

LEARNING FROM MISTAKES

It goes without saying that no human being is flawless. It is the ability to learn from mistakes and implement corrective action to overcome the flaws that is important. The case of the post-1945 Canadian Army and Foulkes' role in its structure provides us with an example of this. The reduction of the Canadian Army from two corps plus supporting troops to a single brigade group plus an additional armoured regiment within almost one year following the Second World War generated significant problems during the Cold War. This reduction was conducted under the CGS' auspices and within governmental guidelines. That established mobilization of the Reserve Forces as the future Canadian strategic concept in 1946.[16]

Foulkes should have known, based on his interwar experiences, that the cadre force of a single brigade group was inadequate, given the technological competence needed to retain war-fighting skills bought in blood from 1939 to 1945. The situation was compounded between 1947 and 1950. Once the Cold War was underway and continental defence commitments were accepted by the Government, the cadre brigade group was converted to an airportable formation, the Mobile Striking Force (MSF), to carry out tasks established by the Military Co-operation Committee (MCC). The brigade group retained its training tasks as well. Foulkes should have insisted that

Claxton consider raising a second formation to handle this new task and not double-hat it.

When the Korean War started in 1950, the Government decided to deploy a brigade group to fight against Communist aggression in Korea. The built-in inflexibility of Canada's force structure meant that the MSF could not be deployed to Korea since it was committed to and structured for continental defence. Foulkes and Simonds, the new CGS, proposed creating a special brigade (25th Brigade) and reinforcement group mobilized off the street to fight in Korea. The implementation of this plan was problematic which resulted in a ten-month delay in deploying the force to Korea, thus demonstrating that mobilization was a flawed concept for Canada at a time when forces in-being were necessary for rapid reaction.[17]

The West saw Korea as a feint by the Soviets and their allies to draw forces into the Far East in order to permit attack on NATO. Consequently, NATO decided to amalgamate several regional planning groups and form the Supreme Headquarters Allied Powers Europe (SHAPE) under Supreme Allied Commander Europe (SACEUR). General Eisenhower proceeded to create the Integrated Force to deter Soviet aggression. Canada agreed to provide land and air force contingents after a lengthy debate. The main problem was similar to the 25th Brigade problem in that the mobilization framework was flawed. The MSF was already tasked with continental defence under the MCC and Canada-US Regional Planning Group, and 25th Brigade was in Korea. The problems with mounting 25th Brigade were examined, and it was concluded that a composite regular and militia force could be formed and sent to West Germany. The 27th Brigade was formed by screening composite militia battalions and it deployed in November 1951. Even when deployed it took eight months to get the formation battle ready.[18]

It would have been easy to make Simonds, his rival and subordinate, a scapegoat for the attendant problems with 25th Brigade and 27th Brigade. However, finger pointing was never part of Foulkes' repertoire. He felt some responsibility and took rigorous steps to correct the faults. Foulkes noted that the main flaw was the lack of a national strategic concept. Another problem was the lack of a link between the elected political officials, their understanding of the application of military force in foreign policy, and the intricacies of creating a force structure capable of its execution. The detonation of a hydrogen device by the United States in 1952 and its subsequent projected impact on Western strategic re-appraisals gave Foulkes the opportunity to correct these problems. In effect, Canada was confronted and had to deal with a Revolution in Military Affairs (RMA). Foulkes understood that the nature of war was changing from the one he fought in the 1940s and that Canada had to have the ability to keep pace to protect her interests.

In his NATO "hat", Foulkes was the Chairman of the Military Committee, the body which co-ordinated NATO strategy.[19] He educated himself about ongoing American and British analyses of their future national strategies in light of these technological advances. He ensured that Canadians were well placed in the NATO structure to report back on these matters. As a result, Foulkes was able to deal directly with both allies while their new strategies were being formulated. He even was asked by General Omar Bradley, the Chairman of the U.S. Joint Chiefs of Staff (JCS), for his views on what became known as the New Look. The British put together a seminal document called the Global Strategy Paper. As with the Americans, Field Marshal Slim asked for Foulkes' input. Foulkes then was able to brief the Cabinet Defence Committee and keep the political level informed.[20]

Over time it became clear to Foulkes that NATO would need a new strategic concept. He was instrumental in making sure that the Military Committee gave safe passage to an amalgam of American and British concepts. This document, called MC 48, influenced NATO strategy well into the early 1960s. MC 48 provided its readers with an agreed upon pattern of war. It also recommended general steps necessary for the evolution of the Integrated Force into a nuclear-equipped organization to provide a conventional-nuclear deterrent force to stave off Soviet aggression. Once NATO agreed in November 1954 that MC 48 was to be the basis for military planning, Foulkes then turned around and was able to convince Pearson, Solandt, Claxton, and his successor, Ralph Campney, that MC 48 could and should form the basis for Canadian strategy.[21]

Canada's acceptance of MC 48 was a critical step in reversing the convoluted strategy and force structure relationship that had existed prior to 1954. All of Canada's Armed Forces now had to be justified under the new concept and monies were allocated accordingly. The three different armies (MSF, 25th Brigade, and 27th Brigade) were now converted into one army of four interchangeable and interoperable brigade groups capable of operating in conventional and nuclear environments in the defence of Europe. The Royal Canadian Navy constructed the St. Laurent-class Anti-Submarine Warfare (ASW) destroyer, also capable of operating under nuclear conditions against enemy submarines threatening Canada with nuclear missiles. The RCAF's various air defence projects, like the

Avro Arrow, were related to defending the North American mobilization base within the MC 48 concept.[22]

Foulkes and Solandt also understood that Canadian units had to receive nuclear weapons effects information so that they could work within the NATO context. Foulkes used his influence – considerable by now – with the Americans to ensure that Canadian scientists and soldiers participated in nuclear testing so that the experience could be brought home and used to generate doctrine and organizational changes. It is fair to say that by 1955, the 1949 to 1951 "ad hoc" period was put behind the defence establishment and that Foulkes provided critical direction and correction for problems for which he was partially responsible. Canada now had salient, capable forces, which justified her seat at the table and protected her interests, rather than some unco-ordinated force structure and a vague strategic concept.[23]

MAINTAINING CONTINUITY AND CO-ORDINATION

It seems incredible that Foulkes was able to achieve so much. Granted, the Chairman did not operate alone. Foulkes was adept at seeking professional advice whenever he felt a deficiency in his knowledge. These sources included R.L. Raymont, Bud Drury (the Deputy Minister and a confidant from the war), Mike Pearson, Omond Solandt, A.D.P. Heeney (Canada's Ambassador to NATO), and Escott Reid over in External Affairs. There was more to this, however. Trying to get policy agreed to and then implemented is a notoriously difficult process in a fluid environment, perhaps more so when dealing with matters of national security. Without vision, policy co-ordination would be useless. Foulkes frequently applied the first principle of war: selection and maintenance of the aim.

As we have seen, Foulkes' aim after 1952 was to ensure that Canada could field the best equipped and trained military force possible (given budgetary limits) deter and then fight a Third World War alongside her NATO allies. There were many obstacles, usually personality-based, sometimes alliance structure-based. Achieving the aim meant that Foulkes had to carefully consider how policy was influenced as it wound its way through the bowels of the Ottawa bureaucracy.

During the St. Laurent years the Cabinet Defence Committee (CDC) met to consider and determine the Government's course of action on national security matters. The CDC usually had the ministers from

Defence and External Affairs, the chairman of the Chiefs of Staff Committee, occasionally the three service chiefs, and the finance minister. Technically, the Clerk of the PCO, Robert Bryce, set the CDC agenda. However, there were serious co-ordination problems, which emerged during the Korean War scare in 1950 and 1951.

Temporary solutions included having a Department of External Affairs representative sit in on the Chiefs of Staff Committee meetings and the bolstering of the Defence Liaison 1 Section in the Department of External Affairs. This was not enough, however. Foulkes and others decided that a little known body dealing with NATO economic and military aid should be converted into a shadow Cabinet Defence Committee. This group, called the Panel on the Economic Aspects of Defence Questions (hereafter called the Panel), met prior to each Cabinet Defence Committee meeting to co-ordinate defence, external, and economic policy. The Panel consisted of Foulkes (in his COSC capacity), the Chairman of the Bank of Canada, Bryce (representing the PCO), and the deputy ministerial-level people from Defence (Drury), External (Norman Robertson and sometimes A.D.P. Heeney or others), and sometimes Solandt from the DRB.[24]

This placed Foulkes on several important bodies within the national security policy structure: he was Canada's military representative to NATO and sometimes even chairman of the Military Committee; he was the Chairman of the Chiefs of Staff Committee; he was on the DRB; he was a member of the Panel; and he was in the Cabinet Defence Committee. No other individual, including Pearson or even Bryce, was placed in such a way to shepherd an integrated national security vision and strategic concept like MC 48 through the system. The fact that Foulkes remained the COSC and a member of all these bodies for the better part of the 1951-1960 period explains the unprecedented continuity generated by his presence.[25]

POWER BROKERING

It was one thing to be on all of these committees, it was quite another to actually influence what was going on. Foulkes' credibility rested on several pillars. The first was that he established himself as the primary military representative that the Department of External Affairs, the PCO, and the Prime Minister approached for advice during the St. Laurent years, and these men accepted that state of affairs. The second was Foulkes' formal and informal connections as well as the understanding within Canadian circles that Foulkes had access to those connections at will.[26]

These links went back to the Second World War. For example, both General Omar Bradley and General Eisenhower knew Foulkes during the Second World War when, in 1945, Foulkes was essentially commanding the Canadian Army in the Netherlands. Thus, when Bradley was the Chairman of the Joint Chiefs of Staff in the United States, it was natural for Foulkes to carry on communications with him. The same relationship existed when Eisenhower was NATO SACEUR and Foulkes was the Chairman of the Military Committee. Foulkes even met informally with Eisenhower after he became President. A connection of lesser importance was Sir Bernard Law Montgomery, the British Chief of the Imperial General Staff (CIGS), but that was more Simonds' bailiwick than Foulkes'. In any event, the Canada-US relationship was more important at this stage of the Cold War.[27]

Another extremely important connection was with General Walter Bedell Smith, the Director of Central Intelligence (CIA). Smith permitted the establishment of a Canadian liaison officer at the CIA, partly at Foulkes' request. This provided added value to Canadian intelligence relationships outside as well as inside the ABC framework.[28]

In NATO circles Foulkes' credibility was high which, in turn, translated into the ability to broker Canadian power. Generals Al Gruenther and Lauris Norstad, successive SACEURs in the 1950s, had highly developed relationships with Foulkes, as did General Curtis LeMay, the Commander in Chief of the USAF's Strategic Air Command nuclear deterrent force. At Foulkes' prompting, the RCAF leadership developed and improved a small fishing camp at Eagle River, Labrador, as an informal meeting place for Canadian and American generals. The importance of Eagle River as part of the power brokering process cannot be underestimated, though, of course, there were no secretaries to take notes and no records were kept. Eagle River allowed Foulkes and his American and NATO counterparts to relax, fish, co-ordinate, and scheme outside of the Washington-Paris-Ottawa pressure cookers. It also allowed Canada valuable insight into what was going on with the Allies.[29]

Therefore, when Foulkes attended CDC meetings or otherwise provided advice to the St. Laurent government, such advice was understood by the people in that government to rest on a firm basis. Even when the Diefenbaker Government took over in 1957, Foulkes took steps to establish a close working relationship with the Minister of National Defence, Major-General George Pearkes, VC, another wartime colleague. Once Pearkes was briefed on how the system functioned, Foulkes continued as he had before. This situation continued until the Prime Minister demonstrated an inability to firmly control rogue policy-makers, like the Secretary of State for External Affairs, Howard Green. Green and those surrounding him had no respect for, or interest in, professional military and intelligence advice, nor did they have an appreciation for the role of military forces as expressions of Canadian interests. Green's unco-ordinated behaviour and personal ambition eventually made the formulation of coherent Canadian national security policy impossible, despite the existence of a supporting structure and Foulkes' ability to broker power in the Canada-US and NATO systems.[30]

A Higher Loyalty and Moral Courage

At points in his tenure as Chairman, particularly after Howard Green became Secretary of State for External Affairs and pursued his own divergent agenda, Foulkes encountered several moral dilemmas which had to be dealt with. The first of these was whether or not there were long-term and established Canadian interests outside of the short-term political interests as expressed by the Diefenbaker government and driven more by domestic politics than a more sophisticated *Weltanshauung*. If so, how could those interests be maintained and articulated without cutting across what the Government was up to? Foulkes and others decided that there were such long-term interests and attempted to continue as much as possible along that path, despite the entropy generated by Diefenbaker's chaotic decision making system. It would have been easy to just sit back and let the system collapse and the Government with it, which is what eventually happened when Air Marshal Frank Miller took over from Foulkes as CCOS in 1960. For three years, however, Foulkes hung in and successfully "stickhandled" several sensitive issues relating to Strategic Air Command operations over Canada and the matter of nuclear weapons and doctrine in the Canadian armed services.[31]

Regarding NATO, Foulkes did his best to inform the Prime Minister how the system functioned, what Canada wanted, and how Canada went about getting it. This advice was generally ignored because Diefenbaker thought Foulkes was a "Liberal pawn" along with the rest of the "Liberal-created" bureaucracy. Anything dealing with foreign affairs was "manipulated" by "personalities" to the detriment of the Conservative Party. Under these conditions, Foulkes was still able to prevent NATO commanders from imposing a SHAPE-conceived force structure plan on Canadian air units in Europe, a plan which would have been financially unmanageable and counter to Canadian political interests.[32]

Another instance of Foulkes' loyalty and moral courage occurred during the Avro Arrow affair. The story of the CF-105 project and its demise is still the subject of significant controversy, and Foulkes' role in the programme was considerable. The CF-105 was initiated during the St. Laurent government's tenure to counter the Soviet nuclear bomber threat to North America. The complexity of the project in addition to the problems inherent in managing it caused serious cost overruns and delays. Foulkes mediated between the various factions on the defence side of the house. When Diefenbaker took over, the situation had stabilized, but then spun out of control again in the House of Commons as Opposition leader Mike Pearson sought to embarrass the Government.

It was customary for a new federal government not to have access to the records of the decision-making process in the PCO from previous governments. Diefenbaker demanded that a thorough review of the Arrow project be undertaken and that Foulkes was to produce it because he had provided so much continuity. Foulkes could have refused and had legal grounds to do so. This would have prevented the Government from making an informed decision on the Arrow programme which, in turn, would have had negative domestic political ramifications. Foulkes chose to produce the study instead. It was far more critical that the government, no matter how incompetent or poorly led, had access to the facts so that they could decide, particularly during the Cold War period of maximum danger and uncertainty.[33]

Work Ethic

There is not a great deal of information on Charles Foulkes' work habits or how he personally organized his approach to the day-to-day decision making regarding problems of national security policy. We do, however, have an anecdote from Foulkes' neighbour, External Affairs diplomat Escott Reid:

> General Charles Foulkes, the chairman of the chiefs of staff, and I were neighbours. I told him once that my wife often complained to me that she did not see why I did not get home from the office till 6:30 or later

whereas Charles got home a little after four. Charles said "Brooke Claxton ... has also talked to me about going home so early. He said to me one morning: 'Charles, I tried to get you by phone yesterday a little after four and they said you'd gone home.' I said: 'I always leave my office at four. If I can't organize my office well enough that I can leave at four you'd better get yourself another chairman of the chiefs of staff.' By thus conserving his resources Foulkes was able to serve for fifteen tumultuous years.[34]

This sort of behaviour, particularly in the era which spawned *The Organization Man* and *The Man in the Grey Flannel Suit* demonstrated that Foulkes was way ahead of his time in the management field.

CONCLUSION

Charles Foulkes would probably not pass the "peer assessment" process at today's Royal Military College. One must, however, conclude that an individual does not have to be popular to be an effective leader. Being unpopular probably facilitated Foulkes' ability to examine the problems confronting Canada's national security establishment from new perspectives and provide innovative solutions. The one main lesson to extract from Charles Foulkes' tenure as CGS and Chairman of the Chiefs of Staff Committee is that a CDS needs to clearly define Canadian national security aims for himself and then create and implement an integrated vision. The role of the highest Canadian military authority is to provide accurate and timely advice, not to second guess the political authorities. If the political authorities accept the advice, fine. If they don't, the responsibility is theirs for the results. Foulkes gave the governments he served intelligence and scientific and military tools with which they could make decisions. He also provided continuity to the process that presented the options. It was critical that Canada muster her more limited resources effectively in this early part of the long Cold War. Canada had a system which afforded operational and strategic influence to an extent that hasn't been paralleled since, and it was Charles Foulkes' leadership and vision that made it work.

ENDNOTES

CHAPTER 10

1. J.L. Granatstein, *The Generals: The Canadian Army's Senior Commanders in the Second World War* (Toronto: Stoddart, 1993), 175.
2. Tony Foster, *Meeting of Generals* (Toronto: Methuen, 1986), 85.
3. John A. English, *The Canadian Army and the Normandy Campaign: A Study of Failure in High Command* (New York: Praeger, 1991), 191.
4. Granatstein, *The Generals*, 177.
5. Indeed, when the positive aspects of Foulkes' administration in the Department of National Defence were explained at a lecture, the author was approached by a former junior officer who served in Ottawa in the 1950s and was admonished with comments like, "He couldn't have contributed anything significant. Charles Foulkes was an asshole."
6. James Eayrs, *In Defence of Canada: Growing Up Allied* (Toronto: University of Toronto Press, 1980), 135.
7. Granatstein, *The Generals*, 173-175; Dominck Graham, *The Price of Command: A Biography of General Guy Simonds* (Toronto: Stoddart Books, 1993), 229-235.
8. D.J. Goodspeed, *DRB: A History of the Defence Research Board of Canada* (Ottawa: Queen's Printers, 1958), 16-17; John Bryden, *Best Kept Secret: Canadian Secret Intelligence in the Second World War* (Toronto: Lester Publishing, 1993), 286-287.
9. Goodspeed, *DRB*, Chapters 4 and 5.
10. National Archives of Canada (hereafter NAC) MG 32 B5 vol. 222 file BC 1946-54 Defence (8), Claxton memoir, 825-826, 923-929.
11. Directorate of History and Heritage (hereafter DHH), file 193.009 (D 53) box 1, (22 Dec 45) CGS to Distribution List, "A Proposal for the Establishment of a National Intelligence Organization."
12. DHH, The Raymont Collection, file 3170, (Jul 52) "An Informal Study of Intelligence."
13. Sean M. Maloney and Scot Robertson, "The Revolution in Military Affairs: Possible Implications for Canada," *International Journal* Summer 1999, 444-462.

14. Maloney, *Securing Command of the Sea: NATO Naval Planning, 1948-1954* (Annapolis: Naval Institute Press, 1995), Chapter 2.

15. Eayrs, *In Defence of Canada*, 138-141.

16. DHH, file 112.012(D-1) (12 Oct 49) "Brief on Canadian Defence Organization with Particular Reference to Organziation and Training in the Canadian Army."

17. David J. Bercuson, *Blood on the Hills: The Canadian Army in the Korean War* (Toronto: University of Toronto Press, 1999) Chapters 1 and 2.

18. Sean M. Maloney, *War Without Battles: Canada's NATO Brigade in Germany, 1951-1993* (Toronto: McGraw Hill Ryerson, 1997), Chapter 1.

19. The relationship between the Standing Group and the Military Committee is a complex one since the French, British, and Americans affected a certain amount of strategy co-ordination at a level above the Military Committee. In the main, the Standing Group sought to co-ordinate global Cold War strategy outside the NATO Area with NATO Area strategy, not just act as a tripartite control mechanism over the rest of NATO.

20. Sean M. Maloney, *Learning to Love The Bomb: Canada's Cold War Strategy and Nuclear Weapons, 1951-1968* (forthcoming University of British Columbia Press), Chapter 2.

21. Ibid.

22. Ibid.

23. Ibid., Chapter 3; See also *An Identifiable Cult: The Evolution of Combat Development in the Canadian Army 1946-1965*, Directorate of Land Strategic Concepts Report 9905, August 1999.

24. Maloney, *Learning to Love The Bomb*, Chapters 1 and 2.

25. Ibid.

26. See Dominick Graham, *The Price Of Command: A Biography of General Guy Simonds* (Toronto: Stoddart Publishing Co. Ltd, 1993), 244; see also George Ignatieff, *The Making of a Peacemonger* (Toronto: University of Toronto Press, 1983).

27. Maloney, *Learning to Love The Bomb*, Chapters 2 and 6.

28. DHH, The Raymont Collection, file 3170, (7 Mar 51) letter Foulkes to Smith.

29. Note that Eagle River continued to be an important meeting place well into the 1980s. Dwight D. Eisenhower Library (DDEL) Norstad Papers, Foulkes file, (9 Aug 57) memo for Trip File, SACEUR's Visit to US and Canada; (31 Jul 57) letter Foulkes to

Nortsad; DHH Raymont Collection, file 503, (24 Aug 62) letter Norstad to Miller.

30. Maloney, *Learning to Love The Bomb,* Chapters 7 and 8.

31. Ibid.

32. H. Basil Robinson, *Diefenbaker's World: A Populist in Foreign Affairs* (Toronto: University of Toronto Press, 1989), Chapter 5.

33. University of Victoria Archives, transcripts of interviews conducted between Reg Roy and Charles Foulkes in preparation of the George Pearkes biography.

34. Escott Reid, *Radical Mandarin: The Memoirs of Escott Reid* (Toronto: University of Toronto Press, 1989), 244.

Chapter 11

Air Force Architect:
Air Marshal Wilfred Austin Curtis,
Chief of the Air Staff, 1947–1953

Jeff Noakes

In December of 1952, the Minister of National Defence, Brooke Claxton, travelled to Great Britain and Europe to inspect elements of the Canadian Army and Royal Canadian Air Force. At a time of war in Korea and growing NATO fears of the Soviet threat, in Europe, Canada's two fighter wings, one in England and one in France, provided what some have argued was the Alliance's most effective defence against Soviet aircraft.[1] Addressing those gathered at Grostenquin, No.2 Fighter Wing's base in France, on 13 December 1952, Claxton closed his speech by stating:

> I know I voice the feelings of everyone present when I say how sorry we are that Air Marshal Curtis, Chief of Staff of the Royal Canadian Air Force, should be prevented by illness in London from being here. He had come with me from Canada especially to be here and to inspect for himself the build-up of our air forces in Europe. The formation of this air division, twelve squadrons, of which already one-half are in existence with this wing here, was a crowning achievement of his own career in the service of this country in two world wars and in all three services. I know I express your hope for the speedy recovery of Air Marshal Curtis.[2]

Only two days before, Curtis had been rushed to a RAF hospital for emergency abdominal surgery and was thus prevented from completing the tour of bases and squadrons that he had played such an important role in establishing.

Wilfred Austin Curtis had served as a Royal Naval Air Service (RNAS) fighter pilot in the First World War and as a reservist in the Army and RCAF between the wars. Although he never attended a staff college, he has been described as one of the RCAF's best staff officers during the Second World War, at which time he was also a strong proponent of Canadianization.[3] He also held the unusual distinction of having served in the Navy, Army, and Air Force, of being the last Chief of Staff to have served in the First World War, and of being the only reservist ever to become a Chief of Staff of one of Canada's armed services. This last point caused some resentment within the Air Force when he was appointed Chief of the Air Staff (CAS). In fact, Curtis did not become a member of the Regular RCAF until shortly before his appointment as Chief of the Air Staff in September of 1947.[4] Until his retirement in early 1953, Curtis was thus directly involved in the rebuilding of the RCAF from its post-war nadir to a size and strength that have prompted some to describe the early 1950s as the beginning of the "golden years" for the service.[5]

Curtis was prepared and qualified for his appointment as CAS as a result of administrative ability developed in private business, ability proved and shaped into staff officer capability by interwar experience and wartime service. This he combined with an aptitude for hard work that tended on occasion towards overwork. Furthermore, Curtis' interwar acquaintance with other officers who would occupy senior positions during the Second World War also proved helpful. Ironically, Curtis' controversial status as a reservist was seen as a positive attribute by his predecessor, Air Marshal Robert Leckie, who wanted a reserve officer if at all possible to serve as CAS of a post-war RCAF that was expected to be composed in considerable part of auxiliary squadrons. Leckie was also impressed by Curtis' abilities, and Brooke Claxton, the Minister of National Defence (MND), found that Curtis also met many of the requirements of a chief of staff. With credentials and endorsements of this calibre, it is little wonder that Claxton would five years later remark on Curtis' absence at the front line of the air Cold War.

Wilfred Austin Curtis was born in Havelock, Ontario, in 1893, but his family moved to Toronto less than two years later, after fire destroyed the lumber mills owned by his grandfather. He attended Dovercourt Public School from 1898 to 1907, where he participated in cadet training during his final year. He then studied business at Central Technical School, leaving to take a job with the Royal Bank of Canada.[6] Upon the outbreak of the First World War, Curtis, like so many other young men working for the Royal Bank and other institutions, decided to join the military.[7] He applied for pilot training with the Royal Naval Air Service, but was not immediately accepted. In 1915, he joined the 34th Regiment (Non-

Permanent Active Militia – NPAM), and by the end of January 1916 had been transferred to the 21st Regiment (NPAM), appointed Provisionary Second Lieutenant, and had finally been accepted for flying training, which he undertook at the Curtiss Air School in Long Branch.[8] After qualifying as a pilot, Curtis was granted a provisional commission in the Royal Navy and sailed for England shortly thereafter. A serious training accident interrupted his training and kept him from a posting to a combat unit until late June 1917, when he joined No. 6 (N) Squadron in Flanders. Less than two months later, Curtis' squadron was disbanded due to a shortage of RNAS pilots and he joined No. 10 (N) Squadron, where he scored his first victory on 6 September. In January of 1918, Curtis scored his thirteenth and final victory, but was injured during the combat and sent to England on sick leave. At this time, he was awarded a bar to the Distinguished Service Cross he had been awarded in November 1917. Curtis was, however, destined not to return to combat. A series of medical boards granted him sick leave and he was repatriated to Canada. On 11 June 1919, Curtis relinquished his commission due to ill health.[9]

Shortly thereafter, however, Curtis renewed his ties with military aviation as a reservist in the Canadian Air Force (CAF). In the summer of 1920, two of the first students presenting themselves at Camp Borden for refresher courses were Curtis and Harold Edwards, with whom Curtis would serve during the Second World War. Two of the first instructors at the camp, A.A.L. Cuffe and N.R. Anderson, would also feature in Curtis' future.[10] Curtis, Edwards, Cuffe, and Anderson all subsequently occupied senior staff positions during the Second World War, and all served at various times as military members of the Air Council between 1940 and 1944.[11]

Curtis relinquished his commission in the CAF (Non-Permanent) in 1924, and for a short time returned entirely to civilian life. Having decided against returning to banking, Curtis eventually formed the insurance partnership of Moore and Curtis, which later became W.A. Curtis and Co., one of the most successful insurance brokerages in Toronto.[12] In 1926, Curtis joined the Militia as a captain in the Toronto Scottish Regiment and, in the meantime, maintained an involvement in aviation through the Toronto Flying Club, of which he was a founding member and which he helped support both financially and through his personal involvement.[13] Curtis became second-in-command and one of the first members of No. 10 (City of Toronto) Auxiliary Squadron when it was formed in 1933, and became its commanding officer in 1935, shortly after his promotion to Squadron Leader. Curtis devoted more and more time to the squadron and to the club, and in 1933, also made a recommendation at a Royal Canadian Legion convention in Toronto that the RCAF be made an autonomous service with its own chief of staff. In 1938, as the RCAF expanded, two more Ontario auxiliary squadrons were created in London and Hamilton, and Curtis, as one of the most experienced officers in the auxiliary air force, was given command of the wing and promoted to Wing Commander as a non-permanent officer.[14] Curtis later recalled, however, that "the wing, though, was never properly organized before the outbreak of war and never really got going."[15] Although the Air Force was expanding, it was still feeling the legacy of Depression-era parsimony.

In the months leading up to the outbreak of the Second World War, the RCAF began to prepare for the heavy enlistment expected with the outbreak of war, and Curtis was made responsible for preparing accommodations for what would soon become No. 1 Manning Depot on the grounds of the Canadian National Exhibition in Toronto.[16] As a result of the heavy workload associated with this task, Curtis took a few weeks' leave from the Air Force and his insurance business in mid-August 1939, but was called back to service late in the month as the situation in Europe rapidly degenerated.[17]

Curtis' promotion to Wing Commander in 1938, and his responsibility for No. 1 Manning Depot mark the beginning of his maturation as a skilful and invaluable staff officer. Curtis' business career, as well as his experience with the formation and operation of a flying club and an auxiliary squadron, may well have provided as good a preparation for wartime service as an Air Force staff officer as could have been offered by the RCAF until quite late in the interwar period. In fact, volume three of the RCAF official history argues that "his astute business skills translated well to air force administration."[18] In this respect, the fact that many of the senior officers with whom Curtis served and who had themselves attended Staff College recognized him as a good staff officer is significant.

Curtis' rapport with these other officers was also almost certainly affected by relationships that were the product of the very small interwar cadre from which the group of staff officers could be drawn. The small cadre and limited opportunities highlight the problem of preparing officers for senior staff positions in a small force that did not start to become overtly military in nature until its reorganization in 1927.[19] Indeed, not until late 1931 did the RCAF begin to give serious consideration to its requirements for national air defence and the organization necessary to support this task, and it was not until the spring of 1932 that its first officer returned from the Imperial Defence College.[20]

Beginning in the early 1920s, the RCAF had begun to send officers to the United Kingdom for specialist training; some of them were sent to the RAF Staff College. This process was accelerated in the years following 1936, and by 1937 one officer was attending the Imperial Defence College (IDC) while two others had already completed the course. This represented an improvement over earlier conditions, but spaces were still very limited. In addition to IDC work, twenty-two other officers had completed or were attending the RAF Staff College.[21]

The RCAF itself did not become a purely military organization until 1 November 1936, when the Department of Transport was formed to assume responsibility for the creation and implementation of civil aviation policy.[22] In the meantime, the RCAF, like the Navy and Army, had had to cope with the cutbacks prompted by the Depression which brought tremendous limitations on procurement of equipment as well as operations and training and thwarted the process of developing staff officers. Furthermore, the RCAF did not gain full independence from the army until 19 December 1938,[23] a change, as already noted, that Curtis fully supported. This delayed independence also undoubtedly limited opportunities for staff work and experience.

The importance of this staff training and experience was not overlooked. It was Air Commodore A.A.L. Cuffe, one of Curtis' instructors at Camp Borden in 1920, who, in December of 1939 as Air Officer Commanding (AOC) of Air Training Command (ATC), recommended that Curtis receive a posting as Senior Staff Officer Training at Air Training Command in Toronto. Someone with Curtis' qualifications, which Cuffe unfortunately did not specify in his letter, was needed in order to enforce training orders and supervise compliance with them. Although the war was only a few months old, ATC was already encountering problems with officers deviating from the approved system of training. Cuffe, as AOC, did not have sufficient time to address these problems and predicted that controlling the training system would become a greater task as more training stations became operational.[24] As a result, Curtis was posted to Air Training Command Toronto as Senior Staff Officer Training on 16 December 1939.[25] Subsequently, he was sent to RCAF HQ Ottawa and appointed Director of Postings and Careers on 21 January 1940. He was promoted to Group Captain in June of the same year.[26]

In March of 1941, Air Commodore Edwards, who had been Air Member for Personnel (AMP) since 1940 and was one of Curtis' fellow students from the Camp Borden days, recommended that Curtis, who had been ordered on a month's sick leave as the result of overwork connected with his appointment as Director of Postings and Careers,[27] be sent to Bermuda as part of this leave. This would enable Curtis to inspect the RCAF officers and airmen involved in Ferry Command's delivery of PBY Catalinas to Great Britain. Curtis was suggested for this task because the medical officer recommended that part of his leave be spent in a warm climate, but there were other reasons. Edwards considered him the logical choice for inspection duties, due to his knowledge of RCAF procedure and routine, and Curtis himself had been responsible for the posting of personnel to the Bermuda detachment.[28] This detachment had been experiencing a number of problems during its start-up, but these were largely ironed out by the summer of 1941.[29] After returning from sick leave, Curtis was given command of No.2 Service Flying Training School and its base in Uplands, Ontario. Subsequently, he was posted to RCAF Headquarters, Ottawa, 10 August 1941, and promoted to the rank of Air Commodore at the start of November 1941.[30]

Curtis' next posting was to prove both important and challenging. In November of 1941, he was appointed Deputy Air Officer Commanding-in-Chief of the RCAF Overseas, serving under Edwards. Among the significant challenges that Curtis would face was the attempt to attain "Canadianization" – the process whereby RCAF squadrons would be formed overseas, filled with Canadians, and organized into higher formations that would also be under Canadian control. Another crucial element of the Canadianization initiative was the effort to ensure that RCAF personnel serving with the RAF would be governed by Canadian regulations, which ensured them more favourable treatment with respect to pay, promotion, commissioning, and repatriation than was provided by RAF regulations.[31]

The RCAF official history argues that Edwards, who by late 1941 had been promoted to Air Vice Marshal, was chosen because of his experience with RCAF organization and manpower resources, proficiency in administration, and interest in the discipline and welfare of officers and airmen. His earlier expressions of concern about the situation overseas, as well as the recommendation of his predecessor, Air Vice Marshal L.F. Stevenson, also contributed to his appointment.[32] While the official history notes simply that Curtis was appointed Edwards' deputy, Curtis stated in a 1975 interview that he was Edwards' personal choice as Deputy Overseas Commander. The interview also reveals that Curtis and Edwards were on a first name basis and indicated that the two of them were quite close, although whether this friendship significantly predated their overseas postings is not clear.[33]

The Bermuda assignment, mentioned earlier, suggests that Edwards had already formed the opinion that Curtis was a useful staff officer, and his selection of Curtis as his deputy when Edwards was given command of the RCAF Overseas supports this contention. Although this may have been one of the reasons for his selection, Edwards may also have been influenced by the personal relationship that Curtis discussed. In any case, Curtis' administrative talents, as well as his more diplomatic approach, proved useful and were often more effective in dealing with the RAF than Edwards' often blunt and confrontational approach to the British and the concept of Canadianization. Curtis' skills were especially important since Edwards was often sidelined by ill health, and Curtis had to assume his responsibilities. In other cases Curtis found himself smoothing over problems between Edwards and senior RAF officers.[34]

Ill-health forced Edwards to return to Canada in January of 1944, and Curtis accompanied him, returning to RCAF Headquarters in Ottawa to become the Air Member for Air Staff (AMAS), responsible for operations, as well as the Air Member of the Canadian Section of the Permanent Joint Board on Defence (PJBD).[35] As AMAS, Curtis was closely involved in the planning of the RCAF's contribution to "Tiger Force," which was intended for operations against Japan after the defeat of Germany. As part of the process, Curtis, still pursuing the goal of Canadianization, defended the idea of integral RCAF groups or other formations within the air campaign against Japan.[36] As senior Canadian officer on the PJBD, Curtis was also involved in the Working Committee on Post-Hostilities Problems, which examined the future of the Canadian-American defence relationship.[37]

Curtis' experience as a staff officer in the Air Force as well as his administrative skills in general were seen as a useful asset by some outside the RCAF. Shortly before the end of the Second World War, C.D. Howe, as Minister of Reconstruction, attempted to persuade Curtis to become the new head of the Department of National Defence's re-organized Air Services Branch. Howe had a reputation for spotting men of administrative talent, many of whom had business backgrounds, and Curtis was no exception. In a March 1945 letter to Colin Gibson, Minister of National Defence for Air, Howe argued that Curtis was "an ideal appointment to this position.... His knowledge of the capabilities of men being discharged from the Air Force will be invaluable as a means of rebuilding the department. He is also a first class executive, and very much interested in the problems with which our civil aviation will be confronted."[38] Howe also noted that, subject to certain salary readjustments, Curtis was interested in the position.[39] In the days following the request, however, Howe made direct contact with Curtis at which point he was informed that Curtis did not wish to leave the RCAF.[40] Curtis was apparently not the only senior Air Force officer, either retired or who might soon be leaving the service, whom Howe tried to recruit for this position.[41] Howe appears to have made a second attempt to recruit Curtis the following year, Curtis, however, wrote a letter to Howe on 4 July 1946 again turning down the position of Director of Air Services. In the letter, Curtis stated that he had discussed the situation with Air Marshal Robert Leckie, CAS, and suggested that he might eventually accept the position if the RCAF considered that he had completed his work there, but Curtis "felt that it was his [Leckie's] wish that I continue with the RCAF."[42]

Leckie most definitely wanted Curtis to continue with the RCAF, since by 1946 the CAS had decided on Curtis as his replacement. Leckie had been giving considerable thought about whom he should recommend to the Minister of National Defence as his successor. In 1950, he wrote a letter to the Minister of National Defence, Brooke Claxton, reflecting on this choice. It is worth quoting at some length, because it discusses Curtis and it provides some insight into the process whereby one outgoing CAS chose his successor:

> For some time prior to my retirement on pension, I had given earnest thought whom I should recommend to you as my successor as Chief of the Air Staff. Having regard to the fact that the post-war Air Force would consist very largely of non-regular squadrons, it seemed to me appropriate that the senior post in the R.C.A.F. should be filled by an auxiliary officer, if one with suitable qualifications were available. Soon after Air Vice Marshal Curtis's appointment to Headquarters in the capacity of Air Member of Air Council for Air Staff, it became apparent to me that he might be my nomination. For fully two years he was under close observation and at least a year before I retired I had decided to recommend him for the post and steadily

groomed him for the job. However, since I was quite uncertain how you would regard the departure from normal practice in recommending a non-regular officer for appointment as Chief of the Air Staff, and since I could scarcely discuss it with you so long before my own retirement, it was necessary to allow Air Vice Marshal Curtis to assume that he would return to civil life along with other non-regular officers. This he did until such time as you yourself informed him of his pending appointment.[43]

Although Curtis' status as an auxiliary officer, albeit one on full-time duty, seemed an obstacle to his appointment as CAS, Leckie's letter makes it clear that one of the main reasons Leckie supported Curtis as his successor was *because* he was a member of the auxiliary, a trait which Leckie saw as a useful asset for a CAS in a post-war RCAF that was expected to be heavily reliant on auxiliary squadrons.[44] Curtis' abilities as a staff officer, already noted by others, undoubtedly also contributed to Leckie's decision to recommend Curtis as his successor.

If Curtis met Leckie's requirements as CAS, he also met Minister of National Defence Brooke Claxton's personal guidelines for chiefs of staff. Unfortunately, Claxton does not discuss Curtis' appointment in his memoirs, but he does discuss the range of experience required for a successful candidate for a position as a chief of staff, including appointments to the various branches of a service, having charge of a major command, and having experience with international co-operation. Curtis' career, as discussed above, met these requirements, Leckie's endorsement was also helpful, particularly since Claxton wrote in his memoirs that he discussed future chief of staff appointments with current chiefs of staff.[45] Claxton also stated that "it was also desirable that the officers becoming Chiefs of Staff should be over fifty and have a few more years service before retirement so as to give them an adequate pension when they retired."[46]

Leckie's mention of "grooming" a successor is also consistent with the material in Claxton's memoirs – that, during Claxton's ministry at least, efforts were made to formulate a long-term succession plan concerning the appointment of a service's future chiefs of staff, and that measures were taken to groom those officers.[47] It should be noted, however, that Leckie's letter stated that the CAS did not think it was suitable to discuss the appointment of a successor with Claxton or, for that matter, his predecessor Douglas Abbott until the end of his term as CAS drew near. This suggests the possibility of two parallel selection processes going on at some point – one by the CAS and one by the MND. If such parallel processes did exist at some point, they were eventually merged and were dealt with by the MND and Cabinet. Claxton recorded in his memoirs the following:

> Assuming a posting of three or four years in each position, it will be seen that the last ten or eleven years of the service career of a potential chief of staff are planned that far ahead. At least that is the ideal position. Certainly when I was at Defence Headquarters, I discussed with all the various chiefs of staff the careers of their senior officers looking at possible three or even four postings ahead. While many of these could not be carried out owing to one fact or another, it was a desirable objective.[48]

While in 1947 such long-term planning was obviously not possible for Claxton in regards to Curtis, since Curtis became CAS less than a year after Claxton's appointment, these thoughts suggest that the selection of chiefs of staff – during Claxton's tenure at least – was partially determined by criteria established by the MND and by input from the representative outgoing chief of staff.

With Leckie and Claxton supporting his appointment, Curtis was transferred to the RCAF (Regular) with the rank of Air Marshal and became Chief of the Air Staff on 1 September 1947.[49] Once appointed, Curtis served for longer than the usual post-war term of a chief of staff. Chiefs of staff were usually expected to hold their positions for approximately three years in order to "maximize freshness of outlook and vigour of activity, and ... to provide opportunity for others. For each service there should be a group of senior officers qualified to take virtually any post and be physically capable of holding it for at least two or three years in the event of an all-out war."[50] Although in agreement with this principle, Curtis served as CAS for almost twice as long. This extended tenure was the direct result of Claxton's long-term planning as described above. "Air Marshal Curtis," he wrote in his memoirs, "stayed for five and a half years so that his successor Air Vice-Marshal Slemon could have a more varied experience."[51] Curtis' prolonged period of service is another argument for his effectiveness as a commander and an indication that the diplomatic skills and restraint that proved valuable during his service as Deputy Air Officer Commanding-in-Chief of the RCAF Overseas were also of use to him as Chief of the Air Staff.[52]

His skills also prepared him for the post-war challenge. When Curtis took over as CAS in 1947, the country was still in the grip of post-war military retrenchment and contraction, and no serious consideration had been given to deployments outside of Canada, a state of affairs that persisted until the fall of 1948. By mid-1949, however, perceptions of the international situation had changed. In conjunction with the creation of NATO, the RCAF now had to give consideration to overseas commitments.[53] In late June 1950, the Korean War provoked an even stronger reaction. One of Canada's first moves was to commit 426 Squadron to provide trans-Pacific air transport for the UN in Korea – an operation that garnered favourable publicity for Curtis and the RCAF.[54] Korea also brought about more significant changes for the RCAF and Canada's military in general, most notably through the accelerated defence programme announced in 1950. Canada's defence budget increased from approximately 1.4 percent of the GNP in 1947, to 8.8 percent in 1952-53.[55]

A considerable portion of these new expenditures went to the support of Canada's aircraft industry through the procurement of military aircraft, including the Canadian-designed and built CF-100 and the Canadian-built versions of the F-86. Curtis was a strong supporter of a domestic aircraft industry, a stance which he attributed to wartime experience in unsuccessfully attempting to get combat aircraft – including those built in Canada – allocated to Canada. In a 1958 speech to the RCAF Benevolent Association, Curtis stated that this situation "meant that if Canada wants its Air Force to be equipped with the most modern and most suitable aircraft for our special needs, then we must build them ourselves."[56] One of the consequences of strong RCAF support for the aircraft industry at a time of strong defence funding was the development of an insistence on only the best possible equipment for the service.[57] Curtis was involved in this hands-on control of Air Force procurement. Colonel Randy Wakelam convincingly argues that some of the delays in CF-100 delivery were directly related to frequent changes made by the RCAF in the aircraft's operational requirements, and in early July 1950, Curtis himself even acknowledged the problems caused by this state of affairs.[58] During Curtis' time as CAS, the RCAF was also beginning the process of choosing a replacement for the CF-100; a process that ultimately produced the ill-fated Arrow.[59] Senior Air Force officers met in June of 1950 to discuss a replacement for the CF-100, even though the second prototype of that aircraft had yet to fly. Unconcerned about finances, they did worry about duplicating American or British efforts.[60] This approach ultimately contributed to a situation in which military proposals and recommendations could not be readily reconciled with fiscal limitations facing the Government, a problem that became especially acute once defence budgets began to contract after the 1952-1953 fiscal year.[61] Curtis' tenure as CAS was thus a baptism under Cold War fire; none of his predecessors had seen such peacetime pressure on his skills as commander of an air force and as negotiator with his political overlords.

Although the date of his retirement was made public on 8 November 1952, along with the announcement that Air Vice Marshal C.R. Slemon would replace him as CAS, Curtis still had almost three months of service remaining before his scheduled retirement on 31 January 1953.[62] A little over one month later, in the midst of visits by Curtis and Claxton to RCAF bases and squadrons in Great Britain and Europe, the CAS was hospitalized and underwent two emergency surgeries after an ongoing intestinal problem flared up.[63] Claxton acknowledged Curtis' role in establishing the RCAF in Europe, as well as the significance of the visit for Curtis himself in a note sent to the latter's hospital bed: "Knowing how much you have looked forward to the official ceremony at Grostenquin, representing, as it does, one of the crowning achievements of your own fine career in the Air Force and great contribution to its build up, I am particularly sorry that you cannot be there to participate. We shall all miss and be thinking of you."[64] After recuperating from surgery in Florida, Curtis returned to Ottawa, where on 31 January 1953, official ceremonies were held in front of "A" Building, National Defence Headquarters, to mark his retirement. Tributes both public and private flooded in as the new Chief of the Air Staff, Air Vice Marshal Slemon, took command.[65]

Although no longer CAS, Curtis remained involved with the aircraft industry and the Canadian military, in addition to his own business interests.[66] Of the many directorships he accepted after the war, the most notable was with A.V. Roe Canada, which he joined shortly after his retirement. Discussion of a closer association with the company began before Curtis' retirement, and he joined its Board of Directors as Vice-Chairman on 6 June 1953.[67] Grieg Stewart notes that "Curtis had played an intimate role with the development of the CF-100 and it only seemed natural he would be suitably rewarded with a position on the board of the company that received the contract to build nearly 700 of them."[68] Although not in a position of real authority, the Vice-Chairmanship allowed Avro to benefit from his service experience, while Curtis also saw his position as an opportunity to continue his support for the RCAF and to work in a business environment. The appointment also hints at a Canadian version of the military-industrial complex that developed in the United States.[69]

Curtis also maintained an active interest in Canadian defence and the Armed Forces, and was engaged in a number of issues. While some of his contributions were connected with his support of the aviation industry in general and Avro Canada in particular,[70] others were related to Canada's armed forces in general. He, for instance, was one of the retired senior officers who argued against unification in front of the Special Committee on Defence in 1964.[71] He also involved himself in the debate surrounding the provision of nuclear weapons for the Canadian military, supporting their acquisition both publicly in newspapers and privately in correspondence with Lester B. Pearson in the spring of 1962, while the latter was Leader of the Opposition.[72] The former Chief of the Air Staff also fostered a more direct involvement with the military through his appointment as honourary commander of two units with which he had once served. He was appointed Honourary Wing Commander of 400 Squadron in Toronto, as well as Honourary Colonel of the Toronto Scottish Regiment.[73]

Wilfred Austin Curtis died in Toronto on 7 August 1977. He was the last Canadian Chief of Staff to have served in the First World War, and the only reservist to have ever held such a position. Respected by both his predecessor and the Minister with whom he worked, Curtis was prepared and qualified for his appointment as CAS as a result of administrative ability developed in private business, ability that was proven and shaped into staff officer capability by interwar experience and wartime service. During his long tenure as Chief of the Air Staff from 1947 to 1953, the Royal Canadian Air Force was built up from a post-war low to a force that included NATO's most potent fighter force in Europe due, in no small part, to his efforts.

ENDNOTES

CHAPTER 11

1. David Bercuson, "Canada, NATO and Rearmament, 1950-1954: Why Canada Made a Difference (But not for Very Long)," in John English and Norman Hillmer, eds., *Making a Difference? Canada's Foreign Policy in a Changing World Order* (Toronto: Lester Publishing, 1992), 104-105.

2. "Speech by Honourable Brooke Claxton, Minister of National Defence of Canada ... at Grostenquin, Lorraine, France, on Saturday, 13 December 1952," National Archives of Canada (hereinafter referred to as NAC), Wilfred Austin Curtis Papers, MG 31 G9, Vol. 1, file 8.

3. Brereton Greenhous et al., *The Crucible of War, 1939-1945: The Official History of the Royal Canadian Air Force,* Volume III, (Toronto: University of Toronto Press, 1994), 63.

4. Douglas How, "Curtis to Quit Air Force Soon, Slemon Succeeds," *Globe and Mail,* 8 November 1952, 3. Unfortunately, there does not seem to be any readily available documentary evidence of the debate and resentment that Curtis' appointment created within the RCAF, and although it is referred to by both Norman Hillmer and Arthur Bishop, neither provides a source for this information. Some of it was derived from personal interviews, and it is known that some of the available documentary sources have had some controversial documents and statements removed from them, often by those who gave the documents to the various institutions holding them. "Particulars of Service," Curtis personnel file; Norman Hillmer, "Curtis, Wilfred Austin," in *The Canadian Encyclopedia,* Vol. 1 (Edmonton: Hurtig Publishers, 1988), 558; Arthur Bishop, *Salute! Canada's Great Military Leaders from Brock to Dextraze* (Toronto: McGraw-Hill Ryerson, 1997), 228.

5. See, for example, Larry Milberry, ed., *Sixty Years: The RCAF and CF Air Command, 1924-1968* (Toronto: CANAV Books, 1984), 258.

6. Curtis personnel file; Bishop, 228.

7. By 1918, 1,495 Royal Bank men had joined the armed services, a

considerable number when in 1914 the bank had had 2,832 employees. Duncan McDowall, *Quick to the Frontier: Canada's Royal Bank* (Toronto: McClelland & Stewart, 1993), 121.

8. Curtis personnel file.

9. Bishop, 228-232; Handwritten note by Curtis, n.d., NAC, MG 31 G9, Vol. 1, file 1. Other correspondence related to Curtis' efforts to be accepted for pilot training, and his eventual acceptance, can also be found in this file. A number of Curtis' medical histories contained in RCAF medical forms from the mid-1930s also note that in 1918 Curtis had been suffering from neurasthenia. "Report of Medical Re-Examination," 30 March 1938, Curtis personnel file. Curtis also suffered some long-term effects from his 1916 crash during training. Curtis to Officer Paying Imperial Pensions, 23 December 1919, NAC, MG 31 G9, Vol. 1, file 1.

10. W.A.B. Douglas, *The Creation of a National Air Force: The Official History of the Royal Canadian Air Force*, Volume II, (Toronto: University of Toronto Press, 1986), 52. As an interesting sidenote, the medical officer for this training camp was F/L Norman Bethune.

11. "Air Council Members," Memorandum, Hillmer to Douglas, 13 January 1984, Department of National Defence, Directorate of History and Heritage (hereinafter referred to as DHH), Curtis Permanent Reference File (PRF).

12. Bishop, 232.

13. Ibid., 232-233.

14. RCAF Overseas Press Release No. 131, DHH, Curtis PRF file; Bishop, *Salute!*, 232-233; "Particulars of Service, Canadian Armed Forces, 317, Air Marshal Wilfred Austin Curtis," Curtis personnel file; Samuel Kostenuk and John Griffin, *RCAF Squadron Histories and Aircraft, 1924-1968* (Toronto: Samuel Stevens Hakkert & Company, 1977), 40. There are some discrepancies in the dates provided by Bishop and those provided in the personnel file and some other sources. The precise year in which Curtis made his recommendation for an independent RCAF is not entirely certain; some correspondence in his DHH permanent reference file displays some confusion between 1923 and 1933.

15. "Summary of an Interview with Air Marshal W.A. Curtis by R.V. Dodds, F.J. Hatch, Norman Hillmer," July 1975, 2, DHH, Curtis PRF.

16. Bishop, 233; "Particulars of Service," Curtis personnel file.

17. Ibid.

18. Greenhous, 52.

19. Douglas, 122.
20. Ibid., 124.
21. Ibid., 145.
22. Kostenuk and Griffin, 17.
23. Douglas, 134-138; and Kostenuk and Griffin, 17-18.
24. A/C A.A.L. Cuffe to CAS, "Wing Commander W.A. Curtis – Training," 11 December 1939, Curtis personnel file. The deviations from the system of training are not specified in the letter.
25. "Particulars of Service," Curtis personnel file.
26. Ibid.
27. Greenhous, 51; "Medical History of an Invalid," Curtis personnel file.
28. AMP to MND for Air, Memorandum "Visit to Bermuda," 4 March 1941, Curtis personnel file.
29. Carl A. Christie, *Atlantic Bridge: The History of RAF Ferry Command* (Toronto: University of Toronto Press, 1995), 98-121.
30. "Particulars of Service," Curtis personnel file. During his time at Uplands, Curtis made a cameo appearance as himself in the movie "Captains of the Clouds." Larry Milberry and Hugh Halliday, *The Royal Canadian Air Force at War, 1939-1945* (Toronto: CANAV Books, 1990), 22-23.
31. Greenhous, 14. For a discussion of Canadianization, and of general air policy related to the RCAF Overseas during the Second World War, see ibid., 13-124.
32. Greenhous, 44-52.
33. Ibid., 52; Summary of an Interview with Air Marshal W.A. Curtis by R.V. Dodds, F.J. Hatch, Norman Hillmer," July 1975, 3, 6, DHH, Curtis PRF.
34. Greenhous, 52-53; "Summary of an Interview with Air Marshal W.A. Curtis by R.V. Dodds, F.J. Hatch, Norman Hillmer," July 1975, 7, DHH, Curtis PRF. Despite his more diplomatic approach, however, the official history notes that Curtis was a strong supporter of Edwards' efforts. Greenhous, 63.
35. Ibid., 99; "Particulars of Service," Curtis personnel file. The PJBD was (and still is) responsible for considering Canadian-American defence issues.
36. Greenhous, 106-124.
37. Grieg Stewart, *Shutting Down the National Dream: A.V. Roe and the Tragedy of the Avro Arrow* (Toronto: McGraw-Hill Ryerson, 1997), 57.
38. C.D. Howe to Colin Gibson, 10 March 1945, Curtis personnel file.

39. Ibid.

40. Colin Gibson to C.D. Howe, 16 March 1945, Curtis personnel file.

41. A/V/M Thomas Cowley to C.D. Howe, 6 March 1945; Howe to Cowley, 10 March 1945, NAC, C.D. Howe Papers, MG 27 III B20, Vol. 170, file "Family and Personal Correspondence (4), Jan-Aug 1945."

42. Curtis to Howe, 4 July 1946, NAC, MG 31 G9, Vol. 1, file 9.

43. Robert Leckie to Brooke Claxton, 3 August 1950, Curtis personnel file. A copy of this letter is also found in the Curtis papers, NAC, MG 31 G9, Vol. 1, file 9. This letter appears to be the only remaining documentary source providing the reasons for Leckie's choice; the Leckie Papers, (NAC MG 30 E251) consist of a collection of newspaper clippings and are of extremely limited use to researchers. The D.C. Abbott papers (NAC, MG 32 B6) dealing with his tenure at the Department of National Defence (August 1945-December 1946) are also of very limited use.

44. Randall Wakelam, "Flights of Fancy: RCAF Fighter Procurement, 1945 – 1954," unpublished M.A. Thesis, Royal Military College, 1997, 72-106.

45. NAC, Brooke Claxton Papers, MG 32 B5, Vol. 222, file "Memoirs - Defence (9)," 1533-C-1533-D. Claxton was specifically discussing the requirements for a Chief of the General Staff – an Army appointment – but general principles about requirements for Chiefs of Staff can be extracted from his discussion. One of the most frustrating passages in Claxton's memoirs states that he could write a chronological account of the events while he was at DND, but that such an account "would be a book of reference which might occasionally be useful to the file clerks or even to the military historian or the student of departmental organization and administration." Ibid., Vol. 221, file "Memoirs - Defence (4)," 896.

46. Ibid., 1533-E. Claxton's comments about pensions did not hold true here, however; due to most of Curtis' military career having been spent in reserve units, he encountered problems with eligibility for a full pension. See NAC, MG 31 G9, Vol. 1, file 6, and Curtis personnel file for more correspondence and details.

47. Claxton, for example, was already considering successors for Slemon when talking to Ralph Campney immediately before Campney took over as Minister of National Defence, even though Claxton thought Slemon could still serve for a few more years. NAC, MG 32 B5, Vol. 222, file "Memoirs - Defence (9)," alternate ending, 34-35.

48. NAC, MG 32 B5, Vol. 222, file "Memoirs - Defence (9)," 1533-D.
49. "Particulars of Service," Curtis personnel file.
50. NAC, MG 32 B5, Vol. 222, file "Memoirs - Defence (9)," 1533B-1533C.
51. Ibid., 1533-E. See Curtis to Gordon, 20 November 1952, NAC, MG 31 G9, Vol. 1, file 5, for Curtis' agreement with the principle of short terms of service.
52. This includes Curtis' avoidance of controversy through inappropriate public speeches and comments, an action particularly disliked by Claxton. NAC, MG 32 B5, Vol. 221, file "Memoirs - Defence (4)," 897.
53. Wakelam, 135-136.
54. "An Essential of Transport," *Saturday Night*, December 19, 1950, 6. In early December 1950 following the Chinese intervention in the war, 426 was even placed on alert to fly to Korea to airlift troops out should that prove necessary. Memorandum, Claxton to St. Laurent, 05 December 1950, NAC, MG 32 B5, Vol. 123, file "Prime Minister the Rt. Honourable Mr. Louis St. Laurent." From shortly after his posting as CAS began, Curtis also defended the concept of functional, not regional, organization for the RCAF, a stand that Claxton admitted was justified and essential to the proper functioning of the air force, especially when simultaneously facing the Korean War and commitments in Europe. Ibid., Vol. 221, file "Memoirs - Defence (4)," 862-863.
55. Bercuson, "Canada, NATO and Rearmament," 103-104. Bercuson argues that the Korean war temporarily suppressed control of defence spending and priorities by the Ministry of Finance. Ibid., 107-108. Wakelam draws similar conclusions, arguing that prior to Korea the post-war RCAF had been planning, making preparations for expansion and modernization, but that it had been driven and controlled by financial needs and concerns rather than by defence needs and concerns. Wakelam, 141-146, 183-184.
56. "Address delivered to the annual dinner of the RCAF Benevolent Association, Ottawa, 12 May 1958," 2-3, NAC, MG 31 G9, Vol. 2, file 30. This speech was reprinted in the *Financial Post* on May 17, 1958, 3, with the title "The Avro Arrow NOT Obsolete." Stewart, *Shutting Down the National Dream*, 237. This speech is often cited in the literature concerning the Avro Arrow; what is not often cited is Curtis' use of the case of the Ford Edsel as a means of explaining development costs. In all fairness, it should be pointed out that Curtis was speaking at a time when the

Edsel's high development costs were public knowledge but before it gained its reputation as a complete lemon. "Address to the RCAF Benevolent Association," 7. In this speech, Curtis was specifically referring to the attempt to obtain Canadian-built Hurricanes in 1942, but he also referred to other problems with obtaining modern combat aircraft for Canada. Although Curtis used these accounts to justify his support for a Canadian aircraft industry, the RCAF official history considers some of his statements about problems with allocation to be an "imperfect rendering of reality." Greenhous, 94.

57. Stewart, *Shutting Down the National Dream*, 199-200.
58. Wakelam, 135.
59. Stewart, *Shutting Down the National Dream*, 177-179.
60. Wakelam, 155.
61. Glen Berg argues that while the RCAF wanted quality and quantity, politicians weighed the nature of the military threat, considered budgetary limitations, and from 1959 onwards decided that Canada could not afford the "best" aircraft in the numbers that the RCAF wanted. Douglas Bland points to this situation and to similar problems in the Navy and Army. Glen Berg, "Scrambling for Dollars: Resource Allocation and the Politics of Canadian Fighter Aircraft Procurement, 1943-1983," (unpublished M.A. Thesis, Royal Military College of Canada, 1993), 196-197; Douglas Bland, *The Administration of Defence Policy in Canada, 1947 to 1985* (Kingston: Ronald P. Frye and Company, 1987), 153.
62. Directorate of Public Relations, Release No. 8126, 8 November 1952, DHH, Curtis PRF.
63. Curtis personnel file.
64. Handwritten note from Claxton to Curtis, n.d., but obviously between 10 and 13 December 1952, NAC, MG 31 G9, Vol. 1, file 8.
65. See Curtis personnel file for details of Curtis' departure ceremonies, and NAC, MG 31 G9, Vol. 1, file 5 for correspondence and other documents relating to Curtis' retirement. See also Department of Public Relations Release No. 8162, 31 January 1953, DHH, Curtis PRF.
66. Curtis stated in late November 1952 that he had no intention of discontinuing his interest in aviation, and hoped to keep in touch with friends in service and aviation. Curtis to St. Barbe, 20 November 1952, NAC, MG 31 G9, Vol. 1, file 5.
67. James L. Jackson, Assistant Public Relations Officer, A.V. Roe Canada,

to Curtis, 12 June 1952, Curtis personnel file; Gordon to Curtis, 10 November 1952; Curtis to Gordon, 20 November 1952; Smye to Curtis, 10 November 1952; Curtis to Smye, 20 November 1952, NAC, MG 31 G9, Vol. 1, file 5. Several lists of directorships appear in the Curtis Papers as well as his personnel file; the most readily accessible, however, are probably those found in *The Canadian Who's Who* and similar publications. Among Curtis' numerous community involvement's outside of aviation and the military was his work in the establishment of a second university in Toronto – York University, and he was appointed its first Chancellor in 1961. "Vote Air Marshal York Chancellor," *Toronto Star*, April 13, 1961, DHH, Curtis PRF; NAC, MG 31 G9, Vol. 2, files 42-43.

68. Stewart, *Arrow Through the Heart*, 112.

69. For Avro's suggested public explanation of Curtis' acceptance of a directorship, see "Suggested outline of remarks for Air Marshal Curtis on announcing his appointment to Board of Directors A.V. Roe Canada Limited," n.d., NAC, MG 31 G9, Vol. 1, file 6. For instance, Curtis made some overseas trips to support the ultimately successful attempt to persuade the Belgians to acquire the CF-100. Stewart, *Shutting Down the National Dream*, 204. Curtis was not alone among retired senior air force officers in accepting positions with important defence contractors; at Curtis' suggestion A/V/M J.L. Plant joined Avro as executive VP and general manager at the end of 1957, shortly thereafter becoming president and general manager. Ibid., 223.

70. W.A. Curtis, "Developing Canada's Air Defences," *Saturday Night*, May 2, 1953, 7-8; "Address delivered to the annual dinner of the RCAF Benevolent Association, Ottawa, 12 May 1958," NAC, MG 31 G9, Vol. 2, file 30.

71. Bland, *The Administration of Defence Policy in Canada*, 40-44. See also NAC, MG 31 G9, Vol. 2, file 30, for a copy of Curtis' address to the committee, as well as ibid., file 34, for correspondence and other materials related to unification.

72. "Air Marshal Curtis on Nuclear Defence," *The Gazette*, 3 December 1962, DHH, Curtis PRF; Curtis to Pearson, 29 March 1962; Pearson to Curtis, 5 April 1962, NAC, MG 31 G9, Vol. 1, file 10.

73. "Particulars of Service," Curtis personnel file.

CHAPTER 12

AIR MARSHAL ROY SLEMON:
THE *RCAF*'S ORIGINAL[1]

Sandy Babcock

BETWEEN 1945 and 1964, only five Royal Canadian Air Force (RCAF) officers occupied the office of Chief of Air Staff (CAS). They were largely efficient and effective managers of personnel and resources during a period of tremendous challenges. These challenges included the rapid post-war demobilization of the RCAF followed by an impressive period of organizational growth; an increasingly complex and changing technological environment; shifting alliance commitments and partnerships; and growing governmental, military, and public awareness of the threat posed by the Soviet Union from over the polar cap. Yet, despite the competence and professionalism with which they went about their jobs, Robert Leckie, Wilf Curtis, Roy Slemon, Hugh Campbell and C.R. "Larry" Dunlap are today largely unknown outside of the air force community.

The purpose of this chapter is to examine the life of one of these individuals, Air Marshal (AM) Roy Slemon, whose career was legendary within the RCAF. His rise to the top of his profession was swift and sure, his accomplishments were many, and his legacy was substantial. While this review will provide insights into our Air Force heritage, its main purpose is to explore the traits, values, and accomplishments of one of Canada's most outstanding military leaders.

Charles Roy Slemon was born on 7 November 1904, in Winnipeg, Manitoba, to Samuel and Mary (Bonser) Slemon. His mother was a British emigrant who met her future husband during a visit to Canada. Samuel, who was an inspector for the Winnipeg Electric Company, had been widowed after his first wife died from tuberculosis. William, Roy's half-brother, was the product of this previous marriage.[2] The family home was located in the working class area in north Winnipeg. Roy's early education was at Luxton Public School and St. John's Technical High School, where he took engineering courses. In 1921, his interest in engineering led him to enroll at the University of Manitoba to pursue a Bachelor of Science degree in Civil Engineering.[3]

Before joining the Air Force, a young Roy Slemon demonstrated courage and resolve that were beyond his years. While still a teenager, he obtained a job as a streetcar operator in place of striking workers. While there were many bloody encounters during the strike, which at times targeted the replacement workers, Slemon's self-confidence, demeanour, and resourcefulness brought him through the experience unscathed.[4]

Although there was no apparent military tradition in his family, Roy Slemon became interested in the military at an early age. On 1 November 1920, while still in high school and just before his sixteenth birthday, he joined the University of Manitoba contingent of the Canadian Officer Training Corps (COTC). He eventually received Infantry Certificates "A" and "B" and, on 1 May 1923, was commissioned as a Lieutenant on the General List of the Active Militia.[5]

During this period, summer jobs for university engineering students were often with the railway companies. An interesting alternative presented itself in 1923 with the creation of the Provisional Pilot Officer (PPO) programme, which was designed by the Canadian Air Force (CAF) to teach engineering students to fly during three successive summers. The CAF recognized that it had to begin recruiting from the post-World War I generation and considered an engineering degree an essential qualification to be a pilot.[6] This opportunity attracted Slemon, and he was one of nine trainees accepted into the first PPO class beginning in May 1923 at Camp Borden.[7]

From the very beginning, Slemon showed himself to be a very good pilot and favourably impressed his instructors and fellow trainees with his character, personal attributes, and potential. He was described as being "very keen" about flying; his appearance and military bearing met with approval.[8] A life-long friend and future Air Vice Marshal (AVM), Ralph McBurney, who entered the PPO program the following year, noticed that Slemon was the natural leader of his class in the eyes of the instructors and his peers. For example, Slemon often would be made responsible for organizing various class tasks. Slemon had a quiet sense of humour and his reserved nature was at times mistaken for shyness. He tended to keep his opinions to himself until he had something relevant to say; then he had the ability to state an opposing point of view without offending superiors.[9] He was seen as a "very good type of Officer," and his instructors recommended that he be accepted for further training in 1924.[10]

Slemon was so enamoured of flying that he had difficulty waiting for the 1923-24 school year to pass in Winnipeg so that he could return to Camp Borden for the second phase of his training. He became a regular visitor to the Winnipeg Air Station and Repair Depot, where he expressed an enthusiasm for aviation in general with a particular interest in the aircraft then at the station.[11]

The RCAF, which the CAF became on 1 April 1924, was heavily involved at this time in photographic survey operations across Canada on behalf of the Government. Because of a concern about a shortage of pilots to perform these operations, four of the five trainees that returned for the second term over the summer of 1924 were asked to continue with their flying training instead of going back to university. On 22 December 1924, these four students, Slemon, W.C. Weaver, E.J. Durnin, and C.M. Anderson were the first graduates on a RCAF Wings Parade and were confirmed as Pilot Officers in the Non-Permanent RCAF.[12] Slemon, along with the others, was transferred subsequently to the Permanent RCAF with a seniority date of 1 April 1925.[13] In 1931, his seniority date for the Permanent Force was amended to coincide with the 1924 receipt of his pilot's wings.

Slemon's performance during the second and third phases of training, which included time in the Avro 504K and the Sopwith Camel, continued to be outstanding. He was assessed as being "intelligent," "open to instruction," and likely to be "a reliable and efficient pilot."[14]

He finished second during the third phase of training behind Weaver, who was placed on the seniority list just above Slemon. Weaver and Anderson were to die in separate flying accidents in 1927, which was the same year that Durnin resigned from the RCAF after being posted away from an operational unit in Winnipeg to the flying school at Camp Borden.[15] This left Slemon as the sole representative from the RCAF's first graduating class, which provided him with a certain cachet throughout his career. It also meant that he was uncontested as the senior member of the RCAF's post-World War I generation.

Although no one has been singled out as Slemon's mentor, it does appear that three officers in particular helped him along the way. The first of these was George Eric Brookes, who happened to be one of Slemon's flight instructors during all three phases of basic pilot training. Brookes thought highly of his earnest young student, and they were to serve together several times during the next two decades. Every assessment Brookes wrote on Slemon was full of high praise. When No. 6 (RCAF) Bomber Group stood up in 1943 with Brookes as its commander, it was Roy Slemon who served as his deputy as Senior Air Staff Officer (SASO). They respected and had affection for one another, as was demonstrated during Slemon's tenure as CAS, when he took the time during a mess dinner speech to acknowledge affectionately the contribution of a then retired AVM Brookes.[16]

From 6 January 1925 to 7 March 1925, Slemon was provided with a general refresher flying course before proceeding from Borden to RCAF Station Vancouver for seaplane training on the HS2L and Vickers Viking. He demonstrated a strong aptitude for flying this type of aircraft and was assessed as doing "exceptionally well from the start and should prove [to be] an unusually reliable Boat Pilot."[17] On 29 May 1925, 20 year old Pilot Officer Roy Slemon reported to the RCAF sub-station at Victoria Beach, Manitoba, for his first operational tour with the Civil Government Air Operations Branch. Initially he was employed on forest fire detection patrols in order to familiarize him with the area and then was used on photographic survey operations.[18]

Although his work performance was never at issue, Roy Slemon's RCAF career almost ended before it really had a chance to start. During the summer of 1925, he was called into the Winnipeg Air Station Commander's office to be confronted by Wing Commander Stanley Scott, the Director of the RCAF. While acknowledging Slemon's contribution to the RCAF of the day through his flying, Scott was convinced that if Slemon was going to have a role in the future of an increasingly technological organization, then he had to complete his university degree. Upon thinking about it, Slemon agreed.[19] That September, following his participation in flying operations over the summer, Slemon returned to the University of Manitoba to pursue his degree on leave without pay. But, he found the confines of a classroom far less interesting than flying duties: while passing nine courses, he had failing grades in five others during his first year back at school. It was difficult for him to show interest in subjects marginal to his RCAF career, such as theoretical railway design or theory of error and structural design. Since the final year of the degree program focused on matters of even less relevance to his flying career, including steel bridge design, railway engineering, and sewage planning, he expressed a preference not to return to school after the 1926 summer flying season.[20] However, in this, he was not to have his way. Scott, who was still aware that Pilot Officer Slemon had not completed his course of studies, warned "that his future in the Force is certain to be prejudiced" if he did not do so. Also, Slemon was advised that without a degree, he was ineligible for promotion.[21] Accepting the inevitable, he returned to university in September 1926 with renewed focus and managed to complete the Bachelor of Science program over the next two academic years while taking part in flying operations between April and September of each year.

It was at this point that a second senior officer took interest in Slemon's future and helped his career go forward. Squadron Leader G.O. Johnson, the Commanding Officer of No. 1 Wing in Winnipeg, was well satisfied with Slemon's work performance, but he thought that it was unfair for the RCAF to ask Slemon to leave university in 1924 in order to continue flight training and then to deny him career advancement for doing so. In fact, Slemon already had been passed over for promotion to Flying Officer and was losing ground to his peers. In 1926, Johnson had recommended Slemon's promotion to Flying Officer but without any success. The 1927 flying season was about to begin. Johnson wanted to give Slemon additional responsibilities, but could not do so unless the promotion came through. Noting that as "the seniority of young officers vitally affects their future in the Air Force, and may mean a difference of several years to a promotion to a higher rank," Johnson asked that the Department of National Defence give the issue of Slemon's promotion and seniority date further thought.[22] It took the RCAF a year to decided on this matter; finally, in April 1928, Slemon's promotion to Flying Officer was announced with a seniority date of 1 April 1926.[23] This restoration of Slemon to the position of senior and ranking post-World War I RCAF officer would pay dividends for the rest of his career.[24]

Air crashes were a fact of life during this period, as witnessed by the 1927 deaths of Weaver and Anderson, and on the ninth of June of that year, Roy Slemon was to play the pivotal role in averting the loss of life in such an accident. It was a common practice for aircraft to fly in formation due to the frequency of mechanical breakdowns. On that day, Slemon was flying next to a civilian airplane that suddenly experienced a structural breakdown. It crashed in Cross Lake, Manitoba, and rescue of the four occupants from shore appeared unlikely. Disregarding the dangers, Slemon put his flying boat down in the lake's rough waters and taxied next to the sinking aircraft. The survivors were able to hold onto Slemon's plane as he took them to shore. For this act, Squadron Leader Johnson put Pilot Officer Slemon's name forward for recognition. This led the RCAF to nominate him for the McKee Trans-Canada Trophy, which, beginning in 1927, was to be given annually to the individual who had made an outstanding contribution to aviation in Canada. Although he did not win, Slemon does have the distinction of being the first and most junior officer ever nominated by the RCAF for this prestigious award.[25]

Between May 1925 and December 1932, Slemon was mainly employed out of Winnipeg, most often on photographic survey missions. His field of operations stretched from the Lakehead area of Northern Ontario, across the northern segments of Manitoba, Saskatchewan, and Alberta, and into the Northwest Territories. These deployed operations were normally run from small sub-detachments in an environment that required junior officers to demonstrate initiative and to assume responsibilities early in their careers. Moreover, these operations frequently took place in isolated areas, where the flying and landing conditions could be hazardous – errors in judgment or mechanical failures could have lethal consequences. Slemon excelled under these circumstances, and he was consistently praised by his superiors for the quality of his work. Annual assessments by his superiors during these six and a half years included comments regarding his "exceptional" flying abilities,[26] his above average zeal in his approach to duties,[27] his "excellent work," "sound judgment,"[28] and "very high standards."[29] When No. 4 Photographic Detachment was formed in 1928, Flying Officer Slemon was chosen to lead it and his performance soon compared very favourably with that of seven other detachment leaders.[30] This led to his being recommended for accelerated promotion to Flight Lieutenant,[31] which was awarded temporarily in May 1930 and then permanently in November of that year. His seniority was backdated to 1 April 1929, thereby bypassing four World War I veterans who had been senior to him.[32]

Slemon's hallmark characteristic was thorough preparation. He typically would examine an issue from various perspectives until he firmly understood it, sometimes to the distraction of others.[33] An example of this preparedness was provided in 1928, when he wrote to the Director, Civil Government Air Operations, to express concern about conditions to be faced during a forthcoming operation near the junction of the Athabaska and Clearwater Rivers in northern Alberta. Slemon believed that the intended camp location did not provide a safe landing area for flying boats due to a swift current, floating timber and debris, and muddy waters that hid the location of shifting sand bars. Moreover, he believed that the proposed area of flying operations out of this camp site posed an undue risk because it was near the limit of the airplane's range and safe emergency landing sites were absent.[34] While, in the end, he was required to carry on with the mission as planned, this incident demonstrated not only the professional and careful approach he had to his work but also his willingness to challenge authority if the situation warranted. Roy Slemon was no "yes man."

In January 1931, Slemon was temporarily posted to Camp Borden for a few months as an instructor in navigation. In preparation for this, he attended an air pilotage course in Calshot, England, where his overall performance was assessed as outstanding. His course report indicated that he was "[v]ery keen and ha[d] worked very hard" and it was expected that he would make a very good instructor.[35] He lived up to these expectations at Camp Borden, where he was seen as having "complete command of his subject." His superiors also liked his military bearing, as shown by comments indicating that Slemon was a "steady[,] thorough and reliable officer of excellent deportment and strong personality ... Smart on parade and off. A very good type of officer."[36]

Slemon returned to Winnipeg in time for photographic operations during the summer of 1931. Over the next two years, he continued to impress his superiors with the quality of his work and his dedication to duty. This was also a time when he began to address personal development in the area of the military arts.

Members of the RCAF of this period have been referred to as "bush pilots in uniform."[37] Certainly photographic operations and forest fire patrols did little towards preparing its members to fight the forthcoming war. To compensate for this, the RCAF annually sent one or two of its more promising officers to RAF Staff College in Andover, England. However, in order to qualify for this training, officers first were required to pass a difficult Staff College qualifying examination. There were also promotion examinations that helped develop the military skills of officers.

Before attempting the qualifying examination, Slemon was selected to attend the Staff College preparatory course between October 1932 and January 1933 at Royal Military College in Kingston, Ontario. It was evident that, like many other RCAF officers, he was being exposed to a new field in his profession. His instructors appreciated how he applied himself, noting on his course assessment that Slemon had "applied himself and ha[d] made good progress on work entirely new to him."[38]

The reading list for the 1933 Staff College qualifying examination included thirty-one books and manuals, covering works familiar to the military history student of today by such authors as Mahan, Foch, Liddell-Hart, Churchill, and Corbett.[39] The examination consisted of six essays produced over three days on assigned questions.

Slemon was to fail his first attempt at the Staff College qualifying examination, which he attributed later in life to not having the ability to absorb the assigned material.[40] Someone a little less self-critical may have noted that pilots engaged in detached operations across Canada's north rarely were able to obtain copies of the full course readings.[41] In fact, the Commanding Officer of RCAF Station Winnipeg telegraphed RCAF Headquarters (HQ) in Ottawa during October 1932 in an attempt to find the required source material specifically for Slemon to be able to study for the examination scheduled for January 1933.[42] It is also noteworthy that Slemon was ill twice during this period, which likely impacted his ability to study.[43] After taking additional time to study and to gain additional experience, he re-wrote and passed the qualifying examination in 1936.[44]

In 1935, Slemon also failed his first attempt at promotion examination "C", which was required for advancement to Squadron Leader. Of the seven examination subjects, he had to be re-tested for Subject III (administration).[45] He passed this final subject in 1936. Lest he be criticized unduly for this, it is important to note that he was the top-ranked officer for the 1936 promotion examination "C" board and that the difficulty of the examinations were such that only three of the ten officers tested that year passed.[46]

Roy Slemon was a fit individual throughout his life, maintaining a weight of around 170 pounds (77 kg) on his 5 feet 11 inch (151 cm) frame for most of his adult life, and he enjoyed pastimes such as swimming, tennis, and golf. He also had good looks; some compared his appearance to the movie star Errol Flynn. Early in his career, he often made an impression at RCAF social functions by arriving late but always with a beautiful, and different, escort.[47] These footloose ways were to change.

In 1932, while on his way to the Staff College preparatory course in Kingston, Slemon stopped to visit a branch of his family in Bowmanville, Ontario. It was there that he met his second cousin, Marion, who he courted and married on 14 September 1935.[48] From every account, Marion was a gracious and capable partner who fully complemented Roy's personal and professional life.

Between 1933 and 1938, Slemon had a quick series of postings to Camp Borden as a navigation and flight instructor, to RCAF HQ as an Assistant Staff Officer, Air Operations 2, and to a photographic detachment based in Ottawa as Commanding Officer. His annual assessments continued to describe him in glowing terms: "An excellent officer in every respect,"[49] "shows considerable promise. He is smart and intelligent,"[50] and "[t]he outstanding features of his work have been thoroughness, a careful attention to details and sound common sense."[51] In recognition of his performance, in November 1936 he was promoted to Squadron Leader with a seniority date of 1 July 1936, once again bypassing three more senior officers.[52]

A clear signal that he was destined for higher rank came with his selection for the RAF Staff College course at Andover beginning in January 1938. Prior to going, and typical of his professionalism and the forethought with which he approached his job, Slemon arranged for a short tour at RCAF HQ before sailing for England. He had been serving as the Commanding Officer of No. 8 (G.P.) Squadron and wanted to become familiar with the latest headquarters policies and plans so that he could interact on a more informed basis with his English counterparts on course.[53]

His performance at Andover was assessed as average. Instructional staff found him to be a "markedly shy and reserved individual who appears to lack self confidence."[54] Perhaps their lack of familiarity with Slemon led to this assessment, since people that knew him saw a friendly and self-confident individual,[55] or perhaps cultural differences were a factor. Regardless of this, the final report from Andover also indicated that Slemon "[h]as imagination and energy and his judgment is usually well balanced and sound. Appears ready and willing to accept responsibility ... He should do well in the future."[56] For his part, Slemon disliked the rigidity of the tactical air doctrine being taught at the Staff College; a full four decades after attending Andover, he still recalled with regret that two capable RAF officers failed the course for insisting that bombers would require a fighter escort in the next war.[57]

The spectre of war hung heavily over the 1938 RAF Staff College course, an atmosphere heightened by events that caused the college to be shut down for a time during the autumn and students to be sent to war assignments. Slemon found himself on a British destroyer in the North Sea. When he protested that there had been some sort of mistake, the ship's Captain informed him that he had been brought aboard as an expert on anti-submarine warfare and would be expected to provide liaison between the destroyer and an aircraft carrier. Given that his experience in this field was limited to three small exercises conducted in conjunction with the Royal Canadian Navy, Slemon had some reservations about his ability to fill the position. Fortunately, diplomatic efforts defused the 1938 crisis and the military was stooddown from a war footing, thereby allowing the RAF Staff course to reconvene.[58]

In addition to the structured learning environment at Andover, there was the informal and invaluable opportunity to make friends with members of the RAF whom he would later serve with during World War II. In 1938 Slemon also enjoyed professional and personal achievements away from Staff College. In November of that year, the prestigious *Journal of the Royal United Services Institute* published an article by Slemon, one of only two RCAF members to be so honoured.[59] On the personal front, Marion and he began a family with the birth of their daughter Patricia; their son David followed in 1940, and a second daughter, Pamela, arrived in 1947.

Upon completion of Staff College, Slemon again demonstrated his professionalism and the tendency to think in broader, strategic terms by requesting and obtaining authority to be attached for a short period to the RCAF Liaison Officer in London in order to study British Air Ministry organization and methods.[60] Thereafter Slemon returned to Canada with his family and, following a two-month stint at RCAF HQ, he was sent in March 1939 to Western Air Command in Victoria, British Columbia.

Serving first as Air Staff Officer (Operations), Slemon was promoted to Wing Commander and employed as SASO following the outbreak of war in September 1939. As such, he was Deputy Commander to Air Commodore A.E. Godfrey, Air Officer Commanding (AOC) Western Air Command, and was instrumental in preparing Western Canada's air defences for war. Certainly there were challenges for him, from the state of the airplanes available (at the start of the war, the RCAF had only eleven Blackburn Sharks, a biplane outfitted with twin-floats, to defend the West Coast) to the need to establish additional flying bases from which to operate. An example of the difficulties experienced was provided soon after the outbreak of the war when an attempt was made to use the Blackburn Shark in the anti-submarine role. After having four of these aircraft loaded with one hundred pound bombs, Slemon and others watched from a dock at Jericho Beach as the Sharks taxied out to English Bay for takeoff. None of the first three planes could gain more than a hundred feet altitude while carrying the bomb and a full fuel load and had to land quickly. After one of these returning planes somersaulted in the water during landing, the fourth plane was stopped before trying to take off.[61]

Slemon took these challenges head-on, driving himself hard and putting in tremendously long hours. The first assessment of him in Western Air Command highlighted his strengths and weaknesses, indicating that:

> Wing Commander Slemon is a most conscientious officer, who devotes every effort to the interest of the service. He started in the appointment of Air Staff Officer under a handicap owing to the gap of a month between the departure of his predecessor and his arrival, but he overcame ... [this] by hard work ... A little less meticulous accuracy would speed up his work and reduce, to some extent, the strain on his health which cannot stand a prolonged period of work at the long hours which he has put in during the period before and after the outbreak of war.[62]

A medical report on Slemon after he had been in the job for two years bore out Godfrey's concerns: the examining doctor wrote that, "This officer, although the results of the various tests are satisfactory, does not look well. His colour is poor and his face has a tired, drawn appearance. He stated that he has had no annual leave for three years. I am of the opinion that this should be considered."[63]

As part of his efforts to prepare area Air Force units for the job ahead, Slemon made frequent inspection visits of the various dispersed units. Foreshadowing the skills and attributes that he would use later in life, Slemon also established an effective relationship with members of the American military responsible for the air defence of the western US.[64] Following the war, he was recognized for these efforts through the award of the US Legion of Merit.[65]

Air Commodore Godfrey was the third officer to come to the help of Slemon's career. Godfrey appreciated all this good work and asked RCAF HQ to promote Slemon to Group Captain.[66] Although it meant that he would pass over six more senior Wing Commanders, HQ agreed and promoted Slemon to temporary Group Captain effective 25 February 1941.[67] In his first assessment of the newly promoted Group Captain, Godfrey noted that Slemon had performed very well while filling in for four months as AOC, Western Air Command. He also described Slemon as "one of the most capable officers that has ever served under me and ... worthy of accelerated promotion." Godfrey also expressed concerns to RCAF HQ about the future of Slemon's career, observing that "[i]n fairness to [Slemon], he should be given an opportunity of serving Overseas before he is promoted to a rank which practically bars this possibility."[68]

In October 1941, Slemon was moved to RCAF HQ to serve as Director of Operations and within a short period was seen as an "excellent officer in every respect."[69] He was later appointed as Commander, Order of the British Empire, for his work at Western Air Command and as Director of Operations, based upon a recommendation that indicated that he was "[e]nergetic, conscientious and reliable ... [and] exemplifies in his character, his conduct and his all-round proficiency the finest traditions of the Service."[70] But his tenure in Ottawa was to be short. His superior, AVM A.A.L. Cuffe, Air Member for Air Services, wanted someone with experience in air operations under war conditions and also wanted to provide Slemon with the opportunity to obtain such experience. Accordingly, Cuffe recommended to the CAS that Slemon exchange positions with an experienced Group Captain in Great Britain. This was agreed upon, and Slemon was posted to Great Britain in July 1942 to serve as SASO for No. 6 (RCAF) Bomber Group, which was in the process of being formed.[71]

During World War I and the first years of World War II, Canadian air and ground crew were integrated, along with other Commonwealth personnel, into the RAF. While the RAF wished to see this practice continue, Canadian politicians and military leaders wanted to have Canadians serve in a distinctly Canadian formation. This led to the establishment of No. 6 (RCAF) Bomber Group on 1 January 1943. Its first commander, G.E. Brookes, welcomed the arrival of Slemon as his deputy, and the six months leading up to the formation's standup would have been filled with hectic arrangements for personnel, equipment, and accommodations. While the commander's job was to provide higher level policy and direction, the responsibility for implementing these and for day-to-day operations fell to Slemon as SASO. That he was up to the challenge is demonstrated amply in the official history of the RCAF in World War II, which describes Slemon as being an "unequivocal success" in the job.[72]

As with any new military formation, No. 6 (RCAF) Bomber Group went through its share of growing pains. Casualties were high amongst bomber crews during some missions and at times there were morale problems; however, by dint of hard work and hard-gained experience, the Group developed into an effective component of the Allied bombing campaign.[73] While the credit for this must be shared with all those involved, from the Group's commanders, first Brookes and then C.M. "Black Mike" McEwen, to the individual air and ground crew members, there can be no doubt that Slemon played a key role in the organization's development and success. For instance, Brookes credited Slemon with being "in large measure responsible for any success achieved by the group."[74] Slemon's particular strength continued to be his practice of examining issues from a range of perspectives before providing thoughtful and intelligent direction to Group squadrons. As part of this process, he effectively made use of available resources and wouldn't allow himself to be bound by past conventions. For example, he readily made use of the relatively new science of operational research to help improve bombing accuracy and reduce casualties.[75] Ralph McBurney, who in 1945 followed Slemon's replacement as SASO for No. 6 (RCAF) Group, recalls another demonstration of his friend's forward thinking. During a visit to No. 6 (RCAF) Bomber Group late in the war, Slemon questioned the status of a standard operating procedure concerning action to be taken in the event of enemy aircraft being found lurking around home airfields. In such cases, Canadian aircraft returning from bombing missions would be low on fuel and especially vulnerable to attack. McBurney, who reinstated the procedure which called for planes to be diverted to other airfields, credits Slemon with saving many lives after the Germans subsequently tried this very tactic.[76]

It was not uncommon for senior officers to share in the risk taken by aircrew by unofficially joining a bombing mission. Slemon apparently did this on at least one occasion, when he went as second pilot on a mission to the Courtrai marshalling yards.[77]

Brookes thought of Slemon in the highest terms, writing that "[h]e is outstanding in his work, plenty of initiative, and shows very good judgement and he gets things done."[78] Sir Arthur Harris, Air Chief Marshal of Bomber Command, succinctly described Slemon as an "outstanding officer."[79] On 1 March 1943, Slemon's hard work was rewarded with a promotion to temporary Air Commodore;[80] later that year he was made a Companion of the Order of Bath.[81]

Slated for higher command, Slemon was posted late in 1944 to RAF Bomber Command HQ and then to RCAF Overseas HQ as Deputy Air Officer Commanding-in-Chief for the RCAF Overseas. On 22 March 1945, Slemon was promoted to Acting Air Vice Marshal,[82] a rank in which he was confirmed following the war.

A general reality for officers that joined the RCAF in the 1920s was that they were too old and too senior to be employed as commanders of flying units and too young and lacking in seniority to fill the top level command positions, which were taken by World War I veterans. Largely, their fate was to serve in the senior staff positions or as station commanders, providing the experience, leadership, and know-how to keep operations running.[83] Slemon was the first post-World War I pilot to break out of this pattern when, in June 1945, he was offered the prestigious appointment as Air Officer Commanding the Canadian contingent of Tiger Force, which was being formed to carry on the war against Japan.[84] In typically understated fashion, Slemon's response to this offer was limited to "accept deeply honoured."[85] But he would not have the opportunity to see this through. While planning for Tiger Force was going forward, American forces dropped two atomic bombs on Japan, ending the war and thereby finishing any requirement for a RCAF formation in the Far East.

As part of the preparation for Tiger Force, Slemon had been repatriated back to Canada on 7 July 1945[86] and was soon reunited with Marion and their children. In the post-war RCAF, it was evident that Slemon had been chosen to lead the generational change marking the passing of the World War I veterans from active service. (In the words of AVM McBurney, "Who else was there?")[87] Brooke Claxton, Minister of National Defence (MND) from 1946 to 1954, later wrote that the reason AM Wilf Curtis was permitted to remain CAS from 1947 to 1953 was to allow Slemon the time needed to gain "more varied experience" before becoming the head of the RCAF.[88] As part of this process, Slemon was first posted to RCAF HQ as Air Member for Air Services from September 1945 to January 1946. He then became Air Member for Supply and Organization, where he played an important role in the reorganization of the RCAF to a peacetime force. In 1947, he was appointed the Air Member for Operations and Training, where he became involved in issues associated with the operational preparedness and effectiveness of the Air Force. One matter of concern for Slemon was the ability of the RCAF Auxiliary, which was the functional component of the RCAF Reserves, to do its job. Since post-war plans called for eleven Auxiliary fighter squadrons and only a single Regular RCAF fighter-reconnaissance squadron, the protection of Canadian airspace rested squarely with the Auxiliary.[89] But Slemon doubted the Auxiliary's ability to react to threats quickly enough. As a result of his involvement, defence plans changed the Auxiliary's mobilization period from on "short notice" to not later than ninety days.[90] When he later became CAS, Slemon worked towards the full professionalization of the air defence role in Canada by repeatedly arguing for the removal of the Auxiliary from this important function and for an increased involvement of the Regular RCAF in it.[91] Although thwarted in his attempts to implement these changes by a MND concerned about their political ramifications,[92] Slemon set the stage for the shift of the Auxiliary to the less demanding relief assistance role by his successor.[93]

While his practice of thoroughly researching an issue before making a decision usually held him in good stead, this by no means meant that he was faultless. In 1948, while Air Member for Operations and Training, Slemon received Air Council and Cabinet Defence Committee approval for the purchase of a sizeable number of de Havilland Vampires to augment the few already in the RCAF inventory. However, the performance of the F-86 Sabre came to the attention of the Air Member for Air Plans, AVM C.R. Dunlap, who later became an AM and CAS himself. Dunlap was able to convince AM Curtis, CAS, to re-examine the selection of the Vampire which was rapidly becoming technologically obsolete. However, such a change meant returning to the Cabinet Defence Committee for approval and the cancellation of a contract with Toronto-based de Havilland in favour of Montreal-based Canadair. Although reluctant to see his choice of aircraft overturned within days of being approved, Slemon came to accept the arguments put forward and got behind the shift to the Sabre.[94] Given the long, successful service of this aircraft in the RCAF, there is little doubt that this had been the correct decision.

On 1 September 1949, Slemon was given the opportunity to exercise command of a formation during peacetime when he became Air Officer Commanding Training Command in Trenton, Ontario.[95] One of the first things he became involved in was the arrangements for the 30 September 1949 dedication ceremony for the Trenton Memorial Gates, which were to commemorate the contribution and sacrifice of Commonwealth air and ground crew trained under the British Commonwealth Air Training Plan. Finding the plans inadequate, Slemon took over responsibility for the arrangements and was soon involved in the minutest detail.[96] The ceremony went off without a hitch.[97]

Slemon's time in Trenton provided him with additional international experience. In March 1952, he represented Curtis at a RAF CAS conference[98] followed by a wide-ranging visit to European air forces. Also, the Commander of the Allied Air Forces, Central Europe, General Lauris

Norstad, asked Slemon to be leader of the enemy air force during the largest NATO air exercise to that date, Exercise Blue Alliance. Slemon and his staff acquitted themselves very well, receiving high praise from Norstad for the "spirit and enthusiasm shown at all levels," and for Slemon's "outstanding command job."[99]

On 31 January 1953, Slemon was promoted to Air Marshal and succeeded Curtis as CAS.[100] The 1950s have been referred to as the "Golden Years" for the RCAF,[101] as this was a time of great organizational growth, the assumption of a wider range of responsibilities in the defence of Canada, and the integration of Canadian defensive efforts into multi- and bi-lateral military alliances. A nation-wide system of air defence, with radar and interceptor stations reaching into almost every corner of the country, provided the RCAF with a public profile as they never had before. As CAS, Slemon was to be associated with many of these developments.

One of the first initiatives Slemon became involved in was the Avro Arrow project. The RCAF needed a supersonic all-weather interceptor capable of handling the threat from Soviet bombers. In an effort to establish a balance between the need for a domestic aircraft production capability and cost efficiency, the new interceptor project was slated to develop and produce the airframe within Canada and to acquire jet engines, avionics and armament systems from Great Britain or the United States. Slemon was able to obtain Chiefs of Staff Committee support for this initiative,[102] but cost overruns, design and production difficulties, and problems with finding export markets doomed the Arrow. The project was cancelled, much to Slemon's regret, after he left the CAS office in 1957.

The RCAF was well-represented during Slemon's tenure as CAS. The three heads of service, the Deputy Minister, and the head of the Defence Research Board met, usually on a weekly basis, as the Chiefs of Staff Committee. It was within this committee that such matters as defence priorities and budget proposals were negotiated. Slemon was highly successful in these meetings; this is in part attributable to his being "thorough in preparation, [tenacious] in debate, and stubborn as a mule." Typically, he would examine the agenda items from every possible angle to see whether there was any impact on the RCAF and would strongly represent his service's interests. At least one deputy head of another service believed that his boss came out "on the short end of the stick" at times in comparison with Slemon and the RCAF.[103]

As CAS, Slemon was a hard-worker who often took large amounts of work home at the end of a long day. While "preparation, presentation and tenacity" are noteworthy Slemon attributes,[104] he had a practice of giving his personal attention to perhaps too wide a range of issues. MND Claxton believed that Slemon was "a perfectionist and not too ready to delegate authority."[105] As an example of his perfectionism, Slemon would often remain late at his office to produce letter-perfect correspondence; the support staff that was required to stay into the evening with him perhaps didn't fully appreciate the merits of this trait.[106]

An important achievement during this period was the formalization of a bilateral agreement with the United States in the area of North American air defence, an agreement that was politically sensitive in Canada. When Slemon spoke out in favour of it during a speech on 2 June 1955 in Montreal, the Liberal MND, Ralph Campney, reacted quickly the next day in the House of Commons by stating that Slemon's statement was "not a declaration of government policy."[107] Still, there had been Permanent Joint Board on Defence discussions on the nature of the Soviet threat and a joint Canada/US Military Study Group (MSG) had been formed to discuss appropriate countermeasures. In 1957, the newly elected Conservative government of John Diefenbaker supported the idea of an integrated air defence system and on 1 August of that year the formation of the North American Air Defence Command (NORAD), with its HQ in Colorado Springs, Colorado, was announced.[108]

Although Slemon had been closely monitoring MSG discussions and recommendations,[109] it is unlikely that he foresaw how the establishment of NORAD would affect him personally. Just as his term as CAS was drawing to a close in 1957, new career opportunities and challenges became available to him as the first Canadian to serve as Deputy Commander-in-Chief, NORAD.

It took a while to work out the day-to-day sharing of responsibilities in the newly formed NORAD HQ. For instance, in 1957 Canada had no nuclear weapons, and American regulations directed that strict national control be maintained of their nuclear weapons. After about three months of operations, the first American Commander-in-Chief, General E.E. Partridge, found that it was intolerable to exclude his deputy from material needed to do the job. He arbitrarily gave Slemon full access to the nuclear weapons information, thereby paving the way for a meaningful contribution by Canada. This was accomplished in no small part by the close personal relationship Slemon had established with

Partridge.[110] When Partridge left NORAD two years later, he gave credit to Slemon for his contribution:

> [He] helped us avoid many pitfalls in dealing with the Canadian government and in our understanding of the best way to proceed in improving the air defense posture in North America ... Air Marshal Slemon has applied himself to his work with the utmost vigor and determination. His dedication is contagious and is felt through out the NORAD establishment.[111]

An important aspect of the job was the hosting of various dignitaries who visited NORAD. This duty occurred on a frequent basis, often a couple of times a week, and it required polished social skills. Roy and Marion were popular and engaging hosts at these functions; they also became active members of the Colorado Springs social set. As well, Roy became a much sought after public speaker.[112]

Slemon's cool performance under pressure aided his professional acceptance by the Americans. On one occasion when the Commander-in-Chief was away and Slemon was left in charge, NORAD systems detected a large attack coming from the Soviet Union. Since the time between the detection of incoming missiles and their arrival at targets across North America could be as little as 15-20 minutes, NORAD had to act quickly to counter any such threat. Still, Slemon held back, demanding additional information, and it was a good thing that he did. The image of the incoming missiles soon disappeared from the NORAD radar screens; subsequent analysis found that a newly installed system had been miscalibrated – the "incoming missiles" had actually been the rising moon.[113]

Slemon's pride in Canada and in the RCAF demanded that Canada meet its alliance commitments and carry its share of the costs of North American air defence. During the Cuban Missile Crisis in the early part of October, 1962, Slemon sent blistering messages to Ottawa when the Diefenbaker government hesitated about living up to treaty obligations to place the Canadian forces on full alert.[114] He took upon himself the responsibility of educating the Canadian public through speeches about the merits of joint air defence.[115] He also reacted strongly to a suggestion by MND Paul Hellyer that it would not be serious if unification of the three armed services failed because the Americans could be counted upon to protect Canada.[116] Years after his retirement, while attending a dinner to honour Minister of National Defence Barney Danson, Slemon forcefully put forward a case that Canada should contribute to the cost of the B1 bomber since Canada would benefit from the bomber's counter-offensive capabilities.[117]

Although Slemon had reached compulsory retirement age in 1959, his services as Deputy Commander-in-Chief of NORAD were extended on an annual basis until August 1964, when AM C.R. Dunlap replaced him. Following his various leave entitlements, Roy Slemon officially retired from the RCAF effective 8 June 1965.[118] At that time, he still carried his original service number, 71, and had long been the last of the original RCAF members from 1924 to serve.

Following retirement, Marion and he decided to remain in Colorado Springs. They were comfortable in their home of seven years, the local community had embraced them (Roy had been made an honourary citizen of the city in 1963), and their grown children were settling in the area. Roy was asked to become executive vice-president of the US Air Academy Foundation, a position he filled for many years. He kept in touch with the Air Force community and was always on hand in Colorado Springs to welcome a new Canadian Deputy Commander-in-Chief. One such successor, Lieutenant General K.J. Thorneycroft, had the pleasure in the early 1980s of taking Slemon and his wife on a tour of NORAD sites in Canada's North. A special side trip out of Yellowknife was to Slemon Lake, which had been named in honour of Roy's accomplishments during the photographic surveying missions.[119] Following a period of illness, Roy Slemon died at Colorado Springs on 12 February 1992 at the age of 87.[120]

What was it that allowed Roy Slemon to become CAS and what was his legacy? Certainly his position as the senior post-World War I member of the RCAF was a factor in some of his promotions, but to reduce his career to this fact would be an injustice to Slemon and to the RCAF. Without his hard work, intelligence, and drive, seniority would have counted for naught. Wartime service brought quick promotion, but if he hadn't performed well he wouldn't have been entrusted with additional responsibilities. From the earliest stages of his career, Slemon had the appearance, traits, and characteristics that his seniors favoured; however, good looks and a military bearing weren't responsible for his overcoming the various career obstacles encountered along the way. Instead, such traits as dedication, professionalism, and an attention to detail were more important to his overall success. He showed promise early and was provided the opportunity to grow and develop through assignments that afforded greater and greater challenges. Roy Slemon stood on his own two feet, yet he still benefited, on a number of occasions, by the timely intervention of senior officers interested in him getting his due. He probably became too involved in things that should have been delegated, but it was his nature to put his personal touch on a full range of issues. His need to be thoroughly prepared for the task at hand may have been tedious to some, but it meant that he was usually in the right. Certainly the RCAF greatly benefited by his efforts. Moreover, Slemon was not afraid of stating his opinion, regardless of the audience; he was honest and apparently did not temper his opinions because of career concerns. Despite this, Slemon was promoted quickly and often. He served at Air rank for an incredible twenty-two years,[121] more than half his career. His career advancement may have been influenced by a number of factors, but in the end it was based primarily upon merit.

Slemon's career pretty well matched the life span of the RCAF. He was there at the beginning as a Provisional Pilot Officer and was still there when the RCAF was divided into several "Commands" in 1964 before it disappeared as a separate entity altogether with unification in 1968. Slemon grew up as the RCAF evolved as an organization. He thrived on the early mapping and surveying missions. He then had to work with the rest of the RCAF during the 1930s and early 1940s to hone the military skills needed during World War II. Subsequently, he was involved in most major developments for the RCAF, from the establishment of No. 6 (RCAF) Bomber Group onwards. He contributed greatly to the high level of professionalism of the Air Force in the 1950s and was deeply involved in the evolving mission and mandate of the RCAF during its "Golden Years." Later on, Slemon's stature and performance during his seven-year tenure as Deputy Commander-in-Chief, NORAD, clearly helped develop and nurture a special RCAF/USAF relationship.

In conclusion, Roy Slemon deserves to be recognized and remembered for his outstanding service to Canada and the RCAF. He graduated on the RCAF's first Wings Parade, he grew and developed with the Air Force, and he played an integral role in many of the RCAF's achievements over the years. While Slemon has been recognized as the last of the RCAF originals, it is clear that he was much more than that. After more than forty-two years service with the Air Force, in many ways he may be seen as a physical manifestation of what the RCAF was and what it became. He was not only an original, he was *the* original. It is unlikely that we will see another career like his again.

1. Anyone looking to write about Air Marshal Slemon will be struck immediately by the paucity of printed sources concerning him. This chapter would not have been possible without the generous help of many people. Foremost, this includes Marion P. McDermott, Slemon's widow, Air Marshal C.R. Dunlap, and Air Vice Marshal (AVM) R.E McBurney. Others that deserve recognition for their assistance include AVM J. Plant, Lieutenant-General (LGen) R.J. Lane, LGen R.C. Stovel, LGen K.J. Thorneycroft, LCdr R.C. Searle, Peter Hall, Hugh Halliday, Jeff Noakes, Bernie Shaw, Ron Smith, Colonel G. Graham, and Master Warrant Officer K. Rodgers.

2. Samuel Slemon died in 1936, Mary Slemon passed away in 1938, and William Slemon died during World War II in Winnipeg. Letter dated 15 April 2000 from Marion P. McDermott that is in my possession. Hereafter, the annotation "McDermott letter" will be used.

3. National Archive of Canada (NAC) Record Group (RG) 2, file 209263, RCAF Record Sheet – Officers, C.R. Slemon, dated 18 May 1926 and memorandum entitled "Combined Graduation List", dated 8 May 1933. Future references to this file will use the annotation "Slemon Personnel File". The date of 1921 for Slemon's enrolment at the University of Manitoba was most commonly used throughout the Slemon Personnel File. However, a biographical sketch dated 26 May 1951 found in this file indicated that he first attended the University of Manitoba during the Fall of 1920. No university transcript was available to clarify this point. Through the kind permission of Marion McDermott I received access to the Slemon Personnel file. Also, I am indebted to Peter Hall and LCdr R.C. Searle at DAIP for their work in making this file available to me.

4. Letter dated 29 February 2000 from Air Marshal C.R. Dunlap that is in my possession. Future references to this letter will use the annotation "Dunlap letter."

5. Slemon Personnel File, memorandum entitled "Combined Graduation List," dated 8 May 33. A COTC enrolment date of 1 November 1920 was most commonly used throughout AM Slemon's RCAF Personnel File and was used to calculate his pension benefits. On at least two occasions his RCAF Record of Service indicated that he had joined the COTC on 5 October 1921. No COTC documents were located to clarify this point.

6. Interview of Air Vice Marshal (AVM) R.E. (Ralph) McBurney dated 22 February 2000. A video recording of this interview is in my possession. Hereafter the annotation "McBurney interview" will be used.

7. Department of National Defence, Department of History and Heritage (DHH) 77/39, Interview of AM Slemon by Ben Greenhous, 29 September 1976, and Slemon Personnel File, untitled memorandum, no file number, dated 11 September 1923. Eight trainees completed the course after the ninth student was declared medically unfit.

8. Slemon Personnel File, Confidential Report – R. Slemon, dated 30 August 1923.

9. McBurney interview.

10. Slemon Personnel File, Confidential Report – R. Slemon, dated 30 August 1923 and R.1-813, dated 31 August 1923.

11. Slemon Personnel File, 889-2-3, undated.

12. Slemon Personnel File, Precis, no file number, undated.

13. Slemon Personnel File, 866-S-70, dated 16 March 1925.

14. Slemon Personnel File, Confidential Flying Reports dated 29 August 1924 and 24 December 1924.

15. DHH, RCAF Weekly Orders for 2 and 16 July 1927.

16. Dunlap letter.

17. Slemon Personnel File, Seaplane Training Course Confidential Report, dated 22 May 1925.

18. Slemon Personnel File, F/C-115, dated 27 May 1925.

19. DHH 79/128, Interview of AM C.R. Slemon by W.A.B. Douglas and W.J. McAndrew, 20 October 1978.

20. Slemon Personnel File, Letter with no file number from P.O. Slemon to Officer Commanding A Flight, No. 5 Squadron, dated 19 June 1926, and F/415-S-4, dated 24 July 1926.

21. Slemon Personnel File, C.4536, dated 5 June 1926.

22. Slemon Personnel File, C.113, dated 8 April 1927.

23. Slemon Personnel File, 866-S-70, dated 19 April 1928.

24. For instance, eight promotions to Flying Officer were reported at the same time as Slemon's. Since his seniority date was backdated by two years, he was immediately senior to the other seven. DHH, RCAF Weekly Orders, Serial No. 16, dated 21 April 1928.

25. NAC RG 24, Vol. 17795, file 821-4. The winner of the McKee Trophy in 1927 was a civilian, H.A. "Doc" Oaks. I am indebted to Hugh Halliday for bringing this reference to my attention.

26. Slemon Personnel File, Annual Confidential Report (Officers) for 1926, 2.

27. Slemon Personnel File, Annual Confidential Report (Officers) for 1927, 1.

28. Slemon Personnel File, Annual Confidential Report (Officers) for 1929, 3.

29. Slemon Personnel File, Annual Confidential Report (Officers) for 1930, 3.

30. Slemon Personnel File, 866-S-70, dated 27 May 1929. On 1 April 1930, Slemon was transferred to No. 9 Photographic Detachment. DHH RCAF Weekly Orders, Serial No. 9, dated 1 March 1930.

31. Slemon Personnel File, Annual Confidential Report (Officers) for 1929, 3.

32. DHH, RCAF List, 1 January 1931.

33. McBurney interview.

34. NAC RG 24, Vol. 4915, file 1008-18-12, Vol. 2, memorandum dated 4 July 1928, no file number. I am indebted to Bernie Shaw for bringing this reference to my attention.

35. Slemon Personnel File, RAF Form 985, dated 20 May 1930.

36. Slemon Personnel File, Annual Confidential Report (Officers) for 1931, dated 31 December 1931.

37. DHH 77/39, Interview of AM Slemon by Ben Greenhous, 29 September 1976, 7. This quote was attributed to Tommy Lawrence.

38. Slemon Personnel File, Confidential Report for Staff College Preparatory Course, RMC, dated 26 January 1933.

39. DHH, Air Force Orders 1-16/1933, dated 31 January 1933, 5.

40. DHH 77/39, Interview of AM Slemon by Ben Greenhous, 29 September 1976, 4.

41. Telephone interview with AM Dunlap, 16 March 2000.

42. Slemon Personnel File, telegraph dated 13 October 1932.

43. Slemon Personnel File, Medical Examination Report dated 3 May 1940.

44. DHH, Air Force Order 136, dated 30 May 1936, 6.

45. Slemon Personnel File, C.4536, dated 13 June 1935.

46. Slemon Personnel File, 866-S-70, dated 4 March 35 and H.Q.C. 6759, dated 11 February 1937, and DHH Air Force Order No. 16, dated 30 June 1936. Slemon's aggregate score on the examinations was 2760, while the other two successful candidates had scores of 2465 and 2335.

47. McBurney interview.

48. Letter dated 15 April 2000 from Marion P. McDermott and Slemon Personnel File, letter dated 22 August 1935 (no file number).

49. Slemon Personnel File, Annual Confidential Report (Officers) for 1933, dated 30 December 1933, 3.

50. Slemon Personnel File, Annual Confidential Report (Officers) for 1935, dated 17 December 1935, 3.

51. Slemon Personnel File, Annual Confidential Report (Officers) for 1936, dated 16 December 1936, 3.

52. DHH, A.P.&R. No. 21, dated 3 November 1936 and Slemon Personnel File, c.4536, dated 14 September 1936.

53. Slemon Personnel File, 405-S-4, dated 13 November 1937 and 866-S-70, F.D. 395, dated 23 November 1937.

54. Slemon Personnel File, RAF Staff College Final Report, dated 2 December 1938.

55. McDermott letter, McBurney interview and telephone interview of AM C.R. Dunlap, 16 March 2000.

56. Slemon Personnel File, RAF Staff College Final Report, dated 2 December 1938.

57. DHH 79/128, Interview of AM C.R. Slemon by W.A.B. Douglas and W.J. McAndrew, 20 October 1978.

58. Ibid., 5.

59. Squadron Leader C.R. Slemon, "Photographic Operations of the Royal Canadian Air Force", *Journal of the Royal United Services Institute*, Vol. LXXXIII, November 1938, No. 532, 797-804. The other RCAF officer published in the *RUSI Journal* was Flight Lieutenant B.G. Carr-Harris in 1936 on flying operations in the Hudson Strait. The *Canadian Defence Quarterly* (*CDQ*) was more commonly used as a public forum on professional matters within the RCAF. Between 1923 and 1939, forty articles were published by RCAF members in the *CDQ*, none of which was submitted by Slemon.

60. Slemon Personnel File, Telegraph from Canadian Liaison Officer, Air Ministry, to RCAF HQ, dated 23 November 1938.

61. Captain R.J. Tracy, "An Air Marshal Remembers by AM C.R. Slemon as Told to Captain R.J. Tracy," *Sentinel* 1974/3, Volume 10, No. 3, 22-23.

62. Slemon Personnel File, Annual Confidential Report (Officers) for 1939, dated 31 January 1940, 3.

63. Slemon Personnel File, Medical Examination Report, dated 29 March 1941.

64. Slemon Personnel File, letter [partially illegible]G-203-46, dated 4 March 1946.

65. DHH, AFRO 388/46, dated 12 April 1946.

66. Slemon Personnel File, C.405-S-4, dated 29 October 1940.

67. Slemon Personnel File, C.4536, dated 8 December 1940 and A.P.&R. 30, dated 28 February 1941.

68. Slemon Personnel File, Short Confidential Report, dated 27 October 1941.

69. Slemon Personnel File, Short Confidential Report, dated 15 December [1941].

70. Slemon Personnel File, Recommendation for Honours and Awards, dated 6 April 1943.

71. Slemon Personnel File, Memorandum (no file number) dated 15 January 1941 and C-C71 dated 6 July 1942.

72. Brereton Greenhous et al, *The Crucible of War, 1939-1945, the Official History of the Royal Canadian Air Force,* Vol. 3 (University of Toronto Press and Supply and Services Canada: Toronto, 1994), 634.

73. DHH 77/39, Interview of AM Slemon by Ben Greenhous, 29 September 1976, 13-21, and DHH 79/128, Interview of AM C.R. Slemon by W.A.B. Douglas and W.J. McAndrew, 20 October 1978, 1-4.

74. Slemon Personnel File, Confidential Personnel Assessment, dated 6 October 1943.

75. Note from Lieutenant General R.J. Lane included with the Dunlap letter.

76. McBurney interview.

77. Note from Lieutenant General R.J. Lane included with the Dunlap letter.

78. Slemon Personnel File, RAF Confidential Report (Officers), dated 25 February 1944, 2.

79. Slemon Personnel File, RAF Confidential Report (Officers), dated 17 August 1944, 2.

80. Slemon Personnel File, Message P.6693/C.-C71 (DPC), dated 26 May [1943].

81. DHH AFRO 1459/43, dated 30 July 1943. Other postwar honours included being made a Chevalier of the Legion of Honour (France) and receiving the Croix de Guerre avec Palme (France), both AFRO 485/47, dated 12 September 1947. He was also Mentioned in Despatches three times (AFROs 1247/43, dated 2 July 1943, 377/45, dated 23 February 1945 and 322/46, dated 29 March 1946). I am indebted to Hugh Halliday for bringing these citations to my attention.

82. DHH AFRO 144/45, dated 7 May 1945.

83. McBurney interview.

84. Slemon Personnel File, Message C.905, dated 21 June [1945]. This message made note that circumstances had come up that prevented AVM McEwen, who had previously been offered this appointment, from accepting the position as head of Tiger Force. McEwen suffered from diabetes, which first officially came to light when receiving a medical examination required for his appointment to Tiger Force. DHH 77/39, Interview of AM Slemon by Ben Greenhous, 29 September 1976.

85. Slemon Personnel File, Message CX25CX 398, dated 21 June [1945].

86. Slemon Personnel File, Message C71(K5), dated 25 July [1945].

87. McBurney interview.

88. NAC, Brooke Claxton Papers, MG 32 B5, Vol. 221(E), 1533-E. I am indebted to Jeff Noakes for bringing this reference to my attention.

89. DHH 181.004 (D44), Post War Plan for the Royal Canadian Air Force (Plan B), April 1946, 10, 18-20.

90. Correspondence from AVM C.R. Slemon, AMOT, to AVM E.E. Middleton, CAC, 150-64/0, dated 6 Nov [1948], NAC RG 24, Vol. 17826, 840-91, Vol. 1 and A Summary of Requirements and Estimates for Plan "F", Section N, 1, DHH 181.004 (D46).

91. DHH 193.009 (D53), Box 13, TS 096-105-9 (CAS), dated 21 September 1955.

92. Minutes of a Special Meeting of the Chiefs of Staff Committee Held on 23 September 1955, 1-2, DHH 193.009 (D53), Box 13 and Memorandum to Cabinet Defence Committee, dated 29 February 1956, and Minutes of the 590th Meeting of the Chiefs of Staff Committee Held on 5 March 1956, DHH 193.009 (D53), Box 13.

93. C895-100-91/0 (CAS), dated 4 December 1957, entitled "Future Policy for the RCAF Auxiliary," presented at a Special Meeting of the Chiefs of Staff Committee held 3-4 December 1957, DHH 193.009 (D53), Box 13.

94. Dunlap letter.

95. Slemon Personnel File, C71 (DPC), dated 30 June 1949.

96. Letter from Lieutenant-General R.C. Stovel, dated 6 March 2000 that is in my possession. As examples of the details dealt with, Slemon ensured that dignitaries were driven about in limousines and rooms for dignitaries contained a full range of toiletries and items such as silk nylons. Also, a replica of the Memorial Gates was built in case of foul weather causing the ceremony to be held indoors and grand stand seating was situated so that the sun would not be in the audience's eyes. Stovel letter and McBurney interview.

97. Stovel letter and Flight Lieutenant R.J. MacKinnon, "The Trenton Memorial Gates," *The Roundel*, Vol. II, No. 3, December 1949, 44-48.

98. Slemon Personnel File, CAS 390, dated 5 March 1952.

99. Slemon Personnel File, WAA10 191/188, [dated 26 September 1952], and Dunlap letter.

100. Slemon Personnel File, P.C. 4451, dated 5 November 1952.

101. For instance, see Jeff Rankin-Lowe, *Golden Years: The Royal Canadian Air Force in the 1950s* (London, Ontario: Sirius Productions, 1997) and Larry Milberry, ed., *Sixty Years: The RCAF and CF Air Command 1924-1984* (Toronto: CANAV Books, 1984), chapter entitled "The Golden Years".

102. Craig Stewart, *Shutting Down the National Dream – A.V. Roe and the Tragedy of the Avro Arrow* (Toronto: McGraw-Hill Ryerson, 1988), 179.

103. Dunlap letter.

104. Ibid.

105. NAC, Brooke Claxton Papers, MG 32 B5, Vol. 221(E), 1534.

106. Dunlap letter.

107. Joseph T. Jockel, "The Military Establishments and the Creation of NORAD," in B.D. Hunt and R.G. Haycock, *Canada's Defence: Perspectives on Policy in the Twentieth Century* (Toronto: Copp Clark Pitman, 1993).

108. Ibid., 172 and Dunlap letter. Dunlap, as an AVM, was the head of the Canadian Section of the Military Study Group.

109. Ibid.

110. DHH 79/128, Interview of AM C.R. Slemon by W.A.B. Douglas and W.J. McAndrew, 20 October 1978, 17-18.
111. Slemon Personnel File, letter from General E.E. Partridge to the Honourable George R. Pearkes, 24 July 1959.
112. McDermott and Dunlap letters.
113. Dunlap letter and McBurney interview.
114. Pat MacAdam, "Atomic Winter," *The Ottawa Citizen*, 28 June 2000, D5.
115. For example, on 30 August 1963, he spoke at the International Air Show Banquet in Toronto on NORAD. DHH 74/467.
116. DHH 79/128, Interview of AM C.R. Slemon by W.A.B. Douglas and W.J. McAndrew, 20 October 1978, 13.
117. Ibid., 17.
118. Slemon Personnel File, memorandum entitled Release Details, no file number or date.
119. Telephone conversation with Lieutenant General K.J. Thorneycroft, 24 April 2000.
120. The Globe and Mail, 14 February 1992, A15 and McBurney interview.
121. The longest time spent in any one rank was his twelve years as Air Marshal. He also spent almost eight years as an Air Vice Marshal, his second longest time in a rank.

CHAPTER 13
HAIL TO THE ARTIST!
THE ART OF COMMAND AND
GENERAL JEAN V. ALLARD

Serge Bernier

INTRODUCTION

A FEW years ago, during some of the many hours that I devoted to subjects other than history, I took great pleasure in reading a book entitled *Artistes, artisans et technocrates dans nos organisations.*[1] The author, Patricia Pitcher, a professor at the École des Hautes Études Commerciales in Montreal, had just published a translation of her doctoral thesis, *Character and the Nature of Strategic Leadership,* which she wrote at McGill University under the supervision of Henry Mintzberg.

Among other things, Pitcher argued against the notion that leadership seems to have been reduced to a task that anyone can learn in a sort of paint-by-numbers scenario. After studying a number of specific cases, she concluded that this was not how leadership is learned. In fact, she compared a number of major leaders from the world of finance, whom she had studied, and artists in general. She noted that, while the latter group often had a fairly good idea of the final goals they endeavoured to attain, they admitted that their vision was often rethought and corrected along the way. Once the finished product was available, it often proved to be quite different from the original vision.

Mintzberg, who obviously agreed with his student's work, states in the preface to Pitcher's book, "A leader must be … a visionary and a true strategist and he can then do whatever he likes and still get away with it."

When I was asked in the fall of 1999 to write a chapter on General Jean V. Allard, his influence on the Canadian Armed Forces, and his place in "the art of command" in Canada, my thoughts went back to Pitcher's book. After working very closely with General Allard in the writing of his memoirs in the 1980s, I saw no point in merely repeating a chronology of the deeds and actions of one of the few Canadian generals who put his thoughts on paper at such length and during his own lifetime; I needed a special angle of attack,[2] even if only to make the task more attractive to myself. I should mention at the very outset that in wishing to bear witness to his experiences as he did, Allard broke the mould into which Canada's supreme military leaders had fit into in the past.

SOME CHARACTERISTICS OF THE "ARTIST"

A Visionary

One of the qualities found in great leaders and in virtually all analyses of leadership is an ability to develop a vision of what they wish to achieve. If we follow Pitcher's methodology, we obtain the following result: artists know where they are going but the route is like an exploration and the destination seems vague. Their vision is to some extent fragmentary.[3] Allard certainly belongs here.

The visionary side of his nature was probably expressed best in what could be called the position of Canada's francophones in the Canadian Armed Forces. During the Second World War, when senior officers of French-Canadian origin had an opportunity, they reflected on why there were so few French Canadians in the military. After the war, their thinking began to be translated into action, albeit somewhat timidly at first.

In 1951, Allard proposed that a military academy be established in Quebec where young French-speaking Canadians could prepare for entry to the Royal Military College in Kingston. The upshot was the Collège militaire royal in Saint-Jean, an institution Allard was not involved in designing, but he was an important advocate on its behalf when it was being established.[4] Allard's goal was to integrate French Canadians into the Armed Forces during peacetime in order "to avoid the problems that occurred during the mobilizations of 1914 and 1939."[5] He was merely finding his way in this regard in the early 1950s, but in 1952 he proposed to the Chief of the General Staff that French-language units be created in Quebec and not be limited to the infantry. The idea did not go any further because his suggestion was ignored. In 1957, an attempt was made to create French-language sub-units in the artillery and the armoured regiments. Allard was not the originator of this suggestion, but he was involved in its implementation because of his position as Commander of the Eastern Quebec Sector.[6] The whole project failed miserably.

Valcartier was not big enough at that time to allow for complete armoured or artillery units to be housed and trained there. Allard set about the task of expanding the base, which he achieved in 1966 when he was the first commander of Mobile Command. In the meantime, in 1965, realizing that integration and unification were coming, he raised the issue of French Canadians in Canada's Armed Forces generally with the first Chief of the Defence Staff. He proposed to General F.R. Miller that a departmental commission be established to review the role and future of Francophones in the Armed Forces. He also suggested that some of its recommendations could be submitted to the Royal Commission on Bilingualism and Biculturalism. When he had not received a reply after several months, he offered his resignation, which led to his being summoned before the Minister who advised him to be patient. In exchange for Allard's withdrawing his resignation, the Minister promised to review the question of francophones and to find a Canadian solution for the unification of the Armed Forces. One of the fears expressed at the time was that the unified forces would become a kind of United States Marine Corps in which the individuality of each force would be smothered.

In 1966, when he became Chief of the Defence Staff (CDS), Allard had all the freedom he needed to bring to fruition the idea he had been developing for more than ten years: to create French-language units outside the infantry and enable young Francophones to serve in the military of their country in a less hostile atmosphere than that which had existed in the past and, equally as important, under leaders who understood them.

On this issue Allard stood firm over the years even though he often had to change his approach as contrary currents and breezes occasionally forced his vessel off course. However, he seized every opportunity he was given. At first, his actions on behalf of francophones focused primarily on the Army (if we exclude his idea of a military academy in 1951-52). Following the integration of the headquarters, as well as the unification of the Armed Forces, he was able to extend his vision to the Navy and the Air Force as a result of a commission of inquiry into the situation of francophones in the Armed Forces – which produced the Ross Report. He was also assisted by the work done by the Royal Commission on Bilingualism and Biculturalism in Canada, the preliminary report of which was harshly critical of the Canadian Forces. Allard considered his achievement in this regard, which intermittently took up a large part of his military career, to be the finest achievement of his professional life.[7]

Today, it should be noted that Allard launched his program and sketched some of its outlines, including the idea of French-language units, *before* the *Official Languages Act* became law. When the Act was passed, he began preparing a plan to enable the Armed Forces to comply fully with its letter and spirit. An amended and more detailed version of this plan was approved by the Treasury Board in 1972, three years after Allard's retirement. Compare this approach with that taken by some of his successors in dealing with certain provisions of the *Canadian Charter of Rights and Freedoms*, employment equity, access to information, and other issues.

There were, however, many other moments, major and minor, when Allard the visionary came to the fore. Some will be mentioned later in this chapter while others are set out below. Note, for example, the invention he made in the Second World War to control the turrets of armoured vehicles by means of an electrical circuit.[8] Or note the way he brought together the Canadian troops assigned to NATO in the area of Lahr/Baden-Soellingen, which made it possible to reduce, if not to eliminate completely, the last influences of the British Army on our own.[9] The organization of the first Canadian Armed Forces' athletic championships was also his idea in August 1967, despite strong resistance.[10] And the overall development plan for the University of Ottawa – which is still very obvious in the architecture of the university and the city – was Allard's idea when he was Chairman of the University's Board of Governors.[11]

The Strategist/Tactician

Pitcher indicates that a leader must be a strategist and Mintzberg underlines this fact in his preface.[12] In my judgement, the expression tactician fits even better in a military context.

Of all the actions Allard led during the war – note that he was awarded three Distinguished Service Orders (DSOs) – I would select the action at San Fortunato, Italy. Following unsuccessful attempts by other regiments in his brigade, it was the turn of the R22eR to go into action. The orders were clear: they were to attack at 11:00 a.m. Allard knew that this would risk disaster. He requested and obtained an order that zero hour would be postponed to 4:00 p.m., but he was already thinking that he would not attack until dusk (between 6:30 and 7:00 p.m.). By all possible means he secured what he wanted and thus no doubt disconcerted his superiors as much as the enemy. The attack was a complete and rapid success.[13] In Korea, a number of well-thought-out initiatives enabled his brigade to control the "no mans' land" in front of their positions, a sector that the Chinese had used more or less as they wished for many long months.[14]

In a lighter vein, when invited by the Red Army to a celebration in Moscow, Allard swallowed several charcoal tablets, which absorbed some of the alcohol that he consumed. A few hours later it was his Soviet counterpart who fell flat on his face, completely inebriated.[15] As a result, his stock soared among the Russian military authorities, who separated him from the other military attachés. When Allard offered his resignation to the Chief of the Defence Staff in the winter of 1965, after receiving no reply to his questions on the future of francophones, he became involved in a risky but well thought out game of poker that he eventually won.[16]

The strategist came into his own again in 1967, when he foresaw that a rapid withdrawal of Canadian troops serving with the UN in the Sinai between Israeli and Egyptian forces would probably be necessary. Allard prepared to react by sea and air. When Egypt demanded that the peacekeepers leave its territory within forty-eight hours, Canada did so within thirty-six hours. Other countries were not able to act as quickly and lost troops when hostilities began.[17]

During Allard's period as CDS, he sought an inexpensive way to show that the North was indeed a part of Canada when an American submarine used the Northwest Passage without prior consultation. To make it very clear that this northern landmass was not open to just anyone, he arranged for an aerial exercise to be conducted there and distributed small Canadian flags to the inhabitants of the islands in the area. Although this was only a small gesture, it nevertheless made an impact.[18]

Above all, however, it is important to appreciate the way in which Allard brought about the unification of the Armed Forces desired by the politicians and helped to ensure that the three services would continue to exist nevertheless. There was a great danger in this project since the leader risked being separated from his base. After all, how is it possible to lead when there is no support for the leader? Given this question, some senior military authorities at the time saw it as a trap to be avoided, rather than a challenge to be met, and they resigned. It would be quite fascinating to examine the cases of those who resigned; all of them had displayed great courage on many occasions during the war but crumbled miserably when facing a classic question of "intellectual" leadership. After succeeding in adapting unification to make it acceptable to both the politicians, who wanted it, and his men, who would have to implement it, Allard was able to sell the concept to the troops.

Finally, it should be noted how Allard made judicious use of his contacts in the Ontario government to transfer the University of Ottawa to lay control. That move certainly helped the institution to become one of Canada's major universities.[19]

The Charmer

The artist is a charmer. He tells his new subordinates – who regard him with a certain mistrust – that he will not interfere in their decisions. He shakes their hands, shares in their successes, and eats with them. He dispels their fears and wins them over completely.[20]

I am sure that the great majority of those who worked with Allard will confirm this view of him as a charmer. A lover of music who played the piano a little and had a fine voice, he was able to use these talents, even in the worst of battles, as can be seen in some of the testimony of his colleagues published in *La Citadelle*, the magazine of the R22eR Association.

When he was parachuted into the R22eR he was, on the one hand, ready for all challenges, although he knew that he would not be given a rapturous welcome by a group of officers who had been together for more than three years. He quickly realized that this challenge, which he had foreseen, was greater than he had expected: even the commander of the unit was disinclined to speak to him. He acted diplomatically, imposing himself slowly and very politely among the officers, the NCOs, and the troops. Within a few days the ice was broken and Allard felt that he was part of the group.[21]

On 16 September 1944, in the savage battles that followed the breach of the Gothic Line not far from Rimini, Italy, Allard prepared to throw his regiment back into the attack on a plateau near San Lorenzo. His unit had been spearheading the attack for two days, his men were exhausted, and losses were severe. He knew that his company commanders wanted to dissuade him from going back into battle so soon because they felt that everyone needed a good rest. Before they could say a word, Allard pointed out that 16 September was the anniversary of the Battle of Courcelette, in which the R22eR had distinguished itself in 1916, and that it was necessary to live up to those illustrious predecessors. No one dared argue; Allard then explained his plan of action, which met with success.[22]

When he led the 4th Division of the British Army on the Rhine (BAOR) in Germany, his British commanders expected him to improve relations between the troops and the local population among whom they were living. In fact, they had to stop acting as occupying troops, since their official status in that regard had disappeared in 1955. This became another success for Allard.[23]

Above all, however, we must see how, in 1966, Allard embarked upon a battle of the giants in which he gained acceptance of unification by his troops (after he had, in a sense, brought it about). On a visit to the Navy in Halifax in August of 1966, rather than answer the host of questions raised (all questions were submitted anonymously in writing and are preserved in the Directorate of History and Heritage), he decided to speak to his audience "from the bottom of his heart,"[24] which was altogether typical of the man. He also won over a rather hostile group at the annual Conference of Defence Associations in 1967.[25] His visits to the NCOs' messes on board ships gave him another chance to observe how unification was working: it was welcomed much more warmly below decks than in the officers' wardroom.[26]

The Non-Conformist

Artists are non-conformists (not necessarily by what they wear) because they do not use a traditional way of thinking,[27] and they take nothing for granted.

When he was second in command of the Chaudière Regiment, for a very short period in August 1943, Allard refused to reject a number of illiterates who had volunteered. When he joined the R22eR, these young men with little education were offered to him as reinforcements. Their actions in battle fully justified the faith he had shown in them.[28]

In 1960, the countries making up the International Commission for Control and Supervision of the Ceasefire in Vietnam, Laos and Cambodia met in Geneva. The commission's work on the ground was not very productive. Allard was familiar with the Soviets and concluded that as long as the countries guaranteeing the armistice remained together – the USSR was one – the number of incidents in Indochina would be minimal. Thus Allard as Deputy Chief of the Army Staff, with George Ignatieff of External Affairs, succeeded by making outrageous requests and keeping the supervising countries conferring together for almost a whole year. In order to do this, Allard had the representative of the Canadian Army move with his family to Switzerland at the outset of the discussions. Although he was criticized for doing so by some people at first, they later realized why he had done so. That was the price that had to be paid to ensure any kind of peace in Indochina.[29]

When Allard was commanding a British armoured division in the Federal Republic of Germany one year later, he put an end to the tradition by which young soldiers would get up at 5:00 a.m. to water (check the radiators) all of the mounts (tanks) in the units. This archaic practice was supposed to maintain a link between armour and the former cavalry it had replaced.[30]

Finally, I should also mention here the single uniform that the Armed Forces started wearing in 1968-69: a non-conformist like Allard was necessary simply to gain acceptance of this requirement.

The Depressive

One of the characteristics of many artists, according to Pitcher, is that they experience moments of depression followed by moments of euphoria. Since they do not tend to be boastful, they sometimes doubt their own abilities as they work toward their goal. However, they always pull themselves together and move on to conquer new heights with their intuition and imagination.[31]

Jean Allard experienced serious dark moments throughout his life, particularly on the death of his son at age 17. He experienced others in his professional life. I shall consider three of them. He reported the first to me himself, although it is not directly included in his memoirs. I shall summarize what happened. In 1942-43, Major Allard, with his modest background and high school education, was not skilled enough for the job of instructor at the army staff college in Kingston. He wrote, "A large number of militia officers were taking it [the course Allard was giving]. They came from all kinds of professional backgrounds: lawyers, accountants, engineers and many others."[32] They included men like Paul Sauvé, the future Premier of Quebec, and Hugues Lapointe, a future Lieutenant-Governor of the province. Mrs. Allard assured me that her husband was so uncomfortable that he wrote a letter requesting a transfer to other duties to which he felt he was better suited. She persuaded him not to send this letter, and he continued as an instructor until he was seconded to the Headquarters of the 2nd Division in Great Britain. In his memoirs, he draws a line under this part of his life in Kingston by saying, "a wonderful year, albeit full of work, which made heavy demands on me."[33]

The second incident, which is better documented, occurred a few months after he arrived at the headquarters of the 2nd Division in Great Britain and to some extent confirmed his apprehensions in Kingston. He realized that many of his former students, members of the Armoured Corps like himself, had now gained the rank of Lieutenant Colonel, whereas he had been left behind. In fact, his own regiment, the 12th Armoured Regiment (Trois-Rivières) had just been given a new leader who was from Ontario. After making an appointment to see General Crerar, he said, "If that is how I am going to be treated, I would prefer to go back to Canada and finish the war there with my family."[34] Crerar probably recognized the power concealed beneath the façade of uncertainty that Allard had just shown him because he quickly transferred Allard to the infantry, where he made the successful career that is known to many.

Let us now move forward twenty or so years to 1965. After being given oral assurances, admittedly ill defined, concerning improvements in the situation of Francophones in the Armed Forces, Allard was hospitalized for several weeks for treatment of severe back pain. He would soon be 52 years old – he celebrated his birthday in the hospital – and he was sure that he had reached the pinnacle of his military career.[35] However, less than one year later he was appointed CDS.

I shall not examine two other episodes that occurred after Allard left the Canadian Forces, namely the fact that he was not given the title of Honorary Colonel of the R22eR in the 1970s, and the terrible brain embolism he suffered in 1982 that left him severely disabled until the end of his life. I shall simply note that he rebounded from such difficulties and became an Honourary Colonel of the R22eR three years after his medical problem occurred.

The Conciliator

Before giving examples of this aspect of the personality of Jean Allard the leader, let us take a closer look at what Pitcher says about two other types of leaders she observed – namely the artisan and the technocrat – and the relationship between them and the leader who is also an "artist."

Beside the artist there is the artisan. While the artist casts bridges to unexplored shores, the artisan builds them. The artisan is patient and conservative (respectful of tradition), rarely applies anything other than the tricks of the trade, is responsible, sensitive, honest, loyal, direct, likeable, tolerant, and displays judgement. Pitcher, who admires artists, shows a great deal of respect for "artisans," to whom she devotes a chapter with the revealing title, "Ode to the artisan class."[36]

The artisan is located between the artist and the technocrat. About the latter Pitcher does not have very much good to say. She describes technocrats as compulsive, callous, difficult, intransigent, and hung up on convention, which they follow and deify. This does not prevent them from being brilliant, meticulous, and cerebral. They may even appear to know where the future lies and to offer a perfect three-part answer to any question, although this does not mean that the problem will be resolved – far from it. Do you believe that, when confronted by an impulsive leader who creates, eyes the horizon, innovates, and challenges the status quo, a technocrat can trust "an artist long enough to find out whether he is trustworthy? Never in a hundred years."[37]

An artist knows how to feed off the qualities of the artisans surrounding him. He can work harmoniously with everyone, including other artists and even technocrats, particularly those who are most likely to put a spoke in the wheel. Technocrats tend to over-emphasize the technical aspects of a problem to the detriment of the human and social consequences. For them, it is a question of quickly getting rid of the fragmentary and impulsive visionary or his "errors" after he has left. In the minds of technocrats, the ideal situation occurs when they can replace the crazy characters who were there earlier. In this light, Pitcher even goes so far as to say that real leaders have powerful enemies. In the public place there is a real war where "those who are right do not always win."[38] It is revealing simply to examine Pitcher's table of contents. The second part of her book is entitled "Le drame" (the drama) and consists of two chapters, "Le triomphe du technocrate" (triumph of the technocrat) and "L'effondrement de la vision" (collapse of the vision).

It is a fact that Allard was able to agree with everyone while at the same time assessing the weaknesses of certain technocrats. He did not look very kindly on those in the 1st Division who, in May 1944, forced the 3rd Brigade, including the R22eR, to attack the Hitler Line without the necessary preparation and on the basis of false information. In fact, he distrusted them until he was able to move to another unit.[39] When, in the following September, he spent time at division headquarters and noticed that the maps used there were not up to date, he had a better understanding of why some units were bombed by their allies. According to one of those maps, a position held by the R22eR was to be the target of the next attack by the Princess Patricia's Canadian Light Infantry (PPCLI).[40] Despite differences of opinion, he maintained very good relations with his superiors, using his "good friend" Brigadier Bernatchez as a buffer between the R22eR and the Division.

His relations with Lieutenant Harry Pope, whom many people could not stand, deserves to be mentioned here. "Personally," stated Allard, "I never had a problem with him: I liked his intelligence, his gallantry and his great ability."[41] Pope was promoted to major and worked with Allard again in Korea nine years later.

What is more, Allard had confidence in the leadership of the Defence Minister, Paul Hellyer, another "artist"-leader who launched the major reform movement that radically changed the Canadian Armed Forces in the 1960s. The General was tasked to establish Mobile Command practically without instructions as to what he must do. In that case, the artist Hellyer allowed the artist Allard to do as he saw fit, and he in turn relied on the artisans Ramsey Withers and Roger Rowley to build the necessary bridges between the vision of the leaders and its implementation. As the Pitcher model predicts, the artist Allard knew how to pay homage to the achievements of his two artisans.[42] He also had good things to say about Armand Letellier, who on two separate occasions was responsible for official languages at the Department of National Defence.[43]

Part of Allard's vision in the 1960s persisted for thirty years. Some questions relating to the place of francophones in the Armed Forces came to a boil again in the early 1990s after being quiet for a decade or so and continue to develop under the original impulse given to this issue by Allard. It must be admitted, however, that the technocrats have had plenty of opportunity to treat parts of Allard's vision shabbily, especially after his retirement.

The Canadian Airborne Regiment that he created when he was Commander of Force Mobile Command was designed to fill a vacuum in modern warfare. If war broke out abroad, it would go into theatre in advance of a brigade being prepared in Canada and would remain in combat for three to five weeks. The members of the unit were required to be able to parachute, but not necessarily at a professional level. This is what Allard wrote about this regiment in 1984, as it existed at that time *and eight years before the Somali affair*. "Since I left the Forces, the regiment has become a unit of parachutists to be used at the same time as all other units but not for special missions. In my opinion, those who adopted this approach showed their complete ignorance of the need for rapid reaction required in most of today's conflicts."[44] If we adopt Pitcher's reasoning, it is very likely that those who have distorted the concept put forward by Allard and his artisans always thought they had the right answers to the questions that arose. The problem is that, when applied to the original project, the picture that emerged was blank and what followed was a mess.

It is once again in the Army that we find what was probably the "most bitter" failure sustained by Allard during his career. This was the reform of the Reserves. Allard wanted them to play a role in a contemporary context. For him there was no longer any point in having, for example, an infantry unit in Brockville and an armoured unit in Trois-Rivières. No doubt many talents other than those required for infantrymen or cavalrymen existed in those cities, but, as in the nineteenth century, the volunteers from a given area could enlist only in a specific unit, and this was very likely to deprive the Army of certain talents. Allard slowly put his ideas in place between 1966 and 1969. When he retired from the Armed Forces, the technocrats hurried to erase what he had succeeded in putting in place, not without pain and difficulty.[45] What has become of the Reserves today? They face the same demons as in 1960.

As I write this, in the spring of 2000, I find it tragic that the Canadian Forces University has come to nought. According to the concept, there would have been a Board of Governors and a board of education, and all the Canadian Forces colleges, including the three military colleges of that time would have been merged in a single bilingual location – Ottawa-Hull.

On 4 September 1969, the Defence Council approved the report submitted for that purpose by the Officer Development Board (ODB) and the Minister requested the preparation of a memorandum to Cabinet. On September 15th of that year, the day on which Allard left, the ODB report was shelved: the memorandum requested by Léo Cadieux, who would leave only a few months later to become Ambassador to France, was never written.[46] Just under thirty years later the idea of a CF University re-emerged and has gained acceptance. However, no one has the "cheek" to concentrate all military post-secondary education in a single location that is both functional and bilingual. The business plan prepared at the time justified this concentration from a budgetary viewpoint. How much time has been wasted simply because the views of the technocrats were accepted! Imagine the Armed Forces of the year 2000 with their CF University up and running since 1976 at the former Rockcliffe Base, as was projected in 1969.[47]

It should be noted that Allard always refused to point a finger at those who were responsible for the "failure" of large parts of his vision.[48] Of course, he felt regret that the Armed Forces did not really take advantage of what he had prepared for them.

Acceptance of Failure

Pitcher notes that "the beauty of artists and artisans is the fact that they admit their mistakes. That is life."[49] In the introduction to his memoirs, Allard writes, "The view I took of situations in the brief or lengthy periods of thinking required before a person acts has not always been right. As a result, I have often ventured onto thin ice."[50] Thus he ascribes to himself some of the responsibility for the failure of the operations by the Seaforth Highlanders of Canada on 18 September 1944 to relieve the positions held by the R22eR. This failure led to the commander of the Seaforths, at whose feet all the blame was laid, being stripped of his command.[51] Also, Allard's treatment of certain journalists in Korea earned him a slight reprimand from Ottawa in September 1953.[52]

During his early years in office, Allard gained a host of successes in a very short time. However, he also recorded a series of small and large failures. While the most important were mentioned earlier in this chapter, there were others. For example, he failed to improve the educational opportunities in French for the children of francophone servicemen (although he had initially succeeded in the 1940s and 1950s, without any public infrastructure to support him, when he was serving outside Quebec). He also attempted, from 1967 on, to sell the idea of a boarding school for such children that would have been located in Quebec City; it was not to be, but the situation of these children began to improve in the late 1970s as other provisions were made for them.[53] However, Allard continued to fight eagerly for this idea, long after he had left the Armed Forces. The new naval insignia that he presented to the navy on the *Bonaventure* in 1968 did not have the colours that he wanted. The change was made by Hellyer without consultation.[54] The badges of the general officers, which he had approved before retiring, disappeared shortly afterwards. The proposal he made to Prime Minister Pearson in 1967 to create different military orders as part of the brand new system of Canadian honours was rejected,[55] only to find acceptance with a few changes some years later.

CONCLUSION

The many aspects of a human personality cannot be assessed without risk of mistakes. The personal history of a leader and the context in which his leadership is exercised are factors that absolutely must be considered. In this short article, I have barely scratched the surface of the complexity of the leader that Allard was. Some of his assistants at that time, with whom I have often had occasion to talk, have sometimes told me that the man had a hundred good ideas a day, and that they had to pick one or two at a time on which to concentrate. He was well aware of the limitations of those around him, and he did not hesitate to put aside a secondary idea within his great scheme of things if it could not easily be implemented within a reasonable time. This having been said, a review of what the various chiefs of the Defence Staff have achieved since 1969 will strike any objective observer with the scope and the number of changes to which the Armed Forces were subject under Allard's leadership, even more so if we include his time as Commander of Force Mobile Command – his second greatest success achieved, in his view.

Readers should examine closely General Allard's memoirs where he describes his life with all the doubts that inevitably follow the making of combat decisions.[56] To deal with this problem and to ensure that his uncertainty would not spread among his subordinates, he often sought refuge in reading poems in the time between issuing his orders and seeing them executed. This was many years before Pitcher's thesis. Was this not an artistic form of behaviour?

The method I have used to describe this leader is only one among many. Allard left a very great and very visible mark as well as a complete set of memoirs. It is, accordingly, relatively easy to repeat the exercise that I have just completed, using, for example, the characteristics that Abraham Zaleznik ascribes to a leader: a person who innovates, is original, develops and concentrates his attention on the staff, inspires trust, plans for the long term, asks what and why, has his eye firmly fixed on the horizon, creates and challenges the status quo, is his own master, and does what has to be done.

If that model were used, Allard would once again emerge as a leader and not as a manager, to whom Zaleznik ascribes the following qualities: administers, is a copy, maintains, concentrates his attention on systems and structures, exercises tight control, plans for the short term, asks when and how, always has his eye on the net benefit, limits, accepts the status quo, is a good little soldier, and does what he is supposed to do.[57]

I am convinced that he would earn a good ranking in any credible system that might be used to measure a military leader. After all, what is expected of such a leader? Ultimately, that he can lead his troops into battle. All the witnesses I have met conclude their impressions of Allard, usually without being asked, with the comment: "I would have followed him into battle at any time!"[58]

ENDNOTES

CHAPTER 13

1. Patricia Pitcher, *Artistes, artisans et technocrates dans nos organisations. Rêves, réalités et illusions du leadership* (2nd ed.; Montréal: Québec/Amérique et Presses des HEC, 1995), 262.
2. I toyed with the idea of considering the case of a leader whose parents died when he was young, which was true of Allard. However, my knowledge of psychology is limited and I have not come across any books or articles by specialists who list the characteristics of orphans who later became great leaders.
3. Pitcher, 52.
4. Jean V. Allard and Serge Bernier, *Mémoires du général Jean V. Allard* (Boucherville: de Mortagne, 1984), 244.
5. Ibid., 253.
6. Ibid., 295-297.
7. Ibid., 430.
8. Ibid., 70-72 and 75-76.
9. Ibid., 435-436.
10. Ibid., 441.
11. Ibid., 462.
12. Pitcher, preface written by Henry Mintzberg.
13. Allard, 145-148.
14. Ibid., 264-267.
15. Ibid., 191-2.
16. Ibid., 343-344, where Allard accurately describes his goal and the game he played.
17. Ibid., 436-438.
18. Ibid., 433.
19. Ibid., 460-462.
20. Pitcher, 119.
21. Allard, 87-88.
22. Ibid., 139-142.
23. Ibid., 318-319.
24. Ibid., 395-396.

25. Ibid., 399.

26. Ibid., 401-402. See also in this context the support he received against Simonds, 398.

27. Pitcher, 64.

28. Allard, 114.

29. Ibid., 308-310. Allard the tactician is of course also present in this example.

30. Ibid., 317.

31. Pitcher, 65. She adds that they are not suicidal depressives; on the contrary, they love life. I can testify that the General was fond of fine wine, good cheer, and discussions of ideas until a year before his death.

32. Allard, 77. See also how he later analyzed the reasons for his success (371-372).

33. Ibid., 79.

34. Ibid., 81.

35. Ibid., 346, and especially 369.

36. Pitcher, 227-232.

37. Ibid., 101.

38. Ibid., 12, 13, 52, and 53.

39. Allard, 120.

40. Ibid., 143-144.

41. Ibid., 125-126.

42. Ibid., 351-354.

43. Ibid., 415-416 and 477.

44. Ibid., 359.

45. Ibid., 360-362.

46. Ibid., 403-404.

47. For a more detailed analysis of this mess, see Serge Bernier, "Un seul collège militaire ou plusieurs? Une tentative de centralisation qui échoue," *Canadian Defence Quarterly*, Vol. 21, No. 3, winter 1991, 27-37.

48. Here I should add the experience of the biographer: my questions and subterfuges to get the General to express his conciliatory positions met with little success, orally or in writing.

49. Pitcher, 158.

50. Allard, 12.

51. Ibid., 144. According to Allard himself, but, above all, those who ordered this hurried relief operation conducted at night should have shared the blame with Lieutenant-Colonel Thompson.

52. Ibid., 283.
53. Ibid., 417-418. In this case, he did not accept failure until the early 1990s.
54. Ibid., 400.
55. Ibid., 404.
56. Allard, 154-155.
57. Pitcher, 169.
58. This chapter has been translated from the original French.

CHAPTER 14
"MAD JIMMY" DEXTRAZE:
THE TIGHTROPE OF UN COMMAND IN THE CONGO

Sean M. Maloney

FOR soldiers of his generation, Jacques Albert Dextraze is legendary. His military career coincided with several major events in Canadian military history: the Second World War, the Korean War, UN peace operations, and the FLQ Crisis. These varied experiences afforded Dextraze insight into all levels of military activity, insight which he put to good use when he was appointed Chief of the Defence Staff in 1972.

Born in Montreal in 1919, Dextraze attended St. Joseph's College in Berthierville and later worked for the Dominion Rubber Company as a salesman. When the Second World War broke out in 1939, he attempted to enlist in the Canadian Army but was not accepted initially because he had flat feet. Eventually Dextraze persuaded the powers that be to accept him into the Fusiliers de Mont Royal (FMR) as a private soldier. While stationed in Great Britain, he was promoted to Sergeant and, after many junior officers had been killed during the disastrous Dieppe Operation, he was commissioned in the FMR as a Lieutenant.[1]

The FMR deployed to Normandy in 1944, with Major Dextraze commanding "D" Company. In his first action, "D" Company was decimated in an artillery attack during the Verrières Ridge manoeuvre. The FMR's commanding officer, Colonel Guy Gauvreau, consolidated his remaining forces and left Dextraze in command. After regrouping, the FMR company group finally seized their designated objective near Ifs. Moving on southward towards May-sur-Orne, "D" Company was ordered to clean out some cut off sub-units of the 9th SS Panzer Division. When the Canadian assault bogged down, Dextraze took the lead, moved in with his infantry company, and wiped out the SS troops. For this action he won the Distinguished Service Order (DSO). After the action at May-sur-Orne, Dextraze was nicknamed "Mad Jimmy."[2]

Throughout 1944, the FMR fought its way through western France and into Belgium and the Netherlands with the rest of 2nd Canadian Division. In time, the 24 year-old "Mad Jimmy" was promoted to command the regiment once it arrived in Nijmegan. In later operations near Groningen, Dextraze drove a Bren Gun Carrier behind German lines to their local headquarters where he told the German commander that his forces were surrounded. He took the enemy commander in the carrier to the FMR's positions in what amounted to a show of force, and the man surrendered his 800-man defensive position. Dextraze received a bar for his DSO.[3]

Dextraze and his regiment fought through the polders and into the deadly Rhineland campaign. At the conclusion of military operations in northwest Europe, Dextraze volunteered for the Canadian Army Pacific Force, but this deployment was stood down after Japan surrendered. He returned to civilian life and worked for the Singer Manufacturing Company as a forest engineer. Moving rapidly up the corporate ladder, Dextraze eventually was appointed director of Forest Operations. When the Korean War broke out, Dextraze was asked by a minister in the Quebec Government to return to the colours and command the French-speaking battalion of the Canadian Army Special Force (25th Canadian Infantry Brigade Group).[4]

As CO of 2nd Battalion, Royal 22nd Regiment, Dextraze had to take a mixed group of Second World War veterans and inexperienced young men and mould them into an infantry battalion that could withstand the rigours of Chinese Communist human wave attacks, bitter cold, and mountainous conditions. During the work ups at Fort Lewis, "Mad Jimmy" was re-nick-named "JADEX" by his men since he had a penchant for signing documents "JDX".[5]

The 2nd R22eR was involved in numerous operations, many of them involving defending static hilltop positions against superior numbers. Dextraze did not believe in sitting around waiting to be struck, so he initiated an intensive night patrolling programme to disrupt Communist activities before they could build up. As David Bercuson notes in *Blood on the Hills,* "his leadership style was highly charismatic. He believed in maintaining close contact with his company commanders when the bullets were flying, and, if necessary, intervening personally in their direction of the battle."[6]

Dextraze was an extremely demanding man and somewhat of a disciplinarian. Arthur Bishop noted that "he was a stickler for dress, obedience, and behaviour and no one set a better example. He drove himself as hard as he drove his men, sometimes even harder. He believed that casualties could be prevented if his men were trained properly to keep their minds and bodies alert."[7]

The flip side of this was that Dextraze could and did walk the fine line between leader and bully, particularly when he was the Chief of the

Defence Staff in the 1970s. It is acceptable, at the tactical level in wartime or other times of tension, to carry out surprise inspections and random orders groups and expect subordinates to adapt to chaotic conditions hourly. It was another thing entirely to apply these techniques in a peacetime headquarters policy-making environment.

After Korea, Dextraze held a number of positions, including Commandant of the Royal Canadian School of Infantry at Camp Borden and staff officer slots in Army Headquarters. He was responsible for implementing the unpopular National Survival force structure changes when he was promoted to Brigadier and appointed commander of Eastern Quebec Area in 1962.[8] The political rigours of converting the Militia into a post-nuclear strike re-entry rescue organization provided Dextraze with some semblance of what was to come when Chief of the General Staff Geoffrey Walsh asked him to consider serving with the United Nations in the violent and volatile Congo in 1963. It is this period and more specifically, Dextraze's courageous and dynamic actions in response to the chaotic conditions during the conflict, that will be the focus of the remainder of this chapter.

UN operations in the former Belgian Congo have been obscured by a combination of time, lack of historical interest, and problems with developing adequate primary source documentation. Similarly, Canadian involvement in *Operation des Nations Unies au Congo* (ONUC) has been all but ignored, due in part to the relatively small size of the Canadian ONUC contingent, the controversial nature of the operation, the convoluted ONUC *modus operandi,* and the fact that the contingent consisted mostly of signals personnel as opposed to a combat unit. Dextraze was not part of 57th Canadian Signals Unit; he was the Chief of Staff in ONUC HQ, so any history of Canada's involvement would bypass the actions of the integrated UN headquarters and thus his activities. Dextraze, however, played a critical role in ONUC operations and as such his actions merit examination in any study of Canadian generalship.

The Congo crisis was well into its fourth year and ONUC was preparing to withdraw when Dextraze arrived in December 1963. Unlike the more public and extremely dangerous Cold War crises, like the Berlin or Cuban Missile Crisis, the Congo was essentially a closed course proxy fight between the West and the Communist powers. The Congo, almost as large as western Europe in terms of land mass, had been a lucrative Belgian colony. The vicious war over French Algeria convinced the Belgians that independence was the best path for their colony and, to avoid the bloodshed the French were experiencing, they proclaimed independence in the summer of 1960.[9]

The resulting power vacuum in the Congo resembled the 1990s collapse of the former Yugoslavia in many ways. The stabilizing "federal" entity ceased to exist and with it the basic day-to-day services provided by it. Several provinces, particularly the pro-West and mineral-rich Katanga Province which contained copper, diamonds, and uranium, declared independence from the Congolese central government. The new central government was in disarray, with the Soviets and Czechs backing one faction, the Americans and Canadians another faction, and the Belgians, French, and British a third. The removal of centralized Belgian control allowed age-old tribal feuds (which did not recognize the Belgian-imposed territorial boundaries) to re-ignite. Personal ambition as a motivating factor was in as much evidence as ideological fervour in these events. Vile atrocities were committed by all factions. Canada and the United States were able to use ONUC as a vehicle to fill the power vacuum so that the central government could stabilize and prevent the area from falling into the hands of Communist-backed entities.

The UN force was generally employed as a peacemaking force, not a peacekeeping force, though the terminology of the day did not distinguish the differences between the two. ONUC conducted counter-insurgency activities of a low intensity nature against various factions opposed to centralized control from Leopoldville, while at the same time trying to moderate the excesses of central government forces. Most ONUC operations centred in and around Katanga. Multinational UN forces used signals intelligence, Canberra light bombers, close air support, and mobile light armoured columns to bring order in areas which could not be controlled by central government forces. These Congolese forces were relatively untrained (their Belgian Army officers had left) and poorly equipped.[10] In effect, the UN force had credibility problems all around, particularly after the extremely able and courageous UN Secretary General Dag Hammarskjold was killed in a plane crash after he personally intervened in the region time and again to bring peace.

The long term Western strategy in the Congo was to use the UN to buy time while the central Congolese government sorted itself out with covert Western military support and overt Western economic support. The main threat was from Communist-supported elements in the region and on the periphery of the Congo. Cuban, Chinese, East German, and Czech training cadres were active: Guinea acted as a conduit, as did Ghana. These factions sometimes even worked at cross purposes which, in turn, added to the confusion.[11]

The situation on the ground was extremely violent with a savagery not previously seen by UN troops. For example, Congolese factions adhered to the practice of *ratissage* which was essentially a "tradition of brutality towards the vanquished."[12] The bulk of the Congo consists of impenetrable deep jungle where populated areas can generally only be reached by air or river. The road infrastructure was not extensive, and the evacuation of the Belgian technicians during the troubles of 1960 degraded the communications and air traffic control systems. The inability of military forces to respond in a timely fashion facilitated tribal massacres. Though not to the same scale as Rwanda in 1994, there were several nasty events of sheer butchery involving thousands of people.

ONUC was not immune in this environment: an entire platoon of Irish UN troops was surrounded and massacred. In another case, thirteen Italian C-119 pilots were seized and literally cut to pieces while still alive by an enraged mob. Even cannibalism was practised. The female dependants of Belgian settlers were a favoured target for gang rape by marauding armed groups. Canadian UN troops were beaten by mobs on arrival since their rules of engagement were sketchy at best, and their sub-machine-gun magazines only held ten rounds instead of the thirty they were designed for.[13]

Canada's interests generally coincided with those of the Americans and Belgians interests – that is, to deny the region to Communist influences. The main issue revolved around direct Belgian and American involvement. Belgium, the former colonial power, was tainted in the East-West propaganda war, as was the United States. The UN was the perfect surrogate, but its utility in the denial effort was waning because the Soviets were successful in mounting a campaign to shut off the ONUC's funds. Additionally, the individual ONUC contingents were generally effective, but their convoluted and "politically correct" command structures were poor. For example, inexperienced generals from Third World ONUC contingent providers had to be placed in command of the ONUC for the sake of appearances. The target audience was the uncommitted Third World UN members who could influence the ONUC funding issue and who were being courted by the Soviets and the Chinese.[14]

It was this political environment that brought Brigadier Dextraze to the Congo. Both the Congolese and American governments repeatedly asked Canada to provide francophone personnel to help train and professionalize the French-speaking *Armée National Congolese* (ANC) as part of the stability effort. The problem was the undefined relationship between the training missions and the ONUC, something which was never fully sorted out. The issue simmered throughout 1963 and the compromise was to have a Canadian brigadier to act as the Chief of Staff for ONUC. The Force Commander was Nigerian General Ironsi, a man considered by many to be ineffective. Having a Canadian Chief of Staff Brigadier in Leopoldville would stabilize the ONUC HQ, but there was some concern that Communist elements would use this against the UN in the New York jungle as well as the Congolese jungle since Canada was also a NATO member.[15]

Dextraze deployed to the Congo in December 1963. A month later he sent a confidential appraisal of the situation to Lieutenant-General Walsh. It is interesting to note that Dextraze's principles influenced his report: "In as much as the organization of the ONUC HQ is concerned, loyalty prevents me from writing comments. I wish to remain as loyal to my employers here as I am when I serve in Canada." Dextraze, in fact, did not like serving in the Congo (this much one can read between the lines) and wanted to command the West Germany-based brigade group instead. Despite his personal feelings, he carried on in Leopoldville without complaint.[16]

It was evident to all elements dealing with the ONUC HQ that if they wanted to get anything accomplished, they should go to the Chief of Staff rather than the Force Commander. This put Dextraze in "a precarious position" since he even developed personal access to General Mobutu, the Congolese leader, and nobody wanted to deal with Ironsi. He had to continually insist that the Force Commander be given "due consideration" by all concerned to prevent "being placed in such awkward positions."[17]

If this were not enough, Dextraze had to deal with a certain amount of fallout from General Ironsi's experiences as a Staff College student:

> When the General was at the IDC he was, for the purpose of a syndicate discussion, appointed Prime Minister of Canada. The students branded him the Black Canadian Premier. This he resented and has not forgotten it as he often in discussions with me refers to himself as the Black Canadian Premier. All these incidents in the past do not place me in an enviable position.[18]

When Dextraze arrived in 1963, the situation in the Congo was relatively stable. The primary threat to peace in the region from Communist-backed factions had been led by Antoine Gizenga, who led a rebellion after his Soviet-backed predecessor Patrice Lumumba was assassinated by Katangese separatists. Gizenga formed a breakaway "state" in Stanleyville which was immediately recognized by the Soviets, Chinese, and the United Arab Republic. A combined UN-ANC force crushed this rebellion in 1962. There were, however, many disaffected and armed "Gizengaists" who fled to the jungle and prepared for future operations.[19]

Despite UN New York's belief that all was well in the Congo, Dextraze's appreciation of the situation was that ONUC forces had to be prepared for the following: inter-tribal fights, large scale uprisings against the central government, interference with installations vital to UN operations, threats to UN personnel, riots, and banditry.[20]

Enter Pierre Mulele, former cabinet minister for education in the central government led by Cyrille Adoula. Adoula and his Defence Minister, General Mobutu, were trying to get a grip on the Congo's economic problems, but the situation in late 1963 was confused and uncertain. Mulele, trained by the Chinese in the latest variants of Maoist insurgency strategy, re-ignited the Gizengaist flame in Stanleyville. He then chose the Kwilu district east of Leopoldville as a test area for new tactics which included the outright murder of the intelligentsia, the destruction of schools and hospitals, and the terrorization of non-native elements. The objective of the exercise was to undermine the central government's authority and replace it with Mulele's.[21]

Mulele's messengers were the Movement Nationale Congolese party (MNC – the legitimate political "front" party) and its "youth workers", the *jeunesse*. These unfortunate people were manipulated through a mixture of witchcraft, Maoist ideology, and a drug called *dawa* which, when mixed with liberal doses of marijuana, produced a state of euphoria which, at least in the subject's mind, would deflect bullets. The *jeunesse* formed the backbone of Mulele's military forces until they were augmented and then superseded with the vicious *simbas* ("lions") units later in 1964.[22]

The ANC was still retraining when the Kwilu revolt started and those units that were deployed were powerless to stop the drug-crazed *jeunesse*. It was only through the intervention of some CIA-provided Cuban exile pilots that the initial moves were very temporarily checked.[23]

Colonel Mike Hoare, an Irish mercenary serving with the central government forces, recalled stomach-turning incidents on more than one occasion during his service:

> What I saw tore my heart out. The room was full of nuns and priests so badly bruised and beaten that some were difficult to recognise as human beings. They looked like grotesque caricatures. Nuns lay stripped of their clothing, their bodies black and blue with bruises and red with marks of the lash, teeth broken and lips swollen.... A Bishop had been forced to eat his own excreta, nuns had been made to drink urine, whilst many had died under the inhuman and calculated savagery.... Rapings in public, whippings, slow torture and other bestialities had been performed.[24]

The Congo had truly become a modern version of Joseph Conrad's *Heart of Darkness*.

Dextraze was planning the ONUC pull out when inklings that there was trouble in Kwilu made their way to Leopoldville in January 1964. At this point ONUC was not the 20,000-man force it had been the previous January. There were about 5,500 personnel left and most of them were deployed in the eastern part of the Congo.[25] It is important to note that it was not immediately clear to ONUC HQ that the Kwilu revolt was part of a larger Mulele strategy to take down the Adoulla government. Word reached Leopoldville that villages were burning, that the ANC forces were running away, and that the *jeunesse* might be behind it, but there was a lack of any "real time" information. This environment confounded Dextraze's ability to analyze what was going on.

Over time, some Western missionaries emerged rag-tag from the jungle and reported to their embassies, which in turn put in several requests to ONUC HQ for assistance. Dextraze saw a pattern in the killings. Aid workers and missionaries (called "NGOs" today) are critical in any stabilization effort. The effects of their outright elimination were obvious. If some force were directly targeting them, this could only mean that the violence in Kwilu was a calculated revolutionary effort and, given Kwilu's proximity to the capital, a direct threat to the central government.

Within days, the Kwilu revolt was followed by massive uprisings in Stanleyville and other provinces. This pinned down the bulk of the ONUC and, in any event, there was not enough air transport for Dextraze to redeploy ONUC forces west to Kwilu. The ANC was ineffective and General Mobutu was on the verge of calling back his effective but exiled political rival, Moise Tshombe, and employing mercenary land and air forces who worked for Tshombe during the Katangese succession to prop up the ANC.[26]

Dextraze could not stand idly by as report after report of *jeunesse* atrocities poured in. The ONUC was in an unenviable position; its scaling down was predicated on a stabilized situation. Many ONUC contributors, including Canada, had had enough of the Congo. The bulk of the ANC was next to useless. If UN forces acted on their own, there would be charges in the UN that ONUC was siding with the pro-West central government against a "people's national liberation movement." It would have been easy to declare that the ONUC did not have the mandate nor the capability to become involved in the Kwilu revolt.

Dextraze rejected the politically cautious, easy way. There were lives at risk: the aid workers and missionaries were unarmed and completely at the mercy of the *jeunesse* and their brutal tactics. The skills and presence of these endangered people were stabilizing influences. They gave hope to regions which had none. Something had to be done and the "politically correct" solution was morally unacceptable.

Dextraze issued orders for Operation JADEX-1 on 16 January 1964, after "consulting" with General Ironsi.[27] With extremely limited resources, a small composite band was put together: their mission, simply put in the orders, was to "rescue as many missionaries as possible who wish to be rescued."[28] Dextraze selected Lieutenant-Colonel Paul Mayer of the Canadian Guards as the on-scene commander. Mayer, who had served with 25th Brigade in Korea and on the International Control Commission in Cambodia and North and South Vietnam, had studied low intensity conflict and understood the precarious political nature of such operations.[29]

Dextraze and Mayer initially had one Otter propeller aircraft and between two and four ageing S-55 helicopters. Dextraze was able to wrangle two sections of ten men from the 1st Battalion, Nigerian Army ONUC contingent. These men had been trained by British officers and were relatively competent. Each section had two light machine guns plus their small arms. Dextraze was unwilling to commit this small force into the field without some form of preparation. He and Mayer initiated a crash training scheme so that the ground troops could disembark expeditiously from the helicopters and the air and ground elements could communicate.[30] Dextraze's concept of operations was to have the Otter conduct recce flights, while two S-55s would carry the two infantry sections. The other two S-55s would provide fire support. Machine-gun mounts had to be improvised for these aircraft since they were usually used for logistics, re-supply, and liaison flights.

While the training was in progress, a Belgian intelligence source reported to ONUC Sector HQ in Luluabourg that villages near the towns of Kisandji and Kilembe were burning. With no land line or radio communications with the missionary outposts there, Operation JADEX 1 was launched.[31]

The JADEX 1 force deployed to a small aerodrome at Tshipaka and re-fuelled. Dextraze was able to also deploy a small Canadian communications section there to maintain the link back to the Sector and Force headquarters. He even dragooned Captain Trembley, Royal Canadian Signal Corps, to act as his "competent Canadian" at Tshipaka since he had little faith in any other contingent communicator. The ONUC Chief of Staff then used his influence with General Mobutu to gain the services of two ANC T-6 close support aircraft (probably flown by CIA Cuban exile pilots) to assist the rescue effort. He then instructed Mayer that he was to have no compunction about using the T-6s if the situation warranted.[32]

There was the issue of rules of engagement. The ONUC was dogged throughout its existence by the ROE problem which usually involved too much civilian interference from New York in tactical matters. These restrictions were even more constrictive by 1964. Without resorting to overly legalistic language, Dextraze instructed the JADEX force that they were to "use peaceful means [to] try to accomplish your evac[uation] mission but if you are fired upon you will, repeat will, answer back with aimed fire to ensure [the] safety of [the] op[eration]." If this were not enough, the force was also instructed to "not fire for effect unless you are fired upon."[33]

One of the T-6 fighter aircraft reported to the UN team at Tshipaka that a group of Italian missionary sisters were on the run from the pursuing *jeunesse* at Kisandji. The UN Otter, with Mayer on board, then moved in for a close recce. After taking twenty-six rounds from the *jeunesse*, the Otter crew spotted the sisters and dropped a note telling them to stay together. A priest and four sisters with a stretcher, separated from the other group, were being pursued by another bunch of *jeunesse*. An S-55 swooped in and picked up four sisters from the first group, but as a second S-55 came in to get the others, it veered away as the *jeunesse* made threatening gestures. A third S-55 dropped in and Canadian Sergeant Leonce Lessard of the Royal 22nd Regiment jumped out before the wheels touched down. When the *jeunesse* saw the Nigerian troops, they "seemed to go berserk," threw spears at the rescue party and brought sub-machine guns to bear on them.[34]

Grabbing the stretcher, Lessard and the Nigerian troops pushed it and its occupant into the cabin of the helicopter. He was then attacked by several *jeunesse*, who he successfully fought off. Lessard then beat off another *jeunesse* who was attacking a nun and literally threw the nun onto the S-55. As one report noted, "The helicopter was already airborne when he drove off his last assailant and jumped aboard amid a hail of spears and arrows."[35] Lessard received the George Medal for this action.

A similar situation was evident at the Kilembe missionary station. A group of missionaries had been contacted by another UN Otter. A priest with that group attempted to parlay with the local *jeunesse* so that four missionary sisters could be evacuated. Mayer was concerned that it was a set-up for an ambush since he had identified *jeunesse* with firearms on the ground nearby. Mayer asked Dextraze to get Mobutu to drop an ANC parachute company in to clean up the area first. His assessment was that "the partisans are too well organized and so controlled [that] nothing short of a company-sized ground offens[ive] will do."[36] Dextraze agreed with Mayer and wanted the ANC to get involved in the effort, but was unable to convince Mobutu to enlarge ANC operations in Kwilu.

Mayer then proceeded to Kilembe by Otter. There were two villages nearby, one of which contained about four hundred *jeunesse* holding a political rally. Mayer was concerned that they might be on the move to destroy the Kilembe mission and its inhabitants, so he ordered Captain Glanz, the Swedish pilot, to make harassing moves with the Otter by buzzing the *jeunesse* group. On one such run over the village, the Otter took about twenty-seven rounds of fire and lost fuel. The helicopter force, commanded by Swedish Captain Von Bayer, then arrived at the mission. Mayer then "ordered [the helicopters] to form line astern and follow the Otter along the length of the crowded village with all guns firing. We formed up about half a mile from the village, came down to treetop level and went in with every rifle, LMG and SMG in action."[37]

Mayer and Glanz then threw grenades from the Otter in a "bombing run." The helicopters then landed and evacuated the mission.

In another incident, Mayer landed in an S-55 to gather information and negotiate for the lives of a priest and eight nuns who were held by the local *jeunesse* at another mission near Kisandji. He was then assaulted by the hostage-takers. A *jeunesse* grabbed Mayer's pistol, stuck it in his stomach and pulled the trigger. Fortunately for Mayer, there was no round up the spout. Sanity temporarily prevailed and Mayer was able to continue to successfully negotiate with the local tribal council. He ensured that all nine hostages were aboard the helicopter before he got on himself. Like Lessard, Mayer was awarded the George Medal for his actions.[38]

Logistics and command and control problems plus the possibility of expanded UN and ANC involvement in the rescue efforts at Tshipaka (and quite probably a personal desire to get in on the action) prompted Dextraze to leave Leopoldville so that he could direct the operation. A vital ferry re-supply route which supported the aerodrome had been attacked by *jeunesse* and put the rescue operations in jeopardy.[39]

By this time Dextraze and Mayer had developed Standard Operating Procedures (SOPs) for the rescue runs. The command and control plane, usually the Otter, would conduct a general recce of the area and identify the mission site or sites and the threat to them. It would then orbit to keep a general picture of the situation. A second aircraft, usually an S-55 or another Otter, would conduct a close recce to identify people on the ground and potential landing sites. The T-6 fighters would then be commanded from the command and control Otter and tasked to harass any large group of *jeunesse* in the area which could interfere with the rescue. The S-55 fire support helicopters would take up position to cover the transport S-55s which would effect the pick up.[40]

More information from JADEX-1 recce flights continued to be collated at Tshipaka. Most villages overflown by the Otters, T-6s, or the S-55s, were burnt out and deserted. Dextraze and his staff could track the *jeunesse's* movements through the jungle by the smoke palls which betrayed an ugly trail of destruction. Most of the population had fled into the bush and were apparently terrified of the retreating ANC garrison forces as much as the *jeunesse*. Only the small UN force could act effectively.

On 29 January, Dextraze received word that the missionary station at Kishua Nseke was about to be attacked by the *jeunesse*. He boarded the Otter and instructed the S-55s to take off. Flying low over the jungle canopy, Dextraze's Otter repeatedly dipped down into clearings in and around the missionary station to look for an unknown number of nuns and priests who were supposed to be in hiding nearby. Spotting armed *jeunesse* closing in, Dextraze dived into an open clearing and identified the mission staff. He then called in the helicopters which touched down and loaded the missionaries minutes before the partisans closed in and burned the station to the ground in frustration.[41]

The next day, the JADEX 1 force was at it again, this time at two stations at Gungo and Totshi. Accounts of these operations are somewhat hazy. Dextraze apparently commanded the operations up front from an S-55 helicopter since the Otter was employed elsewhere. The tactical scenario was similar to the other rescues, with large groups of *jeunesse* closing in and T-6 aircraft disrupting their movements. At Gungo, however, a small group of *jeunesse* got to the mission and almost captured four missionaries. There was no time to bring in the fire support S-55s, so Dextraze's command and control S-55 landed near the mission. Sub-machine gun fire was exchanged between the UN troops and the partisans. Dextraze put the missionaries aboard and the helicopter took off before reinforcements attempted to prevent it from doing so. Dextraze apparently blazed away with his Sterling SMG on full automatic to keep the *jeunesse* off the machine.[42]

After Gungo and Totshi, the clapped-out S-55s needed a rest since they were far beyond their scheduled maintenance periods. One of the machines even had to be abandoned on one mission when its gearbox failed. Mobutu had finally introduced a better-trained ANC force into the area and the *jeunesse* melted back into the bush for the time being. Dextraze went back to Leopoldville.

On 23 February, the Chief of Staff was out doing his rounds when he visited the ONUC contingent at Kikwit Air Base. Word then came in that the *jeunesse* were about to destroy Kafumba Mission. Flying a UN Otter, Dextraze arrived at Kafumba to find the partisan force attacking the mission complex. Flying in low, he saw there were SOS signs on the ground. An ANC paracommando company was in the area, but they could not be located by ONUC Kikwit, so Dextraze set out to contact them, which he did. The radios were not compatible, so he dropped messages to the ANC force to follow him back to Kafumba. He then flew on to the mission and dropped messages to the missionaries to head towards the ANC troops.[43]

With fuel running low, he returned to Kikwit Air Base and ordered the helicopters there to head to Kafumba to pull out the missionaries. In time, thirty missionaries and staff linked up with the ANC paracommandos, who informed them that there were still UN people in Kafumba. This information made its way to Kikwit and then to Dextraze, who was on the lead helicopter. The S-55s arrived at Kafumba and proceeded to engage the *jeunesse*. Nigerian troops led by Dextraze cleared out the mission and evacuated five wounded missionaries and seventeen teachers who had been held hostage. The bodies of two Belgian UNESCO teachers were also recovered.[44]

Now that it was clear that the *jeunesse* were not finished and that NGO personnel remained at risk, Dextraze instructed Lieutenant-Colonel Mayer to establish a permanent rescue force based on the JADEX 1 organization. General Ironsi was, apparently, not in favour of this because of the political repercussions, so Dextraze camouflaged the mission by calling it Operation Stayput. This operation remained in force throughout March and April 1964. It would rescue more than a hundred NGO personnel during that time using SOPs developed by Dextraze and Mayer during Operation JADEX 1. In time, Operation Stayput would incorporate a C-47 transport aircraft and a full ANC paracommando company under command, as well as additional T-6 fighters.[45]

After all was said and done in Kwilu, Dextraze sent a message through the Sector HQ in Luluabourg to General Ironsi:

> Regret having launched action without your prior approval. However, we are happy now to be able to act positively in an area of enormous tension and difficulties. Therefore most grateful for your approval. We will do our utmost to maintain calmness peace and order in area without committing ourselves into political activities which may disturb [the general situation] in Luluabourg.[46]

For his actions in the Congo, Dextraze was awarded the Commander of the Most Excellent Order of the British Empire.

Efforts to stabilize the Congo would continue throughout 1964. ONUC was withdrawn because it lacked credibility and continuing relevance. American and Belgian efforts to prop up the ANC would also continue. The *jeunesse* would crop up elsewhere after the UN left and centre their revolutionary activity in Stanleyville by the summer. Mulele's people then made the mistake of taking the Belgian population and American consulate in Stanleyville hostage which prompted a series of large-scale Belgian-American airborne operations, Dragon Rouge and Dragon Noir, to rescue them. Colonel Mike Hoare and his "Wild Geese" mercenary group would also conduct a series of valiant missionary and hostage rescue operations in the eastern Congo later that fall.[47]

It is clear, however, that Jacques Dextraze's leadership as Chief of Staff to ONUC positively contributed to the saving of several hundred civilian lives during the spring of 1964. It took moral courage to liberally interpret ONUC's mandate and rules of engagement and to be able to pull off the rescue operations without aggravating an already dangerous and politically charged situation in Kwilu. Fortunately for Dextraze and the UN, the missions were conducted outside of the media spotlight and executed without the direct knowledge of UN New York.

Dextraze's personal courage was also a significant factor, given the hazards of the operational environment and the need to lead the lesser-motivated UN personnel from the front. The success of the operation also rested on the fact that Dextraze selected a highly competent and brave officer to organize and lead the JADEX-1 mission. It is also important to note that once the missions were running smoothly, Dextraze backed off and trusted Mayer enough to continue the Stayput Operations without the Chief of Staff looking over his shoulder every minute.

ENDNOTES

CHAPTER 14

1. "JADEX," *Sentinel*, October 1972, 2-8; Arthur Bishop, *Salute!: Canada's Great Military Leaders from Brock to Dextraze* (Toronto: McGraw-Hill Ryerson, 1977), 242.
2. Bishop, 242.
3. Ibid.
4. "JADEX," *Sentinel*, October 1972, 2-8.
5. Bishop, *Salute!*, 245.
6. David Bercuson, *Blood on the Hills: The Canadian Army in the Korean War* (Toronto: University of Toronto Press, 1999), 50.
7. Bishop, *Salute!*, 244.
8. Canadian Forces Headquarters (CFHQ) Information Services, "Major-General Jacques Dextraze, CBE, DSO, CD," December 1970.
9. Brian Urquart, *Hammarskjold* (New York: W.W. Norton, 1994), Chapter 15.
10. See Conor Cruise O'Brien, *To Katanga and Back: A UN Case History* (New York: Simon and Shuster, 1962).
11. Mike Hoare, *Congo Mercenary* (London: Robert Hale and Co., 1967), Chapters 1 and 2; Thomas P. Odom, *Dragon Operations: Hostage Rescue in the Congo 1964-1965* (Leavenworth: Combat Studies Institute, 1988), 5-6.
12. Odum, 163.
13. Erwin A. Schmidt, *Blue Helm Rotes Koreas: Ads osterreichisch UN-Sanitatskontingent im Kongo, 1960 bis 1963* (Wien: Studien Verlag, 1995).
14. See Carl von Horn, *Soldiering for Peace* (New York: David Mackay and Co., 1966), Chapters 11 through 18.
15. Directorate of History and Heritage (hereinafter DHH), Raymont Collection, file 1081, (25 Feb 63) memo CCOS to USSEA, "Canadian Assistance in the Congo"; (18 Mar 63) message Ottawa to New York, "Congo: ANC Training"; (27 May 63) memo CGS to CCOS, "Congo-Provision of Training Coordinator."

16. DHH, 112.1.009 (D39) (31 Jan 64) letter Dextraze to CGS.

17. Ibid.

18. Ibid.

19. Fred E. Wagoner, *Dragon Rouge: The Rescue of Hostages in the Congo* (Washington D.C.: NDU Press, 1980), 11; Hoare, 13.

20. UN Archives, DAG 1/16500 #3, (22 Jan 64) "ONUC Operation Instruction No. 10."

21. Ibid.

22. Hoare, 19-21.

23. Odom, 5-6.

24. Hoare, 152-153.

25. William Durch, ed. *The Evolution of UN Peacekeeping: Case Studies and Comparatie Analysis* (New York: St. Martin's Press, 1993), 336.

26. Hoare, Chapter 1.

27. UN Archive, DAG 13/1.6.5.2.0:26, Mil Ops file: HQ ONUC JADEX -1, (30 Jan 64) message HQ ONUC to sector commanders.

28. UN Archive, ONUC files, DAG 13/1.6.5.0.0 #3,FC/Ops/3025, file Ops Directives Aug 1960-Jan 1964, (26 Jan 64) "Operation JADEX 1."

29. DHH Biog file, Mayer, P.H., DND Press Release, 2 April 1968.

30. UN Archive, ONUC files, DAG 13/1.6.5.0.0 #3,FC/Ops/3025, file Ops Directives Aug 1960-Jan 1964, (26 Jan 64) "Operation JADEX 1."

31. UN Archive, DAG 13/1.6.5.2.0:26, Mil Ops file: HQ ONUC JADEX -1, (27 Jan 64) message ONUC Lulu to ONUC Leo.

32. UN Archive, DAG 13/1.6.5.2.0:26, Mil Ops file: HQ ONUC JADEX -1, (27 Jan 64) message HQ Leo to HQ Sector Luluabourg.

33. Ibid.

34. UN Archive, DAG 13/1.6.5.2.0:26, Mil Ops file: HQ ONUC JADEX -1, (27 Jan 64) message Mayer to HQ ONUC Leo "Report on Kisandji Phase II."

35. Gerard Baril, "Gallantry Rewarded," *Sentinel* 1981/1, 33.

36. UN Archive, DAG 13/1.6.5.2.0:26, Mil Ops file: HQ ONUC JADEX -1, (29 Jan 64) message Mayer to HQ ONUC Leo.

37. Paul Mayer, "Peacekeeping in the Congo: The Operation at Liembe," *The Canadian Guardsman,* 1965, 136-141.

38. UN Archive, DAG 13/1.6.5.2.0:26, Mil Ops file: HQ ONUC JADEX -1, (29 Jan 64) message Mayer to HQ ONUC Leo; DHH BIOG file Mayer, P.A., "Award of the George Medal."

39. UN Archive, DAG 13/1.6.5.2.0:26, Mil Ops file: HQ ONUC JADEX -1, (4 Feb 64) message ONUC LULU to ONUC LEO.

40. Mayer, 136-141.

41. DHH BIOG file, Dextraze, J.A. "Award of the Most Excellent Order of the British Empire (Military Division); JADEX," *Sentinel,* October 1972, 2-8.

42. Ibid. Dextraze's exact actions during this mission have become the stuff of legend within the CF and it is difficult to acquire specific details. It is highly likely that they occurred, it is probably just a matter of how many *jeunesse* were killed: two or twenty.

43. DHH BIOG file, Dextraze, J.A. "Award of the Most Excellent Order of the British Empire (Military Division).

44. Ibid.

45. UN Archives, DAG 13/1.6.5.2.0: 26 HQ Mil ops Operation "STAYPUT" 6 March 1964.

46. UN Archive, DAG 13/1.6.5.2.0:26, Mil Ops file: HQ ONUC JADEX -1, (31 Mar 64) message HQ Sector Lulu to HQ ONUC Leo.

47. See Hoare, *Congo Mercenary*; Odom, *Dragon Operations: Hostage Rescue in the Congo 1964-1965,* and Wagoner, *Dragon Rouge: The Rescue of Hostages in the Congo.*

CHAPTER 15
MacKenzie in Sarajevo[1]

Carol Off

WHETHER the men and women who make up our Armed Forces like it or not, the Canadian public knows them best – and admires them most – for their work in peacekeeping. This does not dismiss the heroic efforts of Canadians in uniform during the great wars. But for contemporary society, the essential roles of defence and security curiously take a back seat in the Canadian psyche to the seemingly romantic and noble task of intervening in foreign conflict to effect good. Peacekeeping has become part of our national genetic code.

The consummate peacekeeper of our time is Major-General (retired) Lewis MacKenzie, a man who is arguably Canada's best known living soldier. Major-General MacKenzie became the poster boy of the blue berets, representing all the qualities that Canadians would like to represent on the world stage. He is celebrated not just among the general public but within the rank and file of the armed forces as well. People who have served with him and under him give the highest of accolades when they refer to the General as "a real soldier who's always looking out for his men." MacKenzie has spent his retirement on the speaking tour circuit where he peppers his speeches about his personal achievements in the field with tributes to the integrity and honour of our men and women in uniform. He has become the Canadian Armed Forces' most visible booster.

For the past few years, Major-General MacKenzie has been engaged in an informal and rarely publicized debate with another retired general, Romeo Dallaire. Lieutenant-General Dallaire contends that peacekeeping missions should follow the codes of other military operations – most obviously war – where the mission comes first, the soldiers second, and the commander last. It is a classic model that has been followed by generations of commanders. Major-General MacKenzie disputes it – not categorically – but principally in the area of peacekeeping. MacKenzie maintains his first priority is the safety of his soldiers, the second is the mission, and then, lastly, the well-being of the commander.

Dallaire argues: if the priority is the well-being of the soldiers and not the mission, then why are the soldiers even there? MacKenzie counters that the United Nations is such a confused organization that its mandates cannot be trusted and, hence, cannot be made a priority. The soldiers, he says, come first.

And yet, Major-General MacKenzie volunteered Canadian soldiers for – and then commanded them in – one of the most violent and questionable United Nations peacekeeping missions of the 1990s.

In May of 1992, the people of Sarajevo still believed the conflict that enveloped their country would soon be over. They had seen only a month of war, and yet, with barricades around the city and snipers hovering just above the main highways, it was impossible to get in or out. Sarajevo was under siege and it would soon be out of food.

In the capitals of Europe and America, heads of government were wringing their hands, trying to develop a response to the crisis in Bosnia. No one wanted to get involved militarily in this ugly little war, and yet they were faced with the prospect that citizens might soon begin to die of starvation in a modern European city a few hours by air from Bonn and Paris. Something had to be done – or for the more politically savvy – at least there had to be the appearance of something being done.

In May 1992, then Brigadier-General Lewis MacKenzie was in Sarajevo as Chief of Staff for the UN Protection Force in former Yugoslavia (UNPROFOR). The mission was assigned to stabilize the few remaining pockets of disputed territory in Croatia that remained following the 1991 war there. Officials at the United Nations Office of Peacekeeping installed the headquarters of UNPROFOR in Sarajevo where the UN believed it might have a secondary effect of keeping a lid on the boiling cauldron of Bosnia. But there would be no such luck. War was breaking out in that state as well and interfering with UNPROFOR's attempts to establish the peacekeeping mission for Croatia. It was decided that the mission headquarters (HQ) would have to be moved.

The several weeks MacKenzie had spent in Sarajevo had whet his appetite for more, even though he had already found the place dauntingly complex. MacKenzie had not only witnessed but had played a principal role in some of the war's earliest historic moments.

On 2 May 1992, Serb forces at the airport kidnapped the President of Bosnia, Alija Izetbegovic, upon his return to Sarajevo from peace talks in Lisbon. The Serbs held the President and his daughter, Sabina, captive at their Lukavica barracks near the airport while they planned what they would do with them. In downtown Sarajevo, meanwhile,

Bosnian government forces were holding hostage the commander of the Yugoslavian National Army (JNA) for Sarajevo, General Milutin Kukanjac, along with approximately four hundred of his officers and enlisted men.

In these early days of war, the so-called "Bosnian Army" was merely a loose association of military reservists, Sarajevo police, and well-armed criminals – essentially anyone who had a gun and knew how to use it. Their obsession was to increase their supply of weapons and ammunition, something they had very little of. The rag-tag force had captured and surrounded the Bistrik barracks in downtown Sarajevo containing General Kukanjac and his troops, and they were anxious to get access to the enormous JNA arsenal they knew to be inside. But when their president was kidnapped everything changed.

In a dramatic all-night bargaining session – most of it broadcast on Bosnian national TV – Brigadier-General Kukanjac and President Izetbegovic negotiated their own exchange. A general would be traded for a president. Early the next morning, the Vice-President of Bosnia, Ejup Ganic, asked General MacKenzie to provide security for the swap. Brigadier-General MacKenzie agreed, not realizing the operation was far more complicated than it appeared.

When Brigadier-General MacKenzie arrived at Lukavica barracks to pick up the president and bring him downtown for the exchange, he learned the plan had been modified: instead of one president for one general, he was now to supervise the swap of one president for the entire Bistrik barracks! MacKenzie told them it was impossible to take responsibility for such a large group when he had only a handful of Armoured Personnel Carriers (APCs) and staff officers. But President Izetbegovic was trying to save his life and that of his daughter. He gave his word that the operation would be secure. MacKenzie accepted his guarantee. The President, under UNPROFOR escort, made the journey from the airport to Bistrik barracks in the late afternoon.

On the previous day, Serbian forces had staged an armoured invasion of Sarajevo in an effort to cut the city in half. The battle had been fierce, and the results of that fighting were still strewn all over the roads. MacKenzie drove through a thick fog of acrid smoke – burning fuel oil from the bombed out vehicles – and saw bodies strewn on the side of the road. MacKenzie had not known much about the battle (he wrote in his diary for 2 May "a quiet day") and now was surprised by the level of carnage. The war had accelerated overnight, and MacKenzie was seeing the results. At Bistrik barracks, MacKenzie learned that General

Kukanjac was in the process of dismantling and loading everything that was movable, which he said would take seven or eight hours to complete. MacKenzie gave him one hour to pack and crossed his fingers.

At the appointed hour, Brigadier-General MacKenzie's vehicle led the JNA convoy out of Bistrik barracks. In the first APC was the President, his daughter, and General Kukanjac. Reports differ, but it appears that some of the Bosnian Army personnel had heard only the first dispatch of information – that there was to be an exchange between the President and the General. Others, including the Deputy Commander of the Bosnian Territorial Defence Force, General Jovan Divjak, understood the convoy would consist of only thirty trucks, enough to allow the men inside the barracks to leave with only their personal weapons.

But witnesses at the barracks say the convoy attempting to depart Bistrik that day was seventy vehicles long, and it was laden with weapons, equipment, documents, files, even the filing cabinets. The Bosnians – watching in horror as their booty escaped – cut the convoy in half by wedging a Volkswagen Golf into the column. They then proceeded to load as many weapons into their own vehicles as possible – and to kill anyone who resisted.

Before MacKenzie could persuade them to stop, six JNA officers were shot dead and car loads of AK-47s had been confiscated. The remaining JNA troops, still stuck inside the barracks, remained hostage. MacKenzie was quick to declare he had been betrayed by the Bosnian presidency and maintains that view to this day, though it's not clear that the entire leadership of the loosely organized Bosnian forces even knew of the detailed arrangements that had been agreed to. If they had, it's still not apparent they would have complied. In addition, MacKenzie had received a last minute phone call from Vice-President Ganic who demanded that the swap be called off. President Izetbegovic over-ruled his deputy, and MacKenzie decided to proceed with the evacuation of the barracks.

At that time, there were three distinct groups in the Bosnian forces – the Territorial Defence Forces (TDF), the police, and the criminals – plus numerous militias including the Green Berets and the Patriotic Front. But there was no single or co-ordinated chain of command. These government forces had been guarding the barracks for twenty-four hours without sleep and had consumed quantities of alcohol. As the self-declared defenders of the capital, they wanted access to the weapons, without which they would be unable to hold off the JNA forces much longer. No one – not even Izetbegovic – had control over them.

The possibility that the whole operation could have ended in a bloodbath was enormous. Both Serbian and Bosnian snipers were positioned at high points along the route, and the heavy artillery up in the hills had a clear sight-line to the road. Miraculously, President Izetbegovic was safely delivered to the other side, and General Kukanjac made his way to Lukavica. (He was later replaced by General Ratko Mladic.) By all accounts from those who were there that day, a fiasco had been a distinct possibility. But MacKenzie provided one point of agreement between the warring sides: they were both angry with him.

In his diary notes, which later made up the bulk of his book, *Peacekeeper,* MacKenzie wrote that 3 May, the day of the convoy incident, was the worst day of his life. He had almost lost a head of state and a general of the Yugoslavian Army. A half dozen officers were dead and scores of others had been taken hostage.

Later in May, MacKenzie was back in Belgrade planning the move of UNPROFOR HQ out of Bosnia when he learned that a UN delegation was to be dispatched to Sarajevo to negotiate an agreement for opening the airport. MacKenzie asked General Nambiar if he could take part in the negotiations but was refused: the Indian general had determined that MacKenzie had no political capital with the Bosnian Serbs because of the convoy incident and he would simply be a liability.

Cedric Thornberry was the civilian head of UNPROFOR and (then) Colonel John Wilson of Australia commanded the United Nations Military Liaison Office (UNMLOY). They were sent off to make the agreement between the Bosnian Serb leadership of Dr. Radovan Karadzic and the government of President Izetbegovic. (The Bosnian government is frequently characterized as the "Muslim government" when, in fact, the presidency was a coalition of ethnic parties – Croat, Serb and Muslim. The Bosnian Army was also multi-ethnic, both in its personnel and its command. However, it is true to say that this pluralism broke down during three and a half years of war.)

Thornberry and Wilson found Izetbegovic extremely reluctant to enter into any arrangement with the Bosnian Serbs. Izetbegovic did not want Karadzic recognized as a legitimate representative of anything. Bosnia had been accepted internationally as a legal entity and had been granted a seat at the United Nations: Karadzic was the leader of a rogue state waging civil war with the rest of the country.

Furthermore, Izetbegovic did not want an agreement for opening the airport that did not also end the two-month siege of Sarajevo. The President insisted that the Bosnian Serb guns be moved twenty kilometres away from the perimeter of the city before he would agree. With skilled diplomatic manipulation, Thornberry and Wilson convinced Izetbegovic to separate the two issues: open the airport first and then negotiate to move the guns. Wilson suspected (quite rightly) there would never be phase two negotiations, but the tactic did the trick. The Bosnian President agreed.

According to the terms of the agreement, Serb forces would be able to continue their attack on Sarajevo and would encounter little interference with their military operations. Their weapons would be deployed only in concentration points specified by the UN, and the guns would be under UN observation, but as long as they did not shoot at the aircraft (or get caught shooting at the aircraft) the siege of the city could continue unimpeded.

In addition, the Serbs knew they would have ample opportunity to siphon off what they wanted from the humanitarian relief flights, since Serb forces would effectively control the key zones around the airport. (The Serbs even managed to install a checkpoint coming to and from the airport, something Colonel Wilson says was never in the original arrangement.) Thornberry and Wilson returned to Belgrade, triumphant. General Nambiar began the task of installing the contingents of UN soldiers who would administer the agreement.

The story of how Canadian soldiers formed the first battalion to run the airport and how Lewis MacKenzie became the commander of sector Sarajevo is now so well-known it has become legendary. In a meeting on 6 June 1992, Brigadier-General MacKenzie, as Chief of Staff, gave his assessment of troop availability. Everyone in attendance – General Nambiar, Cedric Thronberry, French Major-General Phillipe Morillon (the Deputy Commander of UNPROFOR) and Brigadier-General MacKenzie – knew that it would take months to organize a peacekeeping force for the airport. Sarajevo was not even part of the UNPROFOR mandate. The notoriously slow and bumbling United Nations would never supply the needed troops in time, and the momentum created by Wilson and Thornberry would be lost.

MacKenzie volunteered the Canadian battalion located west of Croatia as the only one available for the mission. As the legend goes, MacKenzie also posited that Ottawa would never allow its troops to go to Sarajevo without a Canadian in command, namely Lewis MacKenzie. Sarajevo was not part of the official mandate, MacKenzie explained in a later interview, and he suspected Canada would never release its soldiers for such a mission without a debate in Parliament.

But if a Canadian led the force, chances were greater that it could happen without much interference from the Government in Ottawa.

Nambiar told him to confirm this statement with the Department of National Defence. MacKenzie went to his office and smoked a cigarette. He did not make the call to Ottawa but returned and told Nambiar that his expectation had been confirmed. Nambiar had no choice. The Canadians were available only if Lewis MacKenzie would lead them.

The UN Secretary General Boutros Boutros-Ghali had declared Sarajevo to be the most dangerous city in the world. The bulls-eye of that danger zone was the Sarajevo airport. Brigadier-General MacKenzie, himself, recognized it as possibly the most dangerous mission Canadians had been on since Korea.

MacKenzie led an advance party to the city in mid-June where he found that the siege, and the violence, had actually intensified since he had left several weeks earlier. The airport agreement had sparked off a fierce battle for as much control of the area around the landing strip as possible, and no one was in any mood to accommodate UNPROFOR's demands to honour the cease-fire. The Serbs were still smarting from the act of "betrayal" they believed MacKenzie had committed during the convoy incident. The Bosnian presidency – for its part– had figured out fairly quickly that it had been duped into accepting the airport agreement and knew there would never be negotiations to move the guns away from the city.

MacKenzie's reconnaissance group could see that they had an airport agreement but no airport. It was almost impossible to function in the area because of the shelling. The remaining ink-spots of Bosnian control were two suburbs, Dobrinja and Butmir, that straddled the road between UNPROFOR headquarters and the airport gate. The Serbs had taken everything else, and they controlled most of the strategic high ground around the city from which they could fire their heavy guns. The Bosnians had only a few heavy guns, but they were making good use of what they had.

On 20 June, three Canadian soldiers in the recce group were wounded when their jeep was hit by shrapnel. The tires were shredded and the engine punctured, but Major Peter Devlin managed to move the vehicle out of the line of fire. Corporal Jim Gordon, who had been driving the jeep, had his leg shattered. Devlin and another passenger had lighter wounds. It was a taste of what UNPROFOR soldiers could expect for the next three years: they would become casualties in continuous cross-fire, and they would be deliberately targeted by both sides of the conflict. When they were not casualties, they would become hostages.

Colonel John Wilson[2] of the observer mission in Sarajevo said in an interview that he had been astonished by the range and scope of General Mladic's arsenal. Mladic was backed up and supplied by one of the largest and best-equipped military machines in Europe – the JNA. Wilson noted that the Serbs would arrange their heavy guns in deployment position and then drive a group of soldiers around from place to place to fire them off. They had more weapons then they knew what to do with, according to Wilson, and no infantry force to follow up their shelling. The Bosnians, on the other hand, were defending themselves with whatever they could steal: an international weapons embargo on Yugoslavia prevented them from purchasing supplies on the open market. But what they lacked in weaponry they made up with in sheer brawn and audacity, often at the expense of UNPROFOR.

On 28 June, in the midst of this violence, Brigadier-General MacKenzie had a surprise visit from a very influential head of state. François Mitterand, President of France, decided to spur on the UNPROFOR mission for Sarajevo by proving to the world that planes could actually land there, and the first aircraft would be his. Instead of admitting there was no way to guarantee the president's safe arrival, MacKenzie ordered UNPROFOR to prepare the runway for the aircraft to land. Mitterand and his entourage arrived in two Super Puma helicopters. One of them took machine gun fire as it landed. Undaunted, the President of France decided to make the best of the visit – and so did Brigadier-General MacKenzie.

In later interviews, MacKenzie stated that the Mitterand visit was the one time in his life when all his military and diplomatic experience jelled into effective action. He believes it was his finest professional moment. MacKenzie knew he had only a few hours to convince Mitterand that the airport could be open for business. "When he and I discussed it and when I asked him to send humanitarian aircraft, I knew the media would cover it. And I knew that every friggin' country in the world watching television would want to be part of the action for their six o'clock news," insisted MacKenzie in an interview. He added, "Nothing would insult the world more than to see French aircraft land first."

During the limited time available to persuade the French President of all of this, the General was successful. Mitterand departed – following a final hail of shells and sniper-fire – having agreed to send French planes to Bosnia. As MacKenzie predicted, other countries followed suit;

soon relief flights were pouring in from all over the world – from countries that had been helplessly watching the deterioration of Sarajevo from a distance.

In early July, the Canadian battalion arrived in Sarajevo under the command of Lieutenant-Colonel Michel Jones. It was actually made up of two companies from the Royal Canadian Regiment and the "Vandoos," the Royal 22nd Regiment. Jones' arrival had been delayed by a Serb force of two thousand troops, backed up by a dozen tanks, under the command of an inebriated Bosnian Serb officer who held the Canadian convoy on the road to Sarajevo for eighteen hours.

The United Nations has very strict rules about the types and quantities of weapons and ammunition allowed in a peacekeeping mission. The point is, after all, to keep the peace and not to engage in combat. Moreover, the UN is ever conscious of the costs.

The UNPROFOR mission was under a chapter six mandate, meaning that soldiers were allowed light arms and were permitted to use them only in self-defence. Lewis MacKenzie rewrote the Rules of Engagement for the Sarajevo mission: "I declared it a chapter six and a half," he stated. MacKenzie also authorized Jones to bring as much fire-power as he could: "I told Michel Jones, bring every friggin' missile you've got. Put every high explosive round you can bring for the mortars, cram those vehicles full of that stuff and bring it to Sarajevo. Cause we're going to need it. Cause you guys are going to have to defend that airport."

There were tanks within a half-mile of the airport, and MacKenzie acknowledges he had no idea what they would do. Within hours of his arrival, MacKenzie had received a call from the notorious Serb paramilitary leader known as Arkan, who informed the General that he would slit MacKenzie's throat and kill all the Canadians if they went near the airport.

MacKenzie had asked Canada to send "through the back door" its relatively new tube-launched, optically-controlled, wire-guided anti-tank missile system, TOW, under armour. The UN could sanction the TOW deployment only because the night-vision system that came with it would be useful for securing the airport. But the UN would not permit any high-explosive ammunition. MacKenzie "cheated," as he describes it, and brought it anyway. "After all, if the situation turned nasty and we had to make a break for the Adriatic coast, we would be three hundred kilometres from the nearest border to the west," MacKenzie wrote in his memoir, "it would be helpful to hold off the tanks in the area of the airport if they took a dislike to us."

MacKenzie told the Sarajevo sector of UNPROFOR that, under his newly devised chapter six and a half mandate, the soldiers could fire, not only when they were in danger but when anyone else in UNPROFOR appeared to be in danger or if the airport operations seemed to be in danger. This was not a "what if" scenario, but a reality. Canadian soldiers at Sarajevo found themselves shooting at assailants not only when fired on but when they believed they were going to be fired on. MacKenzie will not hazard a guess at how many belligerents his soldiers shot – and killed – in defence of themselves and the mission. He says he filed no reports on these incidents and made no investigations. But he believes the numbers were substantial, and all were warranted. "It was an act of peace enforcement," MacKenzie stated in an interview. "I made up the rules as I went along. I knew I shouldn't have done it. But I'd do the same thing again, absolutely." The UN expressed some concern at one point, according to MacKenzie, "but whether it had something to do with me or not, they didn't tell me to stop." MacKenzie says that subsequent commanders rescinded the orders to shoot, "but we couldn't have accomplished what we did otherwise."

In interviews with those who served with then Brigadier-General MacKenzie in Sarajevo, soldiers speak admiringly of "fighting Lew" and his fearless commitment to their safety. The high-explosive ammunition, the rewritten rules of engagement, the shoot first ask questions later policy proved MacKenzie's interest in their well-being. But Canadian soldiers might well have asked what they were doing in Sarajevo in the first place. A mission that was so dangerous as to require the ability of the soldiers to fight their way out through a line of tanks controlled and supplied by the fifth largest army in Europe might have been more closely scrutinized and questioned.

The Sarajevo airport agreement was – at once – among the most ambitious and the most cynical exercises of realpolitik in the UN's history. Over the coming months and years, a series of brave pilots flew into the airport under fire; UNPROFOR and the NGOs unloaded the planes and attempted to transport food and supplies to areas of the city and eventually the country that needed them. Much of what they brought into the country was siphoned off for the war effort of Serbs, Muslims, and Croats. Much of what was left ended up on the Sarajevo black-market. People lost their lives in the operation of the airport and on its relief runs.

But the airport agreement allowed the UN and the European Community (EC) to pretend that the siege of Sarajevo was a humanitarian crisis, like a flood or an earthquake, instead of the brutal attack on an undefended population that history has since described. The international community could point to the airport operation as proof that there was a real effort underway to help the people of Bosnia. John Wilson, who co-negotiated the agreement in the first place, believes that the airport opening and the support that it contributed would never have happened if he had not coerced Izetbegovic into agreeing. But Wilson openly concedes that the agreement meant the end of any plans to take more definitive military action against the attacking Serb forces in order to end the war. As soon as the agreement was signed, the threat of air strikes was over, says Wilson. The Serbs knew that. And they also knew that their siege of the city could continue unhindered.

The Sarajevo airport agreement gave an immense public relations boost to the UN. Lewis MacKenzie told his bosses in New York, "I have been told by those who should know that the airport opening has endured more coverage, and that I have been interviewed more times, over the previous ten days, than anyone else in the world in the last half of this century." MacKenzie had helped the UN evade responsibility to do something more definitive. His soldiers paid the price. They took fire routinely – and gave it back – even though they were peacekeepers in a chapter six mission. It appears that nobody ever asked the key question: Should the mission be cancelled?

The people of Sarajevo came to loathe UNPROFOR for failing to protect them (it was, ironically, the UN Protection Force) and to blame MacKenzie in particular for implementing an agreement that allowed the Serbs to control their city in exchange for the airlifts. Sarajevans – of all ethnicities – complained that the UN simply wanted them to die on a full stomach. The word "MacKenzie" became a noun in the Bosnian language, entering the lexicon as a pejorative term for peacekeeper.

Colonel Patrice Sartre, who commanded the French battalion that arrived in July to take over from the Canadians, says he was shocked by how much the local people hated the peacekeepers. He could not figure it out at first. From what he could see, the Canadians were excellent soldiers and had been cited for bravery during a daring rescue of two Sarajevan women. Even Ejup Ganic, the Vice-President and Izetbegovic's right-hand man, claimed that the Canadians were the best peacekeepers they had. The problem, concluded Sartre, was the airport agreement. It never should have been done. "UNPROFOR was a complicit partner in the Serb siege of Sarajevo," declared Sartre.

In a 1999 report commissioned by UN Secretary General Kofi Annan, the United Nations issued an abject apology to the people of Bosnia. The report concerns the fall of Srebrenica – a UN safe area first under Canadian and then Dutch supervision. It was an impossible task for peacekeepers who were as much under siege as the Bosnians they were supposed to protect. When the Serb forces rolled over Srebrenica, they drove out all its inhabitants and killed many of them, including an estimated seven thousand men and boys.

The United Nations report on Srebrenica – signed by Annan – expands its self-condemnation to include the entire UNPROFOR mission in Bosnia. "With the benefit of hindsight," says Annan, the UN now knows that "none of the conditions for the deployment of peacekeepers" existed. Annan's report goes on to criticize the failed policies: the arms embargo that prevented the Bosnians from defending themselves, the humanitarian aid that was an inadequate response to ethnic cleansing and attempted genocide, and the deployment of peacekeepers to a place where there was no peace to keep. Annan concludes these were "poor substitutes for decisive and forceful action." Annan acknowledges that 117 men lost their lives to the UNPROFOR mission in Bosnia Hercegovina – a mission that never should have happened.

Lewis MacKenzie conceded in recent interviews that the UNPROFOR mission in Sarajevo and the airport agreement were probably wrong. Not only were soldiers placed in the path of a considerable amount of danger, but it was a mission with a larger PR component than a protective one. As the mission continued, it became apparent to the international community that peacekeeping was an inappropriate response to the hostilities in Bosnia. But a more robust reaction that would have included "decisive and forceful action" became impossible without endangering the lives of UNPROFOR personnel. In addition, each threat of force directed at the Serb leadership resulted in hostage taking: the UNPROFOR soldiers were sitting ducks.

How much of this was apparent in June of 1992? MacKenzie maintains they could not have predicted how impossible the mission would be, and how little of the airlifted supplies would end up in the right hands. But it was clear there was no political will to do anything else. John Wilson says the political will evaporated the day the Bosnians and the Serbs signed the airport agreement.

What is clear is that Canadian peacekeepers found themselves wounded and even killed in the most dangerous city in the world on a mission that Lewis MacKenzie volunteered for on their behalf. The job was to placate the Serbs and stay out of the way of a Bosnian Army that could not be placated. The soldiers were subjected to humiliation and danger: they were shot at, kidnapped, and killed. Then Brigadier-General Lewis MacKenzie placed the well-being of his troops ahead of the mission. But, Bosnia was a mission that should never have occurred. Ironically, MacKenzie helped make it happen.

Endnotes

Chapter 15

1. The material for this chapter is the result of approximately fifty interviews with the people directly involved with these events – including Major-General Lewis MacKenzie – and conducted over the past year for the purposes of writing the book, *The Lion, the Fox and the Eagle* for Random House, Canada. It is also the result of five years of on-location research that included interviews with dozens of Canadian soldiers, Bosnian Defence Force personnel, and Bosnian Serbs. In addition, source material came from *The Death of Yugoslavia* by Laura Silber and Allan Little and from *Peacekeeper: The Road to Sarajevo* by Lewis MacKenzie.

2. John Wilson retired from the Australian Army as a Brigadier-General.

CHAPTER 16

DO THE RIGHT THING!
LIEUTENANT-GENERAL ROMEO DALLAIRE
IN THE 1990S

Carol Off[1]

COMMON military wisdom dictates that it is much more difficult to lead in peacetime than in war. It's equally true that no one can really see the merits of an officer outside of the very activity for which he or she is trained – armed conflict. Officers may have the best education money can buy they may be perceived as "the right stuff" by their peers and superiors, they may be highly disciplined and focussed, but only within the theatre of war can one see their true mettle.

The career of Lieutenant-General Romeo Dallaire as an artillery officer with the Canadian Army spans three decades. His résumé as a senior officer is not unlike that of his colleagues, with one exception: Romeo Dallaire was tested in a way that few Canadian generals in peacetime have ever been tested. His strengths and weaknesses were exposed as few in the Canadian Forces (CF) have ever been exposed.

This chapter dwells primarily on General Dallaire's role as force commander for the United Nations Assistance Mission for Rwanda (UNAMIR), an engagement that has been the subject of dozens of articles, books, documentaries, judicial inquiries, and parliamentary reviews throughout the Western World and Africa. Yet, despite all the ink that's been used to analyze the mission and its failures, it's impossible to evaluate Dallaire's performance as leader except by examining it against the moral principals and ethics that guided him in his decisions. This chapter attempts to do that.

It was on 6 April 1994 that Romeo Dallaire discovered what all the years of training and education had ostensibly prepared him to face: he was in the middle of a war.

At 2030 hours, a Falcon 50 aircraft with a three-person French crew attempted to land at Kigali airport. They were returning the presidents of Burundi and Rwanda from an intense day of meetings aimed at bringing stability to the troubled region. As the Falcon made its final decent toward the runway, unknown assailants fired off two rockets – with professional precision – from a location near the airstrip. They scored a direct hit: the jet went down in a ball of flames, killing everyone on board.

Was it an act of sabotage? Was it a coup d'état? Romeo Dallaire subsequently spent the night trying to figure out just what he was up against. "I was very anxious to know with whom I was doing business," Dallaire says of the moment. As the force commander for UNAMIR, he had been in Kigali for the past six months trying to implement the Arusha Accords – a peace agreement that was to bring the rebel Tutsi-led militia, the Rwandan Patriotic Front (RPF), into a co-governing arrangement with the Rwandan government of President Juvenal Habyarimana. With the President now dead, it was clear to Dallaire that was now not going to happen.

Dallaire had decided months earlier that one of his priorities was to protect the country's VIPs. Nowhere in his mandate was he instructed to do this, but, long before the plane crash, Dallaire and his UNAMIR headquarters had received warnings and intelligence about a possible massacre of all political opponents of the Habyarimana dictatorship. Dallaire determined that the legitimate politicians of Rwanda – who had declared to the international community that they wanted peace – were his thin line of defence for the UNAMIR project. If they were killed, there would be no more mission.

Dallaire had assigned a handful of peacekeepers to act as bodyguards for each prominent politician he considered vulnerable. But with the death of Habyarimana, Dallaire determined those VIPs were in even more danger. On the night of 6 April, as he watched the brutal Presidential Guard and the paramilitary *Interahamwe* establish road blocks throughout Kigali, he worried not only about the security of the VIPs, but of the city as well.

Dallaire's biggest problem since the inception of UNAMIR was the appalling weakness of his force. The 2,500 soldiers assigned to him were hardly enough for the task at hand, but within that force, only a few contingents were capable of defending themselves – or anyone else. Before he left for the Africa mission, Dallaire had been told he would have a full battalion of Belgian paracommandos: instead, he got 450 soldiers. His only full battalion was of Bangladeshis – troops that Dallaire had determined could not function as boy scouts, let alone as peacekeepers in a conflict situation. They were a motley crew, pulled from different units of the Bangladeshi armed forces, led by a professor from their military school who would accept only written orders submitted well in advance. The Bangladeshis had no ability to be out for more than twelve hours – they did not even have sleeping bags.

Now, with the possibility of a coup – or a civil war – Dallaire dispatched his only reliable peacekeeping contingent, the Belgians, to secure the premises of key politicians, in particular the country's prime minister, Agathe Uwilingiymana. Madame Agathe, as everyone called her, was the one person Dallaire believed could restore order to the country – if she lived.

A section of ten highly capable Belgian peacekeepers arrived at the home of the Prime Minister in the early morning hours of 7 April. They immediately found themselves under fire from the Presidential Guard who had come to kill Madame Agathe. First Lieutenant Thierry Lotin radioed back to contingent headquarters: "I think they're going to lynch us, my colonel." Their commander, Joe Dewez, thought Lotin was exaggerating. Colonel Dewez told them not to surrender their guns, but two had already done so. Dewez determined the others could do the same. After all, they were peacekeepers in Rwanda to work with the authorities, not fight against them. The paracommandos were immediately captured. Dewez would recognize his mistake only hours later, when it was too late.

On that same day, 7 April, General Dallaire made hundreds of snap decisions, many of them life and death ones. He had no idea what he was facing in Kigali, but he heard that a high-level Rwandan military strategy meeting was to be held in the middle of town that morning. Dallaire knew he had to be at that meeting, even if he was uninvited.

Dallaire had also heard that the Belgian paracommandos, who had been sent to Madame Agathe's, had gone missing. Enroute to the meeting, he took a small detour past the Rwandan Army base of Camp Kigali where he had suspected his soldiers were held captive. Dallaire immediately understood the depth of the trouble his mission was in. At the gate of the camp, he saw two peacekeepers down on the ground. He ordered the driver – a Rwandan Army officer – to stop the car, but the man refused. It was too dangerous.

In that moment, Romeo Dallaire discovered what all the training of his past three decades had been about. He had to decide instantly: what should he do about the Belgian prisoners? He had 2,500 peacekeepers under his command – all of them lightly armed and many of them grossly under-trained and inexperienced. He had hundreds of UN observers in Kigali and throughout the countryside, and he knew there were thousands of ex-patriates – especially

Belgians – living in Rwanda. To stage a rescue operation would bring his peacekeepers into combat with the Rwandan Armed Forces. What would become of everyone else in the mission, particularly the other Belgians?

"I had to make a nanosecond decision," explains Dallaire. "This is what all your years of training are all about." Dallaire determined that a rescue operation would never succeed. He had too much at stake. Only negotiations could possibly free those soldiers, and even that was a remote possibility. Unless the Rwandan Army voluntarily released the soldiers, they would be lost. There would be no rescue mission. Dallaire would have to live with the enormous consequences of that decision for the rest of his life.

He proceeded to the military meeting where, after the session concluded, Dallaire attempted to negotiate the release of the Belgians. The man in charge, Colonel Theoneste Bagosora re-assured Dallaire that he would try, but Dallaire suspected nothing would come of it. He already had a good idea that Bagosora was ordering the political assassinations.

By the end of the day, Dallaire finally gained access to his Belgian paracommandos. They were piled in a heap at the hospital morgue, all dead, many of them showing signs of brutality and torture, some with their testicles severed. He also learned that Madame Agathe had been murdered along with most of the other protected VIPs. Dallaire was devastated. His Belgian contingent was outraged and shattered. The mission was disintegrating around them.

The day of 7 April descended into chaos and war. The RPF punched out of their compound in Kigali and confronted the government forces in all-out combat. Romeo Dallaire was in the midst of a genocide of the Tutsi people. He sent a message to New York – "Do I still have a mandate?" New York's Department of Peacekeeping Operations dithered, but Dallaire had already decided that he did: "I called it operation counter-crimes against humanity," says Dallaire. And he worked under that self-made mission for the next two months.

New York's Department of Peacekeeping Operations, taking instruction from the Secretary General and the UN Security Council, could make no decisions about the future of the UNAMIR mission. Dallaire's orders were merely to seek a cease-fire between the two armies, something everyone in UNAMIR knew to be academic. The genocide was the problem, not the combat, and it would not end until one side or the other – probably the RPF – had won the war.

The Belgian Government ordered the rest of its soldiers withdrawn in the days immediately following the death of the commandos. Dallaire subsequently ordered the Bangladeshis out of the country, since they were simply a liability. With a remaining force of 450 African peacekeepers, Dallaire and his deputy, Ghanaian Brigadier-General Henry Anyidoho, literally held down the fort. The UN wanted most of the other soldiers to leave Rwanda as well, but Dallaire and Anyidoho refused the order. The small, reduced force remained in Kigali for the duration of the war, and took it upon themselves to safeguard a number of security zones housing as many as thirty thousand refugees. Canadian Hercules pilots flew dare-devil missions into Kigali almost daily with the only supplies of food and equipment UNAMIR and the Rwandans would see until the genocide ended.

In addition to the relief flight, Canada contributed twelve officers to bolster Dallaire's mission staff. While the Ghanaians – and other African troops still in UNAMIR – were rock solid under fire, they had not the skills and leadership abilities of Canadian-trained soldiers. Dallaire had been asking Canada to send reinforcements since before the war even began. Dallaire knew his own soldiers at Valcartier were ideal for the mission – bilingual, capable, disciplined. These were the skills he needed now. He never got the battalion he had asked for, but he did get the officers.

Dallaire's concern for those under his command led him to the belief that he should not allow them to think about the circumstances they were in. "I conducted forced stress," he explained later. Dallaire describes this form of management as "ruthless but fair." The textbook on leadership would dispute Dallaire's methods – popular wisdom dictates that soldiers should have opportunities to think and reflect, that their stress should be steamed off as often as possible. But one objective outsider, who watched Dallaire in action during those months of war, saw method in his madness.

James Orbinski is a doctor with Médecins Sans Frontières (MSF) who was based at the Amahoro Hostel where UNAMIR had its headquarters. Orbinski had seen every hell hole in the world by the time he arrived in Kigali in May of 1994. But here he found just about the worst conditions possible. Dallaire and his peacekeepers were surrounded by corpses, filth, and garbage. Wild dogs fed upon the cadavers clogging the streets and doorways while soldiers cooked their bad food in the midst of it all. Water was scarce, and toilets had long ago ceased to function. They were shelled frequently. They had almost no petrol and only a handful of functioning vehicles.

"People were profoundly traumatized," recalls Orbinski. "But Dallaire was clear, firm, strong and uncompromising." Orbinski recognized immediately what the General was doing within his command role: "I had been in Somalia, Zaire, Afghanistan – everywhere. What people needed was the semblance of clarity. What are you trying to do here? Dallaire knew and acted upon it." Orbinski says that UNAMIR mission had to maintain a charade. "When you are a handful of UN soldiers with a lorry full of people and you come up against this veil of force [the Hutu Power death squads], you're operating with the tenuous promise of support from the international community that you know, and they know, is a delusion. And you are standing against thirty or forty *Interahamwe* who are drunk and have more equipment than the pea-shooter that's on your shoulder – the last thing you want to do is shatter the delusion."

Dallaire kept sending his men out into the danger and, even when they returned traumatized, they had to write up their reports. The headquarters was as strictly regimented as any normal mission would be, with reveille, morning prayers, and specific hours for meetings and debriefings. But all of this amidst – not only a combat zone – but the wholesale slaughter of civilians. The bodies of dead Rwandans littered the fields, filled the streets, and floated ashore in the river.

In late June, Dallaire presented a series of medals to his soldiers and commended them for their work. But he added: "It must be pointed out ... that there are blurred moments ahead of us. I can only advise that you all hold your composure and continue to perform your duties to the best of your ability. I am always ready and willing to give direction that will lead to the attainment of the mission goal."

Throughout the three months of slaughter, Dallaire spent all the hours he could spare devising a military plan to stop the genocide. In the immediate days following the President's assassination, Dallaire told New York that he would need five thousand equipped and well-motivated soldiers to stop the killing. The UN turned him down. He continued to revise the strategy and later requested a Chapter VII mission with a force capable of blowing through the Hutu Power barricades, securing the countryside, holding firm in downtown Kigali, and sabotaging the Hutu Power radio broadcasts which gave hourly instruction to the Rwandan citizenry in their "work obligation" to destroy the Tutsi. The Security Council, particularly the United States, decided that Dallaire's plan was ill-conceived. Long after the war, a panel of experts, assembled by the Carnegie Commission, would determine that Dallaire's plan would have worked and probably could have saved hundreds of thousands of lives. It's doubtful that the UN even seriously considered it.

On 4 July, Colonel Paul Kagame and his RPF concluded its cleverly manoeuvred sweep through the countryside and arrived in Kigali to join their fellow rebels. The war was over. The genocide ended as well and the perpetrators fled the country. Within weeks of Colonel Kagame's victory, Dallaire contacted General John de Chastelain, Chief of the Defence Staff in Ottawa, and informed him that he was incapable of continuing in the position. He had to leave, even as the reinforcements he had asked for finally began to arrive. By the middle of August, Dallaire's horrific adventure in Rwanda had come to its conclusion.

Major-General Romeo Dallaire (he was promoted to the new rank while he was still in Rwanda) was back at work in Canada on 3 October 1994. He took over the position of Deputy Commander of the Army just as the Somalia affair was beginning to explode. Dallaire had no idea what a mess that mission had become: a Canadian peacekeeper had tortured to death a Somali youth – among other questionable occurrences of the mission – and the Department of National Defence was accused of trying to cover it up. Successive budget cuts to the DND had decimated the entire organization and that, as well as a series of scandals, sent the senior ranks into self-preservation mode. Dallaire was completely unprepared for the bureaucratic, political, and legal battles the Canadian Forces now faced.

It was not just problems with leadership that plagued the CF. By 1996, the UN had established twenty-four new peacekeeping missions – six more than the total for the preceding forty-three years combined. Canadians served on almost all twenty-four of them. Dallaire was extremely conscious of how ill-prepared Canadian soldiers were for these often violent and nasty missions. Rwanda had been his first experience in peacekeeping, but he had visited his soldiers on their own respective missions in Bosnia and elsewhere. Dallaire was developing a sense of where the Canadian Forces were headed – into more and more missions such as the one he had just faced.

At the 1995 Vimy Awards, where Dallaire was honoured for his service in Africa, he poured out his anguish over what he had witnessed in Rwanda, describing his days in the genocide and confronting the "Dante devils" of the death squads.

I have seen fear in the eyes of officers and watched soldiers cower in mortal dread. I was – as others were – on occasion left for lost in battle behind belligerent lines. Many Canadian military personnel are living these types of experiences. These experiences have matured our army, have scarred all those involved, and created a new, more serious, more withdrawn no-nonsense soldier ethos. These peacekeepers are the new breed of full-fledged veterans of Canada.

In 1996, Romeo Dallaire was promoted Lieutenant-General and appointed Chief of Staff (Personnel) and later Assistant Deputy Minister Human Resources – Military (ADM HR-Mil). His most onerous task in Ottawa was the high profile initiative called the Quality of Life project. This was a Canadian Forces wide examination of the living conditions of Canadian service personnel and their families. It had revealed the central rot and decay of an organization whose personnel were living in poverty and had completely lost faith in their leadership. Dallaire's new position should have been an opportunity to change things, but it was one of the most depressing assignments of his career. Though the project ultimately produced some results, the CF was in a crisis: the down-sizing continued under the command of a risk-averse leadership. "It was very, very nasty" recalled Dallaire.

While funding dried up through successive budget cuts, the leadership became even less willing to take chances. The Department of National Defence (DND) was supposed to be bringing the Canadian Forces into the twenty-first century. The CF was stuck in the Dark Ages, as far as officers like Dallaire could see, and the command structure was all wrong. "I was trying to move a 1960s philosophy into a modern one, attempting to change things from a tight central control to giving authority to those in the field."

Dallaire argued that the emphasis for the forces should be on peacekeeping – a controversial issue in its own right – and he insisted that officers needed better and different education, with an emphasis on subjects like military history, sociology, philosophy, and anthropology. "Soldiers need to know more about the places they are going into," Dallaire argued. It was a marked contrast from the institutional thinking at the time. Ironically, in 1992, Major-General Lewis MacKenzie told the Royal United Services Institute, "The last thing that a peacekeeper wants to know is the history of the region he's going into. It complicates the task of mediation."

Dallaire was frequently criticized by those who worked under and around him of being "all over the map." He spouted a plethora of ideas on how to fix the forces but seemed unable to focus on any one. It was, in part, the difficulty of trying to change a conservative and often reactionary organization. But even those who wanted to follow found the General difficult to pin down.

In his scatter-gun approach, Dallaire struggled against the institutional thinking, insisting that the Canadian Forces had to be prepared for complex and confusing peacekeeping missions and operations other than war (OOTW), where they would encounter impenetrable social situations, high levels of violence, and the constant scrutiny of the international media. He wrote: "I maintain that commanders who insist on clear mandates and unambiguous decision processes should not be involved in conflict resolutions, because the challenges they will face will be too complex and subtle to be explicitly addressed through simple short-term tactics and readily definable milestones."

To an outsider, it's difficult to assess what effect Lieutenant-General Dallaire's interventions and arguments had on the group-think of the CF at the time. But it was becoming clear what effect the experiences of the UNAMIR mission in Rwanda were having on General Dallaire. In the latter half of the 1990s, the General slid into depression and despair. His condition was hardly a new one, but it was something that the CF was only just learning about in any detail. Post Traumatic Stress Disorder (PTSD) is surely an illness soldiers have suffered from for as long as there have been wars. As Dallaire sunk into its grips, he remembered, as a boy, that he would visit his father at the legion hall, only to see one or more men quietly crying into his beer. The others maintained a respectful silence as the veteran suffered his moment. He now knew what they had been suffering.

If he would have no other influence on the CF, Dallaire decided at least he would not quietly drift off into early retirement without making a big noise about the condition from which he – and countless others in the forces – were suffering. A number of CF personnel contributed disturbing testimony for an in-house video called *Witness the Evil* that was commissioned by the Chief of Defence Staff (CDS). Dallaire gives one of the most powerful interventions in the film, describing his condition, and admitting publicly that he had contemplated suicide. He urged those who had been traumatized by the missions of the 1990s to seek professional help. The plea was meaningful but hardly therapeutic: his condition persisted.

Within the PTSD, Dallaire began to review every decision, every moment of his time in Rwanda, and concluded that he had failed to do enough to prevent the disaster. Ironically, Dallaire never second-guessed any of his decisions or orders that were in the interest of protecting the Rwandan people and its legitimate political leaders. His regrets were almost exclusively directed at what he failed to do to get more help for them.

The one decision he never doubted was his order to send the Belgian peacekeepers to Madame Agathe's house that day, and the subsequent nanosecond decision not to send in a rescue mission. It's astonishing that he could remain so adamant, given his condition of self-doubt and the fact that the Belgian Government was then lashing out at Dallaire and the United Nations for the death of the ten peacekeepers. A military panel in Brussels ordered a court martial of Colonel Luc Marchal, Dallaire's deputy in Rwanda, and the panel regretted that the force commander, as a Canadian, was beyond their jurisdiction.

Dallaire's actions as force commander in Rwanda are perplexing not just to personnel in Belgium but to many in the Canadian Forces as well. They have been the subject of review from Washington to Nairobi. Why did Dallaire make the decisions he made? Why did he dispatch the Belgians? Another force commander may have ordered his troops back to barracks immediately following the crash of the President's plane – declaring that there was no longer a mandate. But Dallaire did not. Did this demonstrate good judgement or bad? Was it model generalship or failed generalship?

The answer depends entirely on what is regarded as the necessary attributes of a military leader. In all of his writing and in interviews, it appears Lieutenant-General Dallaire believed he had a moral obligation to act as he did. His decisions and commands were based on an ethical position – that he had the security of the Rwandan state to consider and he had to take all the calculated risks possible in order to secure the area under his mandate, even if it resulted in the death of his soldiers. While his orders may have been strategic and informed by his military training, Dallaire acted according to his conscience. Can a leader be effective and not be ethical? Dallaire would argue that he cannot. This ethos lies deeply in an old-fashioned concept of public service in which Dallaire was indoctrinated by first his father and then his father-in-law, both World War Two veterans. The Belgians argue that Dallaire was reckless with the lives of their peacekeepers: he counters that his priority was civil security.

Dallaire asked a group of officers a few years after he returned from Rwanda a provocative question: "Is Canada at war?" Not in a traditional way, was his own answer, but perhaps there is a war against tyranny which is no less relevant than the great wars. "We're on a terribly steep learning curve in this village," Dallaire told a CBC interviewer. "We fought the Second World War because there was a threat to us. Now we've gone to, 'We have to do something because there's a threat to humanity.' That's a big step." Correctly or not, Dallaire saw his role in Rwanda as a battle against tyranny no less relevant than that of the great wars. And he acted accordingly.

Dallaire's final position within the Canadian Forces was to act as special advisor to the CDS where he, and a small staff, prepared a forward looking document that was to be "a blueprint for future officer training." *Canadian Officership in the 21st Century* embodies many of the ideas Dallaire has for a better trained and educated officer class that is prepared for the evolving role of the Canadian Armed Forces. But the one characteristic Dallaire knows cannot be taught or trained into an officer is, simply, a sense of what is right and wrong. Dallaire refused to withdraw the peacekeepers serving under him in Rwanda, even when he was told to by the United Nations. He created his own self-styled mission and followed it. Dallaire has said that he could not have looked himself in the mirror had he done otherwise, and he assumed – correctly or not – that those who served under him felt the same way.

Lieutenant-General Romeo Dallaire once remarked that "no one is ever ready for war, especially the one they end up fighting." He made this quip at an Royal Military College dinner in 1991, two and a half years before he would find himself in a devastating war. Yet Dallaire learned that the properly trained officer *is* ready: the training and discipline does not fail you. Dallaire relied on it every moment that he was in Rwanda during those chaotic months in 1993 and 1994. But Dallaire fell back on something else during that one hundred days of slaughter that he witnessed: a personal sense of right and wrong. He made his leadership and command decisions based on his own moral convictions. It saved neither the people of Rwanda, who were murdered in the hundreds of thousands, nor his own sanity. But it raised a crucial question for the Canadian Forces and for the military of many other countries as well. What are we willing to risk in the interest of human rights?

Lieutenant-General Dallaire resigned from the Canadian Forces in April of 2000, leaving another generation to answer the question.

ENDNOTES

CHAPTER 16

1. The material for this chapter is derived from interviews with dozens of people from Rwanda, Belgium, and Canada who were directly involved in the events. It's also the result of correspondence and conversations with Lieutenant-General Romeo Dallaire conducted over the spring and summer of 2000 for the purposes of writing a book. I have also borrowed heavily from a few excellent accounts of the Rwandan crisis, particularly *Leave None to Tell the Story*, published by Human Rights Watch and Doctor Jacques Castonguay's book, *Les casques bleu au Rwanda.*

CHAPTER 17
A PERSONAL PERSPECTIVE ON COMMAND

General (Retired) John de Chastelain

INTRODUCTION

I JOINED the Canadian Army Militia as a private in January 1956 and retired forty years later in December 1995 as Chief of the Defence Staff. Seventeen of those years were spent as a general officer with a gap year in the Supplementary Reserve as Canadian Ambassador in Washington. In none of those seventeen years was I personally engaged in combat operations. Any thoughts I have on generalship should be viewed in that light.

The *Concise Oxford Dictionary* defines generalship as: *the art or practice of exercising military command; military skill, strategy; skilful management, tact, diplomacy.* In this definition there is no mention of Generals and Admirals. Generalship might be said to define military professionalism regardless of rank.

When I was promoted to Brigadier-General I was surprised to find myself invited to Rideau Hall to be given a General Officer's Commission by the Governor General. The commission I received as a Second Lieutenant (signed by the Minister of Defence who was once a Major-General and who had the Victoria Cross, as well as other gallantry medals) said in part: "You are therefore carefully and diligently to discharge your Duty as such in the Rank of Second Lieutenant or in such other Rank as We may from time to time hereafter be pleased to promote or appoint you to." If I had thought about it at the time, which I had no reason to, I would probably have assumed that the reference to "such other Rank" included the various grades of general officer.

Leadership is leadership, regardless of rank. I believe that all junior officers need a comprehensive understanding of the operational requirements of their classification, the ability to lead effectively, and manage resources carefully. That remains equally true at all rank levels. But the ranks of general officer bring higher visibility, greater responsibilities, and unique requirements. My aim in this chapter is to say what my personal experience leads me to believe these are.

THE OPERATIONAL IMPERATIVE

Unique to the profession of arms is the requirement of being capable of waging war – the raison d'être of all armed forces. I believe it follows that the most important obligation for all officers is to know the operational requirements of their profession, whether these are in the combat, combat support, or combat service support categories. As an officer rises in rank, the scope of that understanding must broaden. At the general officer level it calls for a knowledge of the role of every branch of the service and the requirements of combined operations.

General officers who work predominantly in non-operational headquarters or on the staff must still remain abreast of the operational aspects of their profession.

In wartime, some rise to senior rank in field or sea appointments and spend all their time there. During the two world wars, performance and experience gained in combat were frequently the reasons for promotion and why many spent their wartime experience in combat roles. But most who reach general officer rank do so in peacetime and spend most of their time exercising responsibility over issues short of war. They too must understand the operational imperative of their profession, but they must also have a comprehensive understanding of other key aspects of it, even if these may be less dramatic or less appealing.

Other than operational knowledge, the factors that I believe are particularly significant for general officers include: credibility, visibility, accountability, responding to the effect of changes in society, and interfacing with politicians, civilians, and the media.

CREDIBILITY

In the Armed Forces, as in most professions, the credibility of those at the top has an internal and external dimension. Internally, subordinates need to know their leaders have had the training and experience to qualify them for the positions they hold, so that they fully understand the impact of the orders and instructions they give. Subordinates at various levels may not be happy with the dangers or disadvantages inherent in some of their leaders' decisions, but, if these are made by those whose experience is not in doubt and if they are well-explained, there should be little ground for reasoned complaint. Life in the Armed Forces involves inherent risk – which is accepted by those who join – but not needless risk.

Within the profession, those who rise to senior rank must be seen by their subordinates to have gained their promotion through merit. Outside the profession it is taken for granted that generals and admirals hold their rank because their experience and capability warrant it. Performance must demonstrate that is so. More and more today, rank or privilege is viewed with suspicion, and the performance and credibility of senior leaders is under ever-increasing scrutiny. It is right that performance should be constantly reviewed in the normal course of events. But in the post-Cold War era, reductions in defence funding and the consequent closure of bases and cutbacks in personnel have affected internal morale in such a way as to make the scrutiny of general officers' performance today even more intense than had been usual.

Credibility suffers when those in lower ranks believe their superiors are powerless to influence government decisions that disadvantage them. When changes in government policy appear to be in conflict with the interests of subordinates – such as reduction in personnel, the freezing of pay, or the cancellation of operational capabilities – I believe that senior leaders must first make every effort possible to defend those interests. But if the changes remain, then leaders must make clear to their subordinates what they imply and why they are necessary. If a senior leader is incapable of supporting and implementing policies the Government makes on behalf of the electorate, he or she should consider resigning.

Visibility

I once heard an American officer use the expression "lightening strikes" when talking about promotion to general officer rank. What I took from that was the conclusion that rising to that rank brings attention of a unique nature. I believe that is true. Promotion to general officer rank brings with it instant visibility, both within the Armed Forces and without. Seen as the interface between the Armed Forces and the Government, or between headquarters and the operational units, those in the general officer classification inevitably attract more attention than those in any other rank.

The titles "General" or "Admiral" provoke varying reactions. One view is that people in these ranks constitute the ultimate arbiters of military decision-making. Another is that they constitute a category of "brass" that is out of touch with the rank and file. Some shallow-thinking members of the public and the media like to characterize all senior officers as narrow-minded and mired in the past. Their observations have created in the minds of some an impression that lack of imagination or unjustified privilege go hand in hand with general officer rank. I think that those who believe this are few, but they seem to be at one with those whose observation of things military is based on the facile assessment that privates are good because they take orders and generals are bad because they give them. Privates are good – at least most of them are. The same is true of generals and admirals.

It is sufficient, I believe, for those who reach very senior rank to know they will be the subject of more than usual scrutiny. Their conduct, their decisions, and their actions will quite properly be the focus of attention by members of society and the military alike. They should act accordingly.

A mechanical aspect of visibility for all officers, and I believe especially for general officers, is that of being seen by those they command. Whether the command is a unit, a formation, or a staff division, it is important that its members see those at the top whenever possible and, preferably, that they have the chance to communicate directly with them. Not only should leaders care for their subordinates' interests, they should be seen by them doing so. Geography and time may be impediments, but they should not be insuperable ones. Video speeches do little to rally the troops or convince them of the attention of their leaders. Face to face contact is definitely more likely to do so.

ACCOUNTABILITY

Everyone is accountable for his or her actions, and in the Armed Forces all but those in the lowest rank are accountable both upwards and downwards.

There are obvious aspects of accountability that need no repetition: we are all responsible for our decisions and actions. But leaders at all levels are also accountable for the performance and behaviour of their subordinates. Accountability should mean that leaders credit their subordinates for any success achieved and that they accept blame for failure or misadventure. This should be the case at any level, and certainly at the most senior levels.

Accountability for the actions of subordinates should not be allowed to stand in the way of delegating authority. At most levels of leadership, the delegation of authority is a requirement, along with effective management and the education of subordinates. This is especially true at the most senior levels of the Armed Forces, where the very wide span of responsibility and the need for timely operational decisions make it imperative. It is a fundamental requirement of generalship that leaders must have confidence that immediate subordinates will take required actions as and when necessary. If they do not have that confidence, they should motivate those subordinates to the point that they do, or else get rid of them. Notwithstanding, leaders should accept the responsibility for their decisions.

The question of accountability raises the issue of resignation. I believe that, while there may be good reasons and sometimes an obligation why a senior officer should resign, there are times when he or she does not have the automatic right to such an option. Improper conduct is one good reason for resignation. Accepting the blame for unacceptable actions of subordinates may be another. Simply disagreeing with a change in policy should not automatically be one. Governments have the right to expect that those in whom they have invested experience, knowledge, trust, and senior rank will carry out the policies and decisions they make on behalf of the people. Clearly if a senior officer cannot in conscience support a policy, he or she may be obliged to leave. But it is a decision that should take account of the individual's obligations as much as their preferences.

The best final arbiter of accountability may be one's own conscience. Facing the reflection in the mirror every morning, honestly and objectively, is as good a guide as any.

Responding to Change

The history of the world and of its armed forces is one of change. Being capable of responding effectively to change is a major requirement of generalship. Military leadership is often accused of being opposed to change and harbouring a conservative approach to any new development, but in some respects such conservatism is entirely appropriate. Unless apparent alterations are demonstrably more effective, tried military doctrine should not be cast aside.

In the operational category, history is replete with examples where reluctance at the highest level to accept innovation has proved costly. The long-bow and machine-gun had dramatic impacts on warfare and caused huge numbers of casualties before military leaders of the day accepted that changes were needed in technology and tactics to adapt to their existence. On the other hand, recent history demonstrates the danger of rushing too soon to judgement. Those who believed in 1945 that the mere existence of nuclear weapons would change warfare completely, and prepared to engage in wars based on that belief, soon found out they were wrong.

But the need to be responsive to change goes beyond the realm of strategy and tactics. The end of the Cold War, and the defence budget reductions which followed, made it imperative for Canada to adapt its defence capability from one centred on the high intensity battlefields of Central Europe and the North Atlantic to one in which its remaining field capabilities could respond to a variety of tasks. Unpalatable as it was to many in uniform, this change in approach was vital if even a minimal land, sea, and air combat capability was to be maintained in a climate of reduced defence spending. It is a function of generalship to understand the need for change, to develop the appropriate response, and then to sell this to civilian decision-makers and to those in uniform alike.

The most dramatic challenge for Canadian generals in addressing change in recent years has been in the social and constitutional areas. Legislation affecting human rights and individual issues in Canada in the past quarter century have called for a dramatic re-assessment of longstanding Armed Forces' policies. Advising the Government on the effect that implementing radical change may have on operational capability and the morale of the Forces' while implementing these changes, presents a considerable challenge to senior leaders' judgement and determination. Having a clear understanding of the professional implications of change, as well as an appreciation of the requirement to accept change and to implement it – however unpopular it may be – is an exacting test of leadership.

The armed forces of another country I once served with continue to place a premium on the ability of an officer to be ruthless. That they do so does not imply support for pugnacity, cruelty, or excess. It does recognize that to be effective, a leader must at times make unpopular decisions and be vigorous in seeing them through to completion.

INTERFACE WITH POLITICIANS

In Canada, as in other democratic countries, control over the Armed Forces by the people is exercised through the politicians elected to run the country. Politicians are accountable to the electorate for the handling of their departments, and senior officers are accountable to the Minister of National Defence for the running of the Armed Forces. While it is important that senior officers in operational organizations have a complete understanding of their role and how to execute it, it is equally important that those who are responsible for advising political leaders have a complete understanding of how the Defence Department works in all its facets.

Most officers, and I was one, prefer to spend as much time as possible in operational assignments. The operational aspect of military life is the reason most have chosen a military career over one less vigorous, adventurous, or challenging. But an important part of generalship is understanding all aspects of the profession and being able to give sound advice to politicians. The earlier this understanding is formed the better. My initial assignment to National Defence Headquarters (NDHQ) did not happen until I was a Brigadier-General, and then only after two postings in that rank elsewhere. That NDHQ assignment lasted only one year before I was sent back to "the field." Thus I was faced with a learning curve that meant I was not able to work at an optimum level during my first year in Ottawa nor in subsequent appointments there.

It is entirely understandable that officers prefer to seek employment in their operational specialties and units rather than at a desk. But it is up to personnel managers to ensure that officers get the appropriate headquarters experience as their careers progress, and it is up to those who aspire to move ahead to welcome, and not avoid, such assignments.

As uninteresting as work at National Defence Headquarters may seem to some, it is important that those who may eventually rise to senior rank have the opportunity to serve there as early as their required operational postings permit. Each of the fields of strategic planning, policy, personnel, procurement, and finance have a system that must be understood if informed advice on them is to be given to politicians and if the interests of the Armed Forces are to be served. Ministers of Defence can only run the Department and the Armed Forces effectively if they have sound advice from knowledgeable and experienced officers and public servants. It is a requirement of generalship that their knowledge be comprehensive and their advice well founded.

I believe it is equally important that senior officers and politicians have a working relationship that is based on a clear understanding of the responsibilities of each and of the primacy of civilian control. Senior officers will be required to meet with Parliamentary and Senate committees as well as with individual ministers. They will have to deal with different government departments on the subject of their particular assigned role. On occasion they may be required to appear before Cabinet on issues dealing with the sending of operational units to war or on other operational tasks at home or overseas. In each case it is important that the advice they give is clear, based on a sound understanding of military imperatives, and unaffected by other than purely military considerations.

It has been my experience that politicians listen carefully to military advice and accord it respect. While Cabinet did not always follow all the operational courses of action I might have preferred when I was CDS, I was never asked to have the Armed Forces do something that I and my military colleagues believed was not within their capability or willingness to do, or that we were not prepared to see done.

Some believe that politicians and the military officers who work for them must always agree. I do not. Ideally, and most frequently, agreement will be the case. But generalship calls for senior officers to give the advice they believe in, whether it is appreciated or not. As CDS, I worked for a number of ministers and agreed with them on the vast majority of the decisions they took after receiving advice from me. But occasions did occur when they made decisions within their authority that were not my preference. Equally, on occasion I made decisions within my remit that they may not have liked. But ministers and other politicians need untrammelled advice, not what they might like to hear. Senior officers have an obligation to provide it.

INTERFACE WITH CIVILIANS

All defence departments employ public servants and civilian employees to exercise the "civilian-control" aspect of policy, finance, and procurement or to do functions that do not require uniformed personnel. Canada has chosen to integrate the public service component of the Department of National Defence with the military one at NDHQ to the extent that some branches there have civilians presiding over military staff and vice versa. This situation has existed for almost half a century and, in the minds of some, remains controversial. Others, including the government, regard it as the logical and economic way to structure the Department of National Defence so that it operates efficiently. It is a function of generalship – and of civilian leadership – to ensure that a military-civilian divide is not allowed to interfere with the effective running of the Department and the Armed Forces.

This chapter is not the place to discuss the pros and cons of departmental structure, though I would say my experience has been that the NDHQ system has a clear enough delineation of authority on each side to make it work efficiently and effectively. It will do so only as long as civilian and military members understand and respect each other's role.

It is also an important part of generalship that senior officers make themselves familiar with other departments of government, especially those that have an important relationship with the Department of National Defence. Foremost among these, and in no particular order, I would include Foreign Affairs, Finance, Treasury Board, Supply and Services, Justice, Environment, Fisheries and Oceans, Veterans' Affairs, and the Solicitor General's Department. Further, senior officers should develop, as a matter of priority and where appropriate, good working relationships with members of these departments at the equivalent levels. Such relationships can only contribute to better mutual understanding and to a more informed response by those departments to the Armed Forces' needs.

Interface with the Media

We are all consumers of media products, whether written, oral, or visual. In this age of information, the greatly expanded role played by the media in everyday life places a special focus on all areas of government activity including the Armed Forces. The innovation of around-the-clock television news services, with their voracious appetite for anything classified as "news," coupled with the changes engendered by the end of the Cold War, the impact of human rights legislation, and the huge increase in peacekeeping operations worldwide, have made the activities of the Armed Forces a special area of media and public interest.

In spite of the media's expanded role, armed forces in Canada and elsewhere have generally maintained their traditional suspicion of journalists and their intentions. It is unclear whether this suspicion is borne of a belief that journalists will seek to over-dramatize the events they cover or a concern – particularly regarding operations – that two of the key principles of war, namely security and surprise, will be jeopardized by the overriding requirement to "get the story and tell it." What is clear is that many members of the Armed Forces, including senior officers, still mistrust the media and avoid contact with journalists whenever possible.

This situation results in the double disadvantage of increasing media suspicion of military motives and of keeping senior officers from developing a familiarity and confidence in dealing with media representatives.

It has been my experience that the vast majority of journalists are principled and professional individuals who seek to carry out their role responsibly and accurately. Increasingly, many of them are losing their lives doing so, whether through covering war, crime, or corrupt government. The few who may find it hard to be objective, or who are simply incompetent, are soon found out by their editors or producers, or by those who read, see, or hear their product.

The people have a right to know what their Armed Forces are doing, and members of the Armed Forces are keen to have their story told. Obvious limits must be observed where the security of operations is concerned or where limits on the passage of information has been defined in legislation. But it is a part of generalship to understand the role played by the media and to know how to deal with media representatives effectively. It is also a part of generalship to encourage and prepare subordinates to do likewise. If we have a good story to tell, we should tell it. If we have a story we would rather see not told, and if we seek to obstruct its telling, we must realize that it will be told nonetheless and not sympathetically.

CONCLUSION

It is said that leadership can be hard to define, but that you know it when you see it. I believe the same is true of generalship; this is not surprising, perhaps because generalship is all about leadership. When people think about generalship, it is most often in the context of war, as in the accomplishments of those like Charlemagne, Marlborough, Napoleon, Foche, Currie, and MacArthur. And it is true that in warfare on a grand scale the question of generalship faces its most dramatic test and has its most enduring results. Equally important in peacetime is that facet of generalship which ensures that the men and women are trained and equipped to fight the nation's wars if called upon.

It may be true to say that, with the possible exception of situations that exist within totalitarian regimes, there have been no circumstances in history where the application of generalship has been simple or straightforward. The period during which I served as a general officer turned out to be complex for all the reasons I have mentioned, and it was complicated by a number of unusual operations or events, some of which enhanced the public view of the Armed Forces (and made life simpler), and some of which did not (and made it more complicated).

Generalship involves dedication, determination, and hard work. While there may be some truth in the saying that leaders are born and not made, there are no short cuts to providing the rounded leadership that the Armed Forces, the Department, and the country deserves and needs. It is fortunate that the history of Canada's armed forces over many decades, in war and in peace, shows there has been no shortage of able men and women to provide the generalship needed.

CONTRIBUTORS
WARRIOR CHIEFS

Sandy Babcock is a serving Canadian Forces officer who is presently completing his PhD in Canadian History at Carleton University in Ottawa.

Dr. Serge Bernier is the Director of the Department of National Defence Directorate of History and Heritage.

General (Retired) John de Chastelain is a former Chief of the Defence Staff and is presently the Chairman of the Independent International Commission on Decommissioning for Northern Ireland.

Dr. Stephen J. Harris is the Chief Military Historian with the Department of National Defence Directorate of History and Heritage.

Dr. Ron Haycock is a Professor of History and Dean of Arts at the Royal Military College of Canada.

Lieutenant-Colonel, Dr. Bernd Horn is a serving Canadian Forces officer who is presently teaching history at the Royal Military College of Canada.

Dr. A.M. (Jack) Hyatt is a Professor Emeritus at the University of Western Ontario in the Department of History.

Lieutenant-Colonel, Dr. R.J. Jarymowycz teaches history in Montreal and is the Dean of the Militia Staff College in Kingston.

Captain (Navy) (Retired) Wilfred Lund holds a PhD from the University of Victoria. His interest is senior leadership and personnel policy of the Royal Canadian Navy.

Dr. Sean M. Maloney teaches War Studies and is a Social Sciences and Humanities Research Council (SSHRC) Post Doctoral Fellow at the Royal Military College of Canada.

Jeff Noakes is a doctoral candidate at Carleton University in Ottawa.

Carol Off writes and reports for the CBC flagship TV current affairs program "The National Magazine."

Dr. Dean Oliver is the Senior Historian at the Canadian War Museum.

Dr. Bill Rawling is a Military Historian with the Department of National Defence Directorate of History and Heritage.

Dr. Roger Sarty is the Director, Historical Research and Exhibit Development, at the Canadian War Museum.

Dr. Yves Tremblay is a Military Historian with the Department of National Defence Directorate of History and Heritage.

Michel Wyczynski is a Reservist and Archivist with the National Archives of Canada.

INDEX